SOUPS
STARTERS & SALADS

SOUPS
STARTERS & SALADS

Create the perfect start to a meal
with over 400 recipes for
fabulous first courses

HERMES
HOUSE

This edition is published by Hermes House

© Anness Publishing Limited 2002, 2003

Hermes House is an imprint of Anness Publishing Limited
Hermes House, 88–89 Blackfriars Road, London SE1 8HA
tel. 020 7401 2077; fax 020 7633 9499; info@anness.com

Printed and bound in China

A CIP catalogue record for this book is available from the British Library.

Publisher: Joanna Lorenz; *Managing Editor:* Judith Simons;
Project Editor: Felicity Forster; *Editor:* Linda Doeser.
Recipes: Catherine Atkinson, Alex Barker, Steve Baxter, Michelle Berriedale-Johnson, Angela Boggiano, Janet Brinkworth,
Carla Capalbo, Kit Chan, Jacqueline Clarke, Maxine Clarke, Frances Cleary, Carole Clements, Andi Cleveley, Trish Davies,
Roz Denny, Patrizia Diemling, Matthew Drennan, Sarah Edmonds, Joanne Farrow, Rafi Fernandez, Silvano Franco, Christine France,
Uasako Fukuoka, Sarah Gates, Shirley Gill, Brian Glover, Nicola Graimes, Rosamund Grant, Carole Handslip, Rebekah Hassan,
Deh-Ta Hsiung, Shehzad Husain, Judy Jackson, Peter Jordan, Emi Kasuko, Sheila Kimberley, Lucy Knox, Masaki Ko, Elisabeth Lambert Ortiz,
Ruby Le Bois, Clare Lewis, Sara Lewis, Gilly Love, Leslie Mackley, Norma MacMillan, Kathy Man, Sally Mansfield, Sue Maggs,
Sallie Morris, Annie Nichols, Maggie Pannell, Katherine Richmond, Kieth Richmond, Anne Sheasby, Marlena Spieler, Jenny Stacey,
Liz Trigg, Hilaire Walden, Laura Washburn, Steven Wheeler, Kate Whiteman, Elizabeth Wolf-Cohen, Jenni Wright.
Photographers: Karl Adamson, Edward Allwright, David Armstrong, Steve Baxter, James Duncan, John Freeman, Ian Garlick,
Michelle Garrett, Peter Henley, John Hesseltine, Amanda Heywood, Janine Hosegood, David Jordan, Maria Kelly, Dave King,
Don Last, William Lingwood, Patrick McLeary, Michael Michaels, Thomas Odulate, Juliet Piddington, Peter Reilly, Sam Stowell.
Designer: Michael Morey; *Editorial Reader:* Jonathan Marshall; *Production Controller:* Ben Worley.

Previously published in separate volumes, *Appetizers, Starters and Hors d'Oeuvres, Best-Ever Salads* and *The Soup Bible.*

1 3 5 7 9 10 8 6 4 2

Notes

Bracketed terms are intended for American readers.

For all recipes, quantities are given in both metric and imperial measures and,
where appropriate, measures are also given in standard cups and spoons.
Follow one set, but not a mixture, because they are not interchangeable.

Standard spoon and cup measures are level.

1 tsp = 5ml, 1 tbsp = 15ml, 1 cup = 250ml/8fl oz

Australian standard tablespoons are 20ml. Australian readers should use 3 tsp
in place of 1 tbsp for measuring small quantities of gelatine, flour, salt, etc.

Medium (US large) eggs are used unless otherwise stated.

CONTENTS

INTRODUCTION

Careful thought often goes into planning a main course, especially when we are entertaining, but often less consideration is given to what to serve first. Yet, in some ways, the first course makes or breaks a dinner party or informal supper because it sets the mood, stimulates the appetite and promises that exciting things are to come.

There are a number of aspects to consider. If you are planning a substantial main course, then a light appetizer, such as a mousse or consommé, might be the best choice. On a cold winter's evening, on the other hand, a steaming bowl of chunky vegetable soup or a hot soufflé would fit the bill. Some element of contrast between the different courses makes for an interesting meal, but obviously it would be unsuitable to serve a fiery hot starter that will drown the subtlety of a delicate main course.

You could create a theme for your meal, based on the main ingredients; following a lobster soup or prawn (shrimp) cocktail with a fish dish, for example, or centred on a specific cuisine, such as French, Thai or Indian.

Also, think about practicalities. If the main course will require last-minute attention, a chilled soup or cold hors d'oeuvre that can be prepared in advance is ideal. Nibbles, canapés and dips that can be served with drinks may make catering for a large number of guests

easier. If you have only an hour between rushing in from work and your guests arriving, choose from the Instant Salads.

There are hundreds of recipes for soups, starters and salads in this book, grouped to make these choices as simple as possible. Whatever the occasion, from a sophisticated dinner party (try Warm Salads) to an *al*

fresco lunch (try Chilled Soups), and whatever your tastes, from a family gathering (try Pasta, Noodle and Pulse Salads) to a night in with the

girls (try Vegetable and Cheese Starters), you can guarantee a great start.

Each of the three main sections begins with a guide to ingredients and their preparation. SOUPS includes recipes for those all-important stocks, plus some easy-to-make garnishes. STARTERS also offers some decorative flourishes, as well as advice on how to make marinades, oils and dressings. SALADS will guide you through the large variety of vegetables, fruit, herbs, spices, oils and vinegars available.

With all this information and this huge collection of mouthwatering recipes, the world's best soups, starters and salads are at your fingertips.

SOUPS

Home-made soup is always a treat and turns any
meal into a special occasion. It is not difficult to
make and success is guaranteed if you use one of the
fresh stock recipes that begins this section. It is
immensely versatile and this huge collection of recipes
includes something perfect for all occasions and every
season – hearty winter soups, luxurious seafood bisques,
creamy chowders, filling vegetarian broths and chilled
soups for *al fresco* dining.

Making your own stocks

Fresh stocks are indispensable for creating good home-made soups. They add a depth of flavour that plain water just cannot achieve.

Although many supermarkets now sell tubs of fresh stock, these can work out expensive, especially if you need large quantities for your cooking. Making your own is surprisingly easy and much more economical, particularly if you can use leftovers – the chicken carcass from Sunday lunch, for example, or the shells you're left with once you've peeled prawns

(shrimp). But home-made stocks aren't just cheaper, they're also tastier and much more nutritious, precisely because they're made with fresh, natural ingredients.

You can, of course, use stock (bouillon) cubes or granules, but be sure to check the seasoning, as these tend to be high in salt.

One good idea for keen and regular soup makers is to freeze home-made stock in plastic freezer bags, or ice cube trays, so you always have a supply at your disposal whenever you need some.

Frozen stock can be stored in the freezer for up to six months. Make sure that you label each stock carefully for easy identification.

Use the appropriate stock for the soup you are making. Onion soup, for example, is improved with a good beef stock. Be particularly careful to use a vegetable stock if you are catering for vegetarians.

Recipes are given on the following pages for vegetable stock, chicken stock, meat stock, fish stock and basic stocks for Chinese and Japanese soups.

Vegetable Stock

Use this versatile stock as the basis for all vegetarian soups.

INGREDIENTS

Makes 2.5 litres/4½ pints/11 cups

2 leeks, coarsely chopped

3 celery sticks, coarsely chopped

1 large onion, unpeeled, chopped

2 pieces fresh root ginger, chopped

1 yellow (bell) pepper, seeded
  and chopped

1 parsnip, chopped

mushroom stalks

tomato peelings

45ml/3 tbsp light soy sauce

3 bay leaves

bunch of parsley stalks

3 fresh thyme sprigs

1 fresh rosemary sprig

10ml/2 tsp salt

freshly ground black pepper

3.5 litres/6 pints/15 cups water

1 Put all the ingredients into a very large pan. Gradually bring to the boil, then lower the heat and simmer for 30 minutes, stirring occasionally.

2 Leave to cool. Strain, then discard the vegetables. The stock is ready to use. Alternatively, chill or freeze the stock and keep it to use as required.

Fish Stock

Fish stock is much quicker to make than poultry or meat stock. Ask your fishmonger for heads, bones and trimmings from white fish.

INGREDIENTS

Makes about 1 litre/1¾ pints/4 cups

675g/1½lb heads, bones and trimmings
    from white fish
1 onion, sliced
2 celery sticks with leaves, chopped
1 carrot, sliced
½ lemon, sliced (optional)
1 bay leaf
a few fresh parsley sprigs
6 black peppercorns
1.35 litres/2¼ pints/6 cups cold water
150ml/¼ pint/⅔ cup dry white wine

1 Rinse the fish heads, bones and trimmings well under cold running water. Put in a stockpot with the vegetables and lemon, if using, the herbs, peppercorns, water and wine. Bring to the boil, skimming the surface frequently, then reduce the heat and simmer for 25 minutes.

2 Strain the stock without pressing down on the ingredients in the sieve. If not using immediately, leave to cool and then store in the refrigerator. Fish stock should be used within 2 days, or it can be frozen for up to 3 months.

Chicken Stock

A good home-made poultry stock is invaluable in the kitchen. If poultry giblets are available, add them (except the livers) with the wings. Once made, chicken stock can be kept in an airtight container in the refrigerator for 3–4 days, or frozen for up to 6 months.

INGREDIENTS

Makes about 2.5 litres/4 ½ pints/11 cups

1.2–1.5kg/2½–3lb chicken or turkey
    (wings, backs and necks)

2 onions, unpeeled, quartered

1 tbsp olive oil

4 litres/7 pints/17½ cups cold water

2 carrots, coarsely chopped

2 celery sticks, with leaves if possible,
    coarsely chopped

small handful of fresh parsley

few fresh thyme sprigs or
    3.5ml/¾ tsp dried thyme

1 or 2 bay leaves

10 black peppercorns, lightly crushed

1 Combine the poultry wings, backs and necks in a stockpot with the onion quarters and the oil. Cook over a moderate heat, stirring occasionally, until the poultry and onions are lightly and evenly browned.

2 Add the water and stir well to mix in the sediment on the base of the pan. Bring to the boil and skim off the impurities as they rise to the surface of the stock.

3 Add the chopped carrots and celery, fresh parsley, thyme, bay leaf and black peppercorns. Partly cover the stockpot and gently simmer the stock for about 3 hours.

4 Strain the stock through a sieve into a bowl and leave to cool, then chill in the refrigerator for an hour.

5 When cold, carefully remove the layer of fat that will have set on the surface. Store in the refrigerator for 3–4 days or freeze until required.

Meat Stock

The most delicious meat soups rely on a good home-made stock for success. Once it is made, meat stock can be kept in the refrigerator for 4–5 days, or frozen for longer storage (up to 6 months).

INGREDIENTS

Makes about 2 litres/3½ pints/9 cups

1.75kg/4lb beef bones, such as shin (shank), leg, neck and clod (chuck), or veal or lamb bones, cut into 6cm/2½in pieces

2 onions, unpeeled, quartered

2 carrots, coarsely chopped

2 celery sticks, with leaves if possible, coarsely chopped

2 tomatoes, coarsely chopped

4.5 litres/7½ pints/20 cups water

handful of parsley stalks

few fresh thyme sprigs or 3.5ml/¾ tsp dried thyme

2 bay leaves

10 black peppercorns, lightly crushed

1 Preheat the oven to 230°C/450°F/Gas 8. Put the bones in a roasting pan and roast, turning occasionally, for 30 minutes, until they start to brown.

2 Add the onions, carrots, celery and tomatoes and baste with the fat in the roasting pan. Return the pan to the oven and roast for a further 20–30 minutes, until the bones are well browned. Stir and baste occasionally.

3 Transfer the bones and roasted vegetables to a stockpot. Spoon off the fat from the roasting pan. Add a little of the water to the roasting pan and bring to the boil on the hob (stovetop), stirring well to scrape up any browned sediment. Pour this liquid into the stockpot.

4 Add the remaining water to the pot. Bring just to the boil, skimming frequently to remove all the foam from the surface. Add the parsley, thyme, bay leaves and black peppercorns.

5 Partly cover the stockpot and gently simmer the stock for 4–6 hours. All the bones and vegetables should always be covered with liquid, so top up with a little boiling water from time to time if necessary.

6 Strain the stock through a colander into a bowl, then skim as much fat as possible from the surface. If possible, cool the stock and then chill it in the refrigerator; the fat will rise to the top and set in a layer that can be removed easily.

Stock for Chinese Soups

This stock is an excellent basis for delicate Chinese soups.

Makes 2.5 litres/4¹/₂ pints/11 cups

675g/1¹/₂lb chicken portions

675g/1¹/₂lb pork spareribs

3.75 litres/6 pints/16 cups water

3–4 pieces fresh root ginger, unpeeled and crushed

3–4 spring onions (scallions), each tied into a knot

45–60ml/3–4 tbsp Chinese rice wine

1 Trim off any excess fat from the chicken and spareribs and chop them into large pieces.

2 Place the chicken and sparerib pieces in a large stockpot with the water. Add the ginger and spring onion knots.

3 Bring to the boil and, using a sieve, skim off the froth. Reduce the heat and simmer, uncovered, for 2–3 hours.

4 Strain the stock, discarding the chicken, pork, ginger and spring onions. Add the rice wine and return to the boil. Simmer for 2–3 minutes. Store the stock in the refrigerator when it has cooled. It will keep for up to 4–5 days. Alternatively, it can be frozen in small containers and thawed when it is required.

Stock for Japanese Soups

Dashi is the stock that gives the characteristically Japanese flavour to many dishes. Known as Ichiban-dashi, *it is used for delicately flavoured dishes, including soups. Of course instant stock is available in all Japanese supermarkets, either in granule form, in concentrate or even in a tea-bag style. Follow the instructions on the packet.*

INGREDIENTS

Makes about 800ml/1⅓ pints/3½ cups

10g/¼oz dried kombu seaweed

10–15g/¼–½oz bonito flakes

VARIATION

For vegetarian dashi, just omit the bonito flakes (dried tuna) and follow the same method.

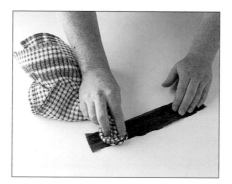

1 Wipe the kombu seaweed with a damp cloth and cut two slits in it with scissors, so that it flavours the stock effectively.

2 Soak the kombu in 900ml/ 1½ pints/3¾ cups cold water for 30–60 minutes.

3 Heat the kombu in its soaking water over a moderate heat. Just before the water boils, remove the seaweed. Then add the bonito flakes and bring to the boil over a high heat, then remove the pan from the heat.

4 Leave the stock until all the bonito flakes have sunk to the base of the pan. Line a strainer with kitchen paper or muslin (cheesecloth) and place it over a large bowl, then gently strain.

V

Garnishes

Sometimes, a soup needs something to lift it out of the ordinary, and garnishes are the answer. They are an important finishing touch; they not only look good, but also add an extra dimension to the flavour. A garnish can be as simple as a sprinkling of chopped parsley, a swirl of cream or some freshly grated cheese. Alternatively, it can be something that requires a little more attention, such as home-made croûtons or sippets. All the garnishes featured here are suitable for vegetarian soups.

DUMPLINGS

These dumplings are easy to make and add an attractive and tasty finishing touch to country soups.

INGREDIENTS

75g/3oz/¹/₂ cup semolina or flour
1 egg, beaten
45ml/3 tbsp milk or water
generous pinch of salt
15ml/1 tbsp chopped fresh parsley

1 Combine all the ingredients into a soft, elastic dough. Leave to stand, covered with clear film (plastic wrap), for 10 minutes.

2 Drop small rounded dessert-spoonfuls of this mixture into the soup and cook for 10 minutes, until firm.

CRISPY CROÛTONS

Croûtons add a lovely crunchy texture to creamy soups and are a good way of using up stale bread. Use thinly sliced ciabatta or French bread for delicious results.

INGREDIENTS

bread
good quality, flavourless oil, such as sunflower or groundnut (peanut) or, for a fuller flavour, extra virgin olive oil or a flavoured oil, such as one with garlic and herbs or chilli

1 Preheat the oven to 200ºC/400ºF/Gas 6. Cut the bread into small cubes and place on a baking sheet.

2 Brush with your chosen oil, then bake for 15 minutes, until golden and crisp. Leave to cool slightly: they crisp up further as they cool down.

3 Store them in an airtight container for up to a week. Reheat in a warm oven, if you like, before serving.

RIVELS

Rivels are pea-size pieces of dough which swell when cooked in a soup.

INGREDIENTS

1 egg
75–115g/3–4oz/³/₄–1 cup flour
2.5ml/¹/₂ tsp salt
freshly ground black pepper

1 Beat the egg in a bowl. Add the flour, salt and pepper to taste and mix with a wooden spoon. Finish mixing with your fingers, rubbing to blend the egg and flour together to form pea-size pieces.

2 Bring the soup back to the boil. Sprinkle in the pieces of dough, stirring gently.

3 Reduce the heat and simmer for about 6 minutes, until the rivels are slightly swollen and cooked through. Serve the garnished soup immediately.

SWIRLED CREAM

An attractive swirl of cream is the classic finish for many soups, such as a smooth tomato soup and chilled asparagus soup. The garnish gives a delightfully professional finish to your soup, although the technique is simplicity itself.

INGREDIENTS

single (light) cream

1 Transfer the cream into a jug (pitcher). Pour a swirl on to the surface of each bowl of soup.

2 Draw the tip of a fine skewer quickly backwards and forwards through the cream to create a delicate pattern. Serve the soup immediately.

SIPPETS

Another good way of using up slightly stale bread, sippets are larger than croûtons and have a more intense flavour because of the addition of fresh herbs. Experiment with the herbs according to the flavour of the soup.

INGREDIENTS

3 slices day-old bread
50g/2 oz/4 tbsp butter
45ml/3 tbsp finely chopped fresh parsley,
    or coriander (cilantro) or basil

1 Cut the bread into fingers about 2.5cm/1in long.

2 Melt the butter in a large frying pan, toss in the small fingers of bread and cook gently until golden brown.

3 Add the fresh herbs and stir well to combine. Cook for a further minute, stirring constantly. Sprinkle the sippets on top of the soup and serve.

LEEK HAYSTACKS

Stacks of golden leek look good served on a creamy soup and the crunchy texture contrasts well with the smoothness of the soup.

INGREDIENTS

1 large leek
30ml/2 tbsp plain (all-purpose) flour
oil, for deep-frying

1 Slice the leek in half lengthways and then cut into quarters. Cut into 5cm/2in lengths and then into very fine strips. Place in a bowl, sprinkle the flour over and toss to coat.

2 Heat the oil to 160ºC/325ºF. Drop small spoonfuls of the floured leeks into the oil and cook for 30–45 seconds, until golden. Drain on kitchen paper. Repeat with the remaining leeks.

3 Serve the soup with a small stack of leeks piled on top of each bowl.

CHILLED SOUPS

There can hardly be a more delightful way to start a summer
lunch or *al fresco* dinner than with a refreshing chilled soup.
Make the most of seasonal vegetables, such as tomatoes and
asparagus, or surprise your guests with a chilled fruit soup.
Choose from classic recipes, such as Gazpacho or Vichyssoise,
or try a more adventurous dish, such as Sorrel and Spinach
Soup or Miami Avocado Soup. All are easy to make, look
fabulous and taste of pure sunshine.

Almond Soup

Unless you are prepared to spend time pounding all the ingredients for this soup by hand, a food processor is essential. Then you'll find that this Spanish soup is simple to make and refreshing to eat on a hot summer's day.

INGREDIENTS

Serves 6

115g/4 oz fresh white bread

750ml/1¼ pints/3 cups water

115g/4oz/1 cup blanched almonds

2 garlic cloves, sliced

75ml/5 tbsp olive oil

25ml/1½ tbsp sherry vinegar

salt and ground black pepper

For the garnish

toasted flaked (sliced) almonds

seedless green and black grapes, halved
  and skinned

1 Break the bread into a bowl and pour 150ml/¼ pint/ ⅔ cup of the water on top. Leave for 5 minutes.

2 Put the almonds and garlic in a blender or food processor and process until finely ground. Blend in the soaked bread.

3 Gradually add the oil until the mixture forms a smooth paste. Add the sherry vinegar, then the remaining cold water and process until smooth.

4 Transfer to a bowl and season with salt and pepper, adding a little more water if the soup is too thick. Chill for at least 2–3 hours. Serve sprinkled with the toasted almonds and grapes.

Tomato and Sweet Pepper Soup

This recipe was inspired by the Spanish gazpacho, the difference being that this soup is cooked first, and then chilled.

INGREDIENTS

Serves 4

2 red (bell) peppers, halved and seeded
45ml/3 tbsp olive oil
1 onion, finely chopped
2 garlic cloves, crushed
675g/1½lb ripe well-flavoured tomatoes
150ml/¼ pint/⅔ cup red wine
600ml/1 pint/2½ cups Chicken Stock
salt and ground black pepper
chopped fresh chives, to garnish

For the croûtons
2 slices white bread, crusts removed
60ml/4 tbsp olive oil

1 Cut each red pepper half into quarters. Place skin side up on a grill (broiler) rack and cook until the skins are charred. Transfer to a bowl and cover with a plate or pop into a plastic bag and seal.

2 Heat the oil in a large pan. Add the onion and garlic and cook gently until soft. Meanwhile, remove the skin from the peppers and coarsely chop the flesh. Cut the tomatoes into chunks.

3 Add the peppers and tomatoes to the pan, then cover and cook gently for 10 minutes. Add the wine and cook for a further 5 minutes, then add the stock and salt and pepper and continue to simmer for 20 minutes.

4 To make the croûtons, cut the bread into cubes. Heat the oil in a small frying pan, add the bread and cook until golden. Drain on kitchen paper and store in an airtight box.

5 Process the soup in a blender or food processor until smooth. Pour into a clean glass or ceramic bowl and leave to cool thoroughly before chilling in the refrigerator for at least 3 hours. When the soup is cold, season to taste with salt and pepper.

6 Serve the soup in bowls, topped with the croûtons and garnished with chopped chives.

V

Gazpacho with Avocado Salsa

Tomatoes, cucumber and peppers form the basis of this classic, chilled soup. Add a spoonful of chunky, fresh avocado salsa and a small sprinkling of croûtons for a delicious summer appetizer. This is quite a substantial soup, so follow with a light main course, such as grilled fish or chicken.

INGREDIENTS

Serves 4–6

2 slices day-old bread

600ml/1 pint/2½ cups chilled water

1kg/2¼ lb tomatoes

1 cucumber

1 red (bell) pepper, seeded and chopped

1 green chilli, seeded and chopped

2 garlic cloves, chopped

30ml/2 tbsp extra virgin olive oil

juice of 1 lime and 1 lemon

few drops of Tabasco sauce

salt and ground black pepper

handful of fresh basil, to garnish

8–12 ice cubes, to serve

For the croûtons

2–3 slices day-old bread, crusts removed

1 garlic clove, halved

15–30ml/1–2 tbsp olive oil

For the avocado salsa

1 ripe avocado

5ml/1 tsp lemon juice

2.5cm/1in piece cucumber, diced

½ red chilli, seeded and finely chopped

1 Make the soup first. In a shallow bowl, soak the day-old bread in 150ml/¼ pint/⅔ cup water for 5 minutes.

COOK'S TIP

For a superior flavour choose Haas avocados with the rough-textured, almost black skins.

---

2 Meanwhile, place the tomatoes in a heatproof bowl; cover with boiling water. Leave for 30 seconds, then peel, seed and chop the flesh.

3 Thinly peel the cucumber, cut in half lengthways and scoop out the seeds with a teaspoon. Discard the seeds and chop the flesh.

4 Place the bread, tomatoes, cucumber, red pepper, chilli, garlic, oil, citrus juices, Tabasco and 450ml/¾ pint/scant 2 cups chilled water in a food processor or blender. Blend until mixed but still chunky. Season and chill well.

5 To make the croûtons, rub the slices of bread with the cut surface of the garlic clove. Cut the bread into cubes and place in a plastic bag with the olive oil. Seal the bag and shake until the bread cubes are coated with the oil. Heat a large non-stick frying pan and cook the croûtons over a medium heat until crisp and golden.

6 Just before serving make the avocado salsa. Halve the avocado, remove the stone (pit), then peel and dice the flesh. Toss the avocado in the lemon juice to prevent it from browning, then mix with the cucumber and chilli.

7 Ladle the soup into bowls, add the ice cubes and top with a spoonful of avocado salsa. Garnish with the basil and hand around the croûtons separately.

Cucumber and Yogurt Soup with Walnuts

V

This is a particularly refreshing cold soup, using a classic combination of cucumber and yogurt.

INGREDIENTS

Serves 5–6

1 cucumber

4 garlic cloves

2.5ml/¹/₂ tsp salt

75g/3oz/³/₄ cup walnut pieces

40g/1¹/₂oz day-old bread, torn into pieces

30ml/2 tbsp walnut or sunflower oil

400ml/14fl oz/1²/₃ cups natural
   (plain) yogurt

120ml/4fl oz/¹/₂ cup cold water

5–10ml/1–2 tsp lemon juice

For the garnish

40g/1¹/₂oz/scant ¹/₂ cup walnuts,
   coarsely chopped

25ml/1¹/₂ tbsp olive oil

fresh dill sprigs

1 Cut the cucumber in half and peel one half of it. Dice the cucumber flesh and set aside.

2 Using a large mortar and pestle, crush together the garlic and salt well, then add the walnuts and bread.

3 When the mixture is smooth, gradually add the walnut or sunflower oil and combine well.

COOK'S TIP

If you prefer your soup smooth, process it in a food processor or blender before serving.

4 Transfer the mixture to a large bowl and beat in the yogurt and diced cucumber. Add the cold water and then stir in lemon juice to taste.

5 Pour the soup into chilled soup bowls to serve. Garnish with the chopped walnuts and drizzle with the olive oil. Finally, arrange the sprigs of dill on top and serve immediately.

V

Green Pea and Mint Soup

Perfect partners, peas and mint really capture the flavours of summer.

INGREDIENTS

Serves 4

50g/2oz/4 tbsp butter

4 spring onions (scallions), chopped

450g/1lb fresh or frozen peas

600ml/1 pint/2½ cups Vegetable Stock

2 large fresh mint sprigs

600ml/1 pint/2½ cups milk

pinch of sugar (optional)

salt and ground black pepper

small fresh mint sprigs, to garnish

single (light) cream, to serve

1 Heat the butter in a large pan, add the chopped spring onions and cook gently on a low heat until they are softened, but not browned.

2 Stir the peas into the pan, add the stock and mint and bring to the boil. Cover and simmer gently for about 30 minutes if you are using fresh peas (15 minutes if you are using frozen peas), until they are tender. Remove about 45ml/3 tbsp of the peas, and set aside to use for a garnish.

3 Pour the soup into a food processor or blender, add the milk and process until smooth. Season to taste, adding a pinch of sugar, if you like. Leave to cool, then chill lightly in the refrigerator.

4 Pour the soup into bowls. Swirl a little cream into each, then garnish with the mint and the reserved peas.

Watercress and Orange Soup

V

This is a healthy and refreshing soup, which is just as good served either hot or chilled.

INGREDIENTS

Serves 4

1 large onion, chopped

15ml/1 tbsp olive oil

2 bunches or bags of watercress

grated rind and juice of 1 large orange

600ml/1 pint/2½ cups Vegetable Stock

150ml/¼ pint/⅔ cup single (light) cream

10ml/2 tsp cornflour (cornstarch)

salt and ground black pepper

a little thick cream or natural (plain)
    yogurt, to garnish

4 orange wedges, to serve

1 Soften the onion in the oil in a large pan. Add the watercress, unchopped, to the onion. Cover and cook for about 5 minutes, until the watercress is wilted.

2 Add the orange rind and juice and the stock to the watercress mixture. Bring to the boil, then lower the heat, cover and simmer for 10–15 minutes.

3 Process the soup thoroughly in a blender or food processor and sieve if you want to increase the smoothness of the finished soup. Blend the cream with the cornflour until no lumps remain, then add to the soup. Season to taste with salt and pepper.

4 Bring the soup gently back to the boil, stirring constantly until just slightly thickened. Check the seasoning.

5 Leave the soup to cool, then chill in the refrigerator. Serve the soup with a swirl of cream or yogurt, and a wedge of orange to squeeze in at the last moment.

6 If serving the soup hot, garnish with a swirl of cream or yogurt and orange wedges, as above, and serve immediately.

Hungarian Sour Cherry Soup

V

Particularly popular in summer, this fruit soup is typical of Hungarian cooking. The recipe makes good use of plump, sour cherries. Fruit soups are thickened with flour, and a touch of salt is added to help bring out the flavour of the cold soup.

INGREDIENTS

Serves 4

15ml/1 tbsp plain (all-purpose) flour

120ml/4fl oz/½ cup sour cream

a generous pinch of salt

5ml/1 tsp caster (superfine) sugar

225g/8oz/1½ cups fresh sour or morello
   cherries, pitted

900ml/1½ pints/3¾ cups water

50g/2oz/¼ cup granulated sugar

1 In a bowl, blend the flour with the sour cream until completely smooth, then add the salt and caster sugar.

2 Put the cherries in a pan with the water and granulated sugar. Gently poach for about 10 minutes.

3 Remove from the heat and set aside 30ml/2 tbsp of the cooking liquid as a garnish. Stir another 30ml/2 tbsp of the cherry liquid into the flour and sour cream mixture, then pour this on to the cherries.

4 Return to the heat. Bring to the boil, then simmer gently for 5–6 minutes.

5 Remove from the heat, cover with clear film (plastic wrap) and leave to cool. Add extra salt if necessary. Serve with the reserved cooking liquid swirled in.

Sorrel and Spinach Soup

This is an excellent Russian summer soup. If sorrel is unavailable, use double the amount of spinach instead and add a dash of lemon juice to the soup just before serving.

Serves 4

25g/1oz/2 tbsp butter

225g/8oz sorrel, washed and
  stalks removed

225g/8oz young spinach, washed and
  stalks removed

25g/1oz fresh horseradish, grated

750ml/1¼ pints/3 cups *kvas* or
  (hard) cider

1 pickled cucumber, finely chopped

30ml/2 tbsp chopped fresh dill

225g/8oz cooked fish, such as pike, perch
  or salmon, skinned and boned

salt and ground black pepper

fresh dill sprig, to garnish

1 Melt the butter in a large pan. Add the sorrel and spinach leaves and fresh horseradish. Cover and cook gently for 3–4 minutes, or until the leaves are wilted.

2 Spoon into a food processor and process to a fine purée. Ladle into a tureen or bowl and stir in the *kvas* or cider, cucumber and dill.

3 Chop the fish into bitesize pieces. Add to the soup, then season with plenty of salt and pepper. Chill for at least 3 hours before serving, garnished with a sprig of dill.

V

Melon and Basil Soup

This is a deliciously refreshing, fruit soup, just right for a hot day.

Serves 4–6

2 Charentais or rock melons

75g/3oz/scant ½ cup caster
   (superfine) sugar

175ml/6fl oz/¾ cup water

finely grated rind and juice of 1 lime

45ml/3 tbsp shredded fresh basil, plus
   whole leaves, to garnish

1 Cut the melons in half across the middle. Scrape out the seeds and discard. Using a melon baller, scoop out 20–24 balls and set aside for the garnish. Scoop out the remaining flesh and place in a blender or food processor.

COOK'S TIP

Add the syrup in two stages, as the amount of sugar needed will depend on the sweetness of the melon.

2 Place the sugar, water and lime rind in a small pan over a low heat. Stir until dissolved, bring to the boil and simmer gently for 2–3 minutes. Remove from the heat and leave to cool slightly. Pour half the mixture into the blender or food processor with the melon flesh. Blend until smooth, adding the remaining syrup and lime juice to taste.

3 Pour the mixture into a bowl, stir in the shredded basil and chill in the refrigerator. Serve garnished with whole basil leaves and the reserved melon balls.

Asparagus Soup

This delicate, pale green soup, garnished with a swirl of cream or yogurt, is as pretty as it is delicious.

INGREDIENTS

Serves 6

900g/2lb fresh asparagus

60ml/4 tbsp butter or olive oil

175g/6oz/1½ cups sliced leeks or spring onions (scallions)

45ml/3 tbsp plain (all-purpose) flour

1.5 litres/2½ pints/6¼ cups Chicken Stock or water

120ml/4fl oz/½ cup single (light) cream or natural (plain) yogurt

15ml/1 tbsp chopped fresh tarragon or chervil

salt and ground black pepper

3 Heat the butter or oil in a heavy pan. Add the sliced leeks or spring onions and cook over a low heat, stirring occasionally, for 5–8 minutes, until softened, but not browned. Stir in the chopped asparagus stalks, cover and cook for a further 6–8 minutes, until the stalks are tender.

4 Add the flour and stir well to blend. Cook for 3–4 minutes, uncovered, stirring occasionally.

5 Add the stock or water. Bring to the boil, stirring frequently, then reduce the heat and simmer for 30 minutes. Season to taste with salt and pepper.

6 Process the soup in a food processor or food mill. If necessary, strain it to remove any coarse fibres. Stir in the asparagus tips, most of the cream or yogurt, and the herbs. Cool, then chill well. Stir before serving and check the seasoning. Garnish each bowl with a swirl of cream or yogurt.

1 Cut the top 6cm/2½in off the asparagus spears and blanch in boiling water for 5–6 minutes, until just tender. Drain thoroughly. Cut each tip into two or three pieces and set aside.

2 Trim the ends of the stalks, removing any brown or woody parts. Chop the stalks into 1cm/½in pieces.

Prawn and Cucumber Soup

If you've never served a chilled soup before, this is the one to try first. Delicious and light, it's the perfect way to celebrate summer.

INGREDIENTS

Serves 4

25g/1oz/2 tbsp butter

2 shallots, finely chopped

2 garlic cloves, crushed

1 cucumber, peeled, seeded and diced

300ml/½ pint/1¼ cups milk

225g/8oz cooked peeled prawns (shrimp)

15ml/1 tbsp each finely chopped fresh
    mint, dill, chives and chervil

300ml/½ pint/1¼ cups whipping cream

salt and ground white pepper

For the garnish

30ml/2 tbsp crème fraîche or sour
    cream (optional)

4 large, cooked prawns (shrimp), peeled
    with tails intact

fresh chives and dill

1 Melt the butter in a pan and cook the shallots and garlic over a low heat until soft but not coloured. Add the cucumber and cook the vegetables gently, stirring frequently, until tender.

2 Stir in the milk, bring almost to the boil, then lower the heat and simmer for 5 minutes. Tip the soup into a blender or food processor and process until very smooth. Season to taste with salt and ground white pepper.

3 Pour the soup into a bowl and set aside to cool. When cool, stir in the prawns, chopped herbs and the whipping cream. Cover, transfer to the refrigerator and chill for at least 2 hours.

4 To serve, ladle the soup into four chilled individual bowls and top each portion with a spoonful of crème fraîche or sour cream, if using. Place a large prawn over the edge of each soup bowl. Garnish with the chives and dill.

COOK'S TIP

For a change try fresh or canned crab meat, or cooked, flaked salmon fillet.

Vichyssoise

This classic leek and potato soup was created by a French chef who named it after his home town.

INGREDIENTS

Serves four

25g/1oz/2 tbsp butter

15ml/1 tbsp vegetable oil

1 small onion, chopped

3 leeks, sliced

2 medium floury potatoes, diced

600ml/1 pint/2½ cups Vegetable Stock

300ml/½ pint/1¼ cups milk

45ml/3 tbsp single (light) cream

a little extra milk (optional)

salt and ground black pepper

60ml/4 tbsp natural (plain) yogurt and
    fried chopped leeks, to serve

1 Heat the butter and oil in a large, heavy pan and add the onion, leeks and potatoes. Cover and cook over a medium heat for 15 minutes, stirring occasionally.

2 Stir in the stock and milk. Bring to the boil, reduce the heat, cover the pan again and simmer for 10 minutes.

3 Ladle the vegetables and liquid into a blender or a food processor, in batches, and process to a smooth purée. Return to the pan, stir in the cream and season to taste with salt and pepper.

4 Leave the soup to cool, and then chill for 3–4 hours. You may need to add a little extra milk to thin down the soup, as it will thicken slightly as it cools.

5 Ladle the soup into soup bowls and serve topped with a spoonful of natural yogurt and a sprinkling of fried leeks.

V

Summer Tomato Soup

The success of this soup depends on having ripe, full-flavoured tomatoes, such as the oval plum variety, so make it when the tomato season is at its peak.

INGREDIENTS

Serves 4

15ml/1 tbsp olive oil

1 large onion, chopped

1 carrot, chopped

1kg/2¼lb ripe tomatoes, quartered

2 garlic cloves, chopped

5 fresh thyme sprigs, or
  1.5ml/¼ tsp dried thyme

4–5 fresh marjoram sprigs, or
  1.5ml/¼ tsp dried marjoram

1 bay leaf

45ml/3 tbsp crème fraîche, sour cream or
  natural (plain) yogurt, plus a little extra
  to garnish

salt and ground black pepper

1 Heat the olive oil in a large, preferably stainless steel pan or flameproof casserole.

2 Add the onion and carrot and cook for 3–4 minutes.

3 Add the quartered tomatoes, chopped garlic and herbs. Reduce the heat and simmer, covered, for 30 minutes.

4 Discard the bay leaf and pass the soup through a food mill or press through a sieve. Leave to cool, then chill in the refrigerator.

VARIATION

If you like, you can use oregano instead of marjoram, and parsley instead of thyme.

Miami Avocado Soup

Avocados are combined with lemon juice, dry sherry and an optional dash of hot pepper sauce, to make this subtle chilled soup.

INGREDIENTS

Serves 4

2 large or 3 medium ripe avocados

15ml/1 tbsp fresh lemon juice

75g/3oz/¾ cup coarsely chopped
    peeled cucumber

30ml/2 tbsp dry sherry

25g/1oz/¼ cup coarsely chopped spring
    onions (scallions), with some of the
    green stems

475ml/16fl oz/2 cups Chicken Stock

5ml/1 tsp salt

hot pepper sauce (optional)

natural (plain) yogurt, to garnish

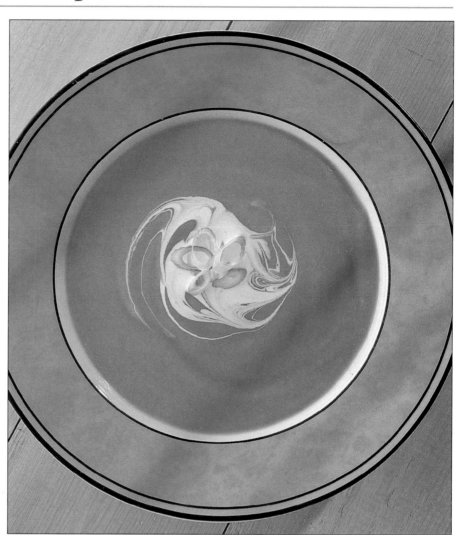

1 Cut the avocados in half, remove the stones (pits) and peel. Coarsely chop the flesh and place in a food processor or blender. Add the lemon juice and process until very smooth.

2 Add the cucumber, sherry and most of the spring onions, reserving a few for the garnish. Process again until smooth.

3 In a large bowl, combine the avocado mixture with the chicken stock. Whisk until well blended. Season with the salt and a few drops of hot pepper sauce, if you like. Cover the bowl with clear film (plastic wrap) and place in the refrigerator to chill thoroughly.

4 To serve, fill four individual bowls with the soup. Place a spoonful of yogurt in the centre of each bowl and swirl with a spoon. Finally, sprinkle with the reserved chopped spring onions.

CREAMED VEGETABLE SOUPS

Whether family favourites, such as Cream of Tomato Soup,
luxurious dinner-party dishes, such as Wild Mushroom Soup,
or international classics, such as Fresh Pea Soup St Germain,
there is something wonderfully comforting and welcoming
about creamy soups. Some are warming and filling, others
are delicate and elegant, still more are rich and colourful.
Whatever the season or occasion, a creamed vegetable
soup is the perfect choice for whetting the appetite and
stimulating the taste buds.

Italian Tomato Soup

This is the perfect soup for late summer when fresh tomatoes are at their most flavoursome.

INGREDIENTS

Serves 4–6

15ml/1 tbsp olive oil

25g/1oz/2 tbsp butter

1 onion, finely chopped

900g/2lb ripe Italian plum tomatoes, coarsely chopped

1 garlic clove, coarsely chopped

750ml/1¼ pints/3 cups Chicken Stock

120ml/4 fl oz/½ cup dry white wine

30ml/2 tbsp sun-dried tomato paste

30ml/2 tbsp shredded fresh basil, plus a few whole leaves to garnish

150ml/¼ pint/⅔ cup double (heavy) cream

salt and ground black pepper

1 Heat the oil and butter in a large pan until foaming. Add the onion and cook gently, stirring frequently, for about 5 minutes, until softened, but not brown.

2 Stir in the chopped tomatoes and garlic, then add the stock, white wine and sun-dried tomato paste and season with salt and pepper to taste.

3 Bring to the boil, then lower the heat, half-cover the pan and simmer gently for 20 minutes, stirring occasionally to stop the tomatoes from sticking to the base of the pan.

4 Process the soup with the shredded basil in a food processor or blender, then press through a sieve into a clean pan.

5 Add the double cream and heat through, stirring. Do not allow the soup to approach boiling point. Check the consistency and add more stock, if necessary. Adjust the seasoning to taste, pour the soup into heated bowls and garnish with whole basil leaves. Serve immediately.

Wild Mushroom Soup

Wild mushrooms are expensive. Dried porcini have an intense flavour, so only a small quantity is needed. Meat stock may seem odd in a vegetable soup, but it helps to strengthen the earthy flavour.

INGREDIENTS

Serves 4

25g/1oz/2 cups dried porcini mushrooms

250ml/8fl oz/1 cup warm water

30ml/2 tbsp olive oil

15g/½oz/1 tbsp butter

2 leeks, thinly sliced

2 shallots, coarsely chopped

1 garlic clove, coarsely chopped

225g/8oz fresh wild mushrooms

1.2 litres/2 pints/5 cups Meat Stock

2.5ml/½ tsp dried thyme

150ml/¼ pint/⅔ cup double
    (heavy) cream

salt and ground black pepper

fresh thyme sprigs, to garnish

3 Chop or thinly slice the fresh mushrooms and add to the pan. Stir over a medium heat for a few minutes until they begin to soften. Pour in the meat stock and bring to the boil. Add the porcini, soaking liquid, dried thyme and salt and pepper. Lower the heat, half-cover the pan and simmer gently for 30 minutes, stirring occasionally.

4 Pour about three-quarters of the soup into a blender or food processor and process until smooth. Return to the soup remaining in the pan, stir in the double cream and heat through. Check the consistency, adding more stock or water if the soup is too thick. Taste and adjust the seasoning. Serve hot, garnished with sprigs of fresh thyme.

1 Put the dried porcini in a bowl, add the warm water and leave to soak for 20–30 minutes. Lift out of the liquid and squeeze to remove as much of the soaking liquid as possible. Strain all the liquid and reserve to use later. Finely chop the porcini.

2 Heat the oil and butter in a large pan until foaming. Add the leeks, shallots and garlic and cook gently for about 5 minutes, stirring frequently, until softened but not coloured.

Cream of Tomato Soup

Tomato soup is an old favourite. This version is made special by the addition of fresh herbs and cream.

INGREDIENTS

Serves 4

25g/1oz/2 tbsp butter or margarine

1 onion, chopped

900g/2lb tomatoes, peeled and quartered

2 carrots, chopped

450ml/¾ pint/scant 2 cups Chicken Stock

30ml/2 tbsp chopped fresh parsley

2.5ml/½ tsp fresh thyme leaves, plus extra
　to garnish

75ml/5 tbsp whipping cream

salt and ground black pepper

1 Melt the butter or margarine in a large, heavy pan. Add the onion and cook for 5 minutes, until softened.

2 Stir in the tomato quarters, carrots, chicken stock, parsley and thyme. Bring to the boil, then reduce the heat to low, cover the pan and simmer gently for about 15–20 minutes, until all the vegetables are tender.

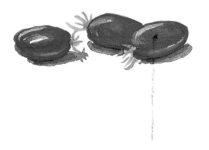

3 Purée the soup in a vegetable mill until it is smooth. Alternatively, process the soup in a blender or food processor, then press through a sieve. Return the puréed soup to the pan.

4 Stir in the cream and reheat gently. Season the soup to taste with salt and ground black pepper. Ladle into warmed soup bowls and serve immediately while piping hot, garnished with fresh thyme leaves.

COOK'S TIP

Meaty and flavourful, Italian plum tomatoes are the best choice for this soup.

Cream of Spring Onion Soup

V

The oniony flavour of this soup is surprisingly delicate.

Serves 4–6

25g/1oz/2 tbsp butter

1 small onion, chopped

bunch of spring onions (scallions), chopped

225g/8oz potatoes, chopped

600ml/1 pint/2½ cups Vegetable Stock

350ml/12fl oz/1½ cups single (light) cream

30ml/2 tbsp lemon juice

salt and freshly ground white pepper

chopped fresh chives, to garnish

1 Melt the butter in a pan and add all the onions. Cover and cook over very low heat for about 10 minutes or until soft.

2 Add the potatoes and the stock. Bring to the boil, then cover again and simmer over a moderately low heat for about 30 minutes. Cool slightly.

3 Process the soup in a blender or food processor.

4 If serving the soup hot, pour it back into the pan. Add the cream and season to taste with salt and pepper. Reheat the soup gently, stirring occasionally. Add the lemon juice.

5 If serving the soup cold, pour it into a bowl. Stir in the cream and lemon juice and season with salt and pepper. Cover the bowl and chill for at least 1 hour.

6 Sprinkle with the chopped fresh chives before serving, whether hot or chilled.

Butternut Squash Bisque

This is a fragrant, creamy and delicately flavoured soup.

INGREDIENTS

Serves 4

25g/1oz/2 tbsp butter or margarine

2 small onions, finely chopped

450g/1lb butternut squash, peeled, seeded and cubed

1.2 litres/2 pints/5 cups Chicken Stock

225g/8oz potatoes, cubed

5ml/1 tsp paprika

120ml/4fl oz/½ cup whipping cream (optional)

25ml/1½ tbsp chopped fresh chives, plus a few whole chives to garnish

salt and ground black pepper

1 Melt the butter or margarine in a large pan. Add the onions and cook over a medium heat for about 5 minutes, until soft.

2 Add the squash, chicken stock, potatoes and paprika. Bring to the boil. Reduce the heat to low, cover the pan and simmer gently for about 35 minutes until all the vegetables are soft.

3 Pour the soup into a food processor or blender and process until smooth. Return the soup to the pan and stir in the cream, if using. Season with salt and pepper. Reheat gently.

4 Stir in the chopped chives just before serving. Garnish each serving with a few whole chives and serve hot.

Cream of Red Pepper Soup

Grilling peppers gives them a sweet, smoky flavour, which is delicious in salads or, as here, in a velvety soup with a secret flavouring of rosemary to add aromatic depth. The soup is equally good served hot or chilled, as you prefer.

INGREDIENTS

Serves 4

4 red (bell) peppers

25g/1oz/2 tbsp butter

1 onion, finely chopped

1 fresh rosemary sprig

1.2 litres/2 pints/5 cups Chicken or
   Vegetable Stock

45ml/3 tbsp tomato purée (paste)

120ml/4fl oz/½ cup double (heavy) cream

paprika

salt and ground black pepper

1 Preheat the grill (broiler). Put the peppers in the grill pan under the grill and turn them regularly until the skins have blackened all around. Put them into plastic bags, sealing them closed. Leave them for 20 minutes.

2 Peel the blackened skin off the peppers. If possible, avoid rinsing them under running water, as this loses some of the natural oil and hence the flavour.

3 Halve the peppers, removing the seeds, stalks and pith, then coarsely chop the flesh.

4 Melt the butter in a deep pan. Add the onion and rosemary and cook gently over a low heat for about 5 minutes. Remove the rosemary and discard.

5 Add the peppers and stock to the onion, bring to the boil and simmer for 15 minutes. Stir in the tomato purée, then process or sieve the soup to a smooth purée.

6 Stir in half the cream and season with paprika, salt, if necessary, and pepper.

7 Serve the soup hot or chilled, with the remaining cream swirled delicately on top. Speckle the cream very lightly with a pinch of paprika.

Corn Soup

This is a simple to make, yet very flavoursome soup. It is sometimes made with sour cream and cream cheese. Poblano chillies may be added, but these are rather difficult to locate outside Mexico. However, you may be able to find them canned in some of the larger supermarkets and delicatessens.

INGREDIENTS

Serves 4

30ml/2 tbsp corn oil

1 onion, finely chopped

1 red (bell) pepper, seeded and chopped

450g/1lb corn kernels, thawed
　if frozen

750ml/1¼ pints/3 cups Chicken Stock

250ml/8fl oz/1 cup single (light) cream

salt and ground black pepper

½ red (bell) pepper, seeded and finely
　diced, to garnish

1 Heat the oil in a frying pan and sauté the onion and red pepper for about 5 minutes, until soft. Add the corn and sauté for 2 minutes.

2 Carefully tip the contents of the pan into a food processor or blender. Process until the mixture is smooth, scraping down the sides and adding a little of the stock, if necessary.

3 Put the mixture into a clean pan and stir in the stock. Season to taste with salt and pepper, bring to a simmer and cook for 5 minutes.

4 Gently stir in the cream. Serve the soup hot or chilled, with the diced red pepper sprinkled over. If serving hot, reheat gently after adding the cream, but do not allow the soup to boil.

Courgette Soup

This soup is so simple – in terms of ingredients and preparation. It would provide an elegant start to a dinner party.

INGREDIENTS

Serves 4

25g/1oz/2 tbsp butter

1 onion, finely chopped

450g/1lb young courgettes (zucchini),
　trimmed and chopped

750ml/1¼ pints/3 cups Chicken Stock

120ml/4fl oz/½ cup single (light) cream,
　plus extra to serve

salt and ground black pepper

1 Melt the butter in a pan and sauté the onion until it is soft. Add the courgettes and cook, stirring, for 1–2 minutes.

2 Add the chicken stock. Bring to the boil over a moderate heat and then simmer for about 5 minutes, or until the courgettes are just tender.

COOK'S TIP

Always use the smallest courgettes (zucchini) available, as these have the best flavour.

3 Strain the stock into a clean pan, saving the vegetable solids in the sieve. Purée the solids in the food processor and add to the pan. Season the soup to taste with salt and pepper.

4 Stir the cream into the soup and heat through very gently without allowing it to boil. Ladle into bowls and serve hot with a little extra cream swirled in.

V

Yogurt Soup

Some communities in India add sugar to this soup.

INGREDIENTS

Serves 4–6

450ml/¾ pint/scant 2 cups natural (plain) yogurt, beaten

25g/1oz/¼ cup gram flour (besan)

2.5ml/½ tsp chilli powder

2.5ml/½ tsp turmeric salt, to taste

2–3 fresh green chillies, finely chopped

60ml/4 tbsp vegetable oil

1 dried red chilli

5ml/1 tsp cumin seeds

3–4 curry leaves

3 garlic cloves, crushed

5cm/2in piece fresh root ginger, crushed

30ml/2 tbsp chopped fresh coriander (cilantro)

1 Mix together the yogurt, flour, chilli powder and turmeric salt and pass through a strainer into a pan. Add the fresh green chillies and cook gently for about 10 minutes, stirring occasionally. Be careful not to let the soup boil over.

2 Heat the oil in a frying pan and fry the dried chilli, cumin seeds, curry leaves, garlic and ginger until the dried chilli turns black. Stir in 15ml/1 tbsp of the chopped fresh coriander.

3 Pour the spices over the yogurt soup, cover the pan and leave to rest for 5 minutes. Mix well and gently reheat for 5 minutes more. Serve hot, garnished with the remaining chopped coriander.

Broccoli and Stilton Soup

*This is a really easy, but rich soup –
choose something simple to follow,
such as plainly roasted or grilled
meat, poultry or fish.*

INGREDIENTS

Serves 4

350g/12oz broccoli

25g/1oz/2 tbsp butter

1 onion, chopped

1 leek, white part only, chopped

1 small potato, cut into chunks

600ml/1 pint/2½ cups hot Chicken Stock

300ml/½ pint/1¼ cups milk

45ml/3 tbsp double (heavy) cream

115g/4 oz Stilton cheese, rind
   removed, crumbled

salt and ground black pepper

1 Break the broccoli into florets,
discarding any tough stems.
Set aside two small florets to
garnish the finished dish.

2 Melt the butter in a large pan
and cook the onion and leek
until soft, but not coloured. Add
the broccoli and potato, then pour
in the stock. Cover and simmer for
15–20 minutes, until the vegetables
are tender.

3 Cool slightly then pour into a
blender or food processor and
process until smooth. Strain the
mixture through a sieve back into
the rinsed pan.

4 Add the milk and double
cream to the pan. Season to
taste with salt and ground black
pepper. Reheat gently. At the last
minute, add the cheese, stirring
until it just melts. Do not boil.

5 Meanwhile, blanch the
reserved broccoli florets and
cut them vertically into thin slices.
Ladle the soup into warmed bowls
and garnish with the sliced
broccoli and a generous grinding
of black pepper.

V

Fresh Pea Soup St Germain

This soup takes its name from a suburb of Paris where peas used to be cultivated in market gardens.

INGREDIENTS

Serves 2–3

small knob (pat) of butter

2–3 shallots, finely chopped

400g/14oz/3 cups shelled fresh peas (from about 1.5kg/3lb garden peas)

500ml/17fl oz/2¼ cups water

45–60ml/3–4 tbsp whipping cream (optional)

salt and ground black pepper

Crispy Croûtons, to garnish

3 When the peas are tender, ladle them into a blender or food processor with a little of the cooking liquid and process until completely smooth.

4 Strain the soup into the pan or casserole, stir in the cream, if using, and heat through without boiling. Add the seasoning and serve hot, garnished with croûtons.

COOK'S TIP

If fresh peas are not available, use frozen peas, but thaw and rinse them before use.

1 Melt the butter in a heavy pan or flameproof casserole. Add the shallots and cook over a medium heat for about 3 minutes, stirring occasionally.

2 Add the peas and water and season with salt and a little pepper. Cover and simmer for about 12 minutes for young peas and up to 18 minutes for large or older peas, stirring occasionally.

Green Bean and Parmesan Soup

V

Fresh green beans and Parmesan cheese make a simple, but delicious combination of flavours.

INGREDIENTS

Serves 4

25g/1oz/2 tbsp butter or margarine

225g/8oz green beans, trimmed

1 garlic clove, crushed

450ml/³⁄₄ pint/scant 2 cups
    Vegetable Stock

40g/1¹⁄₂oz/¹⁄₂ cup grated Parmesan cheese

50ml/2fl oz/¹⁄₄ cup single (light) cream

salt and ground black pepper

30ml/2 tbsp chopped fresh parsley,
    to garnish

1 Melt the butter or margarine in a medium pan. Add the green beans and garlic and cook for 2–3 minutes over a medium heat, stirring frequently.

2 Stir in the stock and season with salt and pepper. Bring to the boil, then simmer, uncovered, for 10–15 minutes, until the beans are tender.

3 Pour the soup into a blender or food processor and process until smooth. Alternatively, purée the soup in a food mill. Return to the pan and reheat gently.

4 Stir in the Parmesan and cream. Sprinkle with the parsley and serve immediately.

Cream of Spinach Soup

This is a deliciously creamy soup that you will make again and again.

INGREDIENTS

Serves 4

25g/1oz/2 tbsp butter

1 small onion, chopped

675g/1½lb fresh spinach, chopped

1.2 litres/2 pints/5 cups Vegetable Stock

50g/2 oz creamed coconut or

    250ml/8fl oz/1 cup coconut cream

freshly grated nutmeg

300ml/½ pint/1¼ cups whipping cream

salt and ground black pepper

long strips of fresh chives, to garnish

3 Return the mixture to the pan and add the remaining stock and the coconut, with salt, pepper and nutmeg to taste. Simmer for 15 minutes to thicken.

4 Add the cream to the pan, stir well and heat through, but do not allow the soup to boil. Serve immediately, garnished with long strips of chives.

1 Melt the butter in a pan over a moderate heat and sauté the onion, stirring occasionally, for a few minutes until soft. Add the spinach, cover the pan and cook gently for 10 minutes, until the spinach has wilted and reduced.

2 Pour the spinach mixture into a blender or food processor and add a little of the stock. Blend until smooth.

Cream of Leek and Potato Soup

Serve this flavourful soup with a spoonful of crème fraîche or sour cream and sprinkle with a few chopped fresh chives – or, for special occasions, with a spoonful of caviar.

INGREDIENTS

Serves 6–8

450g/1lb potatoes, peeled and cubed

1.5 litres/2½ pints/6¼ cups Chicken Stock

350g/12 oz leeks, trimmed

150ml/¼ pint/⅔ cup crème fraîche or sour cream

salt and ground black pepper

45ml/3 tbsp chopped fresh chives, to garnish

1 Put the cubed potatoes and chicken stock in a pan or flameproof casserole and bring to the boil over a medium heat. Reduce the heat and simmer for 15–20 minutes.

2 Make a slit along the length of each leek and rinse well under cold running water to wash away any soil. Slice thinly.

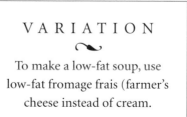
VARIATION

To make a low-fat soup, use low-fat fromage frais (farmer's cheese instead of cream.

3 When the potatoes are barely tender, stir in the leeks. Taste, then season with salt and ground black pepper and simmer. stirring occasionally, for 10–15 minutes, until both the vegetables are soft. If the soup is too thick, thin it down with a little more chicken stock or water.

4 Process the soup in a blender or food processor. If you prefer a very smooth soup, pass it through a food mill or press through a coarse sieve. Stir in most of the cream and reheat gently, but do not boil. Ladle into warmed bowls and garnish with a swirl of cream and the chopped chives.

Cauliflower Cream Soup

V

This delicately flavoured, thick winter soup is enriched at the last minute with chopped hard-boiled eggs and crème fraîche.

INGREDIENTS

Serves 4

1 cauliflower, cut into large pieces

1 large onion, coarsely chopped

1 large garlic clove, chopped

bouquet garni

5ml/1 tsp ground coriander

pinch of mustard powder

900ml/1½ pints/3¾ cups Vegetable Stock

5–10ml/1–2 tsp cornflour (cornstarch)

150ml/¼ pint/⅔ cup milk

45ml/3 tbsp crème fraîche

2 eggs, hard-boiled and coarsely chopped

15ml/1 tbsp chopped fresh coriander (cilantro)

salt and ground black pepper

1 Place the cauliflower in a large pan with the onion, garlic, bouquet garni, coriander, mustard, salt and pepper and stock. Simmer for 10–15 minutes. Cool slightly.

2 Remove and discard the garlic and the bouquet garni. Process the cauliflower and onion with some of the cooking liquid in a food processor. Return to the pan along with the rest of the liquid.

3 Blend the cornflour with a little of the milk to make a smooth paste, then add to the soup with the rest of the milk.

4 Return to the heat and cook until thickened, stirring constantly. Season to taste and, just before serving, turn off the heat and blend in the crème fraîche. Stir in the chopped egg and coriander and serve immediately.

Creamy Courgette and Dolcelatte Soup

V

The beauty of this soup is its delicate colour, its creamy texture and its subtle taste. If you prefer a more pronounced cheese flavour, use Gorgonzola instead of Dolcelatte.

INGREDIENTS

Serves 4–6

30ml/2 tbsp olive oil

15g/¹/₂oz/1 tbsp butter

1 onion, coarsely chopped

900g/2lb courgettes (zucchini), sliced

5ml/1 tsp dried oregano

about 600ml/1 pint/2¹/₂ cups
    Vegetable Stock

115g/4 oz Dolcelatte cheese, diced

300ml/¹/₂ pint/1¹/₄ cups single
    (light) cream

salt and ground black pepper

To garnish

fresh oregano sprigs

extra Dolcelatte cheese

1 Heat the olive oil and butter in a large, heavy pan until foaming. Add the onion and cook over a medium heat for about 5 minutes, stirring frequently, until softened, but not brown.

2 Add the courgettes and oregano and season with salt and pepper to taste. Cook over a medium heat for 10 minutes, stirring frequently.

3 Pour in the stock and bring to the boil, stirring frequently. Lower the heat, half-cover the pan and simmer gently, stirring occasionally, for about 30 minutes. Stir in the diced Dolcelatte until it is melted.

4 Process the soup in a blender or food processor until smooth, then press through a sieve into a clean pan.

5 Add two-thirds of the cream and stir over a low heat until hot, but not boiling. Check the consistency and add more stock if the soup is too thick. Taste and adjust the seasoning if necessary.

6 Pour into heated bowls. Swirl in the remaining cream, garnish with fresh oregano and extra Dolcelatte cheese, crumbled, and serve immediately.

Tomato and Blue Cheese Soup

The concentrated flavour of roasted tomatoes strikes a great balance with strong blue cheese.

INGREDIENTS

Serves 4

1.5kg/3lb ripe tomatoes, peeled, quartered
   and seeded
2 garlic cloves, crushed
30ml/2 tbsp vegetable oil or butter
1 leek, chopped
1 carrot, chopped
1.2 litres/2 pints/5 cups Chicken Stock
115g/4 oz blue cheese, crumbled
45ml/3 tbsp whipping cream
several large fresh basil leaves or 1–2 fresh
   parsley sprigs, plus extra to garnish
salt and ground black pepper
175g/6 oz bacon, cooked and crumbled,
   to garnish

1 Preheat the oven to 200°C/
400°F/Gas 6. Spread the
tomatoes in a shallow ovenproof
dish. Sprinkle with the garlic and
some salt and pepper. Place in the
oven and bake for 35 minutes.

2 Heat the oil or butter in a large
pan. Add the leek and carrot
and season lightly with salt and
pepper. Cook over a low heat,
stirring frequently, for about
10 minutes, until softened.

3 Stir in the stock and baked
tomatoes. Bring to the boil,
then lower the heat, cover and
simmer for about 20 minutes.

4 Add the blue cheese, cream
and basil or parsley. Transfer
to a food processor or blender and
process until smooth (work in
batches if necessary). Taste and
adjust the seasoning.

5 Reheat the soup, but do not
boil. Serve garnished with
bacon and a sprig of fresh herbs.

Cream of Mushroom Soup

A good mushroom soup makes the most of the subtle and sometimes rather elusive flavour of mushrooms. Button mushrooms are used here for their pale colour; chestnut or, better still, field mushrooms give a fuller flavour, but turn the soup brown.

INGREDIENTS

Serves 4

275g/10oz button (white) mushrooms
15ml/1 tbsp sunflower oil
40g/1½oz/3 tbsp butter
1 small onion, finely chopped
15ml/1 tbsp plain (all-purpose) flour
450ml/¾ pint/scant 2 cups Vegetable Stock
450ml/¾ pint/scant 2 cups milk
pinch of dried basil
30–45ml/2–3 tbsp single (light) cream
salt and ground black pepper
fresh basil leaves, to garnish

1 Separate the mushroom caps from the stalks. Finely slice the caps and finely chop the stalks.

2 Heat the oil and half the butter in a large, heavy pan and add the onion, mushroom stalks and about three-quarters of the sliced mushroom caps. Cook for about 1–2 minutes, stirring frequently, then cover and sweat over a gentle heat for 6–7 minutes, stirring occasionally.

3 Stir in the flour and cook for about 1 minute. Gradually add the stock and milk, stirring to make a smooth, thin sauce. Add the dried basil, and season to taste. Bring to the boil and simmer, partly covered, for 15 minutes.

4 Cool the soup slightly and then pour into a blender or food processor and process until smooth. Melt the remaining butter in a frying pan, add the remaining mushroom caps and cook gently for 3–4 minutes, until they are just tender.

5 Pour the soup into a clean pan and stir in the fried mushrooms. Heat until very hot. Taste and adjust the seasoning if necessary. Stir in the cream and heat briefly, but do not boil. Serve sprinkled with fresh basil leaves.

Cream of Avocado Soup

Avocados make wonderful soup – pretty, delicious and refreshing.

Serves 4

2 large ripe avocados
1 litre/1¾ pints/4 cups Chicken Stock
250ml/8fl oz/1 cup single (light) cream
fresh coriander (cilantro) leaves
salt and freshly ground white pepper

1 Cut the avocados in half, remove the stones (pits) and scoop out the flesh. Mash the flesh, then put it into a sieve and press it through the sieve with a wooden spoon into a warm soup tureen.

2 Heat the chicken stock with the cream in a pan. When the mixture is hot, but not boiling, whisk it into the puréed avocado in the tureen.

3 Season to taste with salt and pepper. Serve immediately, sprinkled with the fresh coriander. The soup may be served chilled, if you like.

Carrot Soup with Ginger

The zing of fresh ginger is an ideal complement to the sweetness of cooked carrots.

INGREDIENTS

Serves 6

25g/1oz/2 tbsp butter or margarine

1 onion, chopped

1 celery stick, chopped

1 potato, chopped

675g/1½lb carrots, chopped

10ml/2 tsp crushed fresh root ginger

1.2 litres/2 pints/5 cups Chicken Stock

105ml/7 tbsp whipping cream

good pinch of freshly grated nutmeg

salt and ground black pepper

1 Put the butter or margarine, onion and celery into a large pan and cook for about 5 minutes, until softened.

2 Stir in the potato, carrots, ginger and stock. Bring to the boil. Reduce the heat to low, cover and simmer for about 20 minutes.

3 Pour the soup into a blender or food processor and process until it is smooth. Alternatively, use a vegetable mill to purée the soup. Return the soup to the pan. Stir in the cream and nutmeg and season with salt and pepper to taste. Reheat gently, but do not allow the soup to boil. Serve hot.

Pear and Watercress Soup

The sweetness of the pears in the soup is complemented beautifully by Stilton croûtons. Their flavours make them natural partners.

INGREDIENTS

Serves 6

1 bunch of watercress

4 pears, peeled, cored
   and sliced

900ml/1½ pints/3¾ cups Chicken Stock

120ml/4fl oz/½ cup double (heavy) cream

juice of 1 lime

salt and ground black pepper

For the croûtons

25g/1oz/2 tbsp butter

15ml/1 tbsp olive oil

200g/7oz/3 cups cubed stale bread

150g/5oz/1 cup chopped Stilton cheese

1 Reserve about a third of the watercress leaves. Place the rest of the leaves and stalks in a pan with the pears, stock and a little seasoning. Simmer for about 15–20 minutes. Reserving some watercress leaves for garnishing, add the rest of the leaves and then process in a blender or food processor until smooth.

2 Put the mixture into a bowl and stir in the cream and the lime juice to mix the flavours thoroughly. Taste and adjust the seasoning if necessary. Pour all the soup back into a clean pan and reheat, stirring gently until warmed through.

3 To make the croûtons, melt the butter with the olive oil in a frying pan and cook the bread cubes until golden brown. Drain on kitchen paper. Put the cheese on top and heat under a hot grill (broiler) until bubbling. Reheat the soup and pour into bowls. Divide the croûtons and the reserved watercress leaves among the bowls and serve immediately.

Spiced Parsnip Soup

*This pale, creamy textured soup
is given a special touch with an
aromatic, spiced garlic and
coriander garnish.*

INGREDIENTS

Serves 4–6

40g/1½oz/3 tbsp butter

1 onion, chopped

675g/1½lb parsnips, diced

5ml/1 tsp ground coriander

2.5ml/½ tsp ground cumin

2.5ml/½ tsp ground turmeric

1.5ml/¼ tsp chilli powder

1.2 litres/2 pints/5 cups Chicken Stock

150ml/¼ pint/⅔ cup single (light) cream

15ml/1 tbsp sunflower oil

1 garlic clove, cut into julienne strips

10ml/2 tsp yellow mustard seeds

salt and ground black pepper

1 Melt the butter in a large pan,
add the onion and parsnips
and cook gently for 3 minutes.

2 Stir in the spices and cook for
1 minute more. Add the stock,
season with salt and pepper to
taste and bring to the boil.

3 Reduce the heat, cover and
simmer for about 45 minutes,
until the parsnips are tender. Cool
slightly, then process the soup in a
blender or food processor until
smooth. Return the soup to the
pan, add the cream and heat
through gently over a low heat, but
do not allow to boil.

4 Heat the oil in a small pan,
add the julienne strips of
garlic and the yellow mustard
seeds and fry quickly until the
garlic is beginning to brown and
the mustard seeds start to pop and
splutter. Remove from the heat.

5 Ladle the soup into warmed
soup bowls and pour a little of
the hot spice mixture over each
one. Serve immediately.

V

Mushroom and Bread Soup with Parsley

Thickened with bread, this rich mushroom soup will warm you up on cold winter days.

INGREDIENTS

Serves 8

75g/3 oz/6 tbsp unsalted (sweet) butter

900g/2lb field (portabello) mushrooms, sliced

2 onions, coarsely chopped

600ml/1 pint/2½ cups milk

8 slices white bread

60ml/4 tbsp chopped fresh parsley

300ml/½ pint/1¼ cups double (heavy) cream

salt and ground black pepper

1 Melt the butter in a large pan, add the sliced mushrooms and chopped onions and cook over a low heat, stirring occasionally, for about 10 minutes, until soft but not browned. Add the milk.

2 Tear the bread into pieces, drop them into the soup and leave to soak for 15 minutes. Purée the soup and return it to the pan. Add 45ml/3 tbsp of the parsley, the cream and seasoning. Reheat, without boiling. Serve garnished with the remaining parsley.

Baby Carrot and Fennel Soup

Sweet tender carrots find their moment of glory in this delicately spiced soup. Fennel provides a very subtle aniseed flavour that does not overpower the carrots.

INGREDIENTS

Serves 4

50g/2oz/4 tbsp butter

1 small bunch of spring onions (scallions), chopped

150g/5oz fennel bulb, chopped

1 celery stick, chopped

450g/1lb baby carrots, grated

2.5ml/½ tsp ground cumin

150g/5oz new potatoes, diced

1.2 litres/2 pints/5 cups Chicken Stock

60ml/4 tbsp double (heavy) cream

salt and ground black pepper

60ml/4 tbsp chopped fresh parsley, to garnish

1 Melt the butter in a large pan and add the spring onions, fennel, celery, carrots and cumin. Cover and cook over a low heat, stirring occasionally, for about 5 minutes, or until soft.

2 Add the diced potatoes and chicken stock, and gently simmer the mixture for a further 10 minutes.

3 Purée the soup in the pan with a hand-held blender. Stir in the cream and season to taste. Serve in individual soup bowls and garnish with chopped parsley.

COOK'S TIP

For convenience, you can freeze the soup in portions before adding the cream, seasoning and parsley.

Squash Soup with Horseradish Cream

The combination of cream, curry powder and horseradish makes a wonderful topping for this beautiful golden soup.

INGREDIENTS

Serves 6

1 butternut squash
1 cooking apple
25g/1oz/2 tbsp butter
1 onion, finely chopped
5–10ml/1–2 tsp curry powder, plus extra to garnish
900ml/1½ pints/3¾ cups Vegetable Stock
5ml/1 tsp chopped fresh sage
150ml/¼ pint/⅔ cup apple juice
salt and ground black pepper
lime shreds, to garnish (optional)

For the horseradish cream
60ml/4 tbsp double (heavy) cream
10ml/2 tsp horseradish sauce
2.5ml/½ tsp curry powder

1 Peel the squash, remove the seeds and chop the flesh. Peel, core and chop the apple.

2 Melt the butter in a large pan. Add the onion and cook over a medium heat, stirring frequently, for 5 minutes, until soft. Stir in the curry powder. Cook to bring out the flavour, stirring constantly, for 2 minutes.

3 Add the stock, squash, apple and sage. Bring to the boil, lower the heat, cover and simmer for 20 minutes, until the squash and apple are soft.

4 Meanwhile, make the horseradish cream. Whip the cream in a bowl until stiff, then stir in the horseradish sauce and curry powder. Cover and chill until required.

5 Process the soup in a blender or food processor. Return to the clean pan and add the apple juice, with salt and pepper to taste. Reheat gently, without boiling.

6 Serve the soup in warm bowls, topped with a spoonful of horseradish cream and a dusting of curry powder. Garnish with a few lime shreds, if you like.

Simple Cream of Onion Soup

This wonderfully soothing soup has a deep, buttery flavour that is complemented by crisp croûtons or chopped chives, sprinkled over just before serving.

INGREDIENTS

Serves 4

115g/4oz/½ cup unsalted (sweet) butter
1kg/2¼lb yellow onions, sliced
1 fresh bay leaf
105ml/7 tbsp dry white vermouth
1 litre/1¾ pints/4 cups Chicken or
　Vegetable stock
150ml/¼ pint/⅔ cup double (heavy) cream
a little lemon juice (optional)
salt and ground black pepper
croûtons or chopped fresh chives,
　to garnish

1 Melt 75g/3oz/6 tbsp of the butter in a large, heavy pan. Set about 200g/7oz of the onions aside and add the rest to the pan with the bay leaf. Stir to coat in the butter, then cover and cook very gently for about 30 minutes. The onions should be very soft and tender, but not browned.

COOK'S TIP

Adding the second batch of onions gives texture and a lovely buttery flavour to this soup. Make sure the onions do not brown.

2 Add the vermouth, increase the heat and boil rapidly until the liquid has evaporated. Add the stock, 5ml/1 tsp salt and pepper to taste. Bring to the boil, lower the heat and simmer for 5 minutes, then remove from the heat.

3 Leave the soup to cool, then remove and discard the bay leaf. Process the soup in a blender or food processor. Return the soup to the rinsed pan.

4 Meanwhile, melt the rest of the butter in another pan and add the remaining onions, cover and cook gently until soft but not browned. Uncover and continue to cook gently until the onions are golden yellow.

5 Add the cream to the soup and reheat it gently until hot, but do not allow it to boil. Taste and adjust the seasoning, adding a little lemon juice if you like. Add the buttery onions and stir for 1–2 minutes, then ladle the soup into bowls. Sprinkle with croûtons or chopped chives and serve.

Jerusalem Artichoke Soup

Topped with saffron cream, this soup is wonderful on a chilly day.

INGREDIENTS

Serves 4

50g/2oz/4 tbsp butter

1 onion, chopped

450g/1lb Jerusalem artichokes, peeled and cut into chunks

900ml/1½ pints/3¾ cups Chicken Stock

150ml/¼ pint/⅔ cup milk

150ml/¼ pint/⅔ cup double (heavy) cream

good pinch of saffron powder

salt and ground black pepper

chopped fresh chives, to garnish

1 Melt the butter in a large, heavy pan and cook the onion for 5–8 minutes, until soft but not browned, stirring occasionally.

2 Add the Jerusalem artichokes to the pan and stir until coated in the butter. Cover and cook gently for 10–15 minutes, but do not allow the artichokes to brown.

3 Pour in the chicken stock and milk, then cover and simmer for 15 minutes. Cool slightly, then process in a blender or food processor until smooth.

4 Strain the soup back into the pan. Add half the cream, season to taste with salt and pepper and reheat gently. Lightly whip the remaining cream and the saffron powder. Ladle the soup into warmed soup bowls and put a spoonful of saffron cream in the centre of each. Sprinkle the chopped chives over the top and serve immediately.

Watercress Soup

A delicious and nutritious soup which should be served with crusty bread.

INGREDIENTS

Serves 4

15ml/1 tbsp sunflower oil

15g/½oz/1 tbsp butter

1 onion, finely chopped

1 potato, diced

about 175g/6oz watercress

400ml/14fl oz/1⅔ cups Vegetable Stock

400ml/14fl oz/1⅔ cups milk

lemon juice, to taste

salt and ground black pepper

sour cream, to serve

1 Heat the oil and butter in a large, heavy pan and cook the onion over a gentle heat for about 5 minutes, until soft, but not browned. Add the potato, cook gently for 2–3 minutes and then cover and sweat for 5 minutes over a gentle heat, stirring occasionally.

2 Strip the watercress leaves from the stalks and coarsely chop the stalks.

COOK'S TIP

Provided you leave out the sour cream, this is a low-calorie soup.

3 Add the stock and milk to the pan, stir in the chopped watercress stalks and season to taste with salt and pepper. Bring to the boil, lower the heat and simmer gently, partially covered, for 10–12 minutes, until the potatoes are tender. Add all but a few of the watercress leaves and simmer for 2 minutes more.

4 Process the soup in a blender or food processor, then pour into a clean pan and heat gently with the reserved watercress leaves.

5 Taste the soup when hot, add a little lemon juice and adjust the seasoning.

6 Pour the soup into warmed soup bowls and garnish with a little sour cream in the centre just before serving.

SMOOTH VEGETABLE SOUPS

What better way to persuade fussy children – or awkward adults – to eat a healthy portion of vegetables than to make any of these superb soups? Their deliciously smooth texture makes them really moreish and there are recipes to suit all tastes, from hot and spicy to rich and warming and from exotic and sweet to substantial and earthy. All you need is this marvellous collection of recipes and a blender, food processor or food mill and you will truly be a "whizz" in the kitchen.

V

Fresh Mushroom Soup with Tarragon

This is a light mushroom soup, subtly flavoured with tarragon.

INGREDIENTS

Serves 6

15g/½oz/1 tbsp butter or margarine

4 shallots, finely chopped

450g/1lb/6 cups chestnut mushrooms, finely chopped

300ml/½ pint/1¼ cups Vegetable Stock

300ml/½ pint/ 1¼ cups semi-skimmed (low-fat) milk

15–30ml/1–2 tbsp chopped fresh tarragon

30ml/2 tbsp dry sherry (optional)

salt and ground black pepper

fresh tarragon sprigs, to garnish

1 Melt the butter or margarine in a large pan, add the shallots and cook over a low heat, stirring occasionally, for 5 minutes. Add the mushrooms and cook gently for 3 minutes, stirring. Add the stock and milk.

2 Bring to the boil, then cover and simmer gently for about 20 minutes, until the vegetables are soft. Stir in the chopped tarragon and season to taste with salt and pepper.

3 Leave the soup to cool slightly, then process in a blender or food processor, in batches if necessary, until smooth. Return the soup to the rinsed pan and reheat gently.

4 Stir in the sherry, if using, then ladle into soup bowls and serve garnished with tarragon.

VARIATION

If you like, use a mixture of wild and button (white) mushrooms instead.

Italian Pea and Basil Soup

V

Plenty of crusty country bread is a must with this fresh-tasting soup.

INGREDIENTS

Serves 4

75ml/5 tbsp olive oil

2 large onions, chopped

1 celery stick, chopped

1 carrot, chopped

1 garlic clove, finely chopped

400g/14oz/3½ cups frozen petit pois
  (baby peas)

900ml/1½ pints/3¾ cups Vegetable Stock

25g/1oz/1 cup fresh basil leaves, coarsely
  torn, plus extra to garnish

salt and ground black pepper

freshly grated Parmesan cheese,
  to serve

1 Heat the oil in a large pan and add the onions, celery, carrot and garlic. Cover the pan and cook over a low heat, stirring occasionally, for 45 minutes, or until the vegetables are soft.

2 Add the peas and stock to the pan and bring to the boil. Reduce the heat, add the basil and season to taste, then simmer gently for 10 minutes.

3 Spoon the soup into a food processor or blender and process until smooth. Ladle into warm bowls, sprinkle with grated Parmesan, garnish with basil and serve immediately.

COOK'S TIP

It is always sensible to leave the hot soup to cool slightly before processing to avoid steam being forced out of the top and, possibly, scalding you severely.

VARIATION

Use mint or a mixture of parsley, mint and chives in place of the basil.

V

Broccoli and Almond Soup

The creaminess of the toasted almonds combines perfectly with the slightly bitter taste of the broccoli.

INGREDIENTS

Serves 4–6

50g/2oz/¹⁄₂ cup ground almonds

675g/1¹⁄₂lb broccoli

900ml/1¹⁄₂ pints/3³⁄₄ cups Vegetable Stock
   or water

300ml/¹⁄₂ pint/1¹⁄₄ cups skimmed milk

salt and ground black pepper

1 Preheat the oven to 180°C/ 350°F/ Gas 4. Spread the ground almonds evenly on a baking sheet and toast in the oven for about 10 minutes, until golden. Reserve one quarter of the toasted almonds and set aside to garnish the finished dish.

2 Cut the broccoli into small florets and steam for about 6–7 minutes, until tender.

3 Place the remaining toasted almonds, broccoli, vegetable stock or water and milk in a blender or food processor and process until smooth. Season with salt and pepper to taste.

4 Pour the soup into a pan and heat gently. Ladle into warm bowls and serve sprinkled with the reserved toasted almonds.

Fresh Tomato Soup

Intensely flavoured sun-ripened tomatoes need little embellishment in this fresh-tasting soup. If you buy from the supermarket, choose the juiciest looking ones and add the amount of sugar and vinegar necessary, depending on their natural sweetness. On a hot day, this Italian soup is also delicious chilled.

INGREDIENTS

Serves 6

1.3–1.6kg/3–3½lb ripe tomatoes

400ml/14fl oz/1⅔ cups Chicken or
   Vegetable Stock

45ml/3 tbsp sun-dried tomato paste

30–45ml/2–3 tbsp balsamic vinegar

10–15ml/2–3 tsp caster (superfine) sugar

small handful of basil leaves

salt and ground black pepper

basil leaves, to garnish

toasted cheese croûtes and crème fraîche,
   to serve

1 Plunge the tomatoes into boiling water for 30 seconds, then refresh in cold water. Peel off the skins and quarter the tomatoes

2 Put the tomatoes in a large pan and pour over the chicken or vegetable stock. Bring just to the boil, reduce the heat, cover and simmer the mixture gently for about 10 minutes, until the tomatoes are pulpy.

3 Stir in the sun-dried tomato paste, vinegar, sugar and basil. Season with salt and pepper, then cook gently, stirring, for 2 minutes. Process the soup in a blender or food processor, then return to the pan and reheat gently. Serve in warm bowls topped with one or two toasted cheese croûtes and a spoonful of crème fraîche and garnished with basil leaves.

Nettle Soup

A country-style soup which is a tasty variation of the classic Irish potato soup. Use wild nettles if you can find them, or a washed head of round lettuce if you prefer.

Serves 4

115g/4oz/½ cup butter
450g/1lb onions, sliced
450g/1lb potatoes, cut into chunks
750ml/1¼ pints/3 cups Chicken Stock
25g/1oz/1 cup nettle leaves
small bunch of fresh chives, chopped
salt and ground black pepper
double (heavy) cream, to serve

2 Wearing rubber (latex) gloves, remove the nettle leaves from their stalks. Wash the leaves under cold running water, then dry on kitchen paper. Add to the pan and cook for a further 5 minutes.

3 Ladle the soup into a blender or food processor and process until smooth. Return to a clean pan and season well. Stir in the chives and serve with a swirl of cream and a sprinkling of pepper.

1 Melt the butter in a large pan and add the sliced onions. Cover and cook over a low heat for about 5 minutes, until softened. Add the potatoes to the pan with the chicken stock. Cover and cook for 25 minutes.

COOK'S TIP

If you like, cut the vegetables finely and leave the cooked soup chunky rather than puréeing it.

Mushroom, Celery and Garlic Soup

A robust soup in which the dominant flavour of mushrooms is enhanced with garlic, while celery introduces a contrasting note.

INGREDIENTS

Serves 4

350g/12oz/4½ cups chopped mushrooms

4 celery sticks, chopped

3 garlic cloves

45ml/3 tbsp dry sherry or white wine

750ml/1¼ pints/3 cups Chicken Stock

30ml/2 tbsp Worcestershire sauce

5ml/1 tsp freshly grated nutmeg

salt and ground black pepper

celery leaves, to garnish

1 Place the mushrooms, celery and garlic in a pan and stir in the sherry or wine. Cover and cook over a low heat for 30–40 minutes, until the vegetables are tender.

2 Add half the stock and process in a food processor or blender until smooth. Return to the pan and add the remaining stock, the Worcestershire sauce and nutmeg.

3 Bring to the boil and season to taste with salt and pepper. Ladle the soup into warm bowls and serve immediately, garnished with celery leaves.

Cauliflower and Walnut Soup

This classic combination works well in a number of dishes – especially this richly flavoured soup.

Serves 4

1 cauliflower

1 onion, coarsely chopped

450ml/¾ pint/scant 2 cups Chicken or Vegetable Stock

450ml/¾ pint/scant 2 cups skimmed milk

45ml/3 tbsp walnut pieces

salt and ground black pepper

paprika and chopped walnuts, to garnish

1 Trim the cauliflower of outer leaves and break into small florets. Place the cauliflower, onion and stock in a large pan.

2 Bring to the boil, cover and simmer for about 15 minutes, until soft. Add the milk and walnut pieces, then process in a blender or food processor until smooth.

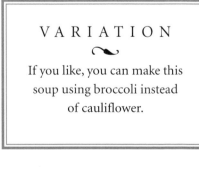

3 Season the soup to taste with salt and pepper, then reheat and bring to the boil. Serve hot sprinkled with a dusting of paprika and chopped walnuts.

VARIATION

If you like, you can make this soup using broccoli instead of cauliflower.

Pumpkin Soup

V

The sweet flavour of pumpkin is excellent in soups, teaming well with other savoury ingredients, such as onions and potatoes, to make a warm and comforting dish. For added flavour, try roasting the pumpkin chunks instead before adding to the soup with the stock.

INGREDIENTS

Serves 4–6

15ml/1 tbsp sunflower oil

25g/1oz/2 tbsp butter

1 large onion, sliced

675g/1½lb pumpkin, cut into
  large chunks

450g/1 1b potatoes, sliced

600ml/1 pint/2½ cups Vegetable Stock

good pinch of freshly grated nutmeg

5ml/1 tsp chopped fresh tarragon

600ml/1 pint/2½ cups milk

5–10ml/1–2 tsp lemon juice

salt and ground black pepper

1 Heat the oil and butter in a heavy pan, add the onion and cook for 4–5 minutes over a gentle heat until soft but not browned, stirring frequently.

2 Add the pumpkin and sliced potatoes, stir well, then cover and sweat over a low heat for about 10 minutes, until the vegetables are almost tender, stirring occasionally to stop them sticking to the pan.

3 Stir in the vegetable stock, grated nutmeg and tarragon and season to taste with salt and pepper. Bring to the boil, then lower the heat and simmer for about 10 minutes, until the vegetables are completely tender.

4 Leave the soup to cool slightly, then pour into a blender or food processor and process until smooth. Pour back into a clean pan and add the milk. Heat gently and then taste, adding lemon juice to taste and extra seasoning, if necessary. Serve piping hot.

Moroccan Vegetable Soup

*Creamy parsnip and pumpkin give
this soup a wonderfully rich texture.*

Serves 4

15ml/1 tbsp olive or sunflower oil

15g/½oz/1 tbsp butter

1 onion, chopped

225g/8oz carrots, chopped

225g/8oz parsnips, chopped

225g/8oz pumpkin

about 900ml/1½ pints/3¾ cups Vegetable
   or Chicken Stock

lemon juice, to taste

salt and ground black pepper

For the garnish

7.5ml/1½ tsp olive oil

½ garlic clove, finely chopped

45ml/3 tbsp chopped fresh parsley and
   coriander (cilantro), mixed

good pinch of paprika

1 Heat the oil and butter in a
large pan and cook the onion,
stirring occasionally, for about
3 minutes, until softened. Add the
carrots and parsnips, stir well,
cover and cook over a gentle heat
for a further 5 minutes.

2 Cut the pumpkin into chunks,
discarding the skin and pith,
and stir into the pan. Cover and
cook for a further 5 minutes, then
add the stock and seasoning and
gradually bring to the boil. Cover
and simmer for 35–40 minutes,
until the vegetables are tender.

3 Leave the soup to cool slightly,
then pour in to a blender or
food processor and process until
smooth, adding a little extra water
or stock if the soup seems too
thick. Pour back into a clean pan
and reheat gently.

4 To make the garnish, heat the
oil in a small pan and cook the
garlic and herbs for 1–2 minutes.
Add the paprika and stir well.

5 Taste and adjust the seasoning
of the soup and stir in lemon
juice to taste. Pour into bowls and
spoon a little of the prepared
garnish on top, which should then
be swirled carefully into the soup.

Sweet Potato and Parsnip Soup

V

*The natural sweetness of these
two popular root vegetables comes
through very strongly in this
delicious soup.*

INGREDIENTS

Serves 6

15ml/1 tbsp sunflower oil

1 large leek, sliced

2 celery sticks, chopped

450g/1lb sweet potatoes, diced

225g/8oz parsnips, diced

900ml/1½ pints/3¾ cups Vegetable Stock

salt and ground black pepper

For the garnish

15ml/1 tbsp chopped fresh parsley

roasted strips of sweet potatoes
   and parsnips

1 Heat the oil in a large pan and
add the leek, celery, sweet
potatoes and parsnips. Cook gently
for about 5 minutes, stirring to
prevent them from browning or
sticking to the pan.

2 Stir in the vegetable stock and
bring to the boil, then cover
and simmer over a low heat for
about 25 minutes, or until the
vegetables are tender, stirring
occasionally. Season to taste with
salt and pepper . Remove the pan
from the heat and leave the soup to
cool slightly.

3 Process the soup in a blender
or food processor until
smooth, then return it to the pan
and reheat gently. Ladle into
warmed soup bowls to serve and
sprinkle over the chopped fresh
parsley and roasted strips of sweet
potatoes and parsnips.

V

Sweet Potato and Red Pepper Soup

As colourful as it is good to eat, this soup is a sure winner, whether for a midweek family supper or a dinner-party first course.

INGREDIENTS

Serves 6

2 red (bell) peppers (about 225g/8 oz) seeded and cubed

500g/1¼lb sweet potatoes, cubed

1 onion, coarsely chopped

2 large garlic cloves, coarsely chopped

300ml/½ pint/1¼ cups dry white wine

1.2 litres/2 pints/5 cups Vegetable Stock

Tabasco sauce, to taste

salt and ground black pepper

fresh country bread, to serve

1 Dice a small quantity of red pepper for the garnish and set aside. Put the rest into a pan with the sweet potato, onion, garlic, wine and vegetable stock. Bring to the boil, lower the heat and simmer for 30 minutes, or until all the vegetables are quite soft. Leave to cool slightly.

2 Transfer the mixture to a blender or food processor and process until smooth. Season to taste with salt, pepper and a generous dash of Tabasco.

3 Leave to cool to serve warm or at room temperature. Garnish with the reserved diced red pepper.

Roasted Garlic and Butternut Squash Soup

This is a wonderful, richly flavoured dish. A spoonful of the hot and spicy tomato salsa gives bite to the sweet-tasting squash and garlic soup.

INGREDIENTS

Serves 4–5

2 garlic bulbs, outer papery skin removed

75ml/5 tbsp olive oil

a few fresh thyme sprigs

1 large butternut squash, halved and seeded

2 onions, chopped

5ml/1 tsp ground coriander

1.2 litres/2 pints/5 cups Vegetable or
  Chicken Stock

30–45ml/2–3 tbsp chopped fresh oregano

salt and ground black pepper

For the salsa

4 large ripe tomatoes, halved and seeded

1 red (bell) pepper, halved and seeded

1 large fresh red chilli, halved and seeded

30–45ml/2–3 tbsp extra virgin olive oil

15ml/1 tbsp balsamic vinegar

pinch of caster (superfine) sugar

1 Preheat the oven to 220°C/ 425°F/Gas 7. Place the garlic bulbs on a piece of foil and pour over half the olive oil. Add the thyme sprigs, then fold the foil around the garlic bulbs to enclose them completely. Place the foil parcel on a baking sheet with the butternut squash and brush the squash with 15ml/1 tbsp of the remaining olive oil. Add the tomatoes, red pepper and fresh chilli for the salsa.

2 Roast the vegetables for 25 minutes, then remove the tomatoes, pepper and chilli. Reduce the temperature to 190°C/ 375°F/Gas 5 and cook the squash and garlic for 20–25 minutes more, or until the squash is tender.

3 Heat the remaining oil in a large, heavy pan and cook the onions and ground coriander gently for about 10 minutes, or until softened.

4 Peel the pepper and chilli and process in a food processor or blender with the tomatoes and 30ml/2 tbsp olive oil. Stir in the vinegar and seasoning to taste, adding a pinch of caster sugar, if necessary. Add the remaining oil if you think the salsa needs it.

5 Squeeze the roasted garlic out of its papery skin into the onions and scoop the squash out of its skin, adding it to the pan. Add the stock, 5ml/1 tsp salt and plenty of black pepper. Bring to the boil and simmer gently for 10 minutes.

6 Stir in half the oregano and cool the soup slightly, then process it in a blender or food processor. Alternatively, press the soup through a fine sieve.

7 Reheat the soup without allowing it to boil, then taste for seasoning before ladling it into warmed bowls. Top each with a spoonful of salsa and sprinkle over the remaining chopped oregano. Serve immediately.

V

Cauliflower, Flageolet and Fennel Seed Soup

The sweet, anise-liquorice flavour of the fennel seeds gives a delicious edge to this hearty soup.

INGREDIENTS

Serves 4–6

15ml/1 tbsp olive oil

1 garlic clove, crushed

1 onion, chopped

10ml/2 tsp fennel seeds

1 cauliflower, cut into small florets

2 x 400g/14 oz cans flageolet or cannellini beans, drained and rinsed

1.2 litres/2 pints/5 cups Vegetable Stock or water

salt and ground black pepper

chopped fresh parsley, to garnish

toasted slices of French bread, to serve

3 Bring the mixture to the boil. Reduce the heat and simmer for about 10 minutes, or until the cauliflower is tender. Leave to cool slightly, then pour the soup into a blender or food processor and process until smooth.

4 Stir in the remaining beans and season to taste with salt and pepper. Reheat the soup and pour into warmed bowls. Sprinkle with chopped parsley and serve immediately with toasted slices of French bread.

1 Heat the olive oil. Add the garlic, onion and fennel seeds and cook gently for 5 minutes, or until the onion is softened.

2 Add the cauliflower florets, half the beans and the vegetable stock or water.

Root Vegetable Soup

V

Simmer a selection of popular and inexpensive winter root vegetables together for a wonderfully warming and satisfying soup.

INGREDIENTS

Serves 6

3 carrots, chopped

1 large potato, chopped

1 large parsnip, chopped

1 large turnip or small swede
   (rutabaga), chopped

1 onion, chopped

30ml/2 tbsp sunflower oil

25g/1oz/2 tbsp butter

1.5 litres/2½ pints/6¼ cups Vegetable
   Stock or water

1 piece fresh root ginger, grated

300ml/½ pint/1¼ cups milk

45ml/3 tbsp crème fraîche or fromage
   frais

30ml/2 tbsp chopped fresh dill

15ml/1 tbsp lemon juice

salt and ground black pepper

fresh dill sprigs, to garnish

1 Put the carrots, potato, parsnip, turnip or swede and onion into a large pan with the oil and butter. Cook lightly, then cover and sweat the vegetables over a low heat for 15 minutes, shaking the pan occasionally.

2 Pour in the stock or water, bring to the boil and season to taste with salt and pepper. Cover and simmer for 20 minutes until the vegetables are soft.

3 Strain the vegetables, reserving the cooking liquid, add the ginger and vegetables to a food processor or blender and process until smooth. Return the puréed mixture and cooking liquid to the pan. Add the milk and stir while the soup gently reheats.

4 Remove the pan from the heat and stir in the crème fraîche or fromage frais, plus the dill and lemon juice. Taste and adjust the seasoning if necessary. Reheat the soup, but do not allow it to boil or it may curdle. Serve garnished with sprigs of dill.

V

Celeriac and Spinach Soup

Celeriac has a wonderful flavour that is reminiscent of celery, but also adds a slightly nutty taste. Here, it is combined with spinach to make a delicious soup.

INGREDIENTS

Serves 6

1 litre/1¾ pints/4 cups water

250ml/8fl oz/1 cup dry white wine

1 leek, thickly sliced

500g/1¼lb celeriac, diced

200g/7 oz fresh spinach leaves

freshly grated nutmeg

salt and ground black pepper

25g/1oz/¼ cup pine nuts,
    to garnish

1 Mix the water and wine in a jug (pitcher). Place the leek, celeriac and spinach in a deep pan and pour the liquid over the top. Bring to the boil, lower the heat and simmer for 10–15 minutes, until the vegetables are soft.

2 Pour the celeriac mixture into a blender or food processor and process until smooth, in batches if necessary. Return to the clean pan and season to taste with salt, pepper and grated nutmeg. Reheat gently.

3 Heat a non-stick frying pan (do not add any oil) and add the pine nuts. Dry-fry until golden brown, stirring occasionally so that they do not stick. Sprinkle them over the soup and serve.

COOK'S TIP

If the soup is too thick, thin with a little water or semi-skimmed (low-fat) milk when processing.

Spicy Carrot Soup with Garlic Croûtons

Carrot soup is given a touch of spice with coriander, cumin and chilli powder.

INGREDIENTS

Serves 6

15ml/l tbsp olive oil

1 large onion, chopped

675g/1½ lb carrots, sliced

5ml/1 tsp ground coriander

5ml/1 tsp ground cumin

5ml/1 tsp hot chilli powder

900ml/1½ pints/3¾ cups Vegetable Stock

salt and ground black pepper

fresh coriander (cilantro) sprigs, to garnish

For the garlic croûtons

4 slices bread, crusts removed

a little olive oil

2 garlic cloves, crushed

1 To make the soup, heat the oil in a large pan, add the onion and carrots and cook over a low heat for 5 minutes, stirring occasionally. Add the ground spices and cook gently for 1 minute, stirring constantly.

2 Stir in the stock, bring to the boil, then cover and simmer gently for about 45 minutes, until the carrots are tender.

3 Meanwhile, make the garlic croûtons. Cut the bread into 1cm/½in cubes. Heat the oil in a frying pan, add the garlic and cook gently for 30 seconds, stirring constantly. Add the bread cubes, turn them over in the oil and fry over a medium heat for a few minutes, until they are crisp and golden brown all over, turning frequently. Drain on kitchen paper and keep warm.

4 Process the soup in a blender or food processor until smooth, then season to taste with salt and pepper. Return the soup to the rinsed pan and reheat gently. Serve hot, sprinkled with garlic croûtons and garnished with fresh coriander sprigs.

Curried Carrot and Apple Soup

The combination of carrot, curry and apple is a highly successful one. Curried fruit is delicious.

INGREDIENTS

Serves 4

10ml/2 tsp sunflower oil

15ml/1 tbsp mild korma curry powder

500g/1¼lb carrots, chopped

1 large onion, chopped

1 large cooking apple, chopped

750ml/1¼ pints/3 cups Chicken Stock

salt and ground black pepper

natural (plain) yogurt and carrot curls, to garnish

1 Heat the oil in a large, heavy pan and gently cook the curry powder for 2–3 minutes.

2 Add the chopped carrots and onion and the cooking apple, stir well until coated with the curry powder, then cover the pan.

3 Cook over a low heat for about 15 minutes, shaking the pan occasionally, until the vegetables are softened. Spoon the vegetable mixture into a food processor or blender, add half the stock and process until smooth.

4 Return the mixture to the pan and pour in the remaining chicken stock. Bring the soup to the boil, then taste and adjust the seasoning. Ladle into warm bowls and serve, garnished with a swirl of yogurt and curls of raw carrot.

Leek, Parsnip and Ginger Soup

A flavoursome winter warmer, with the added spiciness of fresh ginger, this unusual soup is destined to become a family favourite.

INGREDIENTS

Serves 4–6

30ml/2 tbsp olive oil

225g/8oz leeks, sliced

25g/1oz fresh root ginger, finely chopped

675g/1½lb parsnips, coarsely chopped

300ml/½ pint/1¼ cups dry white wine

1.2 litres/2 pints/5 cups Vegetable Stock
   or water

salt and ground black pepper

fromage blanc and paprika,
   to garnish

1 Heat the oil in a large pan and add the leeks and ginger. Cook gently for 2–3 minutes, until the leeks start to soften.

2 Add the parsnips and cook for a further 7–8 minutes, until they are beginning to soften.

3 Pour in the wine and stock or water and bring to the boil. Reduce the heat and simmer gently for 20–30 minutes, or until the parsnips are tender. Leave the soup to cool slightly.

4 Process the soup in a blender or food processor until smooth. Season to taste with salt and pepper. Reheat and garnish with a swirl of fromage blanc and a light dusting of paprika.

Curried Celery Soup

An unusual, but stimulating combination of flavours, this warming soup is an excellent way to transform celery. Serve with warm wholemeal bread rolls.

INGREDIENTS

Serves 4–6

10ml/2 tsp olive oil

1 onion, chopped

1 leek, sliced

675g/1½lb celery, chopped

15ml/1 tbsp medium or hot
   curry powder

225g/8 oz unpeeled potatoes, washed
   and diced

900ml/1½ pints/3¾ cups Vegetable Stock

1 bouquet garni

30ml/2 tbsp chopped fresh mixed herbs

salt

celery seeds and leaves, to garnish

COOK'S TIP

For a change, use celeriac and
sweet potatoes in place of celery
and standard potatoes.

1 Heat the oil in a large pan. Add
the onion, leek and celery, cover
and cook over a low heat for about
10 minutes, stirring occasionally.

2 Sprinkle in the curry powder
and cook gently, stirring
occasionally, for 2 minutes.

3 Add the potatoes, vegetable
stock and bouquet garni, cover
and bring to the boil. Reduce the
heat and simmer gently for about
20 minutes, until the vegetables
are tender, but not too soft.

4 Remove and discard the
bouquet garni and set the
soup aside to cool slightly before
processing it.

5 Transfer the soup to a blender
or food processor and process,
in batches, until smooth.

6 Add the mixed herbs, season
to taste with salt and process
briefly again. Return to the pan
and reheat gently until piping hot.
Ladle into warm bowls and
garnish each one with a sprinkling
of celery seeds and a few celery
leaves before serving.

CHUNKY VEGETABLE SOUPS

It isn't really surprising that many of the world's best-known
and best-loved soups are based on vegetables, for few other
ingredients can offer so much versatility and variety.
Some, such as the classic French Onion Soup, feature
a single vegetable in a starring role, while others, such
as Minestrone Genoese, glory in a veritable cornucopia.
Take a culinary trip around the world with mouth-watering
recipes from places as diverse as Japan, Russia, Spain,
North Africa, Italy, China and the Caribbean.

French Onion Soup with Gruyère Croûtes

This is perhaps the most famous of all onion soups. Traditionally, it was served as a sustaining early morning meal to the porters and workers of Les Halles market in Paris.

INGREDIENTS

Serves 6

50g/2oz/¼ cup butter

15ml/1 tbsp olive oil

2kg/4½lb yellow onions, peeled and sliced

5ml/1 tsp chopped fresh thyme

5ml/1 tsp caster (superfine) sugar

15ml/1 tbsp sherry vinegar

1.5 litres/2½ pints/6¼ cups Meat or
    Chicken Stock

25ml/1½ tbsp plain (all-purpose) flour

150ml/¼ pint/⅔ cup dry white wine

45ml/3 tbsp brandy

salt and ground black pepper

For the croûtes

6–12 thick slices day-old French stick or
    baguette, about 2.5cm/1in thick

1 garlic clove, halved

15ml/1 tbsp French mustard

115g/4oz/1 cup coarsely grated
    Gruyère cheese

COOK'S TIP

The long slow cooking of the onions is the key to success with this soup. If the onions brown too quickly the soup will be bitter.

1 Melt the butter with the oil in a large pan. Add the onions and stir to coat them in the fat. Cook over a medium heat for 5–8 minutes, stirring once or twice, until the onions begin to soften. Stir in the thyme.

2 Reduce the heat to very low, cover the pan and cook the onions for 20–30 minutes, stirring frequently, until they are very soft and golden yellow.

3 Uncover the pan and increase the heat slightly. Stir in the sugar and cook for 5–10 minutes, until the onions start to brown. Add the sherry vinegar and increase the heat again, then continue cooking, stirring frequently, until the onions turn a deep, golden brown – this could take up to 20 minutes.

4 Meanwhile, bring the stock to the boil in another pan. Stir the flour into the onions and cook, stirring constantly, for about 2 minutes, then gradually pour in the hot stock. Add the wine and brandy and season the soup to taste with salt and pepper. Simmer for 10–15 minutes.

5 For the croûtes, preheat the oven to 150°C/300°F/Gas 2. Place the slices of bread on a greased baking tray and bake for 15–20 minutes, until dry and lightly browned. Rub the bread with the cut surface of the garlic and spread with the mustard, then sprinkle the grated Gruyère cheese over the slices.

6 Preheat the grill (broiler) on the hottest setting. Ladle the soup into a large flameproof tureen or six flameproof bowls. Float the croûtes on the soup, then grill (broil) until the cheese melts, bubbles and turns golden brown. Serve immediately.

Green Pea Soup with Spinach

This lovely green soup was invented by the wife of a seventeenth-century British Member of Parliament, and it has stood the test of time.

INGREDIENTS

Serves 6

450g/1lb/generous 3 cups podded fresh or
    frozen peas
1 leek, finely sliced
2 garlic cloves, crushed
2 rindless back (lean) bacon rashers,
    finely diced
1.2 litres/2 pints/5 cups Chicken Stock
30ml/2 tbsp olive oil
50g/2 oz fresh spinach, shredded
40g/1½oz/⅓ cup white cabbage,
    finely shredded
½ small lettuce, finely shredded
1 celery stick, finely chopped
large handful of parsley, finely chopped
½ carton mustard and cress
20ml/4 tsp chopped fresh mint
pinch of ground mace
salt and ground black pepper

1 Put the peas, leek, garlic and bacon in a large pan. Add the chicken stock, bring to the boil, then lower the heat and simmer for 20 minutes.

2 About 5 minutes before the pea mixture is ready, heat the oil in a deep frying pan.

3 Add the spinach, cabbage, lettuce, celery and herbs to the frying pan. Cover and sweat the mixture over a low heat until soft.

4 Transfer the pea mixture to a blender or food processor and process until smooth. Return to the clean pan, add the sweated vegetables and herbs and heat through. Season with mace, salt and pepper and serve.

Leek and Thyme Soup

This heart-warming soup can be processed to a smooth purée or served in its original peasant style.

INGREDIENTS

Serves 4

900g/2lb leeks
450g/1lb potatoes
115g/4oz/¹⁄₂ cup butter
1 large fresh thyme sprig, plus extra to
  garnish (optional)
300ml/¹⁄₂ pint/1¹⁄₄ cups milk
salt and ground black pepper
60ml/4 tbsp double (heavy) cream,
  to serve

3 Melt the butter in a large pan and add the leeks and 1 sprig of thyme. Cover and cook for 4–5 minutes, until softened. Add the potato pieces and just enough cold water to cover the vegetables. Re-cover and cook over a low heat for 30 minutes.

4 Pour in the milk and season to taste with salt and pepper. Cover and simmer for a further 30 minutes. You will find that some of the potato breaks up, leaving you with a semi-puréed and rather lumpy soup.

5 Remove the sprig of thyme (the leaves will have fallen into the soup) and serve, adding 15ml/ 1 tbsp cream and a garnish of thyme to each portion, if using.

1 Trim the leeks. If you are using large winter leeks, strip away all the coarse outer leaves, then cut the leeks into thick slices. Wash thoroughly under cold running water to remove any traces of soil.

2 Cut the potatoes into coarse dice, about 2.5cm/1in, and dry on kitchen paper.

Borscht

Beetroot is the main ingredient of borscht, and its flavour and colour dominate this well-known soup. It is a classic of both Russia and Poland.

INGREDIENTS

Serves 4–6

900g/2lb uncooked beetroot
   (beet), peeled
2 carrots, peeled
2 celery sticks
40g/1½oz/3 tbsp butter
2 onions, sliced
2 garlic cloves, crushed
4 tomatoes, peeled, seeded
   and chopped
1 bay leaf
1 large fresh parsley sprig
2 cloves
4 whole peppercorns
1.2 litres/2 pints/5 cups Meat or
   Chicken Stock
150ml/¼ pint/⅔ cup beetroot (beet) *kvas*
   (see *Cook's Tip*) or the liquid from
   pickled beetroot (beet)
salt and ground black pepper
sour cream, garnished with chopped fresh
   chives or fresh dill sprigs, to serve

1 Cut the beetroot, carrots and celery into fairly thick strips. Melt the butter in a large pan and cook the onions over a low heat for 5 minutes, stirring occasionally.

COOK'S TIP

Beetroot (beet) *kvas*, fermented beetroot juice, adds an intense colour and a slight tartness. If unavailable, peel and grate 1 beetroot, add 150ml/¼ pint/⅔ cup stock and 10ml ½ tsp lemon juice. Bring to the boil, cover and leave for 30 minutes. Strain before using.

2 Add the beetroot, carrots and celery and cook for a further 5 minutes, stirring occasionally.

3 Add the garlic and chopped tomatoes to the pan and cook, stirring, for 2 more minutes.

4 Place the bay leaf, parsley, cloves and peppercorns in a piece of muslin (cheesecloth) and tie with string.

5 Add the muslin bag to the pan with the stock. Bring to the boil, reduce the heat, cover and simmer for 1¼ hours, or until the vegetables are very tender. Discard the bag. Stir in the beetroot *kvas* and season. Bring to the boil. Ladle into bowls and serve with sour cream garnished with chives or dill.

Leek and Potato Soup

These two vegetables make a really tasty and substantial, simple soup, and are readily available and inexpensive throughout the year.

INGREDIENTS

Serves 4

50g/2oz/4 tbsp butter

2 leeks, chopped

1 small onion, finely chopped

350g/12oz floury potatoes, chopped

900ml/1½ pints/3¾ cups Vegetable Stock

salt and ground black pepper

crusty bread, to serve

1 Heat 25g/1oz/2 tbsp of the butter in a large, heavy pan, add the chopped leeks and onion and cook over a low heat, stirring occasionally so that they do not stick to the base of the pan, for about 7 minutes, until softened but not browned.

2 Add the potatoes to the pan and cook, stirring occasionally, for 2–3 minutes.

3 Add the stock and bring to the boil, then reduce the heat to very low, cover and simmer gently for 30–35 minutes until the vegetables are very tender.

4 Season to taste with salt and pepper, remove the pan from the heat and stir in the remaining butter in small pieces at a time. Ladle the soup into warm bowls and serve immediately with slices of thick crusty bread.

V

Spinach and Rice Soup

Use very fresh, young spinach leaves and risotto rice to prepare this surprisingly light, refreshing soup.

INGREDIENTS

Serves 4

675g/1½lb fresh spinach, washed

45ml/3 tbsp extra virgin olive oil

1 small onion, finely chopped

2 garlic cloves, finely chopped

1 small fresh red chilli, seeded and
    finely chopped

115g/4oz/generous ½ cup risotto rice

1.2 litres/2 pints/5 cups Vegetable Stock

salt and ground black pepper

60ml/4 tbsp grated Pecorino cheese,
    to serve

1 Place the spinach in a large pan with just the water that clings to its leaves after washing. Add a large pinch of salt. Heat gently until the spinach has wilted, then remove from the heat and drain, reserving any liquid. Use a knife to chop finely.

2 Heat the oil in a large pan and cook the onion, garlic and chilli over a medium heat, stirring occasionally, for 4–5 minutes, until softened. Stir in the rice until well coated, then pour in the stock and reserved spinach liquid.

3 Bring to the boil, lower the heat and simmer gently for 10 minutes. Add the spinach and cook for 5–7 minutes more, until the rice is tender. Season with salt and freshly ground pepper to taste and serve immediately with the Pecorino cheese.

Apple Soup

A delicious soup that makes the most of freshly picked apples.

INGREDIENTS

Serves 6

45ml/3 tbsp oil

1 kohlrabi, diced

3 carrots, diced

2 celery sticks, diced

1 green (bell) pepper, seeded and diced

2 tomatoes, diced

2 litres/3½ pints/9 cups Chicken Stock

6 large green apples

45ml/3 tbsp plain (all-purpose) flour

150ml/¼ pint/⅔ cup double (heavy) cream

15ml/1 tbsp granulated sugar

30–45ml/2–3 tbsp lemon juice

salt and ground black pepper

lemon wedges and crusty bread, to serve

1 Heat the oil in a large pan. Add the kohlrabi, carrots, celery, green pepper and tomatoes and cook, stirring occasionally, for 5–6 minutes, until just softened.

2 Pour in the chicken stock, bring to the boil, then reduce the heat and simmer for about 45 minutes.

3 Meanwhile, peel and core the apples, then chop into small cubes. Add to the pan and simmer for a further 15 minutes.

4 In a bowl, mix together the flour and cream, then pour slowly into the soup, stirring well, and bring to the boil. Add the sugar and lemon juice before seasoning. Serve immediately with lemon wedges and crusty bread.

V

Pistou

Serve this delicious vegetable soup from Nice, in the south of France, with a sun-dried tomato pesto and fresh Parmesan cheese.

INGREDIENTS

Serves 4

1 courgette (zucchini), diced

1 small potato, diced

1 shallot, chopped

1 carrot, diced

225g/8oz can chopped tomatoes

1.2 litres/2 pints/5 cups Vegetable Stock

50g/2oz green beans, cut into 1cm/ ½in lengths

50g/2oz/½ cup petits pois (baby peas)

50g/2oz/½ cup small pasta shapes

60–90ml/4–6 tbsp pesto, either home-made or ready-made

15ml/1 tbsp sun-dried tomato paste

salt and ground black pepper

grated Parmesan cheese, to serve

1 Place the courgette, potato, shallot, carrot and tomatoes in a large pan. Add the vegetable stock and season with salt and pepper. Bring to the boil, then cover and simmer for 20 minutes.

2 Add the green beans, petits pois and pasta shapes. Cook for a further 10 minutes, until the pasta is tender.

3 Taste the soup and adjust the seasoning as necessary. Ladle the soup into individual bowls. Mix together the pesto and sun-dried tomato paste, and stir a spoonful into each serving.

4 Hand round a bowl of grated Parmesan cheese for sprinkling into each bowl.

Garlic and Coriander Soup

This recipe is based on the wonderful bread soups or açordas *of Portugal. Being a simple soup it should be made with the best ingredients – plump garlic, fresh coriander, high-quality crusty country bread and, of course, extra virgin olive oil.*

INGREDIENTS

Serves 6

25g/1oz fresh coriander (cilantro), leaves
   and stalks chopped separately

1.5 litres/2½ pints/6¼ cups Vegetable or
   Chicken Stock, or water

5–6 plump garlic cloves, peeled

6 eggs

275g/10oz day-old bread, most of the
   crust removed and torn into
   bitesize pieces

salt and ground black pepper

90ml/6 tbsp extra virgin olive oil, plus
   extra to serve

1 Place the coriander stalks in a pan. Add the stock or water and bring to the boil. Lower the heat and simmer for 10 minutes. Cool slightly, then process in a blender or food processor and sieve back into the pan.

2 Crush the garlic with 5ml/ 1 tsp salt, then stir in 120ml/ 4fl oz/½ cup hot soup. Return the mixture to the pan.

3 Meanwhile, poach the eggs separately in a small frying pan of gently simmering water for about 3–4 minutes, until just set.

4 Use a slotted spoon to remove them from the pan and transfer to a warm plate. Trim off any untidy bits of white.

5 Bring the soup back to the boil and add seasoning. Stir in the chopped coriander leaves and remove from the heat.

6 Place the bread in six soup plates or bowls and drizzle the oil over it. Ladle in the soup and stir. Add a poached egg to each bowl and serve immediately, offering olive oil at the table so that it can be drizzled over the soup to taste.

V

Spanish Potato and Garlic Soup

Traditionally served in earthenware dishes, this classic Spanish soup should be savoured.

INGREDIENTS

Serves 6

30ml/2 tbsp olive oil

1 large onion, thinly sliced

4 garlic cloves, crushed

1 large potato, halved and thinly sliced

5ml/1 tsp paprika

400g/14oz can chopped tomatoes, drained

5ml/1 tsp fresh thyme leaves

900ml/1½ pints/3¾ cups Vegetable Stock

5ml/1 tsp cornflour (cornstarch)

salt and ground black pepper

chopped fresh thyme leaves, to garnish

1 Heat the oil in a large pan and cook the onions, garlic, potato and paprika, stirring frequently, for 5 minutes, until the onions have softened, but not browned.

2 Add the tomatoes, thyme and vegetable stock and simmer for 15–20 minutes, until the potatoes have cooked through.

3 Mix the cornflour with a little water to form a paste and stir into the soup, then simmer for 5 minutes, until thickened.

4 Using a wooden spoon break the potatoes up slightly. Season to taste with salt and pepper. Serve hot, garnished with the chopped thyme leaves.

Summer Vegetable Soup

V

This brightly coloured, fresh-tasting soup makes the most of summer's vegetable crop.

INGREDIENTS

Serves 4

45ml/3 tbsp olive oil

1 large onion, finely chopped

15ml/1 tbsp sun-dried tomato paste

450g/1lb ripe Italian plum tomatoes, peeled and finely chopped

225g/8oz green courgettes (zucchini), trimmed and coarsely chopped

225g/8oz yellow courgettes (zucchini), trimmed and coarsely chopped

3 waxy new potatoes, diced

2 garlic cloves, crushed

about 1.2 litres/2 pints/5 cups Vegetable Stock or water

60ml/4 tbsp shredded fresh basil

50g/2oz/²/₃ cup grated Parmesan cheese

salt and ground black pepper

1 Heat the oil in a large pan, add the onion and cook over a low heat for about 5 minutes, stirring constantly, until softened.

2 Stir in the sun-dried tomato paste, chopped tomatoes, courgettes, diced potatoes and garlic. Mix well and cook gently for 10 minutes, uncovered, shaking the pan frequently to stop the vegetables sticking to the base.

3 Pour in the stock or water. Bring to the boil, lower the heat, half-cover the pan and simmer gently for 15 minutes, or until the vegetables are just tender. Add more stock if necessary.

4 Remove the pan from the heat and stir in the basil and half the cheese. Taste and adjust the seasoning. Serve hot, sprinkled with the remaining cheese.

Corn and Sweet Potato Soup

The combination of corn and sweet potato gives this soup a real depth of flavour, as well as making it look very colourful.

INGREDIENTS

Serves 6

15ml/1 tbsp olive oil

1 onion, finely chopped

2 garlic cloves, crushed

1 small fresh red chilli, seeded and
    finely chopped

1.75 litres/3 pints/7½ cups Vegetable Stock

10ml/2 tsp ground cumin

1 medium sweet potato, diced

½ red (bell) pepper, finely chopped

450g/1lb corn kernels

salt and ground black pepper

lime wedges, to serve

1 Heat the oil in a pan and cook the onion for 5 minutes, until softened. Add the garlic and chilli and cook for a further 2 minutes.

2 Add 300ml/½ pint/1¼ cups of the stock, and simmer gently for 10 minutes.

3 Mix the cumin with a little of the stock to form a smooth paste and then stir into the soup. Add the diced sweet potato, stir and simmer for 10 minutes. Season and stir again.

4 Add the pepper, corn and remaining stock and simmer for 10 minutes. Process half of the soup until smooth and then stir into the chunky soup. Adjust the seasoning and serve with lime wedges for squeezing over.

Genoese Minestrone

The variations on this soup are almost endless. This pasta-free version is packed with heaps of vegetables to make a substantial start to any meal.

INGREDIENTS

Serves 6

1.75 litres/3 pints/7½ cups Vegetable
    Stock

1 large onion, chopped

3 celery sticks, chopped

2 carrots, finely diced

2 large floury potatoes, finely diced

½ head of cabbage, very finely diced

225g/8oz green beans, diagonally sliced

2 x 400g/14oz cans cannellini beans,
    drained and rinsed

60ml/4 tbsp ready-made pesto sauce

salt and ground black pepper

crusty bread and freshly grated Parmesan
    cheese, to serve

1 Pour the stock into a large pan. Add the onion, celery and carrots. Simmer for 10 minutes.

2 Add the potatoes, cabbage, and beans and simmer gently for 10–12 minutes, or until the potatoes are tender.

3 Stir in the cannellini beans and pesto, and gradually bring the mixture to the boil. Season to taste with salt and pepper. Ladle into warm bowls or soup plates and serve the soup hot with crusty bread and plenty of freshly grated Parmesan cheese.

V

Italian Rocket and Potato Soup

This filling and hearty soup is based on a traditional Italian peasant recipe. If rocket is unavailable, watercress or baby spinach leaves make an equally delicious alternative.

INGREDIENTS

Serves 4

900g/2lb new potatoes

900ml/1½ pints/3¾ cups Vegetable Stock

1 carrot

115g/4oz rocket (arugula)

2.5ml/½ tsp cayenne pepper

½ loaf stale ciabatta bread, torn into chunks

4 garlic cloves, thinly sliced

60ml/4 tbsp olive oil

salt and ground black pepper

3 Add the cayenne pepper, plus salt and black pepper to taste, then add the chunks of bread. Remove the pan from the heat, cover and leave to stand for about 10 minutes.

4 Meanwhile, sauté the garlic in the olive oil until golden brown. Pour the soup into bowls, add a little of the sautéed garlic to each bowl and serve.

1 Dice the potatoes, then place them in a pan with the stock and a little salt. Bring to the boil and simmer for 10 minutes.

2 Finely dice the carrot and add to the potatoes and stock, then tear the rocket leaves and drop into the pan. Simmer for a further 15 minutes, until the vegetables are tender.

Corn and Potato Chowder

V

This creamy yet chunky soup is rich with the sweet taste of corn. It's excellent served with thick crusty bread and topped with some melted Cheddar cheese.

INGREDIENTS

Serves 4

1 onion, chopped

1 garlic clove, crushed

1 medium baking potato, chopped

2 celery sticks, sliced

1 small green (bell) pepper, seeded, halved and sliced

30ml/2 tbsp sunflower oil

25g/1oz/2 tbsp butter

600ml/1 pint/2½ cups stock or water

300ml/½ pint/1¼ cups milk

200g/7oz can flageolet or cannellini beans

300g/11oz can corn kernels

good pinch of dried sage

salt and ground black pepper

grated Cheddar cheese, to serve

1 Put the onion, garlic, potato, celery and green pepper into a large, heavy pan with the oil and butter.

2 Heat until sizzling, then reduce the heat to low. Cover and cook gently for 10 minutes, shaking the pan occasionally.

3 Pour in the stock or water, season with salt and pepper to taste and bring to the boil. Reduce the heat, cover again and simmer gently for about 15 minutes, until the vegetables are tender.

4 Add the milk, beans and corn – including their can juices – and the sage. Simmer, uncovered, for 5 minutes. Check the seasoning and serve hot, sprinkled with grated cheese.

Plantain and Corn Soup

Here the sweetness of the corn and plantains is offset by a little chilli to create an unusual soup.

INGREDIENTS

Serves 4

25g/1oz/2 tbsp butter or margarine

1 onion, finely chopped

1 garlic clove, crushed

275g/10oz yellow plantains, peeled and sliced

1 large tomato, peeled and chopped

175g/6 oz/1 cup corn kernels

5ml/1 tsp dried tarragon, crushed

900ml/1½ pints/3¾ cups Vegetable or Chicken Stock

1 fresh green chilli, seeded and chopped

pinch of freshly grated nutmeg

salt and ground black pepper

1 Melt the butter or margarine in a pan over a moderate heat, add the onion and garlic and cook, stirring occasionally, for a few minutes until the onion is soft.

2 Add the plantains, tomato and corn kernels, and cook for a further 5 minutes.

3 Add the tarragon, stock, chilli and salt and pepper, then simmer for 10 minutes. or until the plantain is tender. Stir in the grated nutmeg and serve.

Groundnut Soup

Groundnuts or peanuts are widely used in sauces in African cooking. You'll find groundnut paste in health food stores – it makes a wonderfully rich soup – but you could use peanut butter instead if you like.

INGREDIENTS

Serves 4

45ml/3 tbsp groundnut (peanut) paste or peanut butter

1.5 litres/2½ pints/6¼ cups Vegetable Stock or water

30ml/2 tbsp tomato purée (paste)

1 onion, chopped

2 slices fresh root ginger

1.5ml/¼ tsp dried thyme

1 bay leaf

chilli powder

225g/8oz white yam, diced

10 small okra, trimmed (optional)

salt

1 Place the groundnut paste or peanut butter in a bowl, add 300ml/½ pint/1¼ cups of the stock or water and the tomato purée and blend together to make a smooth paste.

2 Spoon the nut mixture into a pan and add the onion, ginger, thyme, bay leaf, chilli powder and salt to taste and the remaining vegetable stock or water.

3 Heat gently until simmering, then cook for 1 hour, whisking occasionally to prevent the nut mixture from sticking.

4 Add the white yam, cook for a further 10 minutes, and then add the okra, if using, and simmer until both vegetables are tender. Ladle the soup into warm bowls and serve immediately.

V

Spicy Peanut Soup

A thick and warming vegetable soup, flavoured with mild chilli and roasted peanuts.

INGREDIENTS

Serves 6

30ml/2 tbsp oil

1 large onion, finely chopped

2 garlic cloves, crushed

5ml/1 tsp mild chilli powder

2 red (bell) peppers, seeded and chopped

225g/8oz carrots, finely chopped

225g/8oz potatoes, finely chopped

3 celery sticks, sliced

900ml/1½ pints/3¾ cups Vegetable Stock

90ml/6 tbsp crunchy peanut butter

115g/4oz/⅔ cup corn kernels

salt and ground black pepper

coarsely chopped unsalted roasted
    peanuts, to garnish

1 Heat the oil in a large pan and cook the onion and garlic for about 3 minutes. Add the chilli powder and cook for a further 1 minute.

2 Add the red peppers, carrots, potatoes and celery. Stir well, then cook for a further 4 minutes, stirring occasionally.

3 Add the vegetable stock, followed by the peanut butter and corn kernels. Stir well until thoroughly combined.

4 Season to taste with salt and pepper. Bring to the boil, cover and simmer for about 20 minutes, until all the vegetables are tender. Taste and adjust the seasoning if necessary before serving, sprinkled with the chopped peanuts.

Caribbean Vegetable Soup

V

This unusual vegetable soup is refreshing and filling.

Serves 4

25g/1oz/2 tbsp butter or margarine

1 onion, chopped

1 garlic clove, crushed

2 carrots, sliced

1.5 litres/2½ pints/6¼ cups
  Vegetable Stock

2 bay leaves

2 fresh thyme sprigs

1 celery stick, finely chopped

2 green bananas, peeled and cut into
  4 pieces

175g/6 oz white yam or eddoe, peeled
  and cubed

25g/1oz/2 tbsp red lentils

1 christophine, peeled and chopped

25g/1oz/2 tbsp macaroni (optional)

salt and ground black pepper

chopped spring onions (scallions),
  to garnish

COOK'S TIP
~

Use other root vegetables or potatoes if yam or eddoes are not available. Add more stock if you want a thinner soup.

1 Melt the butter or margarine and cook the onion, garlic and carrots for a few minutes, stirring occasionally, until beginning to soften. Add the stock, bay leaves and thyme and bring to the boil.

2 Add the celery, green bananas, white yam or eddoe, lentils, christophine and macaroni, if using. Season to taste with salt and pepper and simmer for 25 minutes, until all the vegetables are cooked. Serve garnished with chopped spring onions.

V

North African Spiced Soup

This soup is often served in the evening during Ramadan, the Muslim festival when followers fast during the daytime for a month.

INGREDIENTS

Serves 6

1 large onion, chopped

1.2 litres/2 pints/5 cups Vegetable Stock

5ml/1 tsp ground cinnamon

5ml/1 tsp ground turmeric

15ml/1 tbsp grated fresh root ginger

pinch of cayenne pepper

2 carrots, diced

2 celery sticks, diced

400g/14oz can chopped tomatoes

450g/1lb floury potatoes, diced

5 saffron threads

400g/14oz can chickpeas, drained

30ml/2 tbsp chopped fresh
    coriander (cilantro)

15ml/1 tbsp lemon juice

salt and ground black pepper

fried wedges of lemon, to serve

1 Place the onion in a large pan with 300ml/½ pint/1¼ cups of the vegetable stock. Simmer gently for about 10 minutes.

2 Meanwhile, mix together the cinnamon, turmeric, ginger, cayenne pepper and 30ml/2 tbsp of stock to form a paste. Stir into the onion mixture with the carrots, celery and remaining stock.

3 Bring the mixture to the boil, reduce the heat, then cover and simmer gently for 5 minutes.

4 Add the tomatoes and potatoes, cover again and simmer gently for 20 minutes. Add the saffron, chickpeas, coriander and lemon juice. Season to taste with salt and pepper and when piping hot, serve with fried wedges of lemon.

Tamarind Soup with Peanuts and Vegetables

Known in Indonesia as Sayur Asam, *this is a colourful and refreshing soup from Jakarta with more than a hint of sharpness.*

INGREDIENTS

Serves 4

5 shallots or 1 red onion, sliced

3 garlic cloves, crushed

2.5cm/1in galangal, peeled and sliced

1–2 fresh red chillies, seeded and sliced

25g/1oz/¼ cup raw peanuts

1cm/½in cube shrimp paste, prepared

1.2 litres/2 pints/5 cups Vegetable Stock

50–75g/2–3oz/½–¾ cup salted peanuts,
   lightly crushed

15–30ml/1–2 tbsp dark brown sugar

5ml/1 tsp tamarind pulp, soaked in
   75ml/5 tbsp warm water for 15 minutes

salt

For the vegetables

1 christophine, thinly peeled, seeds
   removed, flesh finely sliced

115g/4 oz green beans, thinly sliced

50g/2 oz corn kernels (optional)

a handful of green leaves, such as
   watercress, rocket (arugula) or
   Chinese leaves (Chinese cabbage),
   finely shredded

1 fresh green chilli, seeded and sliced,
   to garnish

2 Pour in some of the stock to moisten and then pour this mixture into a pan or wok, adding the rest of the stock. Cook for 15 minutes with the crushed salted peanuts and sugar.

4 About 5 minutes before serving, add the christophine slices, beans and corn, if using, to the soup and cook fairly rapidly. At the last minute, add the green leaves and salt to taste.

1 Grind the shallots or onion, garlic, galangal, chillies, raw peanuts and shrimp paste to a paste in a food processor, or using a mortar and pestle.

3 Strain the tamarind pulp, discarding the seeds, and reserve the juice.

5 Add the tamarind juice and adjust the seasoning. Serve immediately, garnished with slices of green chilli.

Miso Broth with Spring Onions and Tofu

The Japanese eat miso broth, a simple, but highly nutritious soup, almost every day – it is standard breakfast fare and it is eaten with rice or noodles later in the day.

INGREDIENTS

Serves 4

1 bunch of spring onions (scallions) or
    5 baby leeks

15g/½ oz/½ cup fresh coriander
    (cilantro)

3 thin slices fresh root ginger

2 star anise

1 small dried red chilli

1.2 litres/2 pints/5 cups Stock for
    Japanese Soup or Vegetable
    Stock

225g/8oz pak choi (bok choy) or other
    Asian greens, thickly sliced

200g/7oz firm tofu, cut into 2.5cm/
    1in cubes

60ml/4 tbsp red miso

30–45ml/2–3 tbsp Japanese soy
    sauce (shoyu)

1 fresh red chilli, seeded and
    shredded (optional)

1 Cut the coarse green tops off the spring onions or baby leeks and reserve. Slice the rest of the spring onions or leeks finely on the diagonal. Place the green tops in a large, heavy pan with the coriander stalks, fresh root ginger, star anise, dried chilli and stock.

2 Heat the mixture gently until boiling, then lower the heat and simmer gently for 10 minutes. Strain, return to the pan and reheat until simmering. Add the green portion of the sliced spring onions or leeks to the soup with the pak choi or greens and tofu. Cook for 2 minutes.

3 Mix 45ml/3 tbsp of the miso with a little of the hot soup in a bowl, then stir it into the soup. Taste the soup and add more miso with soy sauce to taste.

4 Coarsely chop the coriander leaves and stir most of them into the soup with the white part of the spring onions or leeks. Cook for 1 minute, then ladle the soup into warmed serving bowls. Sprinkle with the remaining coriander and the fresh red chilli, if using, and serve immediately.

Japanese Crushed Tofu Soup

The main ingredient for this soup is crushed tofu, which is both nutritious and satisfying.

INGREDIENTS

Serves 4

150g/5oz fresh tofu, weighed
   without water
2 dried shiitake mushrooms
50g/2oz gobo
5ml/1 tsp rice vinegar
½ black or white konnyaku (about 115g/
   4oz)
30ml/2 tbsp sesame oil
115g/4oz mooli (daikon), thinly sliced
50g/2oz carrot, thinly sliced
750ml/1¼ pints/3 cups Stock for Japanese
   Soups or instant dashi
pinch of salt
30ml/2 tbsp sake or dry white wine
7.5ml/1½ tsp mirin
45ml/3 tbsp white or red miso paste
dash of soy sauce
6 mangetouts (snow peas), trimmed,
   boiled and finely sliced, to garnish

1 Crush the tofu coarsely by hand until it resembles lumpy scrambled egg in texture – do not crush it too finely.

2 Wrap the tofu in a clean dishtowel and put it in a sieve, then pour over plenty of boiling water. Leave the tofu to drain thoroughly for 10 minutes.

3 Soak the dried shiitake mushrooms in lukewarm water for 20 minutes, then drain them. Remove their stems and cut the caps into 4–6 pieces.

4 Use a vegetable brush to scrub the skin off the gobo and slice it into thin shavings. Soak the shavings for 5 minutes in plenty of cold water to which the rice vinegar has been added to remove any bitter taste. Drain.

5 Put the konnyaku in a small pan and cover with water. Bring to the boil, then drain and cool. Tear the konnyaku into 2cm/¾in lumps: do not use a knife, as smooth cuts will prevent it from absorbing flavour.

6 Heat the sesame oil in a deep pan. Add all the shiitake mushrooms, gobo, mooli, carrot and konnyaku. Stir-fry for 1 minute, then add the tofu and stir well.

7 Pour in the stock/dashi and add the salt, sake or wine and mirin. Bring to the boil. Skim the broth and simmer it for 5 minutes.

8 In a small bowl, dissolve the miso paste in a little of the soup, then return it to the pan. Simmer the soup gently for 10 minutes, until the vegetables are soft. Add the soy sauce, then remove from the heat. Serve immediately in four bowls, garnished with the mangetouts.

V

Hot-and-sour Soup

A classic Chinese soup, this is a warming and flavoursome start to a meal.

INGREDIENTS

Serves 4

10g/¼oz dried cloud ears
  (wood ears)
8 fresh shiitake mushrooms
75g/3oz tofu
50g/2oz/½ cup sliced, drained, canned
  bamboo shoots
900ml/1½ pints/3¾ cups
  Vegetable Stock
15ml/1 tbsp caster (superfine) sugar
45ml/3 tbsp rice vinegar
15ml/1 tbsp light soy sauce
1.5ml/¼ tsp chilli oil
2.5ml/½ tsp salt
large pinch of ground white pepper
15ml/1 tbsp cornflour (cornstarch)
15ml/l tbsp cold water
1 egg white
5ml/1 tsp sesame oil
2 spring onions (scallions), cut into fine
  rings, to garnish

COOK'S TIP

Cloud ears (wood ears) are a
kind of Chinese mushroom,
valued for their texture more
than for their flavour.

1 Soak the cloud ears in hot
water for 30 minutes or until
soft. Drain, trim off and discard
the hard base from each, and chop
the cloud ears coarsely.

2 Remove and discard the stalks
from the shiitake mushrooms.
Cut the caps into thin strips. Cut
the tofu into 1cm/½in cubes and
shred the bamboo shoots finely.

3 Place the stock, shiitake
mushrooms, tofu, bamboo
shoots and cloud ears in a large
pan. Bring the stock to the boil,
lower the heat and simmer for
about 5 minutes.

4 Stir in the sugar, rice vinegar,
soy sauce, chilli oil, salt and
pepper. Mix the cornflour to a
smooth paste with the water. Add
the mixture to the soup, stirring
until it thickens slightly.

5 Lightly beat the egg white,
then pour it slowly into the
soup in a steady stream, stirring
constantly. Cook, stirring, until the
egg white changes colour.

6 Add the sesame oil just before
serving. Ladle the soup into
four heated bowls and garnish
each portion with a sprinkling of
spring onion rings.

PASTA AND NOODLE SOUPS

The pasta and noodles in these soups are not mere
afterthoughts, but an essential part of the recipes, adding
texture, substance and an attractive appearance. In
some of the dishes, especially the classic Italian pasta
in brodo – literally pasta in broth – and in both Chinese
and Japanese soups, the pasta and noodles play a leading role,
while the soupy component, whether clear, chunky or thick,
is almost subservient. Even when pasta and noodles are only
one of many ingredients, they are no less important.

Broccoli, Anchovy and Pasta Soup

This soup is from Apulia in the south of Italy, where anchovies and broccoli are often used together.

INGREDIENTS

Serves 4

30ml/2 tbsp olive oil

1 small onion, finely chopped

1 garlic clove, finely chopped

1/4–1/3 fresh red chilli, seeded and
   finely chopped

2 canned anchovy fillets, drained

200ml/7fl oz/scant 1 cup passata (bottled
   strained tomatoes)

45ml/3 tbsp dry white wine

1.2 litres/2 pints/5 cups Vegetable Stock

300g/11oz/2 cups broccoli florets

200g/7oz/1¾ cups dried orecchiette

salt and ground black pepper

grated Pecorino cheese, to serve

1 Heat the oil in a large pan. Add the onion, garlic, chilli and anchovies and cook over a low heat, stirring constantly, for 5–6 minutes.

2 Add the passata and white wine and season with salt and pepper to taste. Bring to the boil, cover the pan, then cook over a low heat, stirring occasionally, for 12–15 minutes.

3 Pour in the vegetable stock. Bring to the boil, then add the broccoli and simmer for about 5 minutes. Add the pasta and bring back to the boil, stirring constantly. Simmer for 7–8 minutes, or according to the instructions on the packet, stirring frequently, until the pasta is *al dente*.

4 Taste and adjust the seasoning. Serve hot, in individual warmed bowls. Hand round the grated Pecorino cheese separately.

Clam and Pasta Soup

This soup is a variation of the pasta dish spaghetti alle vongole, *using store-cupboard ingredients. Serve it with hot focaccia or ciabatta for a filling first course.*

Serves 4

30ml/2 tbsp olive oil

1 large onion, finely chopped

2 garlic cloves, crushed

400g/14oz can chopped tomatoes

15ml/1 tbsp sun-dried tomato paste

5ml/1 tsp granulated sugar

5ml/1 tsp dried mixed herbs

about 750ml/1¼ pints/3 cups Fish or
    Vegetable Stock

150ml/¼ pint/⅔ cup red wine

50g/2oz/½ cup small dried pasta shapes

150g/5oz jar or can clams in natural juice

30ml/2 tbsp finely chopped fresh flat leaf
    parsley, plus a few whole leaves
    to garnish

salt and ground black pepper

1 Heat the oil in a large, heavy pan. Add the onion and cook gently for 5 minutes, stirring frequently, until softened.

2 Add the garlic, tomatoes, sun-dried tomato paste, sugar, herbs, stock and wine and season with salt and pepper to taste. Bring to the boil. Lower the heat, half-cover the pan and simmer, stirring occasionally, for 10 minutes.

3 Add the pasta and continue simmering, uncovered, for about 10 minutes, or until the pasta is *al dente*. Stir occasionally to prevent the pasta shapes from sticking together.

4 Add the clams and their juice to the soup and heat through for 3–4 minutes, adding more stock if required. Do not allow it to boil, or the clams will become tough. Remove from the heat, stir in the chopped parsley and adjust the seasoning. Serve hot, sprinkled with coarsely ground black pepper and parsley leaves.

Consommé with Agnolotti

Prawns, crab and chicken jostle for the upper hand in this rich and satisfying consommé.

INGREDIENTS

Serves 4–6

75g/3oz cooked, peeled prawns (shrimp)
75g/3oz canned crab meat, drained
5ml/1 tsp finely grated fresh root ginger
15ml/1 tbsp fresh white breadcrumbs
5ml/1 tsp light soy sauce
1 spring onion (scallion), finely chopped
1 garlic clove, crushed
1 egg white, beaten
400g/14oz can chicken or fish consommé
30ml/2 tbsp sherry or vermouth
salt and ground black pepper

For the pasta dough
200g/7oz/1¾ cups plain (all-purpose) flour
pinch of salt
2 eggs
10ml/2 tsp cold water

For the garnish
50g/2oz cooked, peeled prawns (shrimp)
fresh coriander (cilantro) leaves

1 To make the pasta, sift the flour and salt on to a clean work surface and make a well in the centre with your hand.

2 Put the eggs and water into the well. Using a fork, beat the eggs gently together, then gradually draw in the flour from the sides, to make a thick paste.

3 When the mixture becomes too stiff to use a fork, use your hands to mix to a firm dough. Knead the dough for about 5 minutes until smooth. Wrap in clear film (plastic wrap) to prevent it from drying out and leave to rest for 20-30 minutes.

4 Meanwhile, put the prawns, crab meat, fresh ginger, breadcrumbs, soy sauce, spring onion, garlic and seasoning into a food processor or blender and process until smooth.

5 Roll out the dough into thin sheets. Stamp out 32 rounds 5cm/2in in diameter, with a fluted pastry (cookie) cutter.

6 Place 5ml/1 tsp of the filling in the centre of half the pasta rounds. Brush the edges of each round with egg white and top with a second round. Pinch the edges together to seal.

7 Cook the pasta in a large pan of salted, boiling water for 5 minutes (in batches to stop them sticking together). Remove and drop into a bowl of cold water for 5 seconds before placing on a tray. (You can make these pasta shapes a day in advance. Cover with clear film and store in the refrigerator.)

8 Heat the consommé in a pan with the sherry or vermouth. Add the cooked pasta shapes and simmer for 1–2 minutes.

9 Serve the pasta in soup bowls covered with hot consommé. Garnish with peeled prawns and coriander leaves.

Meatball and Pasta Soup

This soup, which comes from sunny Sicily, is a substantial primo – *a first course that in Italy is considered as important as the second.*

INGREDIENTS

Serves 4
2 x 300g/11oz cans condensed
    beef consommé
90g/3½oz/¾ cup very thin dried pasta,
    such as fidelini or spaghettini
chopped fresh flat leaf parsley, to garnish
grated Parmesan cheese, to serve

For the meatballs
1 very thick slice white bread,
    crusts removed
30ml/2 tbsp milk
225g/8oz/1 cup minced (ground) beef
1 garlic clove, crushed
30ml/2 tbsp grated Parmesan cheese
30–45ml/2–3 tbsp fresh flat leaf parsley
    leaves, coarsely chopped
1 egg
generous pinch of freshly grated nutmeg
salt and ground black pepper

1 Make the meatballs. Break the bread into a small bowl, add the milk and set aside to soak. Meanwhile, put the minced beef, garlic, Parmesan, parsley and egg in another large bowl. Grate the nutmeg liberally over the top and add salt and pepper to taste.

2 Squeeze the bread with your hands to remove as much milk as possible, then add the bread to the meatball mixture and mix everything together well with your hands. Wash your hands, rinse them under cold water, then form the mixture into tiny balls about the size of small marbles.

3 Tip both cans of consommé into a large pan, add water as directed on the labels, then add an extra can of water. Season to taste with salt and pepper, bring to the boil and add the meatballs.

4 Break the pasta into small pieces and add it to the soup. Bring to the boil, stirring gently. Simmer, stirring frequently, for 7–8 minutes or according to the instructions on the packet, until the pasta is *al dente*. Taste and adjust the seasoning.

5 Ladle into warmed bowls and serve immediately, garnished with chopped parsley and freshly grated Parmesan cheese.

Pasta Soup with Chicken Livers

The fried chicken livers in this dish are so delicious that, even if you do not normally like them, you will find yourself lapping them up with enthusiasm in this soup.

INGREDIENTS

Serves 4–6

115g/4oz/¹/₂ cup chicken livers, thawed
    if frozen

15ml/1 tbsp olive oil

knob (pat) of butter

4 garlic cloves, crushed

3 sprigs each of fresh parsley, marjoram
    and sage, chopped

1 fresh thyme sprig, chopped

5–6 fresh basil leaves, chopped

15–30ml/1–2 tbsp dry white wine

2 x 300g/11oz cans condensed
    chicken consommé

225g/8oz/2 cups frozen peas

50g/2oz/¹/₂ cup small dried pasta shapes,
    such as farfalle

2–3 spring onions (scallions),
    sliced diagonally

salt and ground black pepper

1 Cut the chicken livers into small pieces with scissors. Heat the oil and butter in a frying pan, add the garlic and herbs, with salt and ground black pepper to taste, and cook gently for a few minutes. Add the livers, increase the heat to high and stir-fry for a few minutes until they change colour and become dry. Add the wine, cook until it evaporates, then remove from the heat.

2 Tip both cans of chicken consommé into a large pan and add water to the condensed soup as directed on the labels. Add an extra can of water, then stir in a little salt and pepper to taste and bring to the boil.

3 Add the frozen peas to the pan and simmer for about 5 minutes, then add the small pasta shapes and bring the soup back to the boil, stirring constantly. Lower the heat and gently simmer the soup, stirring frequently, for about 5 minutes, or according to the instructions on the packet, until the pasta is *al dente*.

4 Add the fried chicken livers and spring onions and heat through for 2–3 minutes. Taste and adjust the seasoning if necessary. Serve hot, in warmed bowls.

Chicken Soup with Vermicelli

In Morocco, the cook – who is almost invariably the most senior woman of the household – would use a whole chicken for this tasty and nourishing soup, to serve to her large extended family.

INGREDIENTS

Serves 4–6

30ml/2 tbsp sunflower oil

15g/¹⁄₂oz/1 tbsp butter

1 onion, chopped

2 chicken legs or breast portions, halved or quartered

plain (all-purpose) flour, for dusting

2 carrots, cut into 4cm/1¹⁄₂in pieces

1 parsnip, cut into 4cm/1¹⁄₂in pieces

1.5 litres/2¹⁄₂ pints/6¹⁄₄ cups Chicken Stock

1 cinnamon stick

good pinch of paprika

pinch of saffron threads

2 egg yolks

juice of ¹⁄₂ lemon

30ml/2 tbsp chopped fresh coriander (cilantro)

30ml/2 tbsp chopped fresh parsley

150g/5 oz dried vermicelli

salt and ground black pepper

1 Heat the oil and butter in a pan and cook the onion for 3–4 minutes, until softened. Dust the chicken pieces in seasoned flour and cook gently until they are evenly browned.

2 Transfer the chicken to a plate and add the carrots and parsnip to the pan. Cook over a low heat for 3–4 minutes, stirring frequently, then return the chicken to the pan. Add the chicken stock, cinnamon stick and paprika and season well with salt and pepper.

3 Bring the soup to the boil, cover and simmer for 1 hour, until the vegetables are very tender.

4 Meanwhile, blend the saffron in 30ml/2 tbsp boiling water. Beat the egg yolks with the lemon juice in a separate bowl and add the coriander and parsley. When the saffron water has cooled, stir into the egg and lemon mixture.

5 When the vegetables are tender, transfer the chicken to a plate. Spoon away any excess fat from the soup, then increase the heat a little and stir in the vermicelli. Cook for a further 5–6 minutes, until the pasta is *al dente*. Meanwhile, remove the skin and bones from the chicken and chop the flesh into bitesize pieces.

6 When the vermicelli is cooked, stir in the chicken pieces and the egg yolk, lemon and saffron mixture. Cook over a low heat for 1–2 minutes, stirring constantly. Adjust the seasoning and serve.

Pasta Squares and Peas in Broth

*This thick soup is from Lazio, the
region around Rome, where it is
traditionally made with fresh home-
made pasta and peas. In this
modern version, ready-made pasta
is used with frozen peas to save time.*

INGREDIENTS

Serves 4–6

25g/1oz/2 tbsp butter

50g/2oz/¹/₃ cup pancetta or rindless
   smoked streaky (fatty) bacon,
   coarsely chopped

1 small onion, finely chopped

1 celery stick, finely chopped

400g/14oz/3¹/₂ cups frozen peas

5ml/1 tsp tomato purée (paste)

5–10ml/1–2 tsp finely chopped fresh
   flat leaf parsley

1 litre/1³/₄ pints/4 cups Chicken Stock

300g/11oz fresh lasagne sheets

about 50g/2oz/¹/₃ cup prosciutto, diced

salt and ground black pepper

grated Parmesan cheese, to serve

1 Melt the butter in a large pan
and add the pancetta or
bacon, with the onion and celery.
Cook over a low heat, stirring
constantly, for 5 minutes.

COOK'S TIP

Take care when adding salt
because of the saltiness of the
pancetta and the prosciutto.

2 Add the peas and cook,
stirring, for 3–4 minutes. Stir
in the tomato purée and parsley,
then add the stock, with salt and
pepper to taste. Bring to the boil.
Cover the pan, lower the heat and
simmer gently for 10 minutes.
Meanwhile, cut the lasagne sheets
into 2cm/³/₄in squares.

3 Taste the soup and adjust the
seasoning if necessary. Drop in
the pasta, stir and bring to the boil.
Simmer for 2–3 minutes, or until
the pasta is *al dente*, then stir in the
prosciutto. Ladle the soup into
warmed bowls and serve hot, with
grated Parmesan cheese handed
around separately.

Beetroot Soup with Ravioli

Beetroot and pasta make an unusual combination, but this soup is no less good for that.

INGREDIENTS

Serves 4–6

1 quantity of Pasta Dough (see page 118)
1 egg white, beaten, for brushing
plain (all-purpose) flour, for dusting
1 small onion or shallot, finely chopped
2 garlic cloves, crushed
5ml/1 tsp fennel seeds
600ml/1 pint/2½ cups Chicken or
    Vegetable Stock
225g/8oz cooked beetroot (beet)
30ml/2 tbsp fresh orange juice
fresh fennel or dill leaves, to garnish
crusty bread, to serve

For the filling

115g/4oz mushrooms, finely chopped
1 shallot or small onion, finely chopped
1–2 garlic cloves, crushed
5ml/1 tsp chopped fresh thyme
15ml/1 tbsp chopped fresh parsley
90ml/6 tbsp fresh white breadcrumbs
salt and ground black pepper
large pinch of freshly grated nutmeg

1 Put all the filling ingredients in a food processor or blender and process to a paste.

2 Roll the pasta into thin sheets. Lay one piece over a ravioli tray and put 5ml/1 tsp of the filling into each depression. Brush around the edges of each ravioli with egg white. Cover with another sheet of pasta and press the edges together well to seal. Transfer to a floured dishtowel and leave to rest for 1 hour before cooking.

3 Cook the ravioli salted, boiling water for 2 minutes. (Cook in batches to stop them sticking together.) Remove and drop into a bowl of cold water for 5 seconds before placing on a tray. (You can make the ravioli a day in advance and store in the refrigerator.)

4 Put the onion, garlic and fennel seeds into a pan with 150ml/¼ pint/⅔ cup of the stock. Bring to the boil, cover and simmer for 5 minutes, until tender. Peel and finely dice the beetroot, reserving 60ml/4 tbsp for the garnish. Add the rest of it to the soup with the remaining stock, and bring to the boil.

5 Add the orange juice and cooked ravioli and simmer for 2 minutes. Serve in shallow soup bowls, garnished with the reserved diced beetroot and fresh fennel or dill leaves. Serve hot, with crusty bread.

Avgolemono

The name of this popular Greek soup means "egg and lemon", the two key ingredients. It is a light, nourishing soup made with orzo, a Greek rice-shaped pasta, but you can use any very small pasta shape in its place.

INGREDIENTS

Serves 4–6

1.75 litres/3 pints/7½ cups Chicken Stock

115g/4oz/½ cup orzo pasta

3 eggs

juice of 1 large lemon

salt and ground black pepper

lemon slices, to garnish

1 Pour the stock into a large pan and bring to the boil over a medium heat. Add the pasta and cook for 5 minutes.

2 Beat the eggs until frothy, then add the lemon juice and 15ml/1 tbsp cold water.

3 Remove the pan from the heat. Stir a ladleful of the hot chicken stock into the egg and lemon mixture, then stir in 1–2 more. Return this mixture to the pan and stir well. Season and serve immediately, garnished with lemon slices.

Tortellini Chanterelle Broth

The savoury-sweet quality of chanterelle mushrooms combines well in a simple broth with spinach-and-ricotta-filled tortellini. The addition of a little sherry creates a lovely warming effect.

INGREDIENTS

Serves 4

350g/12oz fresh spinach and ricotta
tortellini, or 175g/6oz dried

1.2 litres/2 pints/5 cups Chicken Stock

75ml/5 tbsp dry sherry

175g/6oz fresh chanterelle mushrooms,
trimmed and sliced, or 15g/½oz/½ cup
dried chanterelles

chopped fresh parsley, to garnish

1 Cook the tortellini according to the packet instructions.

2 Bring the chicken stock to the boil, add the dry sherry and fresh or dried mushrooms and simmer for 10 minutes.

3 Strain the tortellini, add to the stock, then ladle the broth into four warmed soup bowls, making sure each contains the same proportions of tortellini and mushrooms. Garnish with the chopped parsley and serve.

Roasted Tomato and Pasta Soup

V

When the only tomatoes you can buy are not particularly flavoursome, make this soup. The roasting compensates for any lack of flavour in the tomatoes, and the soup has a wonderful, smoky taste.

INGREDIENTS

Serves 4

450g/1lb ripe Italian plum tomatoes, halved lengthways

1 large red (bell) pepper, quartered lengthways and seeded

1 large red onion, quartered lengthways

2 garlic cloves, unpeeled

15ml/1 tbsp olive oil

1.2 litres/2 pints/5 cups Vegetable Stock or water

good pinch of granulated sugar

90g/3½oz/scant 1 cup small dried pasta shapes, such as tubetti

salt and ground black pepper

fresh basil leaves, to garnish

1 Preheat the oven to 190°C/ 375°F/Gas 5. Spread out the tomatoes, red pepper, onion and garlic in a roasting pan and drizzle with the olive oil. Roast for 30–40 minutes, until the vegetables are soft and charred, stirring and turning them halfway through cooking.

2 Tip the vegetables into a food processor, add about 250ml/ 8fl oz/1 cup of the stock or water, and process to a purée. Scrape into a sieve placed over a large pan and press the purée through with the back of a spoon into the pan.

3 Add the remaining stock or water, the sugar and salt and pepper to taste. Bring to the boil.

4 Add the pasta and simmer for 7–8 minutes (or according to the instructions on the packet), stirring frequently, until *al dente*. Taste and adjust the seasoning with salt and ground black pepper, if necessary. Serve immediately in warmed bowls, garnished with the fresh basil leaves.

COOK'S TIP
~

You can roast the vegetables in advance, leave them to cool, then store them in a covered bowl in the refrigerator overnight before puréeing.

Tiny Pasta in Broth

In Italy, this filling soup is usually served before a light main course.

Serves 4

1.2 litres/2 pints/5 cups Meat Stock

75g/3oz/¾ cup small soup pasta, such as stellette

2 pieces bottled roasted red (bell) pepper (about 50g/2oz)

salt and ground black pepper

grated Parmesan cheese, to serve

1 Bring the stock to the boil in a large pan. Add salt and pepper to taste, then drop in the soup pasta. Stir well and bring the stock back to the boil.

2 Lower the heat to a simmer and cook for 7–8 minutes, or according to the packet instructions, until the pasta is *al dente*. Stir often during cooking to prevent the pasta shapes sticking together.

3 Drain the pieces of bottled roasted pepper and dice them finely. Place them in the bases of four warmed soup plates and set them aside.

4 Taste the soup and adjust the seasoning if necessary. Ladle it into the soup plates and serve immediately, with a bowl of freshly grated Parmesan cheese handed around separately.

Little Stuffed Hats in Broth

This soup is served in northern Italy on Santo Stefano (St Stephen's Day – 26 December) and on New Year's Day. It makes a welcome change from all the special celebration food, the day before. It is traditionally made with the Christmas capon carcass, but chicken stock works equally well.

Serves 4

1.2 litres/2 pints/5 cups Chicken Stock

90–115g/3½–4oz/1 cup fresh or dried cappelletti

30ml/2 tbsp dry white wine (optional)

about 15ml/1 tbsp finely chopped fresh flat leaf parsley (optional)

salt and ground black pepper

about 30ml/2 tbsp grated Parmesan cheese, to serve

1 Pour the chicken stock into a large pan and bring to the boil. Add a little salt and pepper to taste, then drop in the pasta.

2 Stir well and bring back to the boil. Lower the heat to a simmer and cook according to the instructions on the packet, until the pasta is *al dente*. Stir frequently during cooking to make sure that the pasta cooks evenly.

3 Swirl in the wine and parsley, if using, then taste and adjust the seasoning if necessary. Ladle into four warmed soup plates, then sprinkle with grated Parmesan. Serve immediately.

COOK'S TIP

Cappelletti is just another name for tortellini, which come from Romagna region of Italy. You can either buy them ready-made or make your own.

Minestrone with Pesto

V

In Genoa, they often make minestrone like this, with fresh pesto stirred in towards the end of cooking. It is packed full of vegetables and has a strong, heady flavour, making it an excellent vegetarian dish. There is Parmesan cheese in the pesto, so there is no need to serve any extra with the soup.

INGREDIENTS

Serves 4–6

45ml/3 tbsp olive oil

1 onion, finely chopped

2 celery sticks, finely chopped

1 large carrot, finely chopped

150g/5oz green beans, cut into 5cm/
    2in pieces

1 courgette (zucchini), thinly sliced

1 potato, cut into 1cm/¹⁄₂in cubes

¹⁄₄ Savoy cabbage, shredded

1 small aubergine (eggplant), cut into
    1cm/¹⁄₂in cubes

200g/7oz can cannellini beans, drained
    and rinsed

2 Italian plum tomatoes, chopped

1.2 litres/2 pints/5 cups Vegetable Stock

90g/3¹⁄₂oz dried spaghetti or vermicelli

salt and ground black pepper

For the pesto

about 20 fresh basil leaves

1 garlic clove

10ml/2 tsp pine nuts

15ml/1 tbsp freshly grated
    Parmesan cheese

15ml/1 tbsp freshly grated
    Pecorino cheese

30ml/2 tbsp olive oil

1 Heat the oil in a large, heavy pan, add the chopped onion, celery and carrot, and cook over a low heat, stirring frequently, for 5–7 minutes.

2 Mix in the green beans, courgette, potato and Savoy cabbage. Stir-fry over a medium heat for about 3 minutes. Add the aubergine, cannellini beans and plum tomatoes and stir-fry for 2–3 minutes.

3 Pour in the stock and season with salt and pepper to taste. Bring to the boil. Stir well, cover and lower the heat. Simmer for 40 minutes, stirring occasionally.

4 Meanwhile, process all the pesto ingredients in a food processor until the mixture forms a smooth sauce, adding 15–45ml/ 1–3 tbsp water through the feeder tube if the sauce seems too thick.

5 Break the pasta into small pieces and add it to the soup. Simmer, stirring frequently, for 5 minutes. Add the pesto sauce and stir it in well, then simmer for 2–3 minutes more, or until the pasta is *al dente*. Check the seasoning and serve hot, in warmed soup plates or bowls.

Star-gazer Vegetable Soup

V

For a different flavour, you could also make this soup with chicken or fish stock. All are equally tasty and the soup makes an attractive first course for a dinner party.

INGREDIENTS

Serves 4

1 yellow (bell) pepper

2 large courgettes (zucchini)

2 large carrots

1 kohlrabi

900ml/1½ pints/3¾ cups Vegetable Stock

50g/2oz rice vermicelli

salt and ground black pepper

1 Cut the pepper into quarters, removing the seeds and core. Cut the courgettes and carrots lengthways into 5 mm/¼in slices and slice the kohlrabi into 5 mm/¼in rounds.

2 Using tiny pastry (cookie) cutters, stamp out shapes from the vegetables or use a very sharp knife to cut the slices into stars and other decorative shapes.

COOK'S TIP

Sauté the leftover vegetable pieces in a little oil and mix with cooked brown rice to make a tasty risotto.

3 Place the vegetables and stock in a pan and simmer for 10 minutes, until the vegetables are tender. Season to taste with salt and pepper.

4 Meanwhile, place the rice vermicelli in a bowl, cover with boiling water and set aside for 4 minutes. Drain, then divide among four warmed soup bowls. Ladle the soup over the rice vermicelli and serve immediately.

Seafood Wonton Soup

This is a variation on the popular wonton soup with pork.

INGREDIENTS

Serves 4

50g/2oz raw tiger prawns (jumbo shrimp)

50g/2oz queen scallops

75g/3oz cod fillet, skinned and
   coarsely chopped

15ml/1 tbsp finely chopped fresh chives

5ml/1 tsp dry sherry

1 small (US medium) egg white,
   lightly beaten

2.5ml/½ tsp sesame oil

1.5ml/¼ tsp salt

large pinch of ground white pepper

20 wonton wrappers

2 cos or romaine lettuce leaves, shredded

900ml/1½ pints/3¾ cups Fish Stock

fresh coriander (cilantro) leaves and garlic
   chives, to garnish

1 Peel and devein the prawns. Rinse, pat dry on kitchen paper and cut into small pieces.

2 Rinse and dry the scallops. Chop them into small pieces the same size as the prawns.

3 Place the cod in a food processor and process until a paste is formed. Scrape into a bowl and stir in the prawns, scallops, chives, sherry, egg white, sesame oil, salt and pepper. Mix well, cover and leave in a cool place to marinate for 20 minutes.

4 Make the wontons. Place 5ml/1 tsp of the seafood filling in the centre of a wonton wrapper, then bring the corners together to meet at the top. Twist them together to enclose the filling. Fill the remaining wonton wrappers in the same way. Tie with a fresh chive if you like.

COOK'S TIP

The filled wonton wrappers can be made ahead, then frozen for several weeks and cooked straight from the freezer.

5 Bring a large pan of water to the boil. Drop in the wontons. When the water returns to the boil, lower the heat and simmer gently for 5 minutes or until the wontons float to the surface. Drain the wontons and divide them among four heated soup bowls.

6 Add a portion of shredded lettuce to each bowl. Bring the fish stock to the boil in a pan over a medium heat. Ladle it on top of the lettuce and then garnish each portion with fresh coriander leaves and garlic chives. Serve the wonton soup immediately.

Beef Noodle Soup

Offer your fortunate friends or family a steaming bowl of this soup, packed with delicious and exotic flavours of Asia.

INGREDIENTS

Serves 4

10g/¼oz dried porcini mushrooms

150ml/¼ pint/⅔ cup boiling water

6 spring onions (scallions)

115g/4oz carrots

350g/12oz rump (round) steak

about 30ml/2 tbsp oil

1 garlic clove, crushed

2.5cm/1in piece fresh root ginger, finely chopped

1.2 litres/2 pints/5 cups Meat Stock

45ml/3 tbsp light soy sauce

60ml/4 tbsp dry sherry

75g/3oz thin egg noodles

75g/3oz spinach, shredded

salt and ground black pepper

1 Break the mushrooms into small pieces, place in a bowl and pour over the boiling water. Leave to soak for 15 minutes.

2 Shred the spring onions and carrots into 5cm/2in long, fine strips. Trim any fat off the meat and slice into thin strips.

3 Heat the oil in a large pan and cook the beef, in batches, until browned, adding a little more oil if necessary. Remove the beef with a slotted spoon and drain well on kitchen paper.

4 Add the garlic, ginger, spring onions and carrots to the pan and stir-fry for 3 minutes.

5 Add the meat stock, the pieces of mushroom and their soaking liquid, the soy sauce and sherry. Season generously with salt and ground black pepper. Bring to the boil and simmer, covered, for 10 minutes.

6 Break up the noodles slightly and add them to the pan with the shredded spinach. Simmer gently for 5 minutes, until the beef is tender. Adjust the seasoning to taste if necessary. Ladle into warm bowls and serve immediately.

COOK'S TIP

Dried porcini mushrooms are now widely available in supermarkets. They may seem expensive, but are full of flavour, so a small quantity goes a long way and really gives a lift to a soup like this one.

Udon Noodles with Egg Broth and Ginger

In this Japanese dish, called Ankake Udon, the soup for the udon is thickened with cornflour and retains its heat for a long time.

INGREDIENTS

Serves 4

400g/14oz dried udon noodles

30ml/2 tbsp cornflour (cornstarch)

4 eggs, beaten

50g/2oz mustard and cress

2 spring onions (scallions), finely chopped

2.5cm/1in fresh root ginger, finely grated, to garnish

For the soup

1 litre/1¾ pints/4 cups water

40g/1½oz kezuri-bushi

25ml/1½ tbsp mirin

25ml/1½ tbsp shoyu

7.5ml/1½ tsp salt

1 To make the soup, place the water and the soup ingredients in a pan and bring to the boil over a medium heat. Remove from the heat when it starts boiling. Stand for 1 minute, then strain through muslin (cheesecloth). Check the taste and add more salt if required.

2 Heat at least 2 litres/3½ pints/ 9 cups water in a large pan, and cook the udon noodles for 8 minutes, or according to the packet instructions. Drain under cold running water and wash off the starch with your hands. Leave the noodles in the sieve.

3 Pour the soup into a large pan and bring to the boil. Blend the cornflour with 60ml/4 tbsp water. Reduce the heat to medium and gradually add the cornflour mixture to the hot soup. Stir constantly. The soup will thicken after a few minutes. Reduce the heat to low.

4 Mix the egg, mustard and cress, and spring onions in a small bowl. Stir the soup once again to create a whirlpool. Pour the eggs slowly into the soup pan.

5 Reheat the noodles by pouring hot water over them. Divide among four bowls and pour the soup over the top. Garnish with the ginger and serve hot.

Pot-cooked Udon in Miso Soup

Udon is a white wheat noodle, more popular in the south and west of Japan than the north. It is eaten with various hot and cold sauces and soups. Here, in this dish known as Miso Nikomi Udon, the noodles are cooked in a clay pot with a rich miso soup.

INGREDIENTS

Serves 4

200g/7oz skinless, boneless chicken
   portion

10ml/2 tsp sake

2 abura-age

900ml/1½ pints/3¾ cups water and
   7.5ml/1½ tsp instant dashi

6 large fresh shiitake mushrooms, stalks
   removed, quartered

4 spring onions (scallions), trimmed and
   chopped into 3mm/⅛in lengths

30ml/2 tbsp mirin

about 90g/3½oz aka miso or
   hatcho miso

300g/11oz dried udon noodles

4 eggs

3 To make the soup, heat the second dashi stock in a large pan. When it has come to the boil, add the chicken pieces, shiitake mushrooms and abura-age and cook for 5 minutes. Remove the pan from the heat and add the spring onions.

4 Put the mirin and miso paste into a small bowl. Scoop 30ml/2 tbsp soup from the pan and mix this in well.

5 To cook the noodles, boil at least 2 litres/3½ pints/9 cups water in a large pan. The water should not come higher than two-thirds of the depth. Cook the noodles for 6 minutes and drain.

6 Put the noodles in one large flameproof clay pot or casserole (or divide among four small pots). Mix the miso paste into the soup and check the taste. Add more miso if required. Ladle in enough soup to cover the udon, and arrange the soup ingredients on top of the udon.

7 Put the soup on a medium heat and break an egg on top. When the soup bubbles, wait for 1 minute, then cover and remove from the heat. Leave to stand for 2 minutes before serving.

1 Cut the chicken into bitesize pieces. Sprinkle with sake and leave to marinate for 15 minutes.

2 Put the abura-age in a sieve and thoroughly rinse with hot water to wash off the oil. Drain on kitchen paper and cut each abura-age into 4 squares.

Tokyo-style Ramen Noodles in Soup

Ramen is a hybrid Chinese noodle dish presented in a Japanese way, and there are many regional variations, such as this from Tokyo.

INGREDIENTS

Serves 4
250g/9oz dried ramen noodles

For the soup stock
4 spring onions (scallions)
7.5cm/3in piece of fresh root ginger, quartered
raw bones from 2 chickens, washed
1 large onion, quartered
4 garlic cloves, peeled
1 large carrot, coarsely chopped
1 egg shell
120ml/¼fl oz/½ cup sake
about 60ml/¼ tbsp shoyu
2.5ml/½ tsp salt

For the cha-shu (pot-roast pork)
500g/1¼lb pork shoulder, boned
30ml/½ tbsp vegetable oil
2 spring onions (scallions), chopped
2.5cm/1in piece of fresh root ginger, sliced
15ml/1 tbsp sake
45ml/⅓ tbsp shoyu
15ml/1 tbsp caster (superfine) sugar

For the toppings
2 hard-boiled eggs
150g/5oz menma, soaked for 30 minutes and drained
½ nori sheet, broken into pieces
2 spring onions (scallions), chopped
ground white pepper
sesame oil or chilli oil

1 To make the soup stock, bruise the spring onions and ginger by hitting with the side of a large knife. Pour 1.5 litres/2½ pints/6¼ cups water into a wok and bring to the boil. Add the chicken bones and boil until the colour of the meat changes. Discard the water and wash the bones under water.

2 In a clean wok, bring 2 litres/3½ pints/9 cups water to the boil and add the bones and the other stock ingredients, except for the shoyu and salt. Reduce the heat and simmer until the water has reduced by half, skimming off any scum. Strain into a bowl through a sieve lined with muslin (cheesecloth).

3 Make the cha-shu. Roll the meat up tightly, 8cm/3½in in diameter, and tie with string.

4 Heat the oil to smoking point in a clean wok and add the chopped spring onions and ginger. Cook briefly, then add the meat. Turn often to brown evenly.

5 Sprinkle with sake and add 400ml/14fl oz/1⅔ cups water, the shoyu and sugar. Boil, then reduce the heat and cover. Cook for 25–30 minutes, turning every 5 minutes. Remove from the heat.

6 Slice the pork into 12 thin slices.

7 Shell and halve the boiled eggs, and sprinkle some salt on to the yolks.

8 Pour 1 litre/1¾ pints/4 cups soup stock from the bowl into a large pan. Boil and add the shoyu and salt. Check the seasoning; add more shoyu if required.

9 Wash the wok again and bring 2 litres/3½ pints/9 cups water to the boil. Cook the ramen noodles according to the packet instructions until just soft. Stir constantly to prevent them from sticking. If the water bubbles up, pour in 50ml/2fl oz/¼ cup cold water. Drain well and divide among four bowls.

10 Pour the soup over the noodles to cover. Arrange half a boiled egg, pork slices, menma and nori on top, and sprinkle with spring onions. Serve with pepper and sesame or chilli oil. Season to taste with a little salt, if you like.

Bean, Lentil and Chickpea Soups

Known collectively as pulses, beans, lentils and chickpeas are nutritional powerhouses, full of flavour and very economical, so they are perfect for home-made soups. Some of the recipes are based on fresh beans, while others rely on that useful store-cupboard (pantry) standby, dried pulses. The choice is further extended by using canned beans and chickpeas, which, while a little more expensive than the dried versions, do not require lengthy soaking before cooking and so are conveniently quick for busy cooks.

Lamb, Bean and Pumpkin Soup

This is a hearty soup to warm the cockles of the heart.

Serves 4

115g/4oz/⅔ cup split black-eyed beans
    (peas), soaked overnight
675g/1½lb neck (US shoulder or breast)
    of lamb, cut into medium-sized chunks
5ml/1 tsp chopped fresh thyme or
    2.5ml/½ tsp dried thyme
2 bay leaves
1.2 litres/2 pints/5 cups Meat Stock
1 onion, sliced
225g/8oz pumpkin, diced
2 black cardamom pods
7.5ml/1½ tsp ground turmeric
15ml/1 tbsp chopped fresh
    coriander (cilantro)
2.5ml/½ tsp caraway seeds
1 fresh green chilli, seeded and chopped
2 green bananas
1 carrot
salt and ground black pepper

1 Drain the black-eyed beans, place them in a pan and cover with fresh cold water.

2 Bring the beans to the boil, boil rapidly for 10 minutes and then reduce the heat and simmer, covered, for about 40–50 minutes, until tender, adding more water if necessary. Remove the pan from the heat and set aside to cool.

3 Meanwhile, put the lamb in a large pan, add the thyme, bay leaves and stock and bring to the boil. Cover and simmer over a moderate heat for 1 hour, until the meat is tender.

4 Add the onion, pumpkin, cardamoms, turmeric, coriander, caraway, chilli and seasoning and stir. Bring back to a simmer and cook, uncovered, for 15 minutes, stirring occasionally, until the pumpkin is tender.

5 When the beans are cool, spoon into a blender or food processor with their liquid and process to a smooth purée.

6 Peel the bananas and cut into medium slices. Cut the carrot into thin slices. Stir the banana and carrot slices into the soup with the beans and cook for 10–12 minutes, until the carrot is tender. Adjust the seasoning if necessary, ladle into a warm tureen or individual bowls and serve immediately.

Beef Chilli Soup

This is a hearty dish based on a traditional chilli recipe. It is ideal served with fresh, crusty bread as a warming start to any meal.

INGREDIENTS

Serves 4

15ml/1 tbsp oil

1 onion, chopped

175g/6oz/¾ cup minced (ground) beef

2 garlic cloves, chopped

1 fresh red chilli, sliced

25g/1oz/¼ cup plain (all-purpose) flour

400g/14oz can chopped tomatoes

600ml/1 pint/2½ cups Meat Stock

225g/8oz/2 cups canned kidney beans, drained and rinsed

30ml/2 tbsp chopped fresh parsley

salt and ground black pepper

crusty bread, to serve

1 Heat the oil in a large pan. Add the onion and minced beef and cook for 5 minutes, until brown and sealed.

2 Add the garlic, chilli and flour. Cook for 1 minute. Add the tomatoes and pour in the stock. Bring to the boil.

3 Stir in the kidney beans and season with salt and pepper to taste. Lower the heat and simmer for 20 minutes.

4 Add the chopped parsley, reserving a little to garnish the finished dish. Pour the soup into warm bowls, sprinkle with the reserved parsley and serve with crusty bread.

COOK'S TIP

For a milder flavour, remove the seeds from the chilli after slicing.

V

Fresh Tomato and Bean Soup

This is a rich, chunky tomato soup, with beans and coriander.

INGREDIENTS

Serves 4

900g/2lb ripe plum tomatoes
30ml/2 tbsp olive oil
275g/10oz onions, coarsely chopped
2 garlic cloves, crushed
900ml/1½ pints/3¾ cups Vegetable Stock
30ml/2 tbsp sun-dried tomato paste
10ml/2 tsp paprika
15ml/1 tbsp cornflour (cornstarch)
425g/15oz can cannellini beans, rinsed
    and drained
30ml/2 tbsp chopped fresh
    coriander (cilantro)
salt and ground black pepper
olive ciabatta, to serve

1 First, peel the tomatoes. Using a sharp knife, make a small cross in each one and place in a bowl. Pour over boiling water to cover and leave to stand for 30–60 seconds.

2 Drain the tomatoes and, when they are cool enough to handle, peel off the skins. Quarter them and then cut each piece in half again.

3 Heat the oil in a large pan and cook the onions and garlic for 3 minutes, or until just beginning to soften.

4 Add the tomatoes to the onions and stir in the stock, sun-dried tomato paste and paprika. Season with a little salt and pepper. Bring to the boil and simmer for 10 minutes.

5 Mix the cornflour to a paste with 30ml/2 tbsp water. Stir the beans into the soup with the cornflour paste. Cook for a further 5 minutes.

6 Taste and adjust the seasoning if necessary and stir in the chopped coriander just before serving with olive ciabatta.

V

Tuscan Bean Soup

There are many versions of this wonderful soup. This one uses cannellini beans, leeks, cabbage and good olive oil – and tastes even better when it is reheated.

INGREDIENTS

Serves 4

45ml/3 tbsp extra virgin olive oil

1 onion, coarsely chopped

2 leeks, coarsely chopped

1 large potato, diced

2 garlic cloves, finely chopped

1.2 litres/2 pints/5 cups Vegetable Stock

400g/14oz can cannellini beans, drained and can juice reserved

175g/6oz Savoy cabbage, shredded

45ml/3 tbsp chopped fresh flat leaf parsley

30ml/2 tbsp chopped fresh oregano

75g/3oz/1 cup shaved Parmesan cheese

salt and ground black pepper

For the garlic toasts

30–45ml/2–3 tbsp extra virgin olive oil

6 thick slices country bread

1 garlic clove, peeled and bruised

1 Heat the oil in a large, heavy pan, add the onion, leeks, potato and garlic and cook over a low heat, stirring occasionally, for 4–5 minutes, until they are just beginning to soften.

2 Pour on the vegetable stock and the reserved can juice from the beans. Cover and simmer for 15 minutes.

3 Stir in the cabbage, beans and half the herbs, season and cook for a further 10 minutes. Spoon about one-third of the soup into a food processor or blender and process until fairly smooth. Return to the soup in the pan, adjust the seasoning and heat through for 5 minutes.

4 Make the garlic toasts. Drizzle a little oil over the slices of bread, then rub both sides of each slice with the garlic. Toast until browned on both sides. Ladle the soup into bowls. Sprinkle with the remaining herbs and the Parmesan shavings. Add a drizzle of olive oil and serve with the hot garlic toasts.

Ribollita

Ribollita is rather like minestrone, but includes beans instead of pasta. In Italy, it is traditionally served ladled over bread and a rich green vegetable, although you could omit this for a lighter version.

INGREDIENTS

Serves 6–8

45ml/3 tbsp olive oil

2 onions, chopped

2 carrots, sliced

4 garlic cloves, crushed

2 celery sticks, thinly sliced

1 fennel bulb, trimmed and chopped

2 large courgettes (zucchini), thinly sliced

400g/14oz can chopped tomatoes

30ml/2 tbsp pesto, either home-made or
  ready-made

900ml/1½ pints/3¾ cups Vegetable Stock

400g/14oz can haricot (navy) or borlotti
  beans, drained

salt and ground black pepper

To serve

450g/1 lb young spinach

15ml/1 tbsp extra virgin olive oil, plus
  extra for drizzling

6–8 slices white bread

Parmesan cheese shavings (optional)

1 Heat the oil in a large, heavy pan. Add the onions, carrots, garlic, celery and fennel and cook over a low heat, stirring frequently, for 10 minutes. Add the courgette slices and cook, stirring, for a further 2 minutes.

2 Add the chopped tomatoes, pesto, vegetable stock and beans and bring to the boil. Reduce the heat, cover and simmer gently for 25–30 minutes, until all the vegetables are tender. Season with salt and ground black pepper to taste.

3 To serve, cook the spinach in the oil for 2 minutes, or until wilted. Spoon over the bread in soup bowls, then ladle the soup over the spinach. Serve with extra olive oil for drizzling on to the soup and Parmesan cheese to sprinkle on top, if you like.

Provençal Vegetable Soup

This satisfying soup captures all the flavours of summer in Provence. The basil and garlic purée, pistou, gives it extra colour and a wonderful aroma – so don't leave it out.

INGREDIENTS

Serves 6–8

275g/10oz/1½ cups shelled fresh broad
(fava) beans or 175g/6 oz/¾ cup dried
haricot (navy) beans, soaked overnight
2.5ml/½ tsp dried herbes de Provence
2 garlic cloves, finely chopped
15ml/1 tbsp olive oil
1 onion, finely chopped
1 large leek, thinly sliced
1 celery stick, thinly sliced
2 carrots, finely diced
2 small potatoes, finely diced
115g/4oz green beans
1.2 litres/2 pints/5 cups water
2 small courgettes (zucchini),
finely chopped
3 tomatoes, peeled, seeded and
finely chopped
115g/4oz/l cup shelled garden peas, fresh
or frozen
handful of spinach leaves, cut into
thin ribbons
salt and ground black pepper
fresh basil sprigs, to garnish

For the pistou

1 or 2 garlic cloves, finely chopped
15g/½oz/½ cup basil leaves
60ml/4 tbsp grated Parmesan cheese
60ml/4 tbsp extra virgin olive oil

1 To make the pistou, put the garlic, basil and Parmesan cheese in a food processor and process until smooth, scraping down the sides once. With the machine running, slowly add the olive oil through the feeder tube. Alternatively, pound the garlic, basil and cheese in a mortar with a pestle and stir in the oil.

2 To make the soup, if using dried haricot beans, drain them, place in a pan and cover with water. Boil vigorously for 10 minutes and drain.

3 Place the par-boiled beans, or fresh beans, if using, in a pan with the herbes de Provence and one of the garlic cloves. Add cold water to cover by 2.5cm/1in. Bring to the boil, reduce the heat and simmer over a medium-low heat until tender, about 10 minutes for fresh beans or 1 hour for dried beans. Remove from the heat and set aside in the cooking liquid.

4 Heat the oil in a large pan or flameproof casserole. Add the onion and leek and cook over a low heat for 5 minutes, stirring occasionally, until they are just beginning to soften.

5 Add the celery, carrots and the remaining garlic clove and cook, covered, for 10 minutes, stirring occasionally.

6 Add the potatoes, green beans and water, then season with salt and pepper. Bring to the boil, skimming any foam that rises to the surface. Cover and simmer gently for 10 minutes.

7 Add the courgettes, tomatoes, peas and the reserved beans with their cooking liquid. Simmer for 25–30 minutes, until tender. Add the spinach and simmer for 5 minutes. Season and swirl a spoonful of pistou into each bowl. Garnish with basil and serve.

COOK'S TIP

Both the pistou and the soup can be made 1–2 days in advance and chilled. To serve, reheat gently, stirring occasionally.

Spicy Bean Soup

A filling soup made with two kinds of beans flavoured with cumin.

INGREDIENTS

Serves 6–8

175g/6oz/1 cup dried black beans, soaked
   overnight and drained

175g/6oz/1 cup dried kidney beans,
   soaked overnight and drained

2 bay leaves

90ml/6 tbsp coarse salt

30ml/2 tbsp olive or vegetable oil

3 carrots, chopped

1 onion, chopped

1 celery stick

1 garlic clove, crushed

5ml/1 tsp ground cumin

1.5–2.5ml/¼–½ tsp cayenne pepper

2.5ml/½ tsp dried oregano

50ml/2fl oz/¼ cup red wine

1.2 litres/2 pints/5 cups Meat Stock

250ml/8fl oz/1 cup water

salt and ground black pepper

For the garnish

sour cream

chopped fresh coriander (cilantro)

1 Put the black beans and kidney beans in two separate pans with cold water to cover and a bay leaf in each. Boil rapidly for 10 minutes, then cover and simmer for 20 minutes.

2 Add 45ml/3 tbsp coarse salt to each pan and continue simmering for 30 minutes, until the beans are tender. Drain.

3 Heat the oil in a large, heavy flameproof casserole. Add the carrots, onion, celery and garlic and cook over a low heat for 8–10 minutes, stirring, until softened. Stir in the cumin, cayenne, and oregano and season with salt to taste.

4 Add the red wine, meat stock and water and stir to mix all the ingredients together. Remove the bay leaves from the cooked beans and discard, then add the beans to the casserole.

5 Bring to the boil, reduce the heat, then cover and simmer gently for about 20 minutes, stirring occasionally.

6 Transfer half the soup (including most of the solids) to a food processor or blender. Process until smooth. Return to the pan and stir to combine well.

7 Reheat the soup and adjust the seasoning to taste. Serve hot, garnished with sour cream and chopped coriander.

Beetroot and Butter Bean Soup

This soup is a simplified version of borscht and is prepared in a fraction of the time. Serve with a spoonful of sour cream and a sprinkling of chopped fresh parsley.

INGREDIENTS

Serves 4

30ml/2 tbsp vegetable oil

1 onion, sliced

5ml/l tsp caraway seeds

finely grated rind of ½ orange

250g/9oz cooked beetroot (beet), grated

1.2 litres/2 pints/5 cups Meat Stock
or rassol (see Cook's Tip)

400g/14oz can butter (lima) beans,
drained and rinsed

15ml/1 tbsp wine vinegar

60ml/4 tbsp sour cream

60ml/4 tbsp chopped fresh parsley,
to garnish

1 Heat the oil in a large pan and cook the onion, caraway seeds and orange rind over a low heat until soft, but not coloured.

2 Add the beetroot, stock or rassol, butter beans and vinegar and simmer over a low heat for a further 10 minutes.

3 Divide the soup among four warm bowls, add a spoonful of sour cream to each, sprinkle with chopped parsley and serve.

COOK'S TIP
∾

Rassol is a beetroot (beet) broth, which is used to impart a strong beetroot colour and flavour. You are most likely to find it in Kosher food stores.

White Bean Soup

Use either haricot (navy) or butter (lima) beans for this velvety soup.

Serves 4

175g/6oz/¾ cup dried white beans, soaked in cold water overnight

30–45ml/2–3 tbsp oil

2 large onions, chopped

4 celery sticks, chopped

1 parsnip, chopped

1 litre/1¾ pints/4 cups Chicken Stock

salt and ground black pepper

chopped fresh coriander (cilantro) and paprika, to garnish

1 Drain the beans and boil rapidly in fresh water for 10 minutes. Drain, cover with more fresh water and simmer for 1–2 hours, until soft. Reserve the liquid and discard any bean skins on the surface.

2 Heat the oil in a heavy pan and sauté the onions, celery and parsnip for 3 minutes.

3 Add the cooked beans and chicken stock to the pan and continue cooking until all the vegetables are tender. Remove the pan from the heat, leave the soup to cool slightly, then, using a food processor or hand blender, blend it until it is velvety smooth.

4 Reheat the soup gently, gradually adding some of the bean liquid or a little water if it is too thick. Season to taste.

5 To serve, transfer the soup into wide bowls. Garnish with fresh coriander and paprika.

COOK'S TIP

You can, if you like, use a 400g/14oz can cannellini or butter (lima) beans instead of dried beans. Drain and rinse them before adding to the dish.

Broad Bean and Rice Soup

V

This thick soup makes the most of fresh broad beans while they are in season. It works well with frozen beans for the rest of the year.

INGREDIENTS

Serves 4

1kg/2¼lb broad (fava) beans in their
    pods, or 400g/14 oz shelled frozen
    broad (fava) beans, thawed
90ml/6 tbsp olive oil
1 onion, finely chopped
2 tomatoes, peeled and
    finely chopped
225g/8 oz/1 cup arborio or other
    non-parboiled rice
25g/1oz/2 tbsp butter
1 litre/1¾ pints/4 cups boiling water
salt and ground black pepper
grated Parmesan cheese, to
    serve (optional)

1 Shell the beans if they are fresh. Bring a large pan of water to the boil and blanch the beans, fresh or frozen, for 3–4 minutes. Rinse under cold water and peel off the skins.

2 Heat the oil in a large pan. Add the onion and cook over a low to moderate heat until it softens. Stir in the beans and cook for about 5 minutes, stirring to coat them with the oil.

3 Season to taste with salt and pepper. Add the tomatoes and cook for a further 5 minutes, stirring frequently. Add the rice and cook, stirring constantly, for a further 1–2 minutes.

4 Add the butter and stir until it melts. Pour in the water, a little at a time. Adjust the seasoning to taste. Continue cooking until the rice is tender. Serve with grated Parmesan, if you like.

V

Bean and Pasta Soup

Serve this hearty soup with tasty, pesto-topped French bread croûtons.

INGREDIENTS

Serves 4

115g/4oz/½ cup mixed dried beans,
   soaked overnight and drained
15ml/1 tbsp oil
1 onion, chopped
2 celery sticks, thinly sliced
2–3 garlic cloves, crushed
2 leeks, thinly sliced
1 vegetable stock (bouillon) cube
400g/14oz can or jar pimientos
45–60ml/3–4 tbsp tomato purée (paste)
115g/4oz dried pasta shapes
4 slices French bread
15ml/1 tbsp Pesto Sauce (see page 130)
115g/4oz/l cup baby corn cobs, halved
50g/2oz broccoli florets
50g/2oz cauliflower florets
a few drops of Tabasco sauce
salt and ground black pepper

1 Place the beans in a large pan and cover with water. Bring to the boil and boil rapidly for 15 minutes. Drain and cover with fresh water. Bring to the boil, then simmer for about 45 minutes, or until nearly tender.

2 When the beans are almost ready, heat the oil in a large pan and cook the vegetables for 2 minutes. Add the stock cube and the beans with about 600ml/1 pint/2½ cups of their liquid. Cover and simmer for 10 minutes.

3 Meanwhile, purée the pimientos with a little of their liquid and add to the pan. Stir in the tomato purée and pasta and cook for 15 minutes. Preheat the oven to 200°C/400°F/Gas 6.

4 Meanwhile, make the pesto croûtons. Spread the French bread with the pesto sauce and bake for 10 minutes, or until crisp.

5 When the pasta is just cooked, add the corn cobs, broccoli, cauliflower, Tabasco and seasoning to taste. Heat for 2–3 minutes and serve with the pesto croûtons.

Black and White Bean Soup

V

Although this soup takes a while to prepare, the results are so stunning that it is well worth the effort.

INGREDIENTS

Serves 8

350g/12oz/2 cups dried black beans, soaked overnight and drained

2.4 litres/4¼ pints/10½ cups water

6 garlic cloves, crushed

350g/12oz/2 cups dried white beans, soaked overnight and drained

90ml/6 tbsp balsamic vinegar

4 jalapeño peppers, seeded and chopped

6 spring onions (scallions), finely chopped

juice of 1 lime

50ml/2fl oz/¼ cup olive oil

15g/½oz/¼ cup chopped fresh coriander (cilantro), plus extra to garnish

salt and ground black pepper

1 Place the black beans in a large pan with half the water and garlic. Bring to the boil. Reduce the heat to low, cover the pan, and simmer for about 1½ hours, until the beans are soft.

2 Meanwhile, put the white beans in another pan with the remaining water and garlic. Bring to the boil, cover the pan and simmer for about 1 hour until soft.

3 Process the cooked white beans in a food processor or blender. Stir in the balsamic vinegar, jalapeños, and half the spring onions. Return to the pan and reheat gently.

4 Process the cooked black beans in the food processor or blender. Return to the pan and stir in the lime juice, olive oil, coriander and remaining spring onions. Reheat gently.

5 Season both soups with salt and ground black pepper to taste. To serve, place a ladleful of each puréed soup, side by side, in each of eight warmed soup bowls. Swirl the two soups together with a cocktail stick (toothpick) or skewer. Garnish with chopped fresh coriander and serve.

V

Thai Lentil and Coconut Soup

Hot, spicy and richly flavoured, this is a substantial soup that is perfect for a cold winter evening. Serve with chunks of warmed naan bread.

INGREDIENTS

Serves 4

30ml/2 tbsp sunflower oil

2 red onions, finely chopped

1 fresh bird's eye chilli, seeded and
   thinly sliced

2 garlic cloves, chopped

2.5cm/1in piece of lemon grass, outer
   layers removed and inside thinly sliced

200g/7oz/scant 1 cup red lentils, rinsed

5ml/1 tsp ground coriander

5ml/1 tsp paprika

400ml/14fl oz/1⅔ cups coconut milk

juice of 1 lime

3 spring onions (scallions), chopped

20g/¾oz/scant 1 cup fresh coriander
   (cilantro), finely chopped

salt and ground black pepper

1 Heat the oil in a large pan and add the onions, chilli, garlic and lemon grass. Cook over a low heat for 5 minutes, or until the onions have softened but not browned, stirring occasionally. Add the lentils, ground coriander and paprika.

2 Pour in the coconut milk and 900ml/1½ pints/3¾ cups water, and stir well. Bring to the boil, stir, then reduce the heat and simmer for 40–45 minutes.

3 Pour in the lime juice and add the spring onions and fresh coriander, reserving a little of each. Season to taste with salt and pepper, then ladle the soup into warm bowls. Garnish with the reserved spring onions and coriander.

Indian Spiced Lentil Soup

A subtle blend of spices takes this warming soup to new heights. Serve it with crusty bread for a filling start to a winter supper.

INGREDIENTS

Serves 6

2 onions, finely chopped

2 garlic cloves, crushed

4 tomatoes, coarsely chopped

2.5ml/½ tsp ground turmeric

5ml/1 tsp ground cumin

6 cardamom pods

½ cinnamon stick

225g/8oz/1 cup red lentils, rinsed
    and drained

900ml/1½ pints/3¾ cups water

400g/14oz can coconut milk

15ml/1 tbsp lime juice

salt and ground black pepper

cumin seeds, to garnish

1 Put the onions, garlic, tomatoes, turmeric, cumin, cardamom pods, cinnamon, lentils and water into a pan. Bring to the boil, lower the heat, cover and simmer gently for 20 minutes, or until the lentils are soft.

2 Remove the cardamom pods and cinnamon stick, then process the mixture in a blender or food processor. Press the soup through a sieve, then return it to the clean pan.

3 Reserve a little of the coconut milk for the garnish and add the remainder to the pan with the lime juice. Stir well and season with salt and pepper. Reheat the soup without boiling. Swirl in the reserved coconut milk, garnish with cumin seeds and serve.

Lentil and Pasta Soup

V

Serve this rustic, vegetarian soup before a salad or other light main course. It goes well with Granary or crusty Italian bread.

INGREDIENTS

Serves 4–6

175g/6oz/¾ cup brown lentils
3 garlic cloves
1 litre/1¾ pints/4 cups water
45ml/3 tbsp olive oil
25g/1oz/2 tbsp butter
1 onion, finely chopped
2 celery sticks, finely chopped
30ml/2 tbsp sun-dried tomato paste
1.75 litres/3 pints/7½ cups
　　Vegetable Stock
few fresh marjoram leaves, plus extra
　　to garnish
few fresh basil leaves
leaves from fresh thyme sprig
50g/2oz/½ cup small dried pasta shapes
salt and ground black pepper

1 Put the lentils in a large pan. Smash one of the garlic cloves (there's no need to peel it first) and add it to the lentils. Pour in the water and bring to the boil. Lower the heat to a gentle simmer and cook for about 20 minutes, stirring occasionally, until the lentils are just tender.

2 Tip the lentils into a sieve, remove the cooked garlic clove and set it aside.

3 Rinse the lentils under cold running water, then leave them to drain. Heat 30ml/2 tbsp of the olive oil with half of the butter in a large pan. Add the onion and celery and cook over a low heat, stirring frequently, for 5–7 minutes, until softened.

COOK'S TIP

Use green lentils instead of brown, if you like, but the orange or red ones are not so good for this soup because they tend to go mushy.

4 Crush the remaining garlic and peel and mash the reserved cooked garlic clove. Add them to the vegetables with the remaining oil, the sun-dried tomato paste and lentils. Stir, then add the stock, herbs and salt and pepper to taste. Bring to the boil, stirring. Simmer for 30 minutes, stirring occasionally.

5 Add the pasta and bring to the boil, stirring. Simmer, stirring frequently, for 7–8 minutes, or according to the instructions on the packet, until the pasta is *al dente*. Add the remaining butter and adjust the seasoning. Serve hot in warmed bowls, garnished with marjoram leaves.

Lentil and Bacon Soup

This is a wonderfully hearty German soup, but a lighter version can be made by omitting the frankfurters, if you like.

INGREDIENTS

Serves 6

225g/8oz/1 cup brown lentils

15ml/1 tbsp sunflower oil

1 onion, finely chopped

1 leek, finely chopped

1 carrot, finely diced

2 celery sticks, chopped

115g/4oz piece lean bacon

2 bay leaves

1.5 litres/2½ pints/6¼ cups water

30ml/2 tbsp chopped fresh parsley, plus extra to garnish

225g/8oz frankfurters, sliced

salt and ground black pepper

1 Rinse the lentils thoroughly under cold running water, then drain.

2 Heat the oil in a large pan and gently cook the onion , stirring occasionally, for 5 minutes, until soft. Add the leek, carrot, celery, bacon and bay leaves.

COOK'S TIP

Unlike most pulses, brown lentils do not need to be soaked before cooking.

3 Add the lentils. Pour in the water, then gradually bring to the boil. Skim the surface, then simmer, half-covered, for about 45–50 minutes, or until the lentils are soft.

4 Remove the piece of bacon from the soup and cut into small cubes. Trim off any fat.

5 Return the bacon to the soup with the parsley and sliced frankfurters, and season well with salt and ground black pepper. Simmer for 2–3 minutes, then remove the bay leaves.

6 Transfer to individual soup bowls and serve garnished with chopped parsley.

V

Garlicky Lentil Soup

High in fibre and protein, lentils make a particularly tasty soup and this recipe just couldn't be simpler or easier.

INGREDIENTS

Serves 6

225g/8 oz/1 cup red lentils, rinsed
   and drained

2 onions, finely chopped

2 large garlic cloves, finely chopped

1 carrot, finely chopped

30ml/2 tbsp olive oil

2 bay leaves

generous pinch of dried marjoram
   or oregano

1.5 litres/2½ pints/6¼ cups
   Vegetable Stock

30ml/2 tbsp red wine vinegar

salt and ground black pepper

celery leaves, to garnish

crusty bread rolls, to serve

1 Put all the ingredients except for the red wine vinegar, seasoning and garnish in a large, heavy pan. Bring to the boil over a medium heat, then lower the heat and simmer for 1½ hours, stirring the soup occasionally to prevent the lentils from sticking to the base of the pan.

2 Remove the bay leaves and add the red wine vinegar, with salt and pepper to taste. If the soup is too thick, thin it with a little extra vegetable stock or water. Ladle the soup into heated bowls and garnish with celery leaves. Serve immediately with warmed crusty rolls.

COOK'S TIP

~

If you buy your lentils loose, remember to tip them into a sieve or colander and pick them over, removing any pieces of grit, before rinsing them.

Lentil Soup with Rosemary

A classic rustic Italian soup flavoured with rosemary, this is delicious served with garlic bread.

INGREDIENTS

Serves 4

225g/8oz/1 cup dried green or
 brown lentils
45ml/3 tbsp extra virgin olive oil
3 rindless streaky (fatty) bacon rashers,
 cut into small dice
1 onion, finely chopped
2 celery sticks, finely chopped
2 carrots, finely chopped
2 fresh rosemary sprigs, finely chopped
2 bay leaves
400g/14oz can plum tomatoes
1.75 litres/3 pints/7½ cups
 Vegetable Stock
salt and ground black pepper
fresh bay leaves and fresh rosemary
 sprigs, to garnish

1 Place the lentils in a bowl and cover with cold water. Leave to soak for 2 hours. Rinse and drain.

2 Heat the olive oil in a large, heavy pan. Add the bacon and cook over a medium heat, stirring occasionally, for about 3 minutes, then add the onion and cook, stirring frequently, for 5 minutes, until softened.

3 Stir in the chopped celery, carrots, herbs and lentils. Toss over the heat for 1 minute, until thoroughly coated in the oil.

4 Tip in the tomatoes and stock, and bring to the boil. Lower the heat, half-cover the pan and simmer for about 1 hour, until the lentils are perfectly tender.

5 Remove and discard the bay leaves and season the soup with salt and pepper to taste. Ladle into warm bowls and serve hot with a garnish of fresh bay leaves and sprigs of rosemary.

COOK'S TIP

Keep an eye open for the small, flat green lentils in Italian groceries or delicatessens, as they have an excellent flavour.

Smoked Turkey and Lentil Soup

Lentils seem to enhance the flavour of smoked turkey, and combined with four tasty vegetables they make a fine appetizer.

INGREDIENTS

Serves 4

25g/1oz/2 tbsp butter

1 large carrot, chopped

1 onion, chopped

1 leek, white part only, chopped

1 celery stick, chopped

115g/4oz/1½ cups mushrooms, chopped

50ml/2fl oz/¼ cup dry white wine

1.2 litres/2 pints/5 cups Chicken Stock

10ml/2 tsp dried thyme

1 bay leaf

115g/4oz/½ cup green lentils, rinsed

75g/3oz smoked turkey meat, diced

salt and ground black pepper

1 Melt the butter in a large pan. Add the carrot, onion, leek, celery and mushrooms. Cook over a medium heat, stirring frequently, for 3–5 minutes, until softened and golden brown.

2 Stir in the wine and chicken stock. Bring to the boil and skim off any foam that rises to the surface. Add the thyme and bay leaf. Lower the heat, cover and simmer gently for 30 minutes.

3 Add the lentils, re-cover the pan and continue cooking over a low heat for 30–40 minutes more, until they are just tender. Stir the soup occasionally to prevent the lentils from sticking to the base of the pan.

4 Stir in the smoked turkey and season to taste with salt and pepper. Cook until just heated through. Ladle the soup into bowls and serve immediately.

Chickpea and Pasta Soup

This is a simple, country-style, soup, packed with flavour. The shape of the pasta and the beans complement one another beautifully.

INGREDIENTS

Serves 4–6

60ml/4 tbsp olive oil

1 onion, finely chopped

2 carrots, finely chopped

2 celery sticks, finely chopped

400g/14oz can chickpeas, drained
    and rinsed

200g/7oz can cannellini beans, drained
    and rinsed

150ml/¼ pint/⅔ cup passata (bottled
    strained tomatoes)

120ml/4fl oz/½ cup water

1.5 litres/2½ pints/6¼ cups Vegetable or
    Chicken Stock

1 fresh rosemary sprig, extra to garnish

200g/7oz/scant 2 cups dried conchiglie

salt and ground black pepper

shavings of Parmesan cheese, to serve

1 Heat the olive oil in a large, heavy pan, add the chopped vegetables and cook over a low heat, stirring frequently, for 5–7 minutes.

2 Add the chickpeas and cannellini beans, stir well to mix, then cook for 5 minutes. Stir in the passata and water. Cook, stirring, for 2–3 minutes.

3 Add 475ml/16fl oz/2 cups of the stock, the rosemary sprig and salt and ground black pepper to taste. Bring to the boil, cover, then simmer over a low heat, stirring occasionally, for 1 hour.

VARIATIONS

∾

You can use other pasta shapes, but conchiglie are ideal because they scoop up the chickpeas and beans. If you like, crush 1–2 garlic cloves and cook them with the vegetables.

4 Pour in the remaining stock, add the pasta and bring to the boil. Lower the heat and simmer for 7–8 minutes, or according to the instructions on the packet, until the pasta is *al dente*. Remove the rosemary sprig. Serve the soup sprinkled with rosemary leaves and Parmesan shavings.

Moroccan Harira

This tasty soup is traditionally eaten during the month of Ramadan, when the Muslim population fasts between sunrise and sunset.

INGREDIENTS

Serves 4

25g/1oz/2 tbsp butter
225g/8oz lamb, cut into 1cm/½in pieces
1 onion, chopped
450g/1lb well-flavoured tomatoes
60ml/4 tbsp chopped fresh
   coriander (cilantro)
30ml/2 tbsp chopped fresh parsley
2.5ml/½ tsp ground turmeric
2.5ml/½ tsp ground cinnamon
50g/2oz/¼ cup red lentils
75g/3 oz/½ cup chickpeas,
   soaked overnight
600ml/1 pint/2½ cups water
4 baby (pearl) onions, peeled
25g/1oz/¼ cup soup noodles
salt and ground black pepper

For the garnish
chopped fresh coriander (cilantro)
lemon slices
ground cinnamon

1   Heat the butter in a large pan or flameproof casserole and cook the lamb and chopped onion for 5 minutes, stirring frequently.

2   Peel the tomatoes, if you like, by plunging them into boiling water to loosen the skins. Wait for them to cool a little before peeling off the skins. Then cut them into quarters and add to the lamb with the herbs and spices.

3   Rinse the lentils under cold running water and drain the chickpeas. Add both to the pan with the water. Season with salt and pepper. Bring to the boil, cover and simmer gently for 1½ hours.

4   Add the baby onions and cook for a further 30 minutes. Add the noodles 5 minutes before the end of the cooking time. Serve the soup when the noodles are tender. Ladle into warm bowls, garnish with the coriander, lemon slices and cinnamon.

Chickpea and Parsley Soup

Parsley and a hint of lemon bring freshness to chickpeas.

Serves 6

225g/8oz/1⅓ cups chickpeas,
    soaked overnight
1 small onion
bunch of fresh parsley (about 40g/1½oz)
30ml/2 tbsp olive and sunflower
    oils, mixed
1.2 litres/2 pints/5 cups Chicken Stock
juice of ½ lemon
salt and ground black pepper
lemon wedges and finely pared strips of
    rind, to garnish

3 Heat the olive and sunflower oils in a pan or flameproof casserole and cook the onion mixture over a low heat, stirring frequently, for about 4 minutes until the onion is slightly softened.

4 Add the chickpeas, cook gently for 1–2 minutes, then add the stock. Season with salt and pepper. Bring the soup to the boil, then cover and simmer for 20 minutes, until the chickpeas are tender.

5 Leave the soup to cool a little and then mash the chickpeas with a fork until the soup is thick, but still quite chunky.

6 Reheat the soup gently and stir in the lemon juice. Serve immediately, garnished with lemon wedges and rind.

1 Drain the chickpeas and rinse under cold water. Cook them in boiling water for 1–1½ hours. Drain and rub off the skins.

2 Place the onion and parsley in a food processor or blender and process until finely chopped.

Chickpea and Spinach Soup with Garlic

This thick and creamy soup is richly
flavoured – perfect for vegetarians.

INGREDIENTS

Serves 4

30ml/2 tbsp olive oil

4 garlic cloves, crushed

1 onion, coarsely chopped

10ml/2 tsp ground cumin

10ml/2 tsp ground coriander

1.2 litres/2 pints/5 cups Vegetable Stock

350g/12oz potatoes, finely chopped

425g/15oz can chickpeas, drained

15ml/1 tbsp cornflour (cornstarch)

150ml/¼ pint/⅔ cup double
   (heavy) cream

30ml/2 tbsp light tahini

200g/7 oz spinach, shredded

cayenne pepper

salt and ground black pepper

2 Stir in the ground cumin
and coriander and cook for
1 minute. Add the vegetable stock
and potatoes. Bring to the boil and
simmer for 10 minutes.

3 Add the chickpeas and simmer
for a further 5 minutes, or
until the potatoes are just tender.

4 Blend together the cornflour,
cream, tahini and plenty of
seasoning. Stir into the soup with
the spinach. Bring to the boil,
stirring, and simmer for a further
2 minutes. Adjust the seasoning
with salt, pepper and cayenne to
taste. Serve sprinkled with a little
extra cayenne.

1 Heat the olive oil in a large,
heavy pan and cook the garlic
and onion over a medium heat,
stirring occasionally, for about
5 minutes, or until the onion is
softened and golden brown.

COOK'S TIP

Tahini is sesame seed paste
and is available from many
health food stores.

Eastern European Chickpea Soup

Chickpeas form part of the staple diet in the Balkans, where this soup originates. It is economical to make, and is a hearty and satisfying dish.

INGREDIENTS

Serves 4–6

500g/1¼lb/5 cups chickpeas,
  soaked overnight

2 litres/3½ pints/9 cups Vegetable Stock

3 large waxy potatoes, cut into
  bitesize chunks

50ml/2fl oz/¼ cup olive oil

225g/8oz spinach leaves

salt and ground black pepper

spicy sausage, cooked (optional)

1 Drain the chickpeas and rinse under cold water. Place in a large pan with the vegetable stock. Bring to the boil, then reduce the heat and cook gently for about 1 hour.

2 Add the potatoes and olive oil and season with salt and pepper to taste. Cook for about 20 minutes, until the potatoes are just tender.

3 Add the spinach and sliced, cooked sausage (if using) 5 minutes before the end of the cooking time. Ladle the soup into individual warmed soup bowls and serve immediately.

FISH AND SHELLFISH SOUPS

~

There is something incredibly special about fish soups, even
though many of them originated as inexpensive meals for
fishermen to use up leftovers from the day's catch. Nowadays,
many of these traditional recipes, such as Bouillabaisse, are
luxurious treats reserved for dinner parties and special
occasions. However, not all fish and shellfish soups, bisques
and chowders will strain the family budget and many are
so quick and easy to make that they will provide the perfect
first course for a midweek supper.

Smoked Haddock and Potato Soup

"Cullen Skink" is a classic Scottish dish using one of the country's tastiest fish.

Serves 6

350g/12oz smoked haddock fillet

1 onion, chopped

bouquet garni

900ml/1½ pints/3¾ cups water

500g/1¼lb floury potatoes, quartered

600ml/1 pint/2½ cups milk

40g/1½oz/3 tbsp butter

salt and ground black pepper

chopped chives, to garnish

crusty bread, to serve

3 Strain the fish stock and return to the pan, then add the potatoes and simmer for about 25 minutes. Remove the potatoes from the pan. Add the milk to the pan and bring to the boil over a low heat.

4 Mash the potatoes with the butter, then whisk them into the soup. Add the fish to the pan and heat through. Season to taste. Ladle into bowls, sprinkle with chives and serve with crusty bread.

1 Put the first four ingredients into a large pan and bring to the boil. Skim off any scum that rises to the surface, then cover and poach gently for 10–15 minutes.

2 Lift the haddock from the pan and cool slightly, then remove the skin and bones. Flake the flesh and put to one side. Return the skin and bones to the pan and simmer for 30 minutes.

Fish Soup with Dumplings

V

Use a variety of whatever fish is available in this Czech soup, such as perch, catfish, cod or snapper. The basis of the dumplings is the same, whether you use semolina or flour.

INGREDIENTS

Serves 4–8

3 rindless bacon rashers (strips), diced

675g/1½ lb assorted fresh fish, skinned, boned and diced

15ml/1 tbsp paprika, plus extra to garnish

1.5 litres/2½ pints/6¼ cups Fish Stock or water

3 firm tomatoes, peeled and chopped

4 waxy potatoes, grated

5–10ml/1–2 tsp chopped fresh marjoram, plus extra to garnish

For the dumplings

75g/3oz/½ cup semolina or plain (all-purpose) flour

1 egg, beaten

45ml/3 tbsp milk or water

generous pinch of salt

15ml/1 tbsp chopped fresh parsley

1 Dry-fry the bacon in a large pan until golden brown, then add the pieces of assorted fish. Cook for 1–2 minutes, taking care not to break up the pieces of fish.

2 Sprinkle in the paprika, pour in the fish stock or water and bring to the boil. Reduce the heat and simmer for 10 minutes.

3 Stir the chopped tomatoes, grated potato and marjoram into the pan. Cook for 10 minutes, stirring occasionally.

4 Combine all the dumpling ingredients, then leave to stand, covered with clear film (plastic wrap) for 5–10 minutes.

5 Drop spoonfuls of the mixture into the soup and cook for 10 minutes. Serve hot with a little marjoram and paprika.

Seafood Soup

This is a really chunky, aromatic mixed fish soup from France, flavoured with plenty of saffron and herbs. Rouille, a fiery hot paste, is served separately for everyone to swirl into their soup to flavour.

INGREDIENTS

Serves 6

3 gurnard, red mullet or snapper, scaled
   and gutted
12 large prawns (shrimp)
675g/1½lb white fish, such as cod
225g/8oz fresh mussels
1 onion, quartered
1.2 litres/2 pints/5 cups water
5ml/1 tsp saffron threads
75ml/5 tbsp olive oil
1 fennel bulb, coarsely chopped
4 garlic cloves, crushed
3 strips pared orange rind
4 fresh thyme sprigs
675g/1½lb tomatoes
30ml/2 tbsp sun-dried tomato paste
3 bay leaves
salt and ground black pepper

For the rouille
1 red (bell) pepper, seeded and
   coarsely chopped
1 fresh red chilli, seeded and sliced
2 garlic cloves, chopped
75ml/5 tbsp olive oil
15g/½ oz/¼ cup fresh breadcrumbs

1 To make the *rouille*, process all the ingredients in a blender or food processor until smooth. Transfer to a serving dish and chill.

2 Fillet the gurnard, mullet or snapper by cutting the flesh from the backbone. Reserve the heads and bones. Cut the fillets into small chunks. Peel half the prawns and reserve the trimmings to make the stock. Skin the white fish, discarding any bones, and cut into large chunks. Scrub the mussels, discarding any open ones.

3 Put the fish trimmings and prawn trimmings in a pan with the onion and water. Bring to the boil, then reduce the heat and simmer gently for 30 minutes. Remove the pan from the heat, cool slightly, then strain.

4 Place the saffron in a small bowl and add 15ml/1 tbsp boiling water. Set aside to soak.

5 Heat 30ml/2 tbsp of the olive oil in a large sauté pan or heavy pan. Add the gurnard, mullet or snapper and the white fish and cook over a high heat for 1 minute. Drain well.

6 Heat the remaining oil and cook the fennel, garlic, orange rind and thyme over a medium heat until beginning to colour. Measure the strained stock and make up to about 1.2 litres/2 pints/5 cups with water.

7 Plunge the tomatoes into boiling water for 30 seconds, then refresh in cold water. Peel and chop. Add the stock to the pan with the saffron, tomatoes, tomato paste and bay leaves. Season to taste, bring almost to the boil, then simmer gently, covered, for 20 minutes.

8 Stir in the gurnard, mullet or snapper, the white fish, peeled and unpeeled prawns and add the mussels. Cover the pan and cook for 3–4 minutes. Discard any mussels that do not open. Serve the soup hot with the *rouille*.

Matelote

Traditionally, this fishermen's chunky soup is made from freshwater fish, including eel.

INGREDIENTS

Serves 6

1kg/2¼lb mixed fish, including 450g/1lb
    conger eel if possible
50g/2oz/¼ cup butter
1 onion, thickly sliced
2 celery sticks, thickly sliced
2 carrots, thickly sliced
1 bottle dry white or red wine
1 fresh bouquet garni containing parsley,
    bay leaf and chervil
2 cloves
6 black peppercorns
beurre manié (see Cook's Tip)
salt and cayenne pepper

For the garnish

25g/1oz/2 tbsp butter
12 baby (pearl) onions, peeled
12 button (white) mushrooms
chopped flat leaf parsley

4 Strain the soup through a large sieve placed over a clean pan. Discard the herbs and spices in the sieve, then divide the fish among deep soup plates and keep hot.

3 For the garnish, heat the butter in a pan and sauté the baby onions until golden and tender. Add the mushrooms and cook until golden. Season and keep hot.

COOK'S TIP

To make the beurre manié, mix 15g/½oz/1 tbsp softened butter with 15ml/1 tbsp plain (all-purpose) flour.

---

5 Reheat the soup until it boils. Lower the heat and whisk in the beurre manié, piece by piece, until the soup thickens. Season it and pour over the fish. Garnish each portion with the fried baby onions and mushrooms and sprinkle with chopped parsley.

1 Cut all the fish into thick slices, removing any bones. Melt the butter in a large pan, add the fish and sliced vegetables and stir over a medium heat until lightly browned.

2 Pour in the wine and enough cold water to cover. Add the bouquet garni and spices and season to taste. Bring to the boil, lower the heat and simmer gently for 20–30 minutes, until the fish is tender.

Fish Soup with Rouille

Making this soup is simplicity itself, yet the flavour suggests it is the product of painstaking preparation and complicated cooking.

INGREDIENTS

Serves 6

1kg/2¼ lb mixed fish

30ml/2 tbsp olive oil

1 onion, chopped

1 carrot, chopped

1 leek, chopped

2 large ripe tomatoes, chopped

1 red (bell) pepper, seeded and chopped

2 garlic cloves, peeled

150g/5oz/⅔ cup tomato purée (paste)

1 large fresh bouquet garni, containing
    3 parsley sprigs, 3 small celery sticks
    and 3 bay leaves

300ml/½ pint/1¼ cups dry white wine

salt and ground black pepper

For the rouille

2 garlic cloves, coarsely chopped

5ml/1 tsp coarse salt

1 thick slice of white bread, crust
    removed, soaked in water and then
    squeezed dry

1 fresh red chilli, seeded and
    coarsely chopped

45ml/3 tbsp olive oil

pinch of cayenne pepper (optional)

salt

For the garnish

12 slices of baguette, toasted in the oven

50g/2oz/½ cup finely grated
    Gruyère cheese

1 Cut the fish into 7.5cm/3in chunks, removing any obvious bones. Heat the olive oil in a large pan, then add the prepared fish and chopped vegetables. Stir gently until the vegetables are beginning to colour.

2 Now add all the other soup ingredients, then pour in just enough cold water to cover the mixture. Season well and bring to just below boiling point, then lower the heat so that the soup is barely simmering, cover and cook for 1 hour.

3 Meanwhile, make the rouille. Put the garlic and coarse salt in a mortar and crush to a paste with a pestle. Add the soaked bread and chilli and pound until smooth, or process in a food processor. Whisk in the olive oil, a drop at a time, to make a smooth, shiny sauce that resembles mayonnaise. Add a pinch of cayenne if you like and season to taste with salt. Set aside.

4 Lift out and discard the bouquet garni. Process the soup, in batches, in a food processor, then strain through a fine sieve into a clean pan, pushing the solids through with a ladle.

5 Reheat the soup, but do not boil. Taste and adjust the seasoning if necessary and ladle into individual bowls. Top each with two slices of toasted baguette, a spoonful of rouille and some grated Gruyère, then serve.

COOK'S TIP

Any firm fish can be used for this recipe. If you use whole fish, include the heads, which enhance the flavour of the soup.

Bouillabaisse

Perhaps the most famous of all Mediterranean fish soups, this recipe, originating from Marseilles in the south of France, is a rich and colourful mixture of fish and shellfish, flavoured with tomatoes, saffron and orange.

INGREDIENTS

Serves 4–6

1.5kg/3–3½lb mixed fish and raw shellfish, such as red mullet, John Dory, monkfish, red snapper, whiting, large raw prawns (shrimp) and clams

225g/8oz well-flavoured tomatoes

pinch of saffron threads

90ml/6 tbsp olive oil

1 onion, sliced

1 leek, sliced

1 celery stick, sliced

2 garlic cloves, crushed

1 bouquet garni

1 strip orange rind

2.5ml/½ tsp fennel seeds

15ml/1 tbsp tomato purée (paste)

10ml/2 tsp Pernod

salt and ground black pepper

4–6 thick slices French bread and 45ml/3 tbsp chopped fresh parsley, to serve

COOK'S TIP

Saffron comes from the orange and red stigmas of a type of crocus, which must be harvested by hand and are therefore extremely expensive – the highest-priced spice in the world. However, its flavour is unique and cannot be replaced by any other spice. It is an essential ingredient in traditional bouillabaisse and should not be omitted.

1 Remove the heads, tails and fins from the fish and set the fish aside. Put the trimmings in a large pan with 1.2 litres/2 pints/ 5 cups water. Bring to the boil and simmer for 15 minutes. Strain and reserve the liquid.

2 Cut the fish into large chunks. Leave the shellfish in their shells. Blanch the tomatoes, then drain and refresh in cold water. Peel them and chop coarsely. Soak the saffron in 15–30ml/1–2 tbsp hot water.

3 Heat the oil in a large pan, add the onion, leek and celery and cook until softened. Add the garlic, bouquet garni, orange rind, fennel seeds and chopped tomatoes, then stir in the saffron and its soaking liquid and the reserved fish stock. Season with salt and pepper, then bring to the boil and simmer for 30–40 minutes.

4 Add the shellfish and boil for about 6 minutes. Add the fish and cook for 6–8 minutes more, until it flakes easily.

5 Using a slotted spoon, transfer the fish to a warmed serving platter. Keep the liquid boiling, to allow the oil to emulsify with the broth. Add the tomato purée and Pernod, then check the seasoning and adjust if necessary.

6 Ladle the soup into warm bowls, add the fish and sprinkle with chopped parsley. Serve immediately with French bread.

Spiced Mussel Soup

Chunky and colourful, this Turkish fish soup is like a chowder in its consistency. It is flavoured with harissa, which is more familiar in North African cookery.

INGREDIENTS

Serves 6

1.5kg/3–3½lb fresh mussels

150ml/¼ pint/⅔ cup white wine

30ml/2 tbsp olive oil

1 onion, finely chopped

2 garlic cloves, crushed

2 celery sticks, thinly sliced

bunch of spring onions (scallions),
   thinly sliced

1 potato, diced

7.5ml/1½ tsp harissa

3 tomatoes, peeled and diced

45ml/3 tbsp chopped fresh parsley

ground black pepper

thick natural (plain) yogurt, to serve

1 Scrub the mussels, discarding any damaged ones or any that do not close when tapped.

2 Bring the wine to the boil in a large, pan. Add the mussels and cover tightly with a lid. Cook, shaking the pan occasionally, for 4–5 minutes, until the mussel shells have opened wide. Discard any mussels that remain closed.

3 Drain the mussels, reserving the cooking liquid. Reserve a few mussels in their shells to use as a garnish and shell the rest.

4 Heat the oil in a pan and cook the onion, garlic, celery and spring onions for 5 minutes.

5 Add the shelled mussels, reserved liquid, potato, harissa and tomatoes. Bring to the boil, reduce the heat and cover. Simmer gently for 25 minutes.

6 Stir in the parsley and pepper and add the reserved mussels in their shells. Heat through for 1 minute. Serve immediately with a spoonful of yogurt.

Saffron Mussel Soup

This is one of France's most delicious seafood soups. For everyday eating, the French would normally serve all the mussels in their shells. Serve with plenty of French bread.

INGREDIENTS

Serves 4–6

40g/1½oz/3 tbsp unsalted (sweet) butter

8 shallots, finely chopped

1 bouquet garni

5ml/1 tsp black peppercorns

350ml/12fl oz/l½ cups dry white wine

1kg/2¼lb fresh mussels, scrubbed
    and debearded

2 leeks, trimmed and finely chopped

1 fennel bulb, finely chopped

1 carrot, finely chopped

several saffron threads

1 litre/1¾ pints/4 cups Fish or
    Chicken Stock

30–45ml/2–3 tbsp cornflour (cornstarch),
    blended with 45ml/3 tbsp cold water

120ml/4fl oz/½ cup whipping cream

1 tomato, peeled, seeded and
    finely chopped

30ml/2 tbsp Pernod (optional)

salt and ground black pepper

1 In a large, heavy pan, melt half the butter over a medium-high heat. Add half the shallots and cook, stirring frequently, for 1–2 minutes, until softened but not coloured. Add the bouquet garni, peppercorns and white wine and bring to the boil. Add the mussels, cover tightly with a lid and cook over a high heat for 3–5 minutes, shaking the pan occasionally, until the mussel shells have opened.

2 With a slotted spoon, transfer the mussels to a bowl and set aside. Strain the cooking liquid through a sieve lined with muslin (cheesecloth) to remove any sand or grit and reserve.

3 Pull open the shells and remove most of the mussels. Discard any closed mussels.

4 Melt the remaining butter over a medium heat. Add the remaining shallots and cook for 1–2 minutes. Add the leeks, fennel, carrot and saffron and cook for 3–5 minutes.

5 Stir in the reserved cooking liquid, bring to the boil and cook for 5 minutes, until the vegetables are tender and the liquid is slightly reduced. Add the stock and bring to the boil, skimming any foam that rises to the surface. Season with salt, if needed, and black pepper and cook for a further 5 minutes.

6 Stir the blended cornflour into the soup. Simmer, stirring constantly, for 2–3 minutes, until the soup is slightly thickened, then stir in the cream, mussels and chopped tomato. Add the Pernod, if using, and cook for 1–2 minutes, until hot, then ladle into warm bowls and serve immediately.

Clam and Basil Soup

Subtly sweet and spicy, this soup is an ideal first course for serving as part of a celebration dinner.

INGREDIENTS

Serves 4–6

30ml/2 tbsp olive oil

1 onion, finely chopped

leaves from 1 fresh or dried sprig of
thyme, chopped or crumbled

2 garlic cloves, crushed

5–6 fresh basil leaves, plus extra to garnish

1.5–2.5ml/¼–½ tsp crushed red chillies,
to taste

1 litre/1¾ pints/4 cups Fish Stock

350ml/12fl oz/1½ cups passata (bottled
strained tomatoes)

5ml/1 tsp granulated sugar

90g/3½oz/scant 1 cup frozen peas

65g/2½oz/⅔ cup small dried pasta
shapes, such as chifferini

225g/8oz frozen shelled clams

salt and ground black pepper

1 Heat the oil in a large pan, add
the onion and cook gently for
about 5 minutes, until softened,
but not coloured. Add the thyme,
then stir in the garlic, basil leaves
and chillies.

2 Add the stock, passata and
sugar to the pan and season
with salt and pepper to taste. Bring
to the boil, then lower the heat and
simmer gently for 15 minutes,
stirring occasionally. Add the
frozen peas and cook for a further
5 minutes.

3 Add the pasta to the stock
mixture and bring to the boil,
stirring constantly. Lower the heat
and simmer for about 5 minutes,
or according to the packet
instructions, stirring frequently,
until the pasta is *al dente*.

4 Turn the heat down to low,
add the frozen clams and heat
through for 2–3 minutes. Taste and
adjust the seasoning if necessary.
Serve immediately in warmed
bowls, garnished with basil leaves.

COOK'S TIP

Frozen shelled clams are
available at good fishmongers
and supermarkets. If you can't
get them, use bottled or canned
clams in natural juice (not
vinegar). Italian delicatessens sell
jars of clams in their shells.
These both look and taste
delicious and are not too
expensive. For a special occasion,
stir some into the soup.

Lobster Bisque

Bisque is a luxurious, velvety soup, which can be made with any crustaceans, but lobster is a classic.

INGREDIENTS

Serves 6

500g/1¼ lb fresh lobster, cut into pieces

75g/3oz/6 tbsp butter

1 onion, chopped

1 carrot, diced

1 celery stick, diced

45ml/3 tbsp brandy, plus extra for
    serving (optional)

250ml/8fl oz/1 cup dry white wine

1 litre/1¾ pints/4 cups Fish Stock

15ml/1 tbsp tomato purée (paste)

75g/3oz/scant ½ cup long grain rice

1 fresh bouquet garni

150ml/¼ pint/⅔ cup double (heavy) cream,
    plus extra to garnish

salt, ground white pepper and
    cayenne pepper

1 Melt half the butter in a large pan, add the vegetables and cook over a low heat until soft. Add the lobster and stir until the shell on each piece turns red.

COOK'S TIP

It is best to buy a live lobster, chilling it in the freezer until it is comatose and then killing it just before cooking. If you can't face the procedure, use a cooked lobster; take care not to overcook the flesh.

2 Pour over the brandy and set it alight. When the flames die down, add the wine and boil until reduced by half. Pour in the fish stock and simmer for 2–3 minutes. Remove the lobster.

3 Stir in the tomato purée and rice, add the bouquet garni and cook until the rice is tender. Meanwhile, remove the lobster meat from the shell and return the shells to the pan. Dice the lobster meat and set it aside.

4 When the rice is cooked, discard all the larger pieces of shell. Tip the mixture into a blender or food processor and process to a purée. Press the purée through a fine sieve placed over the clean pan. Stir the mixture, then heat until almost boiling. Season to taste with salt, pepper and cayenne, then lower the heat and stir in the cream.

5 Dice the remaining butter and whisk it into the bisque, a piece at a time. Add the diced lobster meat and serve immediately. If you like, pour a small spoonful of brandy into each soup bowl and swirl in a little extra cream.

Scallop and Jerusalem Artichoke Soup

The subtle sweetness of scallops combines well with the flavour of Jerusalem artichokes in this attractive golden soup. For an even more colourful version, substitute pumpkin for the artichokes and use extra stock instead of the milk.

INGREDIENTS

Serves 6

1kg/2¼lb Jerusalem artichokes

juice of ½ lemon

115g/4oz/½ cup butter

1 onion, finely chopped

600ml/1 pint/2½ cups Fish Stock

300ml/½ pint/1¼ cups milk

generous pinch of saffron threads

6 large or 12 small scallops, with
their corals

150ml/¼ pint/⅔ cup whipping cream

salt and ground white pepper

45ml/3 tbsp flaked (sliced) almonds and
15ml/1 tbsp finely chopped fresh
chervil, to garnish

1 Working quickly, scrub and peel the Jerusalem artichokes, then cut them into 2cm/¾in chunks and drop them into a bowl of cold water, which has been acidulated with the lemon juice. This will prevent the artichokes from discolouring.

2 Melt half the butter in a pan, add the onion and cook over a low heat until softened. Drain the artichokes and add them to the pan. Cook gently for 5 minutes, stirring frequently. Pour in the stock and milk, add the saffron and bring to the boil. Lower the heat and simmer until the artichokes are tender but not mushy.

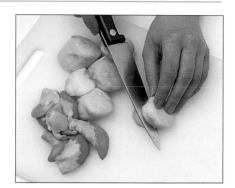

3 Meanwhile, carefully separate the corals from the scallops. Prick the corals and slice each scallop in half horizontally. Heat half the remaining butter in a frying pan, add the scallops and corals and cook very briefly (for about 1 minute) on each side. Dice the scallops and corals, keeping them separate, and set them aside until needed.

4 When the artichokes are cooked, tip the contents of the pan into a blender or food processor. Add half the white scallop meat and process to very smooth purée. Return the soup to the clean pan, season with salt and white pepper and keep hot over a low heat while you prepare the garnish.

5 Heat the remaining butter in a frying pan, add the almonds and toss over a medium heat until golden brown. Add the diced corals and cook for about 30 seconds. Stir the cream into the soup and add the remaining diced white scallop meat.

6 Ladle the soup into warm individual bowls and garnish each serving with the almonds, scallop corals and a sprinkling of chervil.

Saffron Fish Soup

Filling, yet not too rich, this golden soup will make a delicious start to a meal, served with lots of hot fresh bread and a glass of fruity, dry white wine. When mussels are not available use prawns in their shells instead.

INGREDIENTS

Serves 4

1 parsnip, quartered

2 carrots, quartered

1 onion, quartered

2 celery sticks, quartered

2 smoked bacon rashers (strips)

juice of 1 lemon

pinch of saffron threads

450g/1lb fish heads

450g/1lb fresh mussels, scrubbed

1 leek, shredded

2 shallots, finely chopped

30ml/2 tbsp chopped fresh dill, plus extra sprigs to garnish

450g/1lb haddock fillet, skinned

3 egg yolks

30ml/2 tbsp double (heavy) cream

salt and ground black pepper

1 Put the parsnip, carrots, onion, celery, bacon, lemon juice, saffron threads and fish heads in a large, heavy pan with 900ml/1½ pints/3¾ cups water and bring to the boil. Simmer gently for about 20 minutes, or until reduced by half.

2 Discard any mussels that are open and don't close when tapped sharply. Add the mussels to the pan of stock. Cover and cook for about 4 minutes, until they have opened. Strain the soup and return the liquid to the pan. Discard any unopened mussels, then remove the remaining ones from their shells and set aside.

3 Add the leeks and shallots to the soup, bring to the boil, then lower the heat and simmer gently for 5 minutes. Add the dill and haddock, and simmer for a further 5 minutes, until the fish is tender. Remove the haddock, using a slotted spoon, then flake it into a bowl, using a fork.

4 In another bowl, whisk together the eggs and double cream. Whisk in a little of the hot soup, then whisk the mixture back into the hot, but not boiling liquid. Continue to whisk for several minutes, but do not boil.

5 Add the flaked haddock and mussels to the soup and check the seasoning. Garnish with tiny sprigs of dill and serve piping hot.

Corn and Scallop Chowder

Fresh corn is ideal for this chowder, although canned or frozen corn also works well.

INGREDIENTS

Serves 4–6

2 corn cobs or 200g/7 oz/generous
  1 cup frozen or canned corn kernels
600ml/1 pint/2½ cups milk
15g/½oz/1 tbsp butter or margarine
1 small leek or onion, chopped
40g/1½oz/¼ cup smoked streaky (fatty)
  bacon, finely chopped
1 small garlic clove, crushed
1 small green (bell) pepper, seeded
  and diced
1 celery stick, chopped
1 potato, diced
15ml/1 tbsp plain (all-
  purpose) flour
300ml/½ pint/1¼ cups Chicken or
  Vegetable stock
4 scallops
115g/4 oz cooked fresh mussels
pinch of paprika
150ml/¼ pint/⅔ cup single (light)
  cream (optional)
salt and ground black pepper

1 If using fresh corn cobs, slice down them with a sharp knife to remove the kernels. If using canned corn kernels, drain well. Place half the kernels in a food processor or blender and process with a little of the milk. Set the other half aside.

2 Melt the butter or margarine in a large pan and cook the leek or onion, bacon and garlic over a low heat, stirring frequently, for 4–5 minutes, until the leek is soft, but not browned.

3 Add the green pepper, celery and potato and sweat over a gentle heat for 3–4 minutes more, stirring frequently.

4 Stir in the flour and cook for about 1–2 minutes, until golden and frothy. Stir in a little milk and the corn mixture, stock, the remaining milk and corn kernels and seasoning.

5 Bring to the boil, and then simmer, partially covered, for 15–20 minutes, until the vegetables are tender.

6 Pull the corals away from the scallops and slice the white flesh into 5mm/¼in slices. Stir the scallops into the soup, cook for 4 minutes and then stir in the corals, mussels and paprika. Heat through for a few minutes and then stir in the cream, if using. Check the seasoning and serve.

Creamy Fish Chowder

A traditional soup that never fails to please, whether it is made with milk or more luxuriously, with a generous quantity of cream.

INGREDIENTS

Serves 4

3 thick-cut bacon rashers (strips)
1 large onion
675g/1½lb potatoes
1 litre/1¾ pints/4 cups Fish Stock
450g/1lb skinless haddock, cut into
    2.5cm/1in cubes
30ml/2 tbsp chopped fresh parsley
15ml/1 tbsp chopped fresh chives
300ml/½ pint/1¼ cups whipping cream
    or milk
salt and ground black pepper

1 Remove the rind from the bacon and discard it; cut the bacon into small pieces. Chop the onion and cut the potatoes into 2cm/¾in cubes.

2 Fry the bacon in a deep pan until the fat is rendered. Add the onion and potatoes and cook over a low heat, without browning, for about 10 minutes. Season to taste with salt and pepper.

5 Stir the cream or milk into the chowder and reheat gently, but do not bring to the boil. Taste and adjust the seasoning if necessary and serve immediately.

3 Pour off the excess bacon fat from the pan. Add the fish stock to the pan and bring to a boil. Lower the heat and simmer for about 15–20 minutes, until the vegetables are tender.

4 Gently stir in the cubes of haddock, the parsley and chives. Simmer for 3–4 minutes, until the fish is just cooked.

VARIATION

Cod fillets would be equally good in this chowder, or try smoked fillets for a stronger taste.

Corn and Crab Bisque

This is a Louisiana classic, which is certainly luxurious enough for a dinner party and is therefore well worth the extra time required to prepare the fresh crab. The crab shells, together with the corn cobs, from which the kernels are stripped, make a fine-flavoured stock.

INGREDIENTS

Serves 8

4 large corn cobs

2 bay leaves

1 cooked crab (about 1kg/2¼lb)

25g/1oz/2 tbsp butter

30ml/2 tbsp plain (all-purpose) flour

300ml/½ pint/1¼ cups whipping cream

6 spring onions (scallions), shredded

pinch of cayenne pepper

salt and ground black and white pepper

hot French bread or grissini breadsticks,
  to serve

1 Pull away the husks and silk from the cobs of corn and strip off the kernels.

2 Keep the kernels on one side and put the stripped cobs into a deep pan or flameproof casserole with 3 litres/5 pints/12½ cups water, the bay leaves and 10ml/ 2 tsp salt. Bring to the boil, then lower the heat and simmer while you prepare the crab.

3 Pull away the two flaps between the big claws of the crab, stand it on its "nose", where the flaps were, and bang down firmly with the heel of your hand on the rounded end.

4 Separate the crab from its top shell, keeping the shell.

5 Push out the crab's mouth and its abdominal sac immediately below the mouth, and discard.

6 Pull away the feathery gills surrounding the central chamber and discard. Scrape out all the semi-liquid brown meat from the shell and set aside.

7 Crack the claws in as many places as necessary to extract all the white meat. Pick out the white meat from the fragile cavities in the central body of the crab. Set aside all the crab meat, brown and white. Put the spidery legs, back shell and all the other pieces of shell into the pan with the corn cobs. Simmer for a further 15 minutes, then strain the stock into a clean pan and boil hard to reduce to 2 litres/3½ pints/9 cups.

8 Meanwhile, melt the butter in a small pan and sprinkle in the flour. Stir constantly over a low heat until the roux is the colour of rich cream.

9 Remove the pan from the heat and gradually stir in 250ml/ 8fl oz/1 cup of the stock. Return to the heat and stir until it thickens, then stir this thickened mixture into the pan of strained stock.

10 Add the corn kernels, return to the boil and simmer for 5 minutes.

11 Add the crab meat, cream and spring onions and season with cayenne, salt and pepper (preferably a mixture of black and white). Return to the boil and simmer for a further 2 minutes. Serve with hot French bread or grissini breadsticks.

Clam Chowder

If fresh clams are hard to find, use frozen or canned clams for this classic recipe from New England. Large clams should be cut into chunky pieces.

INGREDIENTS

Serves 4

100g/3¾ oz salt pork or thinly sliced unsmoked bacon, diced

1 large onion, chopped

2 potatoes, peeled and cut into 1cm/½ in cubes

1 bay leaf

1 fresh thyme sprig

300ml/½ pint/1¼ cups milk

400g/14oz cooked clams, cooking liquid reserved

150ml/¼ pint/⅔ cup double (heavy) cream

salt, ground white pepper and cayenne pepper

finely chopped fresh parsley, to garnish

1 Put the salt pork or unsmoked bacon in a heavy pan, and heat gently, stirring frequently, until the fat runs and the meat is starting to brown. Add the chopped onion and cook over a low heat until softened but not browned.

2 Add the cubed potatoes, bay leaf and thyme sprig, stir well to coat with fat, then pour in the milk and reserved clam cooking liquid and bring to the boil. Lower the heat and simmer gently for about 10 minutes, until the potatoes are tender but still firm. Lift out the bay leaf and thyme sprig and discard.

3 Remove most of the clams from their shells. Add all the clams to the pan and season to taste with salt, white pepper and cayenne. Simmer over a low heat for 5 minutes more, then stir in the double (heavy) cream. Heat until the soup is very hot, but do not let it boil. Pour into a warm tureen, garnish with the chopped parsley and serve.

Clam, Mushroom and Potato Chowder

The delicate, sweet shellfish taste of clams and the soft earthiness of wild mushrooms combine with potatoes to make this a memorable dish – fit for any occasion.

INGREDIENTS

Serves 4

48 clams, scrubbed

50g/2oz/4 tbsp unsalted (sweet) butter

1 large onion, chopped

1 celery stick, sliced

1 carrot, sliced

225g/8oz assorted wild mushrooms, such as chanterelles, saffron milk-caps, chicken of the woods or St George's mushrooms, sliced

225g/8oz floury potatoes, thickly sliced

1.2 litres/2 pints/5 cups Chicken or Vegetable Stock, boiling

1 fresh thyme sprig

4 fresh parsley stalks

salt and ground black pepper

fresh thyme sprigs, to garnish

1 Place the clams in a large pan, discarding any that are open. Put 1cm/½in of water in the pan, cover tightly, bring to the boil and steam over a medium heat for 6–8 minutes until the clams open. Remove and discard any clams that do not open.

2 Drain the clams over a bowl, remove the shells from each one and chop. Strain the cooking juices into the bowl, add the chopped clams and set aside.

3 Add the butter, onion, celery and carrot to the pan and cook gently for 5 minutes, until softened but not coloured. Add the mushrooms and cook for 3–4 minutes. Add the potatoes, the clams and their juices, the stock, thyme and parsley stalks.

4 Bring to the boil, then reduce the heat, cover and simmer for 25 minutes. Season to taste with salt and pepper, ladle into soup bowls and garnish with thyme.

Smoked Cod and Okra Soup

*The inspiration for this soup came
from a Ghanaian recipe for okra
soup. Here it is enhanced by the
addition of smoked fish.*

INGREDIENTS

Serves 4

2 green bananas

50g/2oz/¼ cup butter or margarine

1 onion, finely chopped

2 tomatoes, peeled and finely chopped

115g/4oz okra, trimmed

225g/8oz smoked cod fillet, cut into
    bitesize pieces

900ml/1½ pints/3¾ cups Fish Stock

1 fresh chilli, seeded and chopped

salt and ground black pepper

fresh parsley sprigs, to garnish

3 Add the cod, fish stock, chilli
and seasoning. Bring to the
boil, then reduce the heat and
simmer for about 20 minutes, or
until the cod is cooked through
and flakes easily.

4 Peel the cooked bananas and
cut into slices. Stir into the
soup, heat through for a few
minutes and ladle into warm soup
bowls. Garnish with parsley and
serve immediately.

1 Slit the skins of the green
bananas and place in a large
pan. Cover with water, bring to the
boil and cook over a moderate heat
for 25 minutes, until the bananas
are tender. Transfer to a plate and
leave to cool.

2 Melt the butter or margarine
in a large pan and cook the
onion for about 5 minutes, until
soft. Stir in the chopped tomatoes
and okra and cook gently for a
further 10 minutes.

Fish and Sweet Potato Soup

The subtle sweetness of the potato, combined with the fish and the aromatic flavour of oregano, makes this an appetizing soup.

INGREDIENTS

Serves 4

¹/₂ onion, chopped

175g/6oz sweet potato, peeled and diced

175g/6oz white fish fillet, skinned

50g/2oz carrot, chopped

5ml/1 tsp chopped fresh oregano or
    2.5ml/¹/₂ tsp dried oregano

2.5ml/¹/₂ tsp ground cinnamon

1.5 litres/2¹/₂ pints/6¹/₄ cups Fish Stock

75ml/5 tbsp single (light) cream

chopped fresh parsley, to garnish

1 Put the chopped onion, diced sweet potato, white fish, chopped carrot, oregano, cinnamon and half of the fish stock in a pan. Bring to the boil, then lower the heat and simmer for 20 minutes, or until the potato is cooked.

2 Leave to cool, then pour into a blender or food processor and process until smooth.

3 Return the soup to the pan, then add the remaining fish stock and gradually bring to the boil. Reduce the heat to low and add the single cream, then gently heat through, without boiling, stirring occasionally.

4 Serve hot in warmed soup bowls, garnished with the chopped fresh parsley.

VARIATION
Garnish with chopped fresh tarragon instead of parsley.

Prawn Creole

Raw prawns are combined with chopped fresh vegetables and cayenne pepper to make this tasty soup.

INGREDIENTS

Serves 4

675g/1½lb raw prawns (shrimp) in the shell, with heads, if available

475ml/16fl oz/2 cups water

45ml/3 tbsp olive or vegetable oil

175g/6oz/1½ cups very finely chopped onions

75g/3oz/½ cup very finely chopped celery

75g/3oz/½ cup very finely chopped green (bell) pepper

25g/1oz/½ cup chopped fresh parsley

1 garlic clove, crushed

15ml/1 tbsp Worcestershire sauce

1.5ml/¼ tsp cayenne pepper

120ml/4fl oz/½ cup dry white wine

50g/2oz/1 cup chopped peeled plum tomatoes

5ml/1 tsp salt

1 bay leaf

5ml/1 tsp sugar

fresh parsley, to garnish

boiled rice, to serve

1 Peel and devein the prawns, reserving the heads and shells. Keep the prawns in a covered bowl in the refrigerator while you make the soup.

2 Put the prawn heads and shells in a pan with the water. Bring to the boil and simmer for 15 minutes. Strain, then measure 350ml/12fl oz/1½ cups of the stock and reserve.

3 Heat the oil in a heavy pan. Add the onions and cook over a low heat for 8–10 minutes, until softened. Add the celery and green pepper and cook for 5 minutes more. Stir in the parsley, garlic, Worcestershire sauce and cayenne. Cook for a further 5 minutes.

4 Raise the heat to medium. Stir in the wine and simmer for 3–4 minutes. Add the tomatoes, reserved prawn stock, salt, bay leaf and sugar and bring to the boil. Stir well, then reduce the heat to low and simmer for about 30 minutes, until the tomatoes have fallen apart and the sauce has reduced slightly. Remove from the heat and cool slightly.

5 Discard the bay leaf. Pour the sauce into a food processor or blender and process until quite smooth. Taste and adjust the seasoning as necessary.

6 Return the tomato soup to the pan and bring to the boil. Add the prawns and simmer for 4–5 minutes, until they turn pink. Ladle into warm individual soup bowls, garnish with fresh parsley and serve with rice.

Fish Ball Soup

The Japanese name for this soup is Tsumire-jiru. Tsumire, *means, quite literally, sardine balls, and these are added to this delicious soup to impart their robust flavour.*

Serves 4

100ml/3½fl oz/generous ⅓ cup sake or
 dry white wine
1.2 litres/2 pints/5 cups instant dashi
60ml/4 tbsp white miso paste

For the fish balls

20g/¾oz fresh root ginger
800g/1¾lb fresh sardines, gutted and
 heads removed
30ml/2 tbsp white miso paste
15ml/1 tbsp sake or dry white wine
7.5ml/1½ tsp sugar
1 egg
30ml/2 tbsp cornflour (cornstarch)
150g/5 oz shimeji mushrooms or
 6 shiitake mushrooms
1 leek or large spring onion (scallion)

1 First make the fish balls. To do this, grate the ginger and squeeze it well to yield 5ml/1 tsp ginger juice.

2 Rinse the sardines under cold running water, then cut them in half along the backbones. Remove and discard all the bones. To skin a boned sardine, lay it skin side down on a board, then run a sharp knife slowly along the skin from tail to head.

3 Coarsely chop the sardines and process with the ginger juice, miso, sake or wine, sugar and egg to a thick paste in a food processor or blender. Transfer to a bowl and mix in the cornflour until thoroughly blended.

4 Trim the shimeji mushrooms and either separate each stem or remove the stems from the shiitake mushrooms and shred them. Cut the leek or spring onion into 4cm/1½in strips.

5 Bring the ingredients for the soup to the boil. Use 2 wet spoons to shape small portions of the sardine mixture into bitesize balls and drop them into the soup. Add the prepared mushrooms and leek or spring onion.

6 Gently simmer the soup until the sardine balls float to the surface. Serve immediately, in individual, deep soup bowls.

Clear Soup with Seafood Sticks

This delicate, Japanese soup, called O-sumashi, which is often eaten with sushi, is very quick to make if you prepare the Japanese stock beforehand or if you use freeze-dried dashi-no-moto – instant dashi.

INGREDIENTS

Serves 4

4 fresh mitsuba sprigs or
   4 fresh chives and a few fresh
   sprigs of mustard and cress
4 seafood sticks
400ml/14fl oz/1⅔ cups Stock for
   Japanese Soups or the same
   amount of water and 5ml/1 tsp
   instant dashi
15ml/1 tbsp shoyu
7.5ml/1½ tsp salt
grated rind of yuzu or lime (optional),
   to garnish

1 Mitsuba leaves are normally sold with the stems and roots on to retain freshness. Cut off the root, then cut 5cm/2in from the top, retaining both the long straw-like stem and the leaf.

2 Blanch the stems by pouring over hot water. If you use chives, choose them at least 10cm/4in in length and blanch, too.

3 Take a seafood stick and carefully tie a mitsuba stem or chive around the middle, holding it in place with a knot. Do not pull too tightly, as the bow will easily break. Repeat the process to make four tied seafood sticks.

4 With your finger, carefully loosen both ends of each seafood stick to make it look like a tassel.

5 Place one seafood stick in each soup bowl, then put the four mitsuba leaves or mustard and cress on top.

6 Heat the stock in a pan and bring to the boil. Add the shoyu and season with salt to taste. Pour the stock gently over the mitsuba and seafood stick. Sprinkle with grated yuzu or lime rind, if using. Serve immediately.

VARIATION

You can use small prawns (shrimp) instead of seafood sticks. Blanch 12 raw prawns in boiling water until they curl up and form a full circle. Drain. Tie mitsuba stems to make four bows. Arrange three prawns, side by side, in each bowl and put the mitsuba bows and leaves on top.

New Year's Soup

Japan's elaborate New Year's Day celebration brunch starts with a tiny glass of spiced warm sake, o-toso. Then, this New Year's soup, o-zoni, and other festive dishes are served.

INGREDIENTS

Serves 4

4 dried shiitake mushrooms

300g/11oz chicken thighs, bones removed and reserved

300g/11oz salmon fillet, skin on, scaled

30ml/2 tbsp sake

50g/2oz satoimo or Jerusalem artichokes

50g/2oz mooli (daikon), peeled

50g/2oz carrots, peeled

4 spring onions (scallions), white part only, trimmed and chopped into 2.5cm/1in lengths

4 fresh mitsuba sprigs, root part removed

1 yuzu or lime

4 large raw tiger prawns (shrimp), peeled, but with tails left on

30ml/2 tbsp shoyu

8 mochi slices

salt

1 First, make the soup stock. Soak the dried shiitake overnight in 1 litre/1¾ pints/ 4 cups cold water. Remove the softened shiitake and pour the water into a pan. Bring to the boil, add the chicken bones, then reduce the heat to medium. Skim frequently to remove any scum. After about 20 minutes, reduce the heat to low. Simmer for 30 minutes, or until the liquid has reduced by a third. Strain the stock into another pan.

2 Chop the chicken thighs and salmon fillet into small, bitesize cubes. Par-boil them both in boiling water with 15ml/1 tbsp sake for 1 minute. Drain and wash off the scum under cold water.

3 Scrub the satoimo or artichokes with a hard brush, and thickly peel. Put in a pan and add enough water to cover. Add a pinch of salt and bring to the boil. Reduce the heat to medium, cook for 15 minutes and drain. Rinse the satoimo or artichokes under running water. Cut the satoimo or artichokes, mooli and carrots into 1cm/½in cubes.

4 Remove and discard the stalks from the soaked shiitake, and slice the caps thinly.

5 Put the mitsuba sprigs into a sieve and pour hot water over them. Divide the leaf and stalk parts. Take a stalk and fold it into two, then tie it in the middle to make a bow. Make four bows.

6 Cut the yuzu or lime into four 3mm/⅛in thick round slices. Hollow out the inside to make rings of peel.

7 Add the remaining sake to the soup stock and boil. Add the mooli, carrot and shiitake, reduce the heat and cook for 15 minutes. Put the prawns, satoimo or artichokes, spring onions, chicken and salmon into the pan. Cook for 5 minutes, then add the shoyu. Reduce the heat to low.

8 Cut the mochi in half crossways. Toast under a medium preheated grill (broiler). Turn every minute until both sides are golden and the pieces have started to swell; this will take about 5 minutes. Place the toasted mochi in individual soup bowls and pour the hot soup over the top. Arrange a mitsuba leaf in the centre of each bowl, put a yuzu or lime ring on top, and lay a mitsuba bow across.

Prawn and Egg-knot Soup

Omelettes and pancakes are often used to add protein to light Asian soups. In this recipe, thin omelettes are twisted into little knots.

INGREDIENTS

Serves 4

1 spring onion (scallion), thinly shredded
800ml/1⅓ pints/3½ cups Stock for
　Japanese Soups or instant dashi
5ml/1 tsp soy sauce
dash of sake or dry white wine
pinch of salt

For the prawn (shrimp) balls
200g/7oz/generous 1 cup raw large
　prawns (shrimp), peeled
65g/2½oz cod fillet, skinned
5ml/1 tsp egg white
5ml/1 tsp sake or dry white wine
22.5ml/4½ tsp cornflour (cornstarch)
2–3 drops soy sauce
pinch of salt

For the omelette
1 egg, beaten
dash of mirin
pinch of salt
oil, for cooking

1 To make the prawn balls, use a pin to remove the black vein running down the back of each prawn. Place the prawns, cod, egg white, sake or dry white wine, cornflour, soy sauce and a pinch of salt in a food processor or blender and process to a thick, sticky paste. Shape the mixture into 4 balls, place in a steaming basket and steam over a pan of vigorously boiling water for about 10 minutes.

2 To make the garnish, soak the spring onion in a small bowl of iced water for about 5 minutes, until the shreds have curled, then drain well.

3 To make the omelette, mix the egg with the mirin and salt. Heat a little oil in a frying pan and pour in the egg mixture, coating the pan evenly. When the omelette has set, turn it over and cook for 30 seconds. Leave to cool.

4 Cut the omelette into strips and tie each in a knot. Heat the stock or dashi, then add the soy sauce, sake or wine and salt. Divide the prawn balls and egg-knots among four bowls and add the soup. Garnish with the spring onion curls and serve.

Coconut and Seafood Soup with Garlic Chives

The long list of ingredients in this Thai-inspired recipe could mislead you into thinking that this soup is complicated. In fact, it is very easy to put together.

INGREDIENTS

Serves 4

600ml/1 pint/2½ cups Fish Stock

5 thin slices fresh galangal or fresh
    root ginger

2 lemon grass stalks, chopped

3 kaffir lime leaves, shredded

25g/1oz garlic chives (1 bunch)

15g/½oz fresh coriander (cilantro), stalks
    and leaves separated

15ml/1 tbsp vegetable oil

4 shallots, chopped

400ml/14fl oz can coconut milk

30–45ml/2–3 tbsp Thai fish sauce

45–60ml/3–4 tbsp Thai green curry paste

450g/1lb raw large prawns (shrimp),
    peeled and deveined

450g/1lb prepared squid

a little lime juice (optional)

salt and ground black pepper

60ml/4 tbsp crisp fried shallot slices,
    to serve

1 Pour the fish stock into a pan and add the slices of galangal or ginger, the lemon grass and half the shredded kaffir lime leaves.

2 Reserve a few garlic chives for the garnish, then chop the remainder. Add half the chopped garlic chives to the pan with the coriander stalks. Bring to the boil, reduce the heat and cover the pan, then simmer gently for 20 minutes. Strain the stock.

3 Rinse the pan. Add the oil and shallots. Cook over a medium heat for 5–10 minutes, until the shallots are softened and just beginning to brown.

4 Stir in the strained stock, coconut milk, the remaining kaffir lime leaves and 30ml/2 tbsp of the fish sauce. Heat gently until simmering and cook over a low heat for 5–10 minutes.

5 Stir in the green curry paste and prawns, then cook for 3 minutes. Add the squid and cook for a further 2 minutes. Add the lime juice, if using, and season, adding more fish sauce to taste.

6 Stir in the remaining chives and the coriander leaves. Serve immediately in warm bowls sprinkled with fried shallots and whole garlic chives.

Hot-and-Sour Prawn Soup

This is a classic Thai seafood soup – Tom Yam Kung – and it is probably the most popular and best-known soup from that country.

INGREDIENTS

Serves 4–6

450g/1lb raw king prawns (jumbo shrimp), thawed if frozen

1 litre/1¾ pints/4 cups Chicken Stock or water

3 lemon grass stalks, root trimmed

10 kaffir lime leaves, torn in half

225g/8oz can straw mushrooms

45ml/3 tbsp Thai fish sauce

60ml/4 tbsp lime juice

30ml/2 tbsp chopped spring onion (scallion)

15ml/1 tbsp fresh coriander (cilantro) leaves

4 fresh red chillies, seeded and thinly sliced

salt and ground black pepper

1 Peel the prawns, putting the shells in a colander. Devein the prawns and set them aside.

2 Rinse the shells under cold water, then put them in a large pan with the stock or water. Bring to the boil.

3 Bruise the lemon grass stalks and add them to the stock with half the lime leaves. Simmer gently for 5–6 minutes, until the stock is fragrant.

4 Strain the stock, return it to the clean pan and reheat. Add the drained mushrooms and the prawns, then cook briefly, until the prawns turn pink.

5 Stir in the fish sauce, lime juice, spring onion, coriander, chillies and the remaining lime leaves. Taste and adjust the seasoning, if necessary. The soup should be sour, salty, spicy and hot. Ladle into warm soup bowls and serve immediately.

Malayan Prawn Laksa

This spicy prawn and noodle soup tastes just as good when made with fresh crab meat or any flaked cooked fish. If you are short of time or can't find all the spice paste ingredients, buy ready-made laksa paste, which is available from Asian stores.

INGREDIENTS

Serves 3–4

115g/4oz rice vermicelli or stir-fry
    rice noodles
15ml/1 tbsp vegetable oil
600ml/1 pint/2½ cups Fish Stock
400ml/14fl oz/1⅔ cups thin coconut milk
30ml/2 tbsp Thai fish sauce
½ lime
16–24 cooked peeled prawns (shrimp)
salt and cayenne pepper
60ml/4 tbsp fresh coriander (cilantro)
    sprigs and leaves, chopped, to garnish

For the spice paste
2 lemon grass stalks, finely chopped
2 fresh red chillies, seeded and chopped
2.5cm/1in piece fresh root
    ginger, sliced
2.5ml/½ tsp shrimp paste
2 garlic cloves, chopped
2.5ml/½ tsp ground turmeric
30ml/2 tbsp tamarind paste

1 Cook the rice vermicelli or noodles in a large pan of salted, boiling water according to the instructions on the packet. Tip into a large sieve or colander, then rinse under cold water and drain. Set aside on a warm plate.

2 To make the spice paste, place all the ingredients in a mortar and pound with a pestle. Or, if you prefer, put the ingredients in a food processor or blender and then process until a smooth paste is formed.

3 Heat the oil in a large pan, add the spice paste and fry, stirring constantly, for a few moments to release all the flavours, but be careful not to let it burn.

4 Add the fish stock and coconut milk and bring to the boil. Stir in the fish sauce, then simmer for 5 minutes. Season with salt and cayenne to taste, adding a squeeze of lime. Add the prawns and heat through for a few seconds.

5 Divide the noodles among three or four soup plates. Pour the soup over, making sure that each portion includes an equal number of prawns. Garnish with coriander and serve piping hot.

Thai Fish Soup

Thai fish sauce, or nam pla, *is rich in B vitamins and is used extensively in Thai cooking. It is available at Thai or Indonesian stores and good supermarkets.*

INGREDIENTS

Serves 4

350g/12oz raw large prawns (shrimp)

15ml/1 tbsp groundnut (peanut) oil

1.2 litres/2 pints/5 cups Chicken or
    Fish Stock

1 lemon grass stalk, bruised and cut into
    2.5cm/1in lengths

2 kaffir lime leaves, torn into pieces

juice and finely grated rind of 1 lime

1/2 fresh green chilli, seeded and
    thinly sliced

4 scallops

24 fresh mussels, scrubbed and debearded

115g/4oz monkfish fillet, cut into
    2cm/3/4in chunks

10ml/2 tsp Thai fish sauce

For the garnish

1 kaffir lime leaf, shredded

1/2 fresh red chilli, thinly sliced

1 Peel the prawns, reserving the shells, and remove the black vein running along their backs.

2 Heat the oil in a pan and fry the prawn shells until pink. Add the stock, lemon grass, lime leaves, lime rind and green chilli. Bring to the boil, simmer for 20 minutes, then strain through a sieve, reserving the liquid.

3 Cut the scallops in half, leaving the corals attached.

4 Return the stock to a clean pan, add the prawns, mussels, monkfish and scallops and cook for 3 minutes. Remove from the heat and add the lime juice and fish sauce.

5 Serve immediately, garnished with the shredded lime leaf and thinly sliced red chilli.

Chinese Crab and Corn Soup

Thawed frozen white crab meat works as well as fresh in this delicately flavoured soup.

INGREDIENTS

Serves 4

600ml/1 pint/2½ cups Fish or
    Chicken Stock
2.5cm/1in piece of fresh root ginger, very
    finely sliced
400g/14oz can creamed corn
150g/5oz cooked white crab meat
15ml/1 tbsp arrowroot or
    cornflour (cornstarch)
15ml/1 tbsp rice wine or dry sherry
15–30ml/1–2 tbsp light soy sauce
1 egg white
salt and ground white pepper
shredded spring onions (scallions),
    to garnish

1 Put the stock and ginger in a large pan and bring to the boil. Stir in the creamed corn and bring back to the boil.

2 Switch off the heat and add the crab meat. Put the arrowroot or cornflour in a cup and stir in the rice wine or sherry to make a smooth paste. Stir the paste into the soup. Cook over a low heat for about 3 minutes, until the soup has thickened and is slightly glutinous in consistency. Add light soy sauce, salt and white pepper to taste.

3 In a bowl, whisk the egg white to a stiff foam. Gradually fold it into the soup. Ladle the soup into warm bowls, garnish each portion with spring onions and serve immediately.

COOK'S TIP

Creamed corn gives a better
texture than whole kernel corn.
If you can't find it in
a can, use thawed frozen
creamed corn instead.

Spinach and Tofu Soup

This is an extremely delicate and mild-flavoured soup, which can be used to counterbalance the heat from a hot Thai curry to follow.

INGREDIENTS

Serves 4–6

30ml/2 tbsp dried shrimp

1 litre/1¾ pints/4 cups Chicken Stock

225g/8oz fresh tofu, drained and cut into
   2cm/¾in cubes

30ml/2 tbsp Thai fish sauce

350g/12oz fresh spinach

ground black pepper

2 spring onions (scallions), thinly sliced,
   to garnish

1 Rinse and drain the dried shrimp. Combine the shrimp with the chicken stock in a large pan and bring to the boil. Add the tofu and simmer for about 5 minutes. Season with fish sauce and black pepper to taste.

2 Wash the spinach leaves and tear into bitesize pieces. Add to the soup and cook for another 1–2 minutes.

3 Pour the soup into warmed bowls, sprinkle the chopped spring onions on top and serve.

Pumpkin and Coconut Soup

Rich and sweet flavours are married beautifully with sharp and hot in this creamy South-east Asian-influenced soup.

INGREDIENTS

Serves 4–6

2 garlic cloves, crushed

4 shallots, finely crushed

2.5ml/½ tsp shrimp paste

15ml/1 tbsp dried shrimp, soaked
   for 10 minutes and drained

1 lemon grass stalk, chopped

2 fresh green chillies, seeded

600ml/1 pint/2½ cups Chicken Stock

450g/1lb pumpkin, cut into thick chunks

600ml/1 pint/2½ cups coconut cream

30ml/2 tbsp Thai fish sauce

5ml/1 tsp sugar

115g/4oz cooked peeled prawns (shrimp)

salt and ground black pepper

For the garnish

2 fresh red chillies, seeded and
   thinly sliced

10–12 fresh basil leaves

1 Using a mortar and pestle, grind the garlic, shallots, shrimp paste, dried shrimp, lemon grass, green chillies and a pinch of salt into a paste.

2 Bring the chicken stock to the boil in a large, add the paste and stir until dissolved.

3 Lower the heat, add the chunks of pumpkin, and simmer for about 10–15 minutes, or until the pumpkin is tender.

4 Stir in the coconut cream, then bring back to a simmer. Add the fish sauce, sugar and ground black pepper to taste.

5 Add the prawns and cook until they are heated through. Serve garnished with the sliced red chillies and basil leaves.

COOK'S TIP

Shrimp paste, which is made from ground shrimp fermented in brine, is used to give food a savoury flavour.

MEAT AND POULTRY SOUPS

European and American soups made with beef, lamb,
pork, chicken or duck are often robust, substantial and
warming – just perfect for taking the edge off a hearty appetite
on a cold winter's day. However, Chinese and Asian
soups are usually more delicate and lighter, although no less
flavoursome. This delicious collection of recipes offers the
best of both worlds and even includes an East-meets-West
duck soup based on a French-Vietnamese tradition.

Chicken, Leek and Celery Soup

This is a substantial soup that is ideal for serving before a light, hot or cold main course. Served with plenty of crusty bread, it would make a meal-in-a-bowl lunch.

INGREDIENTS

Serves 4–6

1.4kg/3lb chicken

1 small head of celery, trimmed

1 onion, coarsely chopped

1 fresh bay leaf

a few fresh parsley stalks

a few fresh tarragon sprigs

2.4 litres/4 pints/10 cups cold water

3 large leeks

65g/2½oz/5 tbsp butter

2 potatoes, cut into chunks

150ml/¼ pint/⅔ cup dry white wine

30–45ml/2–3 tbsp single (light) cream

salt and ground black pepper

90g/3½oz pancetta, grilled (broiled) until crisp, to garnish

1 Cut the breasts off the chicken and set aside. Chop the remainder of the chicken carcass into 8–10 pieces and place in a large pan.

2 Chop 4–5 of the outer sticks of the celery and add them to the pan with the onion. Tie the bay leaf, parsley and tarragon together and add to the pan. Pour in the cold water to cover the ingredients and bring to the boil. Reduce the heat and cover the pan, then simmer for 1½ hours.

3 Remove the chicken and cut off and reserve the meat. Strain the stock, then return it to the pan and boil rapidly until it has reduced to about 1.5 litres/ 2½ pints/6¼ cups.

4 Meanwhile, set about 150g/5oz of the leeks aside. Slice the remaining leeks and the remaining celery, reserving any celery leaves. Chop the celery leaves and set aside to garnish the soup.

5 Melt half the butter in a large, heavy pan. Add the sliced leeks and celery, cover and cook over a low heat for about 10 minutes, or until softened but not browned. Add the potatoes, wine and 1.2 litres/2 pints/5 cups of the chicken stock.

6 Season well with salt and pepper, bring to the boil and reduce the heat. Part-cover the pan and simmer the soup for about 15–20 minutes, or until the potatoes are cooked.

7 Meanwhile, skin the reserved chicken breasts and cut the flesh into small pieces. Melt the remaining butter in a frying pan, add the chicken and cook for 5–7 minutes, until tender.

8 Thickly slice the remaining leeks, add to the pan and cook, stirring occasionally, for a further 3–4 minutes, until just cooked.

9 Process the soup with the cooked chicken from the stock in a blender or food processor. Taste and adjust the seasoning, if necessary, and add more stock if the soup is very thick.

10 Stir in the cream and the chicken and leek mixture. Reheat the soup gently. Serve in warmed bowls. Crumble the pancetta over the soup and sprinkle with the chopped celery leaves to garnish.

Split Pea and Ham Soup

The main ingredient for this dish is bacon hock, which is the narrow piece of bone cut from a leg of ham. You could use a piece of pork belly instead, if you prefer, and remove it with the herbs before serving.

INGREDIENTS

Serves 4

450g/1lb/2½ cups green split peas

4 rindless bacon rashers (strips)

1 onion, coarsely chopped

2 carrots, sliced

1 celery stick, sliced

2.4 litres/4¼ pints/10½ cups water

1 fresh thyme sprig

2 bay leaves

1 large potato, coarsely diced

1 bacon hock

ground black pepper

1 Put the split peas into a bowl, cover with cold water and leave to soak overnight.

2 Cut the bacon rashers into small pieces. In a large pan, dry-fry the bacon for 4–5 minutes. or until crisp. Remove from the pan with a slotted spoon.

3 Add the chopped onion, carrots and celery to the fat in the pan and cook for 3–4 minutes, until the onion is softened but not brown. Return the diced bacon to the pan with the water.

4 Drain the split peas and add to the pan with the thyme, bay leaves, potato and bacon hock. Bring to the boil, reduce the heat, cover and cook gently for 1 hour.

5 Remove the thyme, bay leaves and hock. Process the soup in a blender or food processor until smooth. Return to a clean pan. Cut the meat from the hock and add to the soup and heat through gently. Season with plenty of ground black pepper. Ladle into warm soup bowls and serve immediately.

Chunky Chicken Soup

This thick chicken and vegetable soup is served with garlic-flavoured fried croûtons.

INGREDIENTS

Serves 4

4 skinless, boneless chicken thighs

15g/½oz/1 tbsp butter

2 small leeks, thinly sliced

30ml/2 tbsp long grain rice

900ml/ 1½ pints/3¾ cups Chicken Stock

15ml/1 tbsp chopped mixed fresh parsley
   and mint

salt and ground black pepper

For the garlic croûtons

30ml/2 tbsp olive oil

1 garlic clove, crushed

4 slices bread, cut into cubes

1 Cut the chicken into 1cm/ ½in cubes. Melt the butter in a pan, add the leeks and cook until tender. Add the rice and chicken and cook for 2 minutes.

2 Add the stock, then cover the pan and simmer gently for 15–20 minutes, until tender.

3 To make the garlic croûtons, heat the oil in a large frying pan. Add the crushed garlic clove and bread cubes and cook until the bread is golden brown, stirring constantly to prevent burning. Drain on kitchen paper and sprinkle with a pinch of salt.

4 Add the parsley and mint to the soup and adjust the seasoning to taste. Serve with the garlic croûtons.

Bulgarian Sour Lamb Soup

This traditional sour soup uses lamb, although pork and poultry are popular alternatives.

INGREDIENTS

Serves 4–5

30ml/2 tbsp oil

450g/11b lean lamb, trimmed and cubed

1 onion, diced

30ml/2 tbsp plain (all-purpose) flour

15ml/l tbsp paprika

1 litre/1¾ pints/4 cups hot Meat Stock

3 fresh parsley sprigs

4 spring onions (scallions)

4 fresh dill sprigs

39ml/2 tbsp long grain rice

2 eggs, beaten

30–45ml/2–3 tbsp or more vinegar or lemon juice

salt and ground black pepper

For the garnish

25g/1oz/2 tbsp butter, melted

5ml/1 tsp paprika

a little fresh parsley or lovage and dill

1 In a large pan heat the oil and cook the meat over a medium heat, stirring frequently, for about 8 minutes, until browned all over. Add the diced onion and cook, stirring frequently, for 5 minutes until it has softened. Sprinkle in the flour and paprika. Stir well, then gradually add the stock and cook for 10 minutes.

2 Tie the parsley, spring onions and dill together with kitchen string to make a bouquet garni, then add to the pan with the rice and season to taste with salt and pepper. Bring to the boil, then reduce the heat and simmer for about 30–40 minutes, or until the lamb is tender.

3 Remove the pan from the heat and stir in the eggs. Add the vinegar or lemon juice. Discard the bouquet garni and season to taste.

4 For the garnish, melt the butter in a pan and stir in the paprika. Ladle the soup into warm serving bowls. Garnish with parsley or dill and lovage and a little red paprika butter and serve immediately.

Chicken and Leek Soup with Prunes and Barley

This recipe is based on the famous traditional Scottish soup, Cock-a-leekie. The unconventional combination of leeks and prunes is surprisingly delicious.

INGREDIENTS

Serves 6

1 chicken, weighing about 2kg/4¼lb
900g/2lb leeks
1 fresh bouquet garni containing bay leaf, parsley and thyme
1 large carrot, thickly sliced
2.4 litres/4 pints/10 cups Chicken or Meat Stock
115g/4oz/generous ½ cup pearl barley
400g/14oz ready-to-eat prunes
salt and ground black pepper
chopped fresh parsley, to garnish

1 Cut the breasts off the chicken and set aside. Place the remaining chicken carcass in a large pan. Cut half the leeks into 5cm/2in lengths and add them to the pan. Add the bouquet garni to the pan with the carrot and the stock. Bring to the boil, then reduce the heat and cover. Simmer gently for 1 hour. Skim off any scum when the water first boils and skim occasionally again during simmering.

2 Add the chicken breasts and cook for a further 30 minutes, until they are just cooked. Leave until cool enough to handle, then strain the stock.

3 Reserve the chicken breasts and meat from the chicken carcass. Discard all the skin, bones, cooked vegetables and herbs. Skim as much fat as you can from the stock, then return it to the pan.

4 Meanwhile, rinse the pearl barley thoroughly in a sieve under cold running water, then cook it in a large pan of boiling water for about 10 minutes. Drain, rinse well and drain thoroughly.

5 Add the pearl barley to the stock. Bring to the boil, then lower the heat and simmer very gently for 15–20 minutes, until the barley is just cooked and tender. Season the soup with 5ml/1 tsp salt and black pepper to taste.

6 Add the prunes. Slice the remaining leeks and add them to the pan. Bring to the boil, then simmer for 10 minutes.

7 Slice the chicken breasts and add them to the soup with the remaining chicken meat, sliced or cut into neat pieces. Reheat, then ladle into soup bowls and serve with chopped parsley.

Chicken Minestrone

This is a special minestrone made with fresh chicken. Serve with crusty Italian bread.

INGREDIENTS

Serves 4–6

15ml/1 tbsp olive oil

2 chicken thighs

3 rindless streaky (fatty) bacon rashers (strips) , chopped

1 onion, finely chopped

few fresh basil leaves, shredded

few fresh rosemary leaves, finely chopped

15ml/1 tbsp chopped fresh flat leaf parsley

2 potatoes, cut into 1cm/½in cubes

1 large carrot, cut into 1cm/½in cubes

2 small courgettes (zucchini), cut into 1cm/½in cubes

1–2 celery sticks, cut into 1cm/½in cubes

1 litre/1¾ pints/4 cups Chicken Stock

200g/7oz/1¾ cups frozen peas

90g/3½oz/scant 1 cup stellette or other small soup pasta

salt and ground black pepper

Parmesan cheese shavings, to serve

1 Heat the oil in a large frying pan, add the chicken thighs and cook over a medium heat for about 5 minutes on each side. Remove with a slotted spoon and set aside.

2 Add the bacon, onion and herbs to the pan and cook gently, stirring constantly, for about 5 minutes. Add the potatoes, carrot, courgettes and celery and cook for 5–7 minutes more.

3 Return the chicken thighs to the pan, add the stock and bring to the boil. Cover and cook over a low heat for 35–40 minutes, stirring the soup occasionally.

4 Remove the chicken thighs with a slotted spoon and place them on a board. Stir the peas and pasta into the soup and bring back to the boil. Simmer, stirring frequently, for 7–8 minutes or according to the instructions on the packet, until the pasta is just *al dente*.

5 Meanwhile, remove and discard the chicken skin, then remove the meat from the chicken bones and cut it into small (1cm/½in) pieces.

6 Return the meat to the soup, stir well and heat through. Taste and adjust the seasoning as necessary.

7 Ladle the soup into warmed soup plates or bowls, top with Parmesan shavings and serve immediately, while piping hot.

Galician Broth

This delicious Spanish soup is very similar to the warming, chunky meat and potato broths of cooler climates. For extra colour, a few onion skins can be added when cooking the gammon, but remember to remove them before serving.

INGREDIENTS

Serves 4

450g/1lb piece gammon (cured ham)

2 bay leaves

2 onions, sliced

1.5 litres/2½ pints/6¼ cups water

10ml/2 tsp paprika

675g/1½ lb potatoes, cut into large chunks

225g/8oz spring greens (collards)

400g/14oz can haricot (navy) or cannellini beans, drained and rinsed

salt and ground black pepper

1 Soak the gammon overnight in cold water. Drain and put in a large pan with the bay leaves and onions. Pour the water on top.

2 Bring to the boil, then reduce the heat and simmer gently for about 1½ hours, until the meat is tender. Keep an eye on the pan to make sure it doesn't boil over.

COOK'S TIP

Bacon knuckles can be used instead of the gammon (cured ham). The bones will give the juices a delicious flavour.

3 Drain the meat, reserving the cooking liquid, and leave to cool slightly. Discard the skin and any excess fat from the meat and cut into small chunks. Return to the pan with the paprika and potatoes. Cover and simmer gently for 20 minutes.

4 Cut away the cores from the greens. Roll up the leaves and cut into thin shreds. Add to the pan with the beans and simmer for about 10 minutes. Season with salt and ground black pepper to taste. Ladle into warm soup bowls and serve piping hot.

Mediterranean Sausage and Pesto Soup

This hearty soup brings the summery flavour of basil to midwinter meals. Thick slices of warm crusty bread would make the perfect accompaniment.

INGREDIENTS

Serves 4

15ml/1 tbsp olive oil, plus extra
    for frying
1 red onion, chopped
450g/1lb smoked pork sausages
225g/8oz/1 cup red lentils
400g/14oz can chopped tomatoes
1 litre/1¾ pints/4 cups water
vegetable oil, for deep-frying
salt and ground black pepper
60ml/4 tbsp pesto and fresh basil sprigs,
    to garnish
warm, crusty bread, to serve

1 Heat the oil in a large pan and cook the onion until softened. Coarsely chop all but one of the sausages and add them to the pan. Cook, stirring, for 5 minutes.

2 Stir in the lentils, tomatoes and water, and bring to the boil. Reduce the heat, cover and simmer for about 20 minutes. Cool the soup slightly before processing it in a blender.

3 Cook the remaining sausage in a little oil in a small frying pan, turning frequently. Transfer to a chopping board or plate and leave to cool slightly, then slice thinly.

4 Heat the oil for deep-frying to 190°C/375°F or until a cube of day-old bread browns in about 60 seconds. Deep-fry the sausage slices and basil briefly until the sausages are brown and the basil leaves are crisp. Lift them out using a slotted spoon and drain well on kitchen paper.

5 Reheat the soup, season to taste with salt and pepper, then ladle into warmed individual soup bowls. Sprinkle with the deep-fried sausage slices and basil and swirl a little pesto through each portion. Serve with warm crusty bread.

Onion and Pancetta Soup

This warming winter soup comes from Umbria in Italy, where it is sometimes thickened with beaten eggs and plenty of grated Parmesan cheese. It is then served on top of hot toasted croûtes – rather like savoury scrambled eggs.

INGREDIENTS

Serves 4

115g/4oz pancetta rashers (strips), rinds
    removed, coarsely chopped
30ml/2 tbsp olive oil
15g/½oz/1 tbsp butter
675g/1½lb onions, thinly sliced
10ml/2 tsp granulated sugar
about 1.2 litres/2 pints/5 cups
    Chicken Stock
350g/12oz ripe Italian plum tomatoes,
    peeled and coarsely chopped
few fresh basil leaves, shredded
salt and ground black pepper
grated Parmesan cheese, to serve

1 Put the chopped pancetta in a large pan and heat gently, stirring constantly, until the fat runs. Increase the heat to medium, add the olive oil, butter, sliced onions and granulated sugar and stir well to mix.

2 Half-cover the pan and cook the onions gently for about 20 minutes, until golden. Stir frequently and lower the heat if necessary.

3 Add the stock and tomatoes, season to taste with salt and pepper and bring to the boil, stirring constantly. Lower the heat, half-cover the pan and simmer, stirring occasionally, for about 30 minutes.

4 Check the consistency of the soup and add a little more stock or water if it is too thick.

5 Just before serving, stir in most of the basil and taste adjust the seasoning if necessary. Serve immediately, garnished with the remaining shredded basil. Hand around the freshly grated Parmesan separately.

COOK'S TIP

Look for Vidalia onions to make this soup. They are available at large supermarkets, and have a sweet flavour and attractive, yellowish flesh.

Chicken, Tomato and Christophine Soup

Chicken breast portions and smoked haddock take on the flavours of herbs and spices to produce this tasty soup.

INGREDIENTS

Serves 4

225g/8oz skinless, boneless chicken breast portions, diced

1 garlic clove, crushed

pinch of freshly grated nutmeg

25g/1oz/2 tbsp butter or margarine

½ onion, finely chopped

15ml/1 tbsp tomato purée (paste)

400g/14 oz can tomatoes, puréed

1.2 litres/2 pints/5 cups Chicken Stock

1 fresh chilli, seeded and chopped

1 christophine, peeled and diced (about 350g/12oz)

5ml/1 tsp dried oregano

2.5ml/½ tsp dried thyme

50g/2oz smoked haddock fillet, skinned and diced

salt and ground black pepper

chopped fresh chives, to garnish

1 Dice the chicken, place in a bowl and season with salt, pepper, garlic and nutmeg. Mix well to flavour and then set aside for about 30 minutes.

2 Melt the butter or margarine in a large pan, add the chicken and sauté over a moderate heat for 5–6 minutes. Stir in the onion and cook gently, stirring frequently, for a further 5 minutes, or until the onion is slightly softened.

3 Add the tomato purée, puréed tomatoes, chicken stock, chilli, christophine, oregano and thyme. Bring to the boil, lower the heat, cover and simmer gently for about 35 minutes, or until the chicken and christophine are tender.

4 Add the smoked haddock and simmer for 5 minutes more, or until the fish is cooked through. Adjust the seasoning and pour into warmed soup bowls. Garnish with a sprinkling of chopped fresh chives and serve piping hot.

Lamb and Lentil Soup

Lamb and red lentils go together so well, they seem to have been made for one another.

Serves 4

about 1.5 litres/2½ pints/6¼ cups water

900g/2lb neck (US shoulder or breast) of lamb, cut into chops

½ onion, chopped

1 garlic clove, crushed

1 bay leaf

1 clove

2 fresh thyme sprigs

225g/8oz potatoes, cut into 2.5cm/ 1in pieces

175g/6oz/¾ cup red lentils

salt and ground black pepper

chopped fresh parsley

1 Put about 1.2 litres/2 pints/ 5 cups of the water and the meat in a large pan with the onion, garlic, bay leaf, clove and sprigs of thyme. Bring to the boil, lower the heat and simmer for about 1 hour, until the lamb is tender.

VARIATION

For a richer, fuller flavour, substitute Meat Stock, made with lamb bones, or Chicken Stock for all of some of the water.

2 Add the pieces of potato and the lentils to the pan and season the soup with a little salt and plenty of black pepper. Add the remaining water to come just above surface of the meat and vegetables; you may need to add more if the soup becomes too thick during cooking.

3 Cover and simmer for about 25 minutes, or until the lentils are cooked and well blended into the soup. Taste the soup and adjust the seasoning as necessary. Stir in the parsley and serve.

Spicy Chicken and Mushroom Soup

*This creamy chicken soup makes a
wonderful start to a meal.*

INGREDIENTS

Serves 4

75g/3oz/6 tbsp unsalted (sweet) butter

2.5ml/½ tsp crushed garlic

5ml/1 tsp garam masala

5ml/1 tsp crushed black peppercorns

5ml/1 tsp salt

1.5ml/¼ tsp freshly grated nutmeg

225g/8oz skinless, boneless chicken
    breast portions

1 medium leek, sliced

75g/3 oz/generous 1 cup
    mushrooms, sliced

50g/2 oz/⅓ cup corn kernels

300ml/½ pint/1¼ cups water

250ml/8fl oz/1 cup single (light) cream

30ml/2 tbsp chopped fresh
    coriander (cilantro)

5ml/1 tsp crushed dried red chillies, to
    garnish (optional)

1 Melt the butter in a pan.
Lower the heat slightly and
add the garlic and garam masala.
Lower the heat further and add the
peppercorns, salt and nutmeg.

2 Cut the chicken pieces into
very fine strips and add to the
pan with the leek, mushrooms and
corn. Cook for 5–7 minutes, until
the chicken is cooked through,
stirring constantly.

3 Remove from the heat and
leave to cool slightly. Transfer
three-quarters of the mixture to
a food processor or blender. Add
the water and process for about
1 minute.

4 Pour the resulting purée back
into the pan with the rest of
the mixture and bring to the boil
over a medium heat. Lower the
heat and stir in the cream.

5 Add the fresh coriander. Taste
and adjust the seasoning.
Serve hot, garnished with crushed
red chillies, if you like.

Jalapeño-style Soup

Chicken, chilli and avocado combine to make this simple but unusual soup.

INGREDIENTS

Serves 6

1.5 litres/2½ pints/6¼ cups Chicken
  Stock

2 cooked chicken breast fillets, skinned
  and cut into large strips

1 drained canned chipotle or jalapeño
  chilli, rinsed

1 avocado

COOK'S TIP

When using canned chillies,
it is important to rinse them
thoroughly before adding them
to a dish in order to remove the
flavour of any pickling liquid.

1 Heat the stock in a large pan and add the chicken and chilli. Simmer over a very gentle heat for 5 minutes to heat the chicken through and release the flavour from the chilli.

2 Cut the avocado in half, remove the stone (pit) and peel off the skin. Slice the avocado flesh neatly lengthways.

3 Using a slotted spoon, remove the chilli from the pan and discard it. Pour the soup into heated serving bowls, distributing the chicken evenly among them.

4 Add a few avocado slices to each bowl and serve.

Indian Beef and Berry Soup

The fresh berries give this soup a pleasant kick.

INGREDIENTS

Serves 4

30ml/2 tbsp vegetable oil

450g/1lb tender beef steak

2 onions, thinly sliced

25g/1oz/2 tbsp butter

1 litre/1¾ pints/4 cups Meat Stock

2.5ml/½ tsp salt

115g/4oz/1 cup fresh huckleberries, blueberries or blackberries, lightly mashed

15ml/1 tbsp clear honey

1 Heat the oil in a heavy pan until almost smoking. Add the steak and cook on both sides over a medium-high heat until well browned. Remove the steak from the pan and set aside.

2 Reduce the heat to low and add the sliced onions and butter to the pan. Stir thoroughly, scraping up the meat juices. Cook over a low heat for 8–10 minutes, until the onions are softened.

3 Add the meat stock and salt and bring to the boil, stirring constantly. Mix in the mashed berries and the honey. Simmer for 20 minutes.

4 Cut the steak into thin slivers. Taste the soup and add more salt or honey if necessary. Add the steak to the pan. Cook gently for 30 seconds, stirring, then serve.

Wonton Soup

In China, wonton soup is served as a snack, or dim sum, but is a popular soup course in the West.

INGREDIENTS

Serves 4

175g/6oz pork, coarsely chopped

50g/2oz peeled prawns (shrimp), finely chopped

5ml/1 tsp light brown sugar

15ml/1 tbsp Chinese rice wine

15ml/1 tbsp light soy sauce

5ml/1 tsp finely chopped spring onions (scallions), plus extra to garnish

5ml/1 tsp finely chopped fresh root ginger

24 ready-made wonton skins

about 750ml/1¼ pints/3 cups Stock for Chinese Soups

15ml/1 tbsp light soy sauce

1 In a bowl, mix the pork and prawns with the sugar, rice wine, soy sauce, spring onions and ginger. Set aside for 25–30 minutes for the flavours to blend.

2 Place about 5ml/1 tsp of the pork mixture in the centre of each wonton skin.

3 Wet the edges of each filled wonton skin with a little water and press them together with your fingers to seal. Fold each wonton parcel over.

4 To cook, bring the stock to a rolling boil in a wok, add the wontons and cook for 4–5 minutes. Season with the soy sauce and add the extra spring onions.

5 Transfer to individual soup bowls and serve.

Chinese Chicken and Asparagus Soup

This is a very delicate and delicious soup. When fresh asparagus is not in season, canned white asparagus is an acceptable substitute.

INGREDIENTS

Serves 4

140g/5oz skinless, boneless chicken
    breast portion
5ml/1 tsp egg white
5ml/1 tsp cornflour (cornstarch) mixed to
    a paste with 15ml/1 tbsp water
115g/4oz asparagus
700ml/1¼ pints/3 cups Chicken Stock
salt and ground black pepper
fresh coriander (cilantro) , to garnish

1 Cut the chicken into very thin slices each about 4 × 2.5cm/ 1½ × 1in. Mix with a pinch of salt, then add the egg white, and finally the cornflour paste.

2 Cut off and discard the tough stems of the asparagus, and cut the tender spears diagonally into short, even lengths.

3 In a wok or pan, bring the stock to a rolling boil, add the asparagus, bring back to the boil and cook for 2 minutes. (You do not need to do this if you are using canned asparagus.)

4 Add the chicken, stir to separate and bring back to the boil once more. Taste and adjust the seasoning if necessary. Serve immediately, garnished with fresh coriander leaves.

Clear Soup with Meatballs

A Chinese-style soup, in which meatballs are combined with lightly cooked vegetables in a tasty stock.

INGREDIENTS

Serves 8

4–6 Chinese mushrooms, soaked in warm
water for 30 minutes
30ml/2 tbsp groundnut (peanut) oil
1 large onion, finely chopped
2 garlic cloves, finely crushed
1cm/½in piece fresh root ginger, bruised
2 litres/3½ pints/9 cups Meat or Chicken
stock, including the soaking liquid from
the mushrooms
30ml/2 tbsp soy sauce
115g/4 oz curly kale, spinach or Chinese
leaves (Chinese cabbage), shredded

For the meatballs

175g/6oz/¾ cup minced (ground) beef
1 small onion, finely chopped
1–2 garlic cloves, crushed
15ml/1 tbsp cornflour (cornstarch)
a little egg white, lightly beaten
salt and ground black pepper

1 First prepare the meatballs.
Mix the beef with the onion,
garlic, cornflour and seasoning in a
food processor and then bind with
sufficient egg white to make a firm
mixture. With wet hands, roll into
tiny, bitesize balls and set aside.

2 Drain the mushrooms.
Reserve the soaking liquid.
Trim off and discard the stalks.
Slice the caps thinly and set aside.

3 Heat a wok or large pan and
add the oil. Cook the onion,
garlic and ginger to bring out the
flavour, but do not allow to brown.

4 When the onion is soft, pour
in the stock. Bring to the boil,
then stir in the soy sauce and
mushroom slices and simmer for
10 minutes. Add the meatballs and
cook for 10 minutes.

5 Just before serving, remove the
ginger. Stir in the shredded
curly kale, spinach or Chinese
leaves. Heat through for 1 minute
only – no longer or the leaves will
be overcooked. Ladle the soup into
warm bowls and serve.

Duck Consommé

The Vietnamese community in France has had a profound influence on French cooking, as this soup bears witness – it is light and rich at the same time, with intriguing flavours of South-east Asia.

INGREDIENTS

Serves 4

1 duck carcass (raw or cooked), plus 2 legs or any giblets, trimmed of as much fat as possible

1 large onion, unpeeled, with root end trimmed

2 carrots, cut into 5cm/2in pieces

1 parsnip, cut into 5cm/2in pieces

1 leek, cut into 5cm/2in pieces

2–4 garlic cloves, crushed

2.5cm/1in piece fresh root ginger, sliced

15ml/1 tbsp black peppercorns

4–6 fresh thyme sprigs or
    5ml/1 tsp dried thyme

6–8 fresh coriander (cilantro) sprigs, leaves and stems separated

For the garnish

1 small carrot

1 small leek, halved lengthways

4–6 shiitake mushrooms, thinly sliced

soy sauce

2 spring onions (scallions), thinly sliced

watercress or finely shredded Chinese leaves (Chinese cabbage)

ground black pepper

1 Put the duck carcass and legs or giblets, onion, carrots, parsnip, leek and garlic in a large, heavy pan or flameproof casserole. Add the ginger, peppercorns, thyme and coriander stems, cover with cold water and bring to the boil over a medium-high heat, skimming off any foam that rises to the surface.

2 Reduce the heat and simmer gently for 1½–2 hours, then strain through a sieve lined with muslin (cheesecloth) into a bowl. Discard the bones and vegetables. Cool the stock and chill for several hours. Skim off any congealed fat and blot the surface with kitchen paper to remove any traces of fat.

3 To make the garnish, cut the carrot and leek into 5cm/2in pieces. Cut each piece lengthways into thin slices, then stack and slice into thin julienne strips. Place the carrot and leek strips in a large pan with the sliced mushrooms.

4 Pour over the stock and add a few dashes of soy sauce and some pepper. Bring to the boil over a medium-high heat, skimming any foam that rises to the surface. Adjust the seasoning if necessary. Stir in the spring onions and watercress or Chinese leaves. Ladle the consommé into warmed bowls and sprinkle with the coriander leaves before serving.

Pork and Pickled Mustard Greens Soup

This highly flavoured soup makes an interesting start to a meal.

INGREDIENTS

Serves 4–6

225g/8oz pickled mustard leaves, soaked

50g/2oz cellophane noodles, soaked

15ml/1 tbsp vegetable oil

4 garlic cloves, thinly sliced

1 litre/1¾ pints/4 cups Chicken Stock

450g/1lb pork ribs, cut into large chunks

30ml/2 tbsp Thai fish sauce

pinch of sugar

ground black pepper

2 fresh red chillies, seeded and thinly
    sliced, to garnish

1 Cut the pickled mustard leaves into bitesize pieces. Taste to check the seasoning. If they are too salty, soak them for a little longer.

2 Drain the cellophane noodles, discarding the soaking water, and cut them into pieces about 5cm/2in long.

3 Heat the oil in a small frying pan, add the garlic and stir-fry until golden. Transfer to a bowl and set aside.

4 Pour the chicken stock into a large pan, bring to the boil, then add the pork ribs and simmer gently over a low heat for about 10–15 minutes.

5 Add the pickled mustard leaves and cellophane noodles. Bring back to the boil. Season to taste with fish sauce, sugar and ground black pepper.

6 Pour the soup into individual serving bowls. Garnish with the fried garlic and the red chillies and serve hot.

Ginger, Chicken and Coconut Soup

This aromatic soup is rich with coconut milk and intensely flavoured with galangal, lemon grass and kaffir lime leaves.

INGREDIENTS

Serves 4–6

750ml/1¼ pints/3 cups coconut milk

475ml/16fl oz/2 cups Chicken Stock

4 lemon grass stalks, bruised and chopped

2.5cm/1in piece galangal, thinly sliced

10 black peppercorns, crushed

10 kaffir lime leaves, torn

300g/11oz skinless boneless chicken, cut into thin strips

115g/4oz button (white) mushrooms

50g/2oz/½ cup baby corn cobs

60ml/4 tbsp lime juice

45ml/3 tbsp Thai fish sauce

For the garnish

2 red chillies, seeded and chopped

3–4 spring onions (scallions), chopped

chopped fresh coriander (cilantro)

1 Bring the coconut milk and chicken stock to the boil in a large pan. Add the lemon grass, galangal, peppercorns and half the kaffir lime leaves, reduce the heat and simmer gently for 10 minutes.

2 Strain the stock mixture into a clean pan. Return to the heat, then add the chicken strips, mushrooms and baby corn cobs. Cook for about 5–7 minutes, until the chicken is cooked.

3 Stir in the lime juice, fish sauce to taste and the rest of the lime leaves. Ladle the soup into warm bowls, garnish with red chillies, spring onions and coriander and serve.

Miso Soup with Pork and Vegetables

This is quite a rich and filling soup. Its Japanese name, Tanuki Jiru, means raccoon soup for hunters, but as raccoons are not eaten nowadays, pork is used.

INGREDIENTS

Serves 4

200g/7oz lean boneless pork

1 parsnip

50g/2oz mooli (daikon)

4 fresh shiitake mushrooms

½ konnyaku or ½ x 225–285g/ 8–10¼oz
    firm tofu

a little sesame oil, for stir-frying

600ml/1 pint/2½ cups water and 10ml/
    2 tsp instant dashi

70ml/4½ tbsp miso

2 spring onions (scallions), chopped

5ml/1 tsp sesame seeds

1 Firmly press the meat down on a chopping board using the palm of your hand and slice horizontally into very thin, long strips, then cut the strips crossways into small, neat squares. Set the pork aside.

2 Peel the parsnip with a vegetable peeler, cut it in half lengthways, then cut it into 1cm/½in thick half-moon-shaped slices.

3 Peel and slice the mooli into 1.5cm/⅔in thick discs. Cut the discs into 1.5cm/⅔in cubes. Remove the shiitake stalks and cut the caps into quarters.

4 Place the konnyaku, if using, in a pan of boiling water and cook for 1 minute. Drain and cool. Cut in quarters lengthways, then crossways into 3mm/⅛in thick pieces. If using tofu, cut into 3mm/⅛in thick pieces.

5 Heat a little sesame oil in a heavy, cast-iron or enamelled pan until purple smoke rises. Stir-fry the pork, then add the konnyaku or tofu and all the vegetables, except for the spring onions. When the colour of the meat has changed, add the stock.

6 Bring to the boil over a medium heat and skim off the foam until the soup looks fairly clear. Reduce the heat, cover, and simmer for 15 minutes.

7 Put the miso in a small bowl, and mix with 60ml/4 tbsp hot stock to make a smooth paste. Stir one-third of the miso into the soup. Taste and add more miso if required. Add the spring onion and remove from the heat. Serve very hot in individual soup bowls and sprinkle with sesame seeds.

STARTERS

~

While it may be sensible to plan your main course first,
especially when entertaining, it is still important to give
plenty of thought to the starter. This section is packed
with inspiring first-course ideas for every occasion from
informal suppers to sophisticated dinner parties. You
will find clever suggestions for canapés and tasty morsels
to serve with drinks, hot hors d'oeuvres and fabulous
appetizers based on vegetables, cheese, fish, seafood, meat
and poultry, as well as helpful advice and tips on
garnishes, marinades and dressings.

Garnishes

Many garnishes are delicate works of art which seem almost a shame to eat, and others add a dash of texture or a hint of colour without which the dish would just not be the same.

CREAM SWIRL

Add a swirl of cream, sour cream or yogurt to make a dip look particularly attractive.

To create a delicate pattern draw the tip of a fine skewer back and forth through the swirl.

CROÛTONS

Croûtons are an easy and effective way to use up stale bread whilst adding crunch to any dish, and are always served with classic Caesar salads.

Once you have cut your chosen bread into small cubes either fry them in sunflower oil until they are golden and crisp, or brush them with oil and bake in the oven. They will keep in an airtight container for up to a week.

CUCUMBER FLOWERS

This is a stunning garnish which would grace any dinner party.

1 Cut the cucumber in half lengthways and remove the seeds. Place each half cut side down and then cut at an angle into 7.5cm/3in lengths. Cut into fine slices stopping 5mm/¼in short of the far side, so that the slices remain attached.

2 Fan the slices out. Turn in alternate slices to form a loop. Bend the length into a semicircle so the cucumber loops resemble the petals of a flower.

LEMON TWIST

A classic garnish – so simple but very effective.

Cut a lemon into 5mm/¼in slices. Make a cut in each slice from the centre to the skin. Hold the slice either side of the cut and twist to form an "S" shape.

PARMESAN CURLS

Curls of Parmesan add a delicate touch to pasta or risotto.

Holding a swivel-bladed peeler at a 45° angle, draw it steadily across the block of Parmesan cheese to form a curl.

CHILLI FLOWERS

Make these chilli flowers several hours before needed to allow the "flowers" to open up.

1 Use a small pair of scissors or a slim-bladed knife to cut a chilli carefully lengthways up from the tip to within 1cm/½in of the stem end. Repeat this at regular intervals around the chilli – more cuts will produce more petals. Repeat with the remaining chillies.

2 Rinse the chillies in cold water and remove all the seeds. Place the chillies in a bowl of iced water and chill for at least 4 hours. For very curly flowers leave the chillies overnight.

CHIVE BRAIDS

Try adding a couple of edible braids of chives around your appetizers.

1 Align three chives on a worksurface with a bowl on one end to hold them still. Carefully plait the chives together to within 2.5cm/1in of the end.

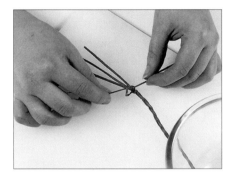

2 Tie a thin chive around the exposed end of the plait. Remove the bowl and tie the other end the same way. Trim both ends with kitchen scissors.

3 Plaice the braid in a bowl and pour boiling water over them. Leave to stand for 20–30 seconds then drain and refresh under cold water. Drain again.

SPRING ONION (SCALLION) TASSELS

You can often find this garnish in Chinese restaurants, where looks are almost as important as taste.

Cut the white part of a spring onion (scallion) into a 6cm/2½in length. Shred one end of each piece, then place in iced water for about 30 minutes until the ends curl.

TOMATO SUNS

Colourful cherry tomato suns look good with pâtés and terrines.

1 Place a tomato stem side down. Cut lightly into the skin across the top, edging the knife down towards the base on either side. Repeat until the skin has been cut into eight separate segments, joined at the base.

2 Slide the top of the knife under the point of each segment and ease the skin away towards the base. Gently fold the petals back to mimic the sun's rays.

AVOCADO FAN

Avocados are amazingly versatile – they can serve as edible containers, be sliced or diced in a salad, or form the foundation of a delicious sauce. They also make very elegant garnishes for appetizers.

1 Halve, stone and peel an avocado. Slice each half lengthways into quarters. Gently draw a cannelle knife across the quarters at 1cm/½in intervals, to create regular stripes.

2 Make four cuts lengthways down each avocado quarter leaving 1cm/½in intact at the end. Carefully fan out the slices and arrange on a plate.

Marinades, Oils and Dressings

Marinades, flavoured oils and dressings can turn a plain piece of fish or a sliced vegetable into a delectable appetizer, starter or hors d'oeuvre. With a few simple ingredients, and in just a few minutes, you can make a fresh herb marinade to tenderize fish or meat, a ginger and garlic oil for fragrant fried dishes, or a sour cream dressing to bring out the flavour of crisp salad vegetables.

SUMMER HERB MARINADE

Make the best of summer herbs in this marinade. Any combination may be used depending on what you have to hand, and it works well with veal, chicken, pork or lamb.

1 Discard any coarse stalks or damaged leaves from a selection of herb sprigs, such as chervil, thyme, parsley, sage, chives, rosemary and oregano, then chop finely.

2 Mix the herbs with 90ml/ 6 tbsp olive oil, 45ml/3 tbsp tarragon vinegar, 1 garlic clove, crushed, 2 spring onions (scallions), chopped, and salt and pepper. Add the meat or poultry, cover and chill for 2–3 hours.

GINGER AND LIME MARINADE

This refreshing marinade is particularly good with chicken.

1 Mix together the rind of one lime and the juice of three limes. Add 15ml/1 tbsp green cardamom seeds, crushed, 1 finely chopped onion, grated fresh root ginger (use a 2.5cm/1in piece and peel before grating), 1 large garlic clove, crushed and 45ml/3 tbsp olive oil.

2 Pour over the meat or fish. Stir gently to coat, cover and leave in a cool place for 1 hour.

CHILLI AND GARLIC MARINADE

Add extra chillies if you like your food to be very spicy.

Combine 4 small chillies, seeded and finely diced, 10ml/2 tsp finely grated fresh root ginger, 1 large garlic clove, crushed, and 45ml/ 3 tbsp light soy sauce in a bowl. Add the meat or fish, cover and chill for 2–4 hours.

CHINESE MARINADE

This marinade is traditionally used to flavour succulent duck breasts.

Mix 15ml/1 tbsp clear honey, 1.5ml/1¼ tsp five spice powder, 1 garlic clove, finely chopped, 15ml/1 tbsp hoisin sauce and a pinch of salt and pepper. Add the duck breasts or other meat, turning them in the marinade. Cover and leave in a cool place to marinate for 2 hours.

AROMATIC SPICE OIL

As well as tasting delicious, aromatic oils make wonderful gifts. Ginger, Garlic and Shallot Oil is simple and delicious, but you could also try using a combination of other spices and flavourings, such as chillies, coriander (cilantro), lemon grass, peppercorns and lime leaves.

Peel and lightly bruise a 6cm/ 2½in piece of fresh root ginger and place in a clean bottle. Fill with groundnut (peanut) oil, 2 garlic cloves (left whole) and 3 small peeled shallots. Cover tightly and leave in a cool dark place for 2 weeks, or until the flavour is sufficiently pronounced, before using.

PARSLEY, SAGE AND THYME OIL

Chop a handful each of fresh parsley, sage and thyme. Place in a bottle and fill up with olive oil. Seal and allow to stand at room temperature for about a week, shaking occasionally. Strain the oil into another sterilized, decorative bottle, discard the chopped herbs but add a fresh sprig or two to decorate.

SOUR CREAM AND DILL DRESSING

This unusual dressing can be made in only a couple of minutes.

Blend together 120ml/4fl oz/ ½ cup sour cream, 10ml/2 tsp creamed horseradish and 15ml/ 1 tbsp chopped fresh dill in a small bowl and season with a little salt and pepper.

SPICY TOMATO DRESSING

This tangy dressing goes very well with a robust salad, such as bean or potato salad. It can also be used as a marinade.

Mix together 5ml/1 tsp ground cumin, 15ml/1 tbsp tomato ketchup, 30ml/2 tbsp olive oil, 15ml/1 tbsp white wine vinegar and 1 garlic clove, crushed in a small bowl. Add a little salt and some hot pepper sauce to taste and stir again thoroughly.

HERB GARDEN DRESSING

The dried mixture will keep throughout the winter until your herbs are growing again. It can also be used to sprinkle over vegetables, casseroles and stews.

1 Mix together 115g/4oz/1 cup dried oregano, 115g/4oz/ 1 cup dried basil, 50g/2oz/½ cup dried marjoram, 50g/2oz/ ½ cup dried dill weed, 50g/ 2oz/½ cup dried mint leaves, 50g/2oz/½ cup onion powder, 30ml/2 tbsp dry mustard, 10ml/ 2 tsp salt and 15ml/1 tbsp freshly ground black pepper and keep in a sealed jar to use as needed.

2 When making a batch of salad dressing, take 2 tbsp of the herb mixture and add it to 350ml/12fl oz/1½ cups of extra virgin olive oil and 120ml/4fl oz/ ½ cup cider vinegar. Mix thoroughly and allow to stand for 1 hour or so. Mix again before using.

NIBBLES AND DIPS

This mouth-watering collection of hot and cold morsels is
designed to tempt the appetite. You can serve them as an hors
d'oeuvre, once you are all seated at the table, or, in many cases,
dispense with formality and serve as canapés with pre-dinner
drinks. Whatever your preference, there is something to set
the taste buds tingling – Tex-Mex dips, Japanese tempura,
Russian blinis, Middle Eastern falafel, French tapenade and
a huge array of tempting treats from around the world.

V

Marinated Olives

For the best flavour, marinate the olives for at least 10 days and serve at room temperature.

INGREDIENTS

Serves 4

225g/8oz/1⅓ cups unpitted, green olives

3 garlic cloves

5ml/1 tsp coriander seeds

2 small fresh red chillies

2–3 thick slices of lemon, cut into pieces

1 fresh thyme or rosemary sprig

75ml/5 tbsp white wine vinegar

1 Spread out the olives and garlic on a chopping board. Using a rolling pin, crack and flatten them slightly.

2 Crack the coriander seeds in a mortar with a pestle.

COOK'S TIP

For a change, use a mix of caraway and cumin seeds in place of the coriander.

3 Mix the olives and the garlic, coriander seeds, chillies, lemon pieces, thyme or rosemary sprigs and white wine vinegar in a large bowl. Toss well, then transfer the mixture to a clean glass jar. Pour in sufficient cold water to cover. Store in the refrigerator for at least 5 days before serving at room temperature.

V

Salted Almonds

These crunchy salted nuts are at their best when fresh so, if you can, cook them on the day you plan to eat them.

INGREDIENTS

Serves 2–4

175g/6oz/1½ cups whole almonds in their skins

15ml/1 tbsp egg white, lightly beaten

2.5ml/½ tsp coarse sea salt

COOK'S TIP

This traditional method of salt-roasting nuts gives a matt, dry-looking finish; if you want them to shine, turn the roasted nuts into a bowl, add 15ml/1 tbsp of olive oil and shake well to coat.

1 Preheat the oven to 180°C/ 350°F/Gas 4. Spread out the almonds on a baking sheet and roast for about 20 minutes, until cracked and golden.

2 Mix the egg white and salt in a bowl, add the almonds and shake well to coat.

3 Tip the almond and egg mixture on to the baking sheet, give a shake to separate the nuts, then return them to the oven for 5 minutes, until they have dried. Set aside until cold, then store in an airtight container until ready to serve.

Assorted Canapés

These elegant party pieces take a little time to make, but they can be prepared in advance with the final touches added when your guests arrive. Each variation makes 12.

TRUFFLE CANAPÉS

INGREDIENTS

225/8oz rich shortcrust (unsweetened)
   pastry dough, thawed if frozen
2 eggs, beaten
15g/½oz/1 tbsp butter
5ml/1 tsp truffle oil or a few slices or
   shreds of fresh truffle
salt and ground black pepper
chopped fresh chives, to garnish

1 Preheat the oven to 190°C/ 375°F/Gas 5. Roll out the pastry very thinly on a lightly floured work surface and use to line 12 very small tartlet tins (muffin pans).

2 Line each pastry case (shell) with baking parchment and bake for 10 minutes. Remove the parchment and bake for a further 5 minutes, until the pastry is crisp and golden.

3 Season the beaten eggs, then melt the butter in a pan, pour in the eggs and stir constantly over a gentle heat. When the eggs are almost set, stir in the truffle oil or fresh truffle. Spoon the mixture into the pastry cases and top with chives.

PRAWN AND TOMATO CANAPÉS

INGREDIENTS

225g/8oz rich shortcrust (unsweetened)
   pastry dough, thawed if frozen
2 tomatoes, peeled, seeded and chopped
12 large cooked prawns (shrimp), peeled
   but with tails left on
60ml/4 tbsp hollandaise sauce
salt and ground black pepper
fresh fennel or chervil sprigs, to garnish

1 Preheat the oven to 190°C/ 375°F/Gas 5. Roll out the pastry very thinly on a lightly floured work surface and use to line 12 very small tartlet tins (muffin pans).

2 Line each pastry case (shell) with baking parchment and bake for 10 minutes. Remove the parchment and bake for a further 5 minutes, until the pastry is crisp and golden.

3 Place some chopped tomato in the base of each pastry case and season with salt and ground black pepper. Top with the prawns and spoon on some hollandaise sauce. Warm through briefly in the oven and serve garnished with fennel or chervil sprigs.

SALMON AND CORIANDER CANAPÉS

INGREDIENTS

3–4 slices dark rye bread
2 eggs, hard-boiled and thinly sliced
115g/4oz poached salmon
few fresh coriander (cilantro) leaves,
   to garnish

For the lime and coriander (cilantro) mayonnaise
45–60ml/3–4 tbsp mayonnaise
5ml/1 tsp chopped fresh
   coriander (cilantro)
5ml/1 tsp lime juice
salt and ground black pepper

1 Cut the slices of rye bread into 12 triangular pieces, using a sharp knife.

2 Make the lime and coriander mayonnaise. In a small bowl, mix together the mayonnaise, chopped coriander and lime juice. Season with salt and ground black pepper to taste.

3 Top each bread triangle with a slice of egg, a small portion of salmon and a teaspoon of mayonnaise. Garnish each with a coriander leaf. Chill the canapés until ready to serve.

WATERCRESS AND AVOCADO CANAPÉS

INGREDIENTS

3–4 slices dark rye bread

1 small ripe avocado

15ml/1 tbsp lemon juice

45ml/3 tbsp mayonnaise

½ bunch of watercress, chopped, reserving a few sprigs to garnish

6 quail's eggs, hard-boiled

1 Cut the bread into 12 rounds, using a plain or fluted biscuit (cookie) cutter.

2 Cut the avocado in half, around the stone (pit). Peel one half, then slice and dip each piece in lemon juice. Place one piece of avocado on each bread round.

3 Scoop the remaining avocado into a bowl and mash. Mix in the mayonnaise and watercress. Spoon a little of the mixture on to each canapé, top with a shelled, halved quail's egg and garnish with a sprig of watercress.

Smoked Salmon and Gravadlax Sauce

Gravadlax is cured fresh salmon: it is marinated in dill, salt and sugar and left for 2–3 days with weights on it. It can now be bought in most supermarkets and delicatessens and you can use it instead of smoked salmon if you like.

INGREDIENTS

Serves 8

25g/1oz/2 tbsp softened butter

5ml/1 tsp grated lemon rind

4 slices rye or pumpernickel bread

115g/4oz smoked salmon

few frisée lettuce leaves

8 lemon slices

8 cucumber slices

60ml/4 tbsp gravadlax sauce

dill sprigs, to garnish

1 Mix the butter and lemon rind together, spread over the bread and cut in half diagonally.

2 Arrange the smoked salmon over the top to cover.

3 Add a little frisée lettuce and a slice each of lemon and cucumber. Spoon over some gravadlax sauce, then garnish with fresh dill sprigs.

Smoked Trout Mousse in Cucumber Cups

This delicious creamy mousse can be made in advance and chilled for 2–3 days in the refrigerator. Serve it in crunchy cucumber cups, or simply with crudités if you like.

INGREDIENTS

Makes about 24

115g/4oz/½ cup cream cheese, softened

2 spring onions (scallions), chopped

15–30ml/1–2 tbsp, chopped fresh dill or parsley

5ml/1 tsp horseradish sauce

225g/8oz smoked trout fillets, flaked and any fine bones removed

30–60ml/2–4 tbsp double (heavy) cream

cayenne pepper, to taste

2 cucumbers

salt

fresh dill sprigs, to garnish

1 Put the cream cheese, spring onions, dill or parsley, and horseradish sauce into a blender or the bowl of a food processor and process until well blended. Add the trout and process until smooth, scraping down the sides of the bowl once.

2 With the machine running, pour in the cream through the feeder tube until a soft, mousse-like mixture forms. Season to taste with salt and cayenne pepper, turn into a bowl, cover and chill for 15 minutes.

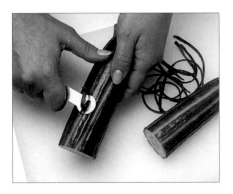

3 Using a canelle knife or vegetable peeler, score the length of each cucumber to create a striped effect on the skin. Cut each cucumber into 2cm/¾in thick rounds. Using a small spoon or melon baller, scoop out the seeds from the centre of each cucumber round.

4 Spoon the smoked trout mousse into a piping (pastry) bag fitted with a medium star nozzle and pipe swirls of the mixture into the prepared cucumber rounds. Chill in the refrigerator until ready to serve. Garnish the cucumber cups with small sprigs of dill.

Tapenade and Quail's Eggs

Tapenade is a purée made from capers, olives and anchovies. It is popularly used in Mediterranean cooking. It complements the taste of eggs perfectly, especially quail's eggs, which look very pretty on open sandwiches.

INGREDIENTS

Serves 8

8 quail's eggs
1 small baguette
45ml/3 tbsp tapenade
frisée lettuce leaves
3 small tomatoes, sliced
black olives
4 canned anchovy fillets, drained and
   halved lengthways
fresh parsley sprigs, to garnish

1 Boil the quail's eggs for 3 minutes, then plunge them straight into cold water to cool. Crack the shells and remove them very carefully.

2 Cut the baguette into slices on the diagonal and spread each one with some of the tapenade.

3 Arrange a little frisée lettuce, torn to fit, and the tomato slices on top.

4 Halve the quail's eggs and place them on top of the tomato slices.

5 Finish with a little more tapenade, the olives and finally the anchovies. Garnish with small parsley sprigs.

COOK'S TIP

To make 300ml/½ pint/1¼ cups of tuna tapenade, put a 90g/3½oz canned drained tuna in a food processor with 25g/1oz/2 tbsp capers, 10 canned anchovy fillets and 75g/3oz/¾ cup pitted black olives and blend until smooth, scraping down the sides as necessary. Gradually add 60ml/ 4 tbsp olive oil through the feeder tube. This purée can be used for filling hard-boiled eggs. Blend the tapenade with the egg yolks then pile into the whites.

Eggs Mimosa

The use of the word mimosa describes the fine yellow and white grated egg which looks not unlike the flower of the same name. It can be used to finish any dish, adding a light summery touch.

INGREDIENTS

Serves 20

12 hard-boiled eggs, shelled

2 avocados, halved and stoned (pitted)

1 garlic clove, crushed

Tabasco sauce, to taste

15ml/1 tbsp virgin olive oil

salt and ground black pepper

20 chicory (Belgian endive) leaves or
    small crisp green lettuce leaves

basil leaves, to garnish

1 Reserve 2 of the eggs, halve the remainder and put the yolks in a mixing bowl. Blend or beat the yolks with the avocados, garlic, Tabasco sauce, oil and salt and pepper. Check the seasoning. Pipe or spoon this mixture back into the halved egg whites.

2 Sieve the remaining egg whites and sprinkle over the filled eggs. Sieve the yolks on top. Arrange each half egg on a chicory or lettuce leaf and place them on a serving platter. Sprinkle the shredded basil over the filled egg halves before serving.

Stuffed Devilled Eggs

These eggs are so simple to make, yet guests will always be impressed by them. They have a wonderful flavour and can be given quite a "kick" too by including the cayenne.

INGREDIENTS

Serves 6

6 hard-boiled eggs, shelled

40g/1½oz/¼ cup minced (ground) cooked ham

6 walnut halves, coarsely ground

15ml/1 tbsp very finely chopped spring onions (scallions)

15ml/1 tbsp Dijon mustard

15ml/1 tbsp mayonnaise

10ml/2 tsp vinegar

1.5ml/¼ tsp cayenne pepper (optional)

salt and ground black pepper

paprika and gherkin slices, to garnish

1 Cut each hard-boiled egg in half lengthways. Put the yolks in a bowl and set the whites aside.

2 Mash the yolks well with a fork, or push them through a sieve. Add all the remaining ingredients, except the garnish, and mix well with the yolks. Taste and season with more salt and pepper if necessary.

3 Spoon the filling into the egg white halves, or pipe it in with a piping (pastry) bag. Garnish with a little paprika and a small star or other shape cut from the gherkin slices. Serve at room temperature.

Stuffed Celery Sticks

The creamy filling contrasts well with the crunchy celery, and the walnuts add a wonderful flavour.

INGREDIENTS

Serves 4–6

12 crisp, tender celery sticks

25g/1oz/¼ cup crumbled blue cheese

115g/4oz/½ cup cream cheese

45ml/3 tbsp sour cream

50g/2oz/½ cup chopped walnuts

1 Trim the celery sticks. Wash them, if necessary, and dry well on kitchen paper. Cut into 10cm/ 4in lengths.

2 In a small bowl, combine the crumbled blue cheese, cream cheese and sour cream. Stir together with a wooden spoon until smoothly blended. Fold in all but 15ml/1 tbsp of the walnuts.

3 Fill the celery pieces with the cheese and nut mixture. Chill before serving, garnished with the reserved walnuts.

COOK'S TIP

Use the same filling to stuff scooped-out cherry tomatoes. Serve together if you like.

Foie Gras Pâté in Filo Cups

This is an extravagantly rich hors d'oeuvre – so save it for a special anniversary or celebration.

INGREDIENTS

Makes 24

3–6 sheets fresh or thawed filo pastry

40g/1½oz/3 tbsp butter, melted

225g/8oz canned foie gras pâté or other fine liver pâté, at room temperature

50g/2oz/4 tbsp butter, softened

30–45ml/2–3 tbsp Cognac or other brandy (optional)

chopped pistachio nuts, to garnish

2 Keeping the rest of the filo squares covered, place one square on a work surface and brush lightly with melted butter, then turn and brush the other side.

5 Bake the filo cups for about 4–6 minutes until crisp and golden, then remove and cool in the tray for 5 minutes. Carefully transfer each filo cup to a wire rack and leave to cool completely.

1 Preheat the oven to 200°C/ 400°F/Gas 6. Grease a bun tray (muffin pan) with 24 x 4cm/1½in cups. Stack the filo sheets on a work surface and cut them into 6cm/2½in squares. Cover with a damp dishtowel.

3 Butter a second square and place it over the first at an angle. Butter a third square and place at an angle over the first two sheets to form an uneven edge.

4 Press the layers into a cup of the bun tray. Continue with the remaining pastry and butter until all the cups in the bun tray have been filled.

6 In a small bowl, beat the pâté with the softened butter until smooth and well blended. Add the Cognac or brandy to taste, if using. Spoon into a piping (pastry) bag fitted with a medium star nozzle and pipe a swirl into each cup. Sprinkle with pistachio nuts. Chill until you are ready to serve, but bring back to room temperature.

COOK'S TIP

The pâté and pastry are best eaten soon after preparation. If preparing ahead of time and then chilling in the refrigerator, be sure to bring back to room temperature before serving.

Pickled Quail's Eggs

V

These Chinese eggs are pickled in alcohol and can be stored in a preserving jar in a cool, dark place for several months. They will make delicious bite-size snacks at a drinks party and are sure to delight guests.

INGREDIENTS

Serves 12

12 quail's eggs

15ml/1 tbsp salt

750ml/1¼ pints/3 cups distilled or
    previously boiled water

15ml/1 tsp Sichuan peppercorns

150ml/¼ pint/⅔ cup spirit such as
    Mou-tal (Chinese brandy), brandy,
    whisky, rum or vodka

dipping sauce (see Cook's Tip) and
    toasted sesame seeds, to serve

1 Boil the eggs for about 4 minutes, until the yolks are soft but not runny.

2 In a large pan, dissolve the salt in the distilled or previously boiled water. Add the peppercorns, then leave the water to cool and add the spirit.

3 Gently tap the eggs all over but do not peel them. Place in a large, airtight, sterilized jar and fill up with the liquid, totally covering the eggs. Seal the jar and leave the eggs to stand in a cool, dark place for 7–8 days.

4 To serve, remove the eggs from the liquid and peel off the shells carefully. Cut each egg in half or quarters and serve whole with a dipping sauce and a bowl of toasted sesame seeds.

COOK'S TIP

• Although you can buy Chinese dipping sauces in the supermarket, it is very easy to make your own at home. To make a quick dipping sauce, mix equal quantities of soy sauce and hoisin sauce.

• Be sure to use only boiled water or distilled water for the eggs, as the water must be completely free of bacteria or they will enter the porous shells.

Buckwheat Blinis with Mushroom Caviar

V

*These little Russian pancakes are
traditionally served with caviar and
sour cream. Here is a vegetarian
alternative that uses a selection of
delicious wild mushrooms in place
of the fish roe. The blinis can be
made ahead of time and warmed in
the oven before topping.*

INGREDIENTS

Serves 4

115g/4oz/1 cup strong white bread flour

50g/2oz/$\frac{1}{2}$ cup buckwheat flour

2.5ml/$\frac{1}{2}$ tsp salt

300ml/$\frac{1}{2}$ pint/1$\frac{1}{4}$ cups milk

5ml/1 tsp dried yeast

2 eggs, separated

200ml/7fl oz/scant 1 cup sour cream or
   crème fraîche

For the mushroom caviar

350g/12oz mixed wild mushrooms. such
   as field (portabello) mushrooms,
   orange birch bolete, bay boletus, oyster
   and St George's mushrooms

5ml/1 tsp celery salt

30ml/2 tbsp walnut oil

15ml/1 tbsp lemon juice

45ml/3 tbsp chopped fresh parsley

ground black pepper

1 To make the caviar, trim and
chop the mushrooms, then
place them in a glass bowl, toss
with the celery salt and cover with
a weighted plate.

2 Leave the mushrooms for
2 hours until the juices have
run out into the base of the bowl.
Rinse the mushrooms thoroughly
to remove the salt, drain and press
out as much liquid as you can with
the back of a spoon. Return them
to the bowl and toss gently with
the walnut oil, lemon juice and
parsley. Season to taste with
pepper. Chill in the refrigerator
until ready to serve.

3 Sift the two flours together
with the salt into a large
mixing bowl. Gently warm the
milk to lukewarm. Add the yeast,
stirring until dissolved, then pour
the mixture into the flour, add
the egg yolks and stir to make a
smooth batter. Cover with a clean
damp dishtowel and leave in a
warm place for 1 hour.

4 Whisk the egg whites in a
clean, grease-free bowl until
stiff, then fold into the risen batter.

5 Heat an iron pan or griddle to
a moderate temperature.
Moisten with oil, then drop
spoonfuls of the batter on to the
surface. When bubbles rise to the
top, turn them over and cook
briefly on the other side. Spoon on
the sour cream or crème fraîche,
top with the mushroom caviar and
serve immediately.

Potato Blinis

These light-as-air pancakes are luxuriously topped with sour cream and smoked salmon.

INGREDIENTS

Serves 6

115g/4oz potatoes, boiled and mashed

15ml/1 tbsp easy-blend (rapid-rise) dried yeast

175g/6oz/1½ cups plain (all-purpose) flour

oil, for greasing

90ml/6 tbsp sour cream

6 slices smoked salmon

salt and ground black pepper

lemon slices, to garnish

COOK'S TIP

These small pancakes can easily be prepared in advance and stored in the refrigerator until ready for use. Simply warm them through in a low oven.

1 In a large bowl, mix together the mashed potatoes, dried yeast, flour and 300ml/½ pint/1¼ cups lukewarm water.

2 Leave to rise in a warm place for about 30 minutes, until the mixture has doubled in size.

3 Heat a non-stick frying pan and add a little oil. Drop spoonfuls of the mixture on to the preheated pan. Cook the blinis for 2 minutes, until lightly golden on the underside, toss with a spatula and cook on the second side for about 1 minute.

4 Season the blinis with some salt and pepper. Serve with a little sour cream and a small slice of smoked salmon folded on top. Garnish with a final grind of black pepper and a small slice of lemon.

Eggy Thai Fish Cakes

These tangy little fish cakes, with a kick of Eastern spice, make a really fabulous appetizer and great party food, too.

INGREDIENTS

Makes about 20

225g/8oz smoked cod or haddock fillet (undyed)

225g/8oz fresh cod or haddock fillet

1 small fresh red chilli, seeded and finely chopped

2 garlic cloves, grated

1 lemon grass stalk, very finely chopped

2 large spring onions (scallions), very finely chopped

30ml/2 tbsp Thai fish sauce

60ml/4 tbsp thick coconut milk

2 large (US extra large) eggs, lightly beaten

15ml/1 tbsp chopped fresh coriander (cilantro)

15ml/1 tbsp cornflour (cornstarch), plus extra for moulding

oil, for frying

soy sauce, rice vinegar or Thai fish sauce, for dipping

1 Place the smoked fish fillet in a bowl of cold water and set aside to soak for 10 minutes. Dry well on kitchen paper. Skin the smoked and fresh fish fillets, then chop them coarsely and place in a food processor.

2 Add the chilli, garlic, lemon grass, spring onions, fish sauce and coconut milk and process until well blended. Add the eggs and coriander and process for a further few seconds. Cover with clear film (plastic wrap) and chill in the refrigerator for 1 hour.

3 To make the fish cakes, flour your hands with cornflour and shape large teaspoonfuls into neat balls, coating them with the flour.

4 Heat 5–7.5cm/2–3in oil in a medium pan until a crust of bread turns golden in about 1 minute. Fry the fish cakes, 5–6 at a time, turning them carefully with a slotted spoon, for 2–3 minutes, until they turn golden all over. Remove with a slotted spoon and drain on kitchen paper. Keep the fish cakes warm in the oven until they are all cooked. Serve them immediately with one or more dipping sauces.

Monti Cristo Triangles

These opulent little sandwiches are stuffed with ham, cheese and turkey, dipped in egg, then fried in butter and oil. They are rich and filling.

INGREDIENTS

Makes 64

16 thin slices firm-textured white bread
120g/4oz/½ cup butter, softened
8 slices oak-smoked ham
45–60ml/3–4 tbsp wholegrain mustard
8 slices Gruyère or Emmenthal cheese
45–60ml/3–4 tbsp mayonnaise
8 slices cooked turkey or chicken breast
4–5 eggs
50ml/2 fl oz/¼ cup milk
5ml/1 tsp Dijon mustard
vegetable oil, for frying
butter, for frying
salt and ground white pepper

For the garnish
pimiento-stuffed green olives
fresh parsley leaves,

1 Arrange 8 of the bread slices on a work surface and spread with half the softened butter. Lay a slice of ham on each slice of bread and spread with a little mustard. Cover with a slice of Gruyère or Emmenthal cheese and spread with a little of the mayonnaise, then cover with a slice of turkey or chicken breast. Butter the rest of the bread slices and use to top the sandwiches. Using a sharp knife, cut off the crusts, trimming to an even square.

2 In a large, shallow, ovenproof dish, beat the eggs with the milk and Dijon mustard until thoroughly combined. Season to taste with salt and pepper. Soak the sandwiches in the egg mixture on both sides until all the egg has been absorbed.

3 Heat about 1cm/½in of oil with a little butter in a large, heavy frying pan, until hot, but not smoking. Gently fry the sandwiches, in batches, for about 4–5 minutes, until crisp and golden, turning once. Add more oil and butter as necessary. Drain on kitchen paper.

4 Transfer the sandwiches to a chopping board and cut each into 4 triangles, then cut each in half again. Make 64 triangles in total. Thread an olive and parsley leaf on to a cocktail stick (toothpick), then stick into each triangle and serve while warm.

Prawn Toasts

These crunchy sesame-topped toasts are simple to prepare using a food processor for the prawn paste.

INGREDIENTS

Makes 64

225g/8oz cooked, peeled prawns (shrimp), well drained and patted dry

1 egg white

2 spring onions (scallions), chopped

5ml/1 tsp chopped fresh root ginger

1 garlic clove, chopped

5ml/1 tsp cornflour (cornstarch)

2.5ml/½ tsp salt

2.5ml/½ tsp sugar

2–3 dashes hot pepper sauce

8 slices firm-textured white bread

60–75ml/4–5 tbsp sesame seeds

vegetable oil, for frying

spring onion (scallion) tassel, to garnish

1 Put the first 9 ingredients in the bowl of a food processor and process until the mixture forms a smooth paste, scraping down the side of the bowl from time to time.

COOK'S TIP

You can prepare these in advance and heat them through in a hot oven before serving. Make sure they are really crisp and hot though, because they won't be nearly so enjoyable if there's no crunch when you bite them!

2 Spread the prawn paste evenly over the bread slices, then sprinkle over the sesame seeds, pressing to make them stick. Remove the crusts, then cut each slice diagonally into 4 triangles, and each in half again. Make 64 triangles in total.

3 Heat 5cm/2in vegetable oil in a heavy pan or wok, until it is hot, but not smoking. Fry the triangles, in batches, for about 30–60 seconds, turning the toasts once. Drain on kitchen paper and keep hot in the oven while you cook the rest. Serve hot with the garnish.

Parmesan Fish Goujons

Use this batter, with or without the cheese, whenever you feel brave enough to fry fish. This is light and crisp and just melts in the mouth.

INGREDIENTS

Serves 4

375g/13oz plaice, flounder or sole fillets, or thicker fish such as cod or haddock
a little plain (all-purpose) flour
oil, for deep-frying
salt and ground black pepper
fresh dill sprigs, to garnish

For the cream sauce
60ml/4 tbsp sour cream
60ml/4 tbsp mayonnaise
2.5ml/½ tsp grated lemon rind
30ml/2 tbsp chopped gherkins or capers
15ml/1 tbsp chopped mixed fresh herbs, or 5ml/1 tsp dried mixed herbs

For the batter
75g/3oz/¾ cup plain (all-purpose) flour
25g/1oz/⅓ cup grated Parmesan cheese
5ml/1 tsp bicarbonate of soda (baking soda)
1 egg, separated
150ml/¼ pint/⅔ cup milk

1 To make the cream sauce, mix the sour cream, mayonnaise, lemon rind, gherkins or capers, herbs and seasoning together, then place in the refrigerator to chill.

2 To make the batter, sift the flour into a bowl. Mix in the other dry ingredients and some salt, and then whisk in the egg yolk and milk to give a thick yet smooth batter. Then gradually whisk in 90ml/6 tbsp water. Season and place in the refrigerator to chill.

3 Skin the fish and cut into thin strips of similar length. Season the flour and then dip the fish lightly in the flour.

4 Heat at least 5cm/2in oil in a large pan with a lid. Whisk the egg white until stiff and gently fold into the batter until just blended.

5 Dip the floured fish into the batter, drain off any excess and then drop gently into the hot oil.

6 Cook the fish, in batches so that the goujons don't stick to one another, for only 3–4 minutes, turning once. When the batter is golden and crisp, remove the fish with a slotted spoon. Place on kitchen paper on a plate and keep warm in a low oven while cooking the remaining goujons.

7 Serve hot garnished with sprigs of dill and accompanied by the cream sauce.

Parmesan Thins

These thin, crisp, savoury biscuits will melt in the mouth, so make plenty for guests. They are a great snack at any time of the day, so don't just keep them for parties.

INGREDIENTS

Makes 16–20

50g/2oz/½ cup plain (all-purpose) flour

40g/1½ oz/3 tbsp butter, softened

1 egg yolk

40g/1½ oz/⅔ cup freshly grated
   Parmesan cheese

pinch of salt

pinch of mustard powder

1 Rub together the flour and the butter in a bowl using your fingertips, then work in the egg yolk, Parmesan cheese, salt and mustard. Mix to bring the dough together into a ball. Shape the mixture into a log, wrap in foil or clear film (plastic wrap) and chill in the refrigerator for 10 minutes.

2 Preheat the oven to 200°C/ 400°F/Gas 6. Cut the Parmesan log into very thin slices, 3–6mm/ ⅛–¼in maximum, and arrange on a baking sheet. Flatten with a fork to give a pretty ridged pattern. Bake for 10 minutes, or until the biscuits (crackers) are crisp, but not changing colour.

Celeriac Fritters with Mustard Dip

The combination of the hot, crispy
fritters and cold mustard dip is
extremely good.

INGREDIENTS

Serves 4

1 egg

115g/4oz/1 cup ground almonds

45ml/3 tbsp freshly grated
    Parmesan cheese

45ml/3 tbsp chopped fresh parsley

1 celeriac, about 450g/1lb

lemon juice

oil, for deep-frying

salt and ground black pepper

sea salt flakes, to garnish

For the dip

150ml/¼ pint/⅔ cup sour cream

15–30ml/1–2 tbsp wholegrain mustard

1 Beat the egg well and pour into
a shallow dish. Mix together
ground the almonds, grated
Parmesan and chopped parsley in
a separate dish. Season with salt
and plenty of ground black pepper.
Set aside.

2 Peel the celeriac and cut into
batons about 1cm/½in wide
and 5cm/2in long. Drop them
immediately into a bowl of water
with a little lemon juice added to
prevent discoloration.

3 Heat the oil to 180°C/350°F or
until a cube of day-old bread
browns in 30 seconds. Drain and
then pat dry half the celeriac
batons. Dip them first into the
beaten egg, then into the ground
almond mixture, making sure that
the pieces are coated completely
and evenly.

4 Deep-fry the celeriac fritters,
in batches, for 2–3 minutes,
until golden. Drain on kitchen
paper. Keep warm while you cook
the remaining fritters.

5 Make the dip. Mix the sour
cream, mustard and salt to
taste. Spoon into a serving bowl.
Sprinkle the fritters with sea salt.

Dates Stuffed with Chorizo

This is a delicious combination from Spain, using fresh dates and spicy chorizo sausage.

INGREDIENTS

Serves 4–6

50g/2oz chorizo sausage

12 fresh dates, stoned (pitted)

6 streaky (fatty) bacon rashers (strips)

oil, for frying

plain (all-purpose) flour, for dusting

1 egg, beaten

50g/2oz/1 cup fresh breadcrumbs

1 Trim the ends of the chorizo sausage and then peel off the skin. Cut into three 2cm/³⁄₄ in slices. Cut these in half lengthways, then into quarters, giving 12 pieces.

2 Stuff each date with a piece of chorizo, closing the date around it. Stretch the bacon, by running the back of a knife along the rasher. Cut each rasher in half, widthways. Wrap a piece of bacon around each date and secure with a wooden cocktail stick (toothpick).

3 In a deep pan, heat 1cm/¹⁄₂ in of oil. Dust the dates with flour, dip them in the beaten egg, then coat in breadcrumbs. Fry the dates in the hot oil, turning them, until golden. Remove the dates with a slotted spoon, and drain on kitchen paper. Serve immediately.

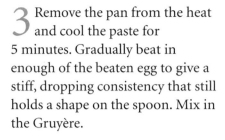

Cheese Aigrettes

Choux pastry is often associated with sweet pastries, such as profiteroles, but these little savoury puffs, flavoured with Gruyère and dusted with grated Parmesan, are just delicious. They are best made ahead and deep-fried to serve. They make a wonderful party snack.

INGREDIENTS

Makes 30

90g/3½ oz/scant 1 cup strong plain (all-purpose) flour

2.5ml/½ tsp paprika

2.5ml/½ tsp salt

75g/3oz/6 tbsp cold butter, diced

200ml/7fl oz/scant 1 cup water

3 eggs, beaten

75g/3oz Gruyère cheese, coarsely grated

corn or vegetable oil, for deep-frying

50g/2oz/⅔ cup freshly grated Parmesan cheese

ground black pepper

1 Mix the flour, paprika and salt together by sifting them on to a large sheet of greaseproof (waxed) paper. Add a generous amount of ground black pepper.

2 Put the diced butter and water into a medium pan and heat gently. As soon as the butter has melted and the liquid starts to boil, quickly tip in all the seasoned flour at once and beat very hard with a wooden spoon until the dough comes away cleanly from the sides of the pan.

3 Remove the pan from the heat and cool the paste for 5 minutes. Gradually beat in enough of the beaten egg to give a stiff, dropping consistency that still holds a shape on the spoon. Mix in the Gruyère.

4 Heat the oil for deep-frying to 180°C/350°F. Take a teaspoonful of the choux paste and use a second spoon to slide it into the oil. Make more aigrettes in the same way. Fry for 3–4 minutes, then drain on kitchen paper and keep warm while you are cooking successive batches. To serve, pile the aigrettes on a warmed serving dish and sprinkle with Parmesan.

COOK'S TIP

Filling these aigrettes gives a delightful surprise as you bite through their crisp shell. Make slightly larger aigrettes by dropping a slightly larger spoonful of dough into the hot oil. Slit them open and scoop out any soft paste. Fill the centres with taramasalata or crumbled Roquefort mixed with a little fromage frais (farmer's cheese).

Pork and Peanut Wontons with Plum Sauce

These crispy filled wontons are delicious served with a sweet plum sauce. The wontons can be filled and set aside for up to 8 hours before they are cooked.

INGREDIENTS

Makes 40–50 wontons

175g/6oz/1½ cups minced (ground) pork
   or 175g/6oz pork sausages, skinned
2 spring onions (scallions), finely chopped
30ml/2 tbsp peanut butter
10ml/2 tsp oyster sauce (optional)
30ml/2 tbsp cornflour (cornstarch)
40–50 wonton wrappers
vegetable oil, for deep-frying
salt and ground black pepper
lettuces and radishes, to garnish

For the plum sauce
225g/8oz/generous ¾ cup dark plum jam
15ml/1 tbsp rice or white wine vinegar
15ml/1 tbsp dark soy sauce
2.5ml/½ tsp chilli sauce

1 Combine the minced pork or skinned sausages, spring onions, peanut butter, oyster sauce, if using, and seasoning, and then set aside.

2 For the plum sauce, combine the plum jam, vinegar, soy and chilli sauces in a serving bowl and set aside.

3 Mix the cornflour with 30–45ml/2–3 tbsp water to a smooth paste in a small bowl.

4 To make the wontons, place 8 wrappers at a time on a work surface, moisten the edges with the cornflour paste and place 2.5ml/½ tsp of the filling on each. Fold in half, corner to corner, and twist.

5 Fill a wok or deep frying pan one-third full with vegetable oil and heat to 190°C/385°F. Have ready a wire strainer or frying basket and a tray lined with kitchen paper. Drop the wontons, 8 at a time, into the hot oil and deep-fry for 1–2 minutes, until golden all over. Lift out on to the paper-lined tray and sprinkle with fine salt. Serve immediately with the plum sauce garnished with lettuce and radishes.

V

Crispy Spring Rolls

These small and dainty spring rolls are ideal served as appetizers or as cocktail snacks. If you like, you could replace the mushrooms with chicken or pork and the carrots with prawns.

INGREDIENTS

Makes 40 rolls

225g/8oz beansprouts

115g/4oz small leeks or spring
    onions (scallions)

115g/4oz carrots

115g/4oz bamboo shoots, sliced

115g/4oz mushrooms

45–60ml/3–4 tbsp vegetable oil

5ml/1 tsp salt

5ml/1 tsp light brown sugar

15ml/1 tbsp light soy sauce

15ml/1 tbsp Chinese rice wine

20 frozen spring roll wrappers, thawed

15ml/1 tbsp cornflour (cornstarch) paste
    (see Cook's Tip)

plain (all-purpose) flour, for dusting

oil, for deep-frying

1 Cut all the vegetables into thin shreds, about the same size and shape as the beansprouts.

2 Heat the oil in a wok and stir-fry the vegetables for about 1 minute. Add the salt, sugar, soy sauce and Chinese rice wine and continue stirring the vegetables for 1½–2 minutes. Remove and drain away the excess liquid, then leave to cool.

3 To make the spring rolls, cut each spring roll wrapper in half diagonally, then place about a tablespoonful of the vegetable mixture one-third of the way down on the wrapper, with the triangle pointing away from you.

> ### COOK'S TIP
> ∿
>
> To make cornflour (cornstarch) paste, mix together 4 parts cornflour with about 5 parts cold water until smooth.

4 Lift the lower edge over the filling and roll once.

5 Fold in both ends and roll once more, then brush the upper pointed edge with a little cornflour paste, and roll into a neat package. Lightly dust a tray with flour and place the spring rolls in a single layer on the tray with the flapside underneath.

6 To cook, heat the oil in a wok or deep-fryer until hot, then reduce the heat to low. Deep-fry the spring rolls, in batches (about 8–10 at a time), for 2–3 minutes, or until golden and crisp, then remove and drain on kitchen paper. Serve the spring rolls hot with a dipping sauce, such as soy sauce, or mixed salt and pepper.

Vegetable Tempura

Tempura is a Japanese type of savoury fritter. Originally prawns were used, but vegetables can be cooked in the egg batter successfully too. The secret of making the incredibly light batter is to use really cold water, and to have the oil at the right temperature before you start cooking the fritters.

INGREDIENTS

Serves 4

2 courgettes (zucchini)

½ aubergine (eggplant)

1 large carrot

½ small Spanish onion

1 egg

120ml/4fl oz/½ cup iced water

115g/4oz/1 cup plain (all-purpose) flour

vegetable oil, for deep-frying

salt and ground black pepper

sea salt flakes, lemon slices and Japanese
    soy sauce (*shoyu*), to serve

1 Using a potato peeler, pare strips of peel from the courgettes and aubergine to give a striped effect.

2 Using a chef's knife, cut the courgettes, aubergine and carrot into strips measuring about 7.5–10cm/3–4in long and 3mm/⅛in wide. Place in a colander and sprinkle with salt. Put a small plate over and weight it down. Leave for 30 minutes, then rinse thoroughly. Drain well, then pat dry with kitchen paper.

3 Thinly slice the onion from top to base, discarding the plump pieces in the middle. Separate the layers so that there are lots of fine, long strips. Mix all the vegetables together and season with salt and pepper.

4 Make the batter immediately before frying. Mix the egg and iced water in a bowl, then sift in the flour. Mix briefly with a fork or chopsticks. Do not overmix: the batter should remain lumpy. Add the vegetables to the batter and mix to combine.

5 Half-fill a wok with oil and heat to 180°C/350°F. Scoop up a heaped tablespoonful of the mixture at a time and carefully lower it into the oil. Deep-fry, in batches, for about 3 minutes, until golden brown and crisp. Drain on kitchen paper.

6 Serve each portion with salt, slices of lemon and a tiny bowl of Japanese soy sauce for dipping.

COOK'S TIP

Other suitable vegetables for tempura include mushrooms and slices of red, green, yellow or orange (bell) peppers.

Spicy Peanut Balls

Tasty rice balls, rolled in chopped peanuts and deep-fried, make a delicious appetizer. Serve them simply as they are, or with a chilli sauce for dipping.

INGREDIENTS

Makes 16

1 garlic clove, crushed

1cm/½in piece fresh root ginger, peeled
    and finely chopped

1.5ml/¼ tsp turmeric

5ml/1 tsp granulated sugar

2.5ml/½ tsp salt

5ml/1 tsp chilli sauce

10ml/2 tsp Thai fish sauce or soy sauce

30ml/2 tbsp chopped fresh
    coriander (cilantro)

juice of ½ lime

225g/8oz/2 cups cooked white long
    grain rice

115g/4oz/1 cup peanuts, chopped

vegetable oil, for deep-frying

lime wedges and chilli dipping sauce, to
    serve (optional)

1 Process the garlic, ginger and turmeric in a food processor or blender until the mixture forms a paste. Add the sugar, salt, chilli sauce and fish sauce or soy sauce, with the chopped coriander and lime juice. Process briefly to mix the ingredients.

2 Add three-quarters of the cooked rice to the paste and process until smooth and sticky. Scrape into a mixing bowl and stir in the remainder of the rice. Wet your hands and shape the mixture into thumb-size balls.

3 Roll the balls in the chopped peanuts, making sure they are evenly coated.

4 Heat the oil in a deep-fryer or wok. Deep-fry the peanut balls until crisp. Drain on kitchen paper and then pile on to a platter. Serve hot with lime wedges and a chilli dipping sauce, if you like.

Guacamole

Avocados discolour quickly so make this delicious dip just before serving. If you do need to keep it for any length of time, cover the surface of the sauce with clear film and chill in the refrigerator.

INGREDIENTS

Serves 6

2 large ripe avocados

2 red chillies, seeded

1 garlic clove

1 shallot

20ml/2 tbsp olive oil,
   plus extra to serve

juice of 1 lemon or lime

salt and ground black pepper

flat leaf parsley leaves, to garnish

1 Halve the avocados, remove the stones (pits) and scoop out the flesh into a large bowl.

2 Using a fork or potato masher, mash the avocado flesh until fairly smooth.

3 Finely chop the chillies, garlic and shallot, then stir them into the mashed avocado with the olive oil and lemon or lime juice. Season to taste with salt and pepper.

4 Spoon the mixture into a small serving bowl. Drizzle over a little olive oil and sprinkle with a few flat leaf parsley leaves. Serve the guacamole immediately.

Basil and Lemon Dip

This lovely dip is based on fresh mayonnaise flavoured with lemon juice and two types of basil. Serve with crispy potato wedges for a delicious appetizer.

INGREDIENTS

Serves 4

2 large (US extra large) egg yolks
15ml/1 tbsp lemon juice
150ml/¼ pint/⅔ cup olive oil
150ml/¼ pint/⅔ cup sunflower oil
4 garlic cloves
handful of fresh green basil
handful of fresh opal basil
salt and ground black pepper

1 Place the egg yolks and lemon juice in a blender or food processor and process them briefly until lightly blended.

2 Stir the oils together in a jug (pitcher). With the machine running, pour in the oil very slowly, a little at a time.

3 Once half of the oil has been added, the remaining oil can be incorporated more quickly. Continue processing to form a thick, creamy mayonnaise.

4 Peel and crush the garlic cloves. Alternatively, place them on a chopping board and sprinkle with salt, then flatten them with the heel of a heavy-bladed knife and chop the flesh. Flatten the garlic again to make a coarse purée.

5 Tear both types of basil into small pieces and then stir them into the mayonnaise with the crushed garlic.

6 Add salt and pepper to taste, then transfer the dip to a serving dish. Cover and chill until ready to serve.

COOK'S TIP
~

For potato wedges, bake a large potato until nearly cooked. Slice thickly, brush one side with oil and grill (broil) for 7–10 minutes.

V

Quail's Eggs with Herbs and Dips

For al fresco *eating or informal entertaining, this platter of contrasting tastes and textures is delicious and certainly encourages a relaxed atmosphere. Choose the best seasonal vegetables and substitute for what is available.*

INGREDIENTS

Serves 6

1 large Italian focaccia or 2–3 Indian
    parathas or other flatbread
extra virgin olive oil, plus extra to serve
1 large garlic clove, finely chopped
small handful of chopped fresh mixed
    herbs, such as coriander (cilantro),
    mint, parsley and oregano
18–24 quail's eggs
30ml/2 tbsp mayonnaise
30ml/2 tbsp thick sour cream
5ml/1 tsp chopped capers
5ml/1 tsp finely chopped shallot
225g/8oz fresh beetroot (beet), cooked in
    water or (hard) cider, peeled and sliced
½ bunch of spring onions (scallions),
    trimmed and coarsely chopped
60ml/4 tbsp red onion or tamarind and
    date chutney
salt and ground black pepper
coarse sea salt and mixed ground
    peppercorns, to serve

1 Preheat the oven to 190°C/375°F/Gas 5. Brush the focaccia or flatbread liberally with olive oil, sprinkle with garlic, your choice of herbs and seasoning and bake for 10–15 minutes, or until golden. Keep warm.

2 Put the quail's eggs into a pan of cold water, bring to the boil and boil for 5 minutes. Transfer to a serving dish. Shell the eggs first if you like or leave guests to shell them themselves.

3 To make the dip, combine the mayonnaise, sour cream, capers, shallot and seasoning.

4 To serve, cut the bread into wedges and serve with dishes of the quail's eggs, mayonnaise dip, beetroot, spring onion and chutney. Serve with tiny bowls of the coarse salt, ground peppercorns and olive oil for dipping.

COOK'S TIP

If you don't have time to make your own mayonnaise, use the best store-bought variety available. You will probably find that you need to add less seasoning to it.

Sesame Seed-coated Falafel with Tahini Dip

V

Sesame seeds are used to give a delightfully crunchy coating to these spicy chickpea patties. Serve with the tahini yogurt dip.

INGREDIENTS

Serves 6

250g/9oz/1⅓ cups dried chickpeas
2 garlic cloves, crushed
1 fresh red chilli, seeded and finely sliced
5ml/1 tsp ground coriander
5ml/1 tsp ground cumin
15ml/1 tbsp chopped fresh mint
15ml/1 tbsp chopped fresh parsley
2 spring onions (scallions), finely chopped
1 large (US extra large) egg, beaten
sesame seeds, for coating
sunflower oil, for frying
salt and ground black pepper

For the tahini yogurt dip
30ml/2 tbsp light tahini
200ml/7fl oz/scant 1 cup natural
   (plain) yogurt
5ml/1 tsp cayenne pepper, plus extra
   for sprinkling
15ml/1 tbsp chopped fresh mint
1 spring onion (scallion), thinly sliced
fresh herbs, to garnish

1 Place the chickpeas in a bowl, cover with cold water and leave to soak overnight. Drain and rinse the chickpeas, then place in a pan and cover with cold water. Bring to the boil and boil rapidly for 10 minutes. Reduce the heat and simmer for about 1½–2 hours, until tender. Drain well.

2 Meanwhile, make the tahini yogurt dip. Mix together the tahini, yogurt, cayenne pepper and mint in a small bowl. Sprinkle the spring onion and extra cayenne pepper on top and chill in the refrigerator until required.

3 Combine the chickpeas with the garlic, chilli, ground spices, herbs, spring onions and salt and pepper, then mix in the egg. Place in a food processor and blend until the mixture forms a coarse paste. If the paste seems too soft, chill it for 30 minutes.

4 Form the chilled chickpea paste into 12 patties with your hands, then roll each one in the sesame seeds to coat thoroughly.

5 Heat enough oil to cover the base of a large frying pan Fry the falafel, in batches if necessary, for 6 minutes, turning once. Serve immediately with the tahini yogurt dip garnished with fresh herbs.

Chilli Bean Dip

*This deliciously spicy and creamy
bean dip is best served warm with
triangles of grilled pitta bread or a
bowl of crunchy tortilla chips.*

INGREDIENTS

Serves 4

2 garlic cloves

1 onion

2 fresh green chillies

30ml/2 tbsp vegetable oil

5–10ml/1–2 tsp hot chilli powder

400g/14oz can kidney beans

75g/3oz/¾ cup grated Cheddar cheese

1 fresh red chilli, seeded

salt and ground black pepper

1 Finely chop the garlic and
onion. Seed and finely chop
the green chillies.

2 Heat the vegetable oil in a large
sauté pan or deep frying pan
and add the garlic, onion, green
chillies and chilli powder. Cook
gently for about 5 minutes, stirring
regularly, until the onions are
softened and translucent, but
not browned.

3 Drain the kidney beans,
reserving the can juice. Process
all but 30ml/2 tbsp of the beans to
a purée in a food processor.

4 Add the puréed beans to the
pan with 30–45ml/2–3 tbsp of
the reserved can juice. Heat gently,
stirring to mix well.

5 Stir in the whole kidney beans
and the Cheddar cheese. Cook
over a low heat for 2–3 minutes,
stirring until the cheese has
melted. Season with salt and
pepper to taste.

6 Cut the red chilli into tiny
strips. Spoon the dip into four
individual serving bowls and
sprinkle the chilli strips over the
top. Serve warm.

COOK'S TIP

For a dip with a coarser texture,
do not purée the beans; instead
mash them with a potato masher.

Hummus

V

Blending chickpeas with garlic and oil creates a surprisingly creamy purée that is delicious as part of a Turkish-style mezze, or as a dip with vegetables. Leftovers make a good sandwich filler.

INGREDIENTS

Serves 4–6

150g/5oz/¾ cup dried chickpeas

juice of 2 lemons

2 garlic cloves, sliced

30ml/2 tbsp olive oil

pinch of cayenne pepper

150ml/¼ pint/⅔ cup tahini

salt and ground black pepper

extra olive oil and cayenne pepper,
   for sprinkling

flat leaf parsley sprigs, to garnish

1 Put the chickpeas in a bowl with plenty of cold water and leave to soak overnight.

2 Drain the chickpeas, place in a pan and cover with fresh cold water. Bring to the boil and boil rapidly for 10 minutes. Reduce the heat and simmer gently for about 1–1½ hours, until soft. Drain in a colander.

3 Process the chickpeas in a food processor to a smooth purée. Add the lemon juice, garlic, olive oil, cayenne pepper and tahini and process until creamy, scraping the mixture down from the sides of the bowl.

4 Season the purée with plenty of salt and ground black pepper and transfer to a serving dish. Sprinkle with a little olive oil and cayenne pepper and serve garnished with a few parsley sprigs.

COOK'S TIP

For convenience, canned chickpeas can be used instead. Allow two 400g/14oz cans and drain them thoroughly. Tahini can now be purchased from most good supermarkets or health food stores.

Baba Ganoush

Baba ganoush is a delectable aubergine dip from the Middle East. Tahini, a sesame seed paste with cumin, is the main flavouring, giving a subtle hint of spice.

INGREDIENTS

Serves 6

2 small aubergines (eggplant)
1 garlic clove, crushed
60ml/4 tbsp tahini
25g/1oz/¼ cup ground almonds
juice of ½ lemon
2.5ml/½ tsp ground cumin
30ml/2 tbsp fresh mint leaves
30ml/2 tbsp olive oil
salt and ground black pepper

For the flatbread

4 pitta breads
45ml/3 tbsp sesame seeds
45ml/3 tbsp fresh thyme leaves
45ml/3 tbsp poppy seeds
150ml/¼ pint/⅔ cup olive oil

1 Start by making the flatbread. Split the pitta breads through the middle with a sharp knife and carefully open them out. Mix the sesame seeds, chopped thyme and poppy seeds in a mortar. Work them lightly with a pestle to release the flavour.

2 Stir in the olive oil. Spread the mixture over the cut sides of the pitta bread. Grill (broil) until golden brown and crisp. When cool, break into pieces.

3 Grill the aubergines, turning them frequently, until the skin is blackened and blistered. Remove the peel, chop the flesh coarsely and leave to drain in a colander.

4 Squeeze out as much liquid from the aubergine as possible. Place the flesh in a blender or food processor, then add the garlic, tahini, ground almonds, lemon juice and cumin, with salt to taste. Process to a smooth paste, then coarsely chop half the mint and stir into the dip.

5 Spoon the paste into a bowl, sprinkle the remaining mint leaves on top and drizzle with the olive oil. Serve at room temperature with the flatbread.

Hors d'Oeuvres

Set the mood with hors d'oeuvres that are delicious enough
to turn any meal into a party. From summery vegetarian
bruschetta to succulent mussels and from exotic smoked duck
wontons to tried-and-tested baked potatoes, there is the
perfect first course for every meal. Although they are sure
to impress your guests, you may be pleasantly surprised to
discover that many of these tasty appetizers are astonishingly
easy to prepare or can be made in advance, allowing you to
relax with your friends and a pre-dinner drink.

Marinated Mussels

This is an ideal recipe to prepare and arrange well in advance. Remove from the refrigerator about 15 minutes before serving to allow the flavours to develop fully.

INGREDIENTS

Makes about 48

1kg/2¼lb fresh mussels, large if possible (about 48)

175ml/6fl oz/¾ cup dry white wine

1 garlic clove, finely crushed

120ml/4fl oz/½ cup olive oil

50ml/2fl oz/¼ cup lemon juice

5ml/1 tsp hot chilli flakes

2.5ml/½ tsp mixed spice

15ml/1 tbsp Dijon mustard

10ml/2 tsp sugar

5ml/1 tsp salt

15–30ml/1–2 tbsp chopped fresh dill or coriander (cilantro)

15ml/1 tbsp capers, drained and chopped if large

ground black pepper

1 Scrub the mussels under cold running water to remove any sand and barnacles; pull out and remove the beards. Discard any open shells that will not shut when they are tapped and any mussels with damaged shells.

2 In a large casserole or pan set over a high heat, bring the white wine to the boil with the garlic and ground black pepper. Add the mussels and cover. Reduce the heat to medium and simmer for 2–4 minutes, until the shells open, stirring occasionally.

3 In a large bowl combine the olive oil, lemon juice, chilli flakes, mixed spice, Dijon mustard, sugar, salt, the chopped dill or coriander and the capers. Stir well, then set aside.

4 Discard any mussels with closed shells. With a small sharp knife, carefully remove the remaining mussels from their shells, reserving the half shells for serving. Add the mussels to the marinade. Toss the mussels to coat well, then cover and chill in the refrigerator for 6–8 hours or overnight, stirring occasionally.

5 With a teaspoon, place one mussel with a little marinade in each shell. Arrange on a platter and cover until ready to serve.

COOK'S TIP

Mussels can be prepared ahead of time and marinated for up to 24 hours. To serve, arrange the mussel shells on a bed of crushed ice, well-washed seaweed or even coarse salt to stop them wobbling on the plate.

Spinach Empanadillas

These are little pastry turnovers from Spain, filled with ingredients that have a strong Moorish influence – pine nuts and raisins. Empanadillas are also very popular throughout South America.

INGREDIENTS

Makes 20

25g/1oz/2 tbsp raisins

25ml/1½ tbsp olive oil

450g/1lb fresh spinach, washed and chopped

6 drained canned anchovies, chopped

2 garlic cloves, finely chopped

25g/1oz/⅓ cup pine nuts, chopped

1 egg, beaten

350g/12oz puff pastry, thawed if frozen

salt and ground black pepper

1 To make the filling, soak the raisins in a little warm water for 10 minutes. Drain, then chop coarsely. Heat the oil in a large sauté pan or wok, add the spinach, stir, then cover and cook over a low heat for about 2 minutes. Uncover, turn up the heat and let any liquid evaporate. Add the anchovies, garlic and seasoning, then cook, stirring, for a further minute. Remove from the heat, add the raisins and pine nuts, and cool.

2 Preheat the oven to 180°C/350°F/Gas 4. Roll out the pastry to a 3mm/⅛in thickness.

3 Using a 7.5cm/3in pastry cutter, cut out 20 rounds, re-rolling the dough if necessary. Place about two teaspoonfuls of the filling in the middle of each round, then brush the edges with a little water. Bring up the sides of the pastry and seal well.

4 Press the edges of the pastry together with the back of a fork. Brush with beaten egg. Place the turnovers on a lightly greased baking sheet and bake for about 15 minutes, until golden. Serve the empanadillas warm.

Prawn and Vegetable Crostini

Use bottled carciofini (tiny artichoke hearts preserved in olive oil) for this simple first course, which can be prepared very quickly.

INGREDIENTS

INGREDIENTS

Serves 4

450g/1lb unpeeled cooked
    prawns (shrimp)

4 slices of ciabatta, cut diagonally across

3 garlic cloves, peeled and
    2 halved lengthwise

60ml/4 tbsp olive oil

200g/7oz/2 cups small button (white)
    mushrooms, trimmed

12 drained bottled carciofini

60ml/4 tbsp chopped flat leaf parsley

salt and ground black pepper

1 Peel the prawns and remove the heads. Rub the ciabatta slices on both sides with the cut sides of the halved garlic cloves, drizzle with a little olive oil and grill (broil) until lightly browned.

2 Finely chop the remaining garlic. Heat the remaining oil in a frying pan and gently cook the chopped garlic until golden, but do not allow it to burn.

3 Add the mushrooms and stir to coat with oil. Season with salt and pepper and sauté for about 2–3 minutes. Gently stir in the drained carciofini, then add the chopped flat leaf parsley.

4 Season again, then stir in the prawns and sauté briefly to warm through. Pile the prawn mixture on to the ciabatta. Pour over any remaining cooking juices and serve immediately.

COOK'S TIP

Don't be tempted to use thawed frozen prawns, especially those that have been peeled. Freshly cooked prawns in their shells are infinitely nicer.

Sautéed Mussels with Garlic and Herbs

These mussels are served without their shells, in a delicious paprika-flavoured sauce. Eat them with cocktail sticks.

INGREDIENTS

Serves 4

900g/2lb fresh mussels

1 lemon slice

90ml/6 tbsp olive oil

2 shallots, finely chopped

1 garlic clove, finely chopped

15ml/1 tbsp chopped fresh parsley

2.5ml/½ tsp sweet paprika

1.5ml/¼ tsp dried chilli flakes

1 Scrub the mussels, discarding any damaged ones that do not close when tapped with a knife. Put the mussels in a large pan, with 250ml/8fl oz/1 cup water and the slice of lemon. Bring to the boil and cook for 3–4 minutes, removing the mussels as they open. Discard any that remain closed. Take the mussels out of the shells and drain on kitchen paper.

2 Heat the oil in a sauté pan, add the mussels and cook, stirring, for 1 minute. Remove from the pan. Add the shallots and garlic and cook, covered, over a low heat for about 5 minutes, or until soft. Remove the pan from the heat and stir in the parsley, paprika and chilli flakes.

3 Return the pan to the heat and stir in the mussels. Cook briefly. Remove from the heat and cover for 1–2 minutes, to let the flavours mingle, before serving.

Cannellini Bean and Rosemary Bruschetta

This variation on the theme of beans on toast makes an unusual but sophisticated hors d'oeuvre.

INGREDIENTS

Serves 6

150g/5oz/²⁄₃ cup dried cannellini beans

5 tomatoes

45ml/3 tbsp olive oil, plus extra
 for drizzling

2 sun-dried tomatoes in oil, drained and
 finely chopped

1 garlic clove, crushed

30ml/2 tbsp chopped fresh rosemary

12 slices Italian-style bread, such
 as ciabatta

1 large garlic clove

salt and ground black pepper

handful of fresh basil leaves, to garnish

1 Put the beans in a bowl, cover with water and soak overnight. Drain and rinse the beans, then place in a pan and cover with fresh water. Bring to the boil and boil rapidly for 10 minutes. Then lower the heat and simmer for about 1 hour, or until tender. Drain, return to the pan and keep warm.

2 Meanwhile, place the tomatoes in a bowl, cover with boiling water, leave for 30 seconds, then peel, seed and chop the flesh. Heat the oil in a frying pan, add the fresh and sun-dried tomatoes, garlic and rosemary. Cook for 2 minutes, until the tomatoes begin to break down and soften.

3 Add the tomato mixture to the cannellini beans and season to taste. Mix together well. Keep the bean mixture warm.

4 Rub the cut sides of the bread slices with the garlic clove, then toast them lightly. Spoon the cannellini bean mixture on top of the toast. Sprinkle with basil leaves and drizzle with a little extra olive oil before serving.

V

Mini Baked Potatoes with Blue Cheese

These miniature potatoes can be eaten with the fingers. They provide a great way of starting off an informal supper party.

Makes 20

20 small new or salad potatoes

60ml/4 tbsp vegetable oil

coarse salt

120ml/4fl oz/½ cup sour cream

25g/1oz blue cheese, crumbled

30ml/2 tbsp chopped fresh chives,
   to garnish

1 Preheat the oven to 180°C/ 350°F/Gas 4. Wash and dry the potatoes. Toss with the oil in a bowl to coat.

2 Dip the potatoes in the coarse salt to coat lightly. Spread the potatoes out on a baking sheet. Bake for 45–50 minutes, until the potatoes are tender.

3 In a small bowl, combine the sour cream and blue cheese, mixing together well.

COOK'S TIP

This dish works just as well as a light snack; if you don't want to be bothered with lots of small potatoes, simply bake an ordinary baking potato.

4 Cut a cross in the top of each potato. Press gently with your fingers to open the potatoes.

5 Top each potato with a spoon of the blue cheese mixture. Place on a serving dish and garnish with the chives. Serve hot or at room temperature.

Potato Skins with Cajun Dip

V

Divinely crisp and naughty, these potato skins are great on their own or served with this piquant dip as a garnish or on the side.

INGREDIENTS

Serves 4

2 large baking potatoes
vegetable oil, for deep-frying

For the dip
120ml/4fl oz/½ cup natural
    (plain) yogurt
1 garlic clove, crushed
5ml/1 tsp tomato purée (paste) or
    2.5ml/½ tsp green chilli purée
    or ½ small fresh green chilli,
    seeded and chopped
1.5ml/¼ tsp celery salt
salt and ground black pepper

1 Preheat the oven to 180°C/350°F/Gas 4. Bake the potatoes for 45–50 minutes, until tender. Cut them in half and scoop out the flesh, leaving a thin layer on the skins. Keep the flesh for another meal. Cut the potato skins in half once more.

2 To make the dip, mix together all the ingredients and chill.

3 Heat a 1cm/½in layer of oil in a pan or deep-fat fryer. Fry the potato skins until crisp and golden on both sides. Drain on kitchen paper, then sprinkle with salt and black pepper. Serve the potato skins with a bowl of dip or a spoon of the dip in each skin.

Asparagus with Salt-cured Ham

Serve this tapas when asparagus is plentiful and not too expensive.

INGREDIENTS

Serves 4

6 slices of Serrano ham

12 asparagus spears

15ml/1 tbsp olive oil

sea salt and coarsely ground black pepper

COOK'S TIP

If you can't find Serrano ham, use Italian prosciutto or Portuguese presunto.

1 Preheat the grill (broiler) to high. Cut each slice of ham in half lengthways and then securely wrap one half around each of the asparagus spears.

2 Brush the ham and asparagus lightly with oil and sprinkle with salt and pepper. Place on the grill rack. Grill (broil), turning frequently, for 5–6 minutes, until the asparagus is tender but still firm. Serve immediately.

King Prawns with Spicy Dip

*The spicy dip served with this dish is
equally good made from peanuts
instead of cashew nuts.*

Serves 4–6

24 raw king prawns (jumbo shrimp)
juice of ½ lemon
5ml/1 tsp paprika
1 bay leaf
1 fresh thyme sprig
vegetable oil, for brushing
salt and ground black pepper

For the spicy dip

1 onion, chopped
4 canned plum tomatoes, plus 60ml/4 tbsp
   of the juice
½ green (bell) pepper, seeded
   and chopped
1 garlic clove, crushed
15ml/1 tbsp cashew nuts
15ml/1 tbsp soy sauce
15ml/1 tbsp desiccated (dry unsweetened
   shredded) coconut

1 Peel the prawns, leaving the
tails on. Place in a shallow dish
and sprinkle with the lemon juice,
paprika and seasoning. Cover and
chill in the refrigerator.

2 Put the shells in a pan with the
bay leaf and thyme, cover with
water, then bring to the boil and
simmer for 30 minutes. Strain the
stock into a measuring jug (cup).
Top up with water, if necessary, to
300ml/½ pint/1¼ cups.

3 To make the spicy dip, place all
the ingredients in a blender or
food processor and process until
the mixture is smooth.

4 Pour into a pan with the
prawn stock and simmer over
a moderate heat for 30 minutes,
until the sauce is fairly thick.

5 Preheat the grill (broiler).
Thread the prawns on to small
skewers, then brush the prawns on
both sides with a little oil and grill
(broil) under a low heat until pink
and cooked, turning once. Serve
immediately with the dip.

COOK'S TIP

If unpeeled raw prawns are not
available, use cooked king prawns
instead. Just grill (broil) them for
a short time, until they are
completely heated through.

Charred Artichokes with Lemon Oil Dip

V

Here is a lip-smacking change from traditional fare.

INGREDIENTS

Serves 4

15ml/1 tbsp lemon juice or white
    wine vinegar

2 artichokes, trimmed

12 garlic cloves, unpeeled

90ml/6 tbsp olive oil

1 lemon

sea salt

flat leaf parsley sprigs, to garnish

1 Preheat the oven to 200°C/400°F/Gas 6. Add the lemon juice or vinegar to a bowl of cold water. Cut each artichoke into wedges. Pull the hairy choke out from the centre of each wedge and discard, then drop the wedges into the water.

2 Drain the wedges and place in a roasting pan with the garlic and 45ml/3 tbsp of the oil. Toss well to coat. Sprinkle with salt and roast for 40 minutes, until tender and a little charred.

COOK'S TIP

Artichokes are usually boiled, but dry-heat cooking also works very well. If you can get young artichokes, try roasting them over a barbecue.

3 Meanwhile, make the dip. Using a small, sharp knife thinly pare away two strips of rind from the lemon. Lay the strips of rind on a board and carefully scrape away any remaining pith. Place the rind in a small pan with water to cover. Bring to the boil, then lower the heat and simmer for 5 minutes. Drain the rind, refresh in cold water, then chop coarsely. Set aside.

4 Arrange the cooked artichokes on a serving plate and leave to cool for 5 minutes. Using the back of a fork gently flatten the garlic cloves so that the flesh squeezes out of the skins. Transfer the garlic flesh to a bowl, mash to a paste, then add the lemon rind. Squeeze the juice from the lemon, then, using a fork, whisk the remaining olive oil and the lemon juice into the garlic mixture. Garnish with the parsley. Serve the artichokes still warm with the lemon oil dip.

Rice Triangles

These rice shapes – Onigiri – are very popular in Japan. You can put anything you like in the rice, so you could invent your own onigiri.

INGREDIENTS

Serves 4

1 salmon steak

15ml/1 tbsp salt

450g/1lb/4 cups freshly cooked sushi rice

¼ cucumber, seeded and cut
 into thin batons

½ sheet yaki-nori seaweed, cut into four
 equal strips

white and black sesame seeds,
 for sprinkling

1 Grill (broil) the salmon steaks on each side, until the flesh flakes easily when tested with the tip of a sharp knife. Set aside to cool while you make other onigiri. When the salmon is cold, flake it, discarding any skin and bones.

2 Put the salt in a bowl. Spoon an eighth of the warm cooked rice into a small rice bowl. Make a hole in the middle of the rice and put in a few cucumber batons. Smooth the rice over to cover.

3 Wet the palms of both hands with cold water, then rub the salt evenly on to your palms.

4 Empty the rice and cucumbers from the bowl onto one hand. Use both hands to shape the rice into a triangular shape, using a firm but not heavy pressure, and making sure that the cucumber is completely encased by the rice. Make three more rice triangles in the same way.

5 Mix the flaked salmon into the remaining rice, then shape it into triangles as before.

6 Wrap a strip of yaki-nori around each of the cucumber triangles. Sprinkle sesame seeds on the salmon triangles.

COOK'S TIP

Always use warm rice to make the triangles. Allow them to cool completely and wrap each in foil or clear film (plastic wrap).

Sushi-style Tuna Cubes

These tasty tuna cubes are easier to prepare than classic Japanese sushi, but retain the same fresh taste.

Makes about 24

675g/1½lb fresh tuna steak

1 large red (bell) pepper, seeded and cut into 2cm/¾in pieces

sesame seeds, for sprinkling

For the marinade

15–30ml/1–2 tbsp lemon juice

2.5ml/½ tsp salt

2.5ml/½ tsp sugar

2.5ml/½ tsp wasabi paste

120ml/4 fl oz/½ cup olive or vegetable oil

30ml/2 tbsp chopped fresh coriander (cilantro)

For the soy dipping sauce

105ml/7 tbsp soy sauce

15ml/1 tbsp rice wine vinegar

5ml/1 tsp lemon juice

1–2 spring onions (scallions), finely chopped

5ml/1 tsp sugar

2–3 dashes hot chilli oil

1 Cut the tuna into 2.5cm/1in pieces and then arrange them in a single layer in a large non-metallic ovenproof dish.

2 Prepare the marinade. In a small bowl, stir the lemon juice with the salt, sugar and wasabi paste. Gradually, whisk in the oil until well blended and slightly creamy. Stir in the coriander. Pour over the tuna cubes and toss to coat. Cover and marinate for about 40 minutes in a cool place.

3 Meanwhile, prepare the soy dipping sauce. Combine all the ingredients in a small bowl and stir until well blended. Cover until ready to serve.

4 Preheat the grill (broiler) and line a baking sheet with foil. Thread a cube of tuna, then a piece of pepper on to each skewer and arrange on the baking sheet.

5 Sprinkle with sesame seeds and grill (broil) for about 3–5 minutes, turning once or twice, until just beginning to colour, but still pink inside. Serve with the soy dipping sauce.

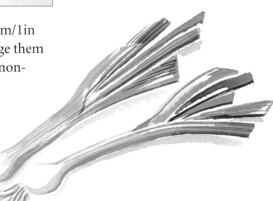

COOK'S TIP

Wasabi is a hot, pungent Japanese horseradish available in powder form (that has to be reconstituted) and as paste in a tube from gourmet and Japanese food stores.

King Prawns in Crispy Batter

Serve these delightfully crispy prawns with an Asian-style dipping sauce, or offer a simple tomato sauce or lemon wedges for squeezing.

INGREDIENTS

Serves 4

120ml/4fl oz/½ cup water

1 egg

115g/4oz/1 cup plain (all-purpose) flour

5ml/1 tsp cayenne pepper

12 raw king prawns (jumbo shrimp)

vegetable oil, for deep-frying

flat leaf parsley, to garnish

lemon wedges, to serve

For the dipping sauce

30ml/2 tbsp soy sauce

30ml/2 tbsp dry sherry

10ml/2 tsp clear honey

3 To make the dipping sauce, stir together the soy sauce, dry sherry and honey in a small bowl until well combined.

4 Heat the oil in a large pan or deep-fryer to 180°C/350°F or until a cube of day-old bread browns in 1 minute.

5 Holding the prawns by their tails, dip them into the batter, one at a time, shaking off any excess. Drop them carefully into the oil and fry for 2–3 minutes, until crisp and golden brown. Drain on kitchen paper and serve with the dipping sauce and lemon wedges, garnished with parsley.

1 In a large bowl, whisk the water with the egg. Add the flour and cayenne and whisk until smooth.

2 Carefully peel the prawns, leaving just the tail sections intact. Make a shallow cut down the back of each prawn, then pull out and discard the dark intestinal tract.

COOK'S TIP

Use leftover batter to coat thin strips of sweet potato, beetroot (beet), carrot or (bell) pepper, then deep-fry until golden.

Tandoori Chicken Sticks

This aromatic chicken dish is traditionally baked in a special clay oven called a tandoor. Here the chicken is grilled.

INGREDIENTS

Makes about 25

450g/1lb skinless, boneless chicken
    breast portions

For the coriander (cilantro) yogurt

250ml/8fl oz/1 cup natural (plain) yogurt

30ml/2 tbsp whipping cream

½ cucumber, peeled, seeded and
    finely chopped

15–30ml/1–2 tbsp fresh chopped mint
    or coriander (cilantro)

salt and ground black pepper

For the marinade

175ml/6fl oz/¾ cup natural (plain) yogurt

5ml/1 tsp garam masala or curry powder

1.5ml/¼ tsp ground cumin

1.5ml/¼ tsp ground coriander

1.5ml/¼ tsp cayenne pepper (or to taste)

5ml/1 tsp tomato purée (paste)

1–2 garlic cloves, finely chopped

2.5cm/1in piece fresh root ginger,
    finely chopped

grated rind and juice of ½ lemon

15–30ml/1–2 tbsp chopped fresh mint
    or coriander (cilantro)

1 Prepare the coriander yogurt. Combine all the ingredients in a bowl and season with salt and ground black pepper. Cover with clear film (plastic wrap) and chill until you are ready to serve.

2 Prepare the marinade. Place all the ingredients in the bowl of a food processor, and process until the mixture is smooth. Pour into a shallow dish.

3 Freeze the chicken for about 5 minutes to firm, then slice in half horizontally. Cut the slices into 2cm/¾in strips and add to the marinade. Toss to coat well. Cover and chill in the refrigerator for 6–8 hours or overnight.

4 Preheat the grill (broiler) and line a baking sheet with foil. Using a slotted spoon, remove the chicken from the marinade and arrange the pieces in a single layer on the baking sheet. Scrunch up the chicken slightly so it makes wavy shapes. Grill (broil), turning once, for 4–5 minutes until brown and just cooked. When it is cool enough to handle, thread pieces on to short skewers and serve with the coriander yogurt dip.

V

Thai Tempeh Cakes with Dipping Sauce

Made from soya beans, tempeh is similar to tofu but has a nuttier taste. Here, it is combined with a fragrant blend of lemon grass, coriander and ginger and formed into small patties.

INGREDIENTS

Makes 8 cakes

1 lemon grass stalk, outer leaves removed, finely chopped

2 garlic cloves, finely chopped

2 spring onions (scallions), finely chopped

2 shallots, finely chopped

2 fresh chillies, seeded and finely chopped

2.5cm/1 in piece fresh root ginger, finely chopped

60ml/4 tbsp chopped fresh coriander (cilantro), plus extra to garnish

250g/9oz/2¼ cups tempeh, thawed if frozen, sliced

15ml/1 tbsp lime juice

5ml/1 tsp caster (superfine) sugar

45ml/3 tbsp plain (all-purpose) flour

1 large (US extra large) egg, lightly beaten

vegetable oil, for frying

salt and ground black pepper

For the dipping sauce

45ml/3 tbsp mirin

45ml/3 tbsp white wine vinegar

2 spring onions (scallions), thinly sliced

15ml/1 tbsp sugar

2 fresh chillies, seeded and finely chopped

30ml/2 tbsp chopped fresh coriander (cilantro)

1 To make the dipping sauce, mix together the mirin, vinegar, spring onions, sugar, chillies, coriander and a large pinch of salt in a small bowl and set aside.

2 Place the lemon grass, garlic, spring onions, shallots, chillies, ginger and coriander in a food processor or blender, then process to a coarse paste.

3 Add the tempeh, lime juice and sugar, then process until thoroughly combined. Add the flour and egg and season well with salt and pepper. Process again until the mixture forms a fairly coarse, sticky paste.

4 Take a heaped serving spoonful of the tempeh paste mixture at a time and form into rounds with your hands. The mixture will be quite sticky.

5 Heat enough oil to cover the base of a large frying pan. Fry the tempeh cakes for 5–6 minutes, turning once, until golden. Drain on kitchen paper and serve warm with the dipping sauce, garnished with chopped fresh coriander.

Aromatic Tiger Prawns

There is no elegant way to eat these aromatic prawns – just hold them by the tails, pull them off the sticks with your fingers and pop them into your mouth.

INGREDIENTS

Serves 4

16 raw tiger prawns (jumbo shrimp) or
   scampi (extra large shrimp) tails
2.5ml/½ tsp chilli powder
5ml/1 tsp fennel seeds
5 Sichuan or black peppercorns
1 star anise, broken into segments
1 cinnamon stick, broken into pieces
30ml/2 tbsp groundnut (peanut) oil
2 garlic cloves, chopped
2cm/¾in piece fresh root ginger,
   finely chopped
1 shallot, chopped
30ml/2 tbsp rice vinegar
30ml/2 tbsp soft brown or palm sugar
salt and ground black pepper
lime slices and chopped spring onion
   (scallion), to garnish

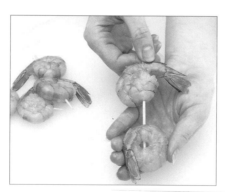

1 Thread the prawns or scampi tails in pairs on to 8 wooden cocktail sticks (toothpicks). Set aside. Heat a frying pan, put in all the chilli powder, fennel seeds, Sichuan or black peppercorns, star anise and cinnamon stick and dry-fry for 1–2 minutes to release the flavours. Leave to cool, then grind coarsely in a grinder or tip into a mortar and crush with a pestle.

2 Heat the groundnut oil in a shallow pan, add the garlic, ginger and chopped shallot and then cook gently until very lightly coloured. Add the crushed spices and seasoning and cook the mixture gently for 2 minutes. Pour in 30ml/2 tbsp water and simmer, stirring constantly, for 5 minutes.

3 Add the rice vinegar and soft brown or palm sugar, stir until dissolved, then add the prawns or scampi tails. Cook for about 3–5 minutes, until the seafood has turned pink, but is still very juicy. Serve hot, garnished with lime slices and spring onion.

COOK'S TIP

If you buy whole prawns, remove the heads before cooking them.

Duck Wontons with Spicy Mango Sauce

These Chinese-style wontons are easy to make using ready-cooked smoked duck or chicken, or even leftovers from the Sunday roast.

INGREDIENTS

Makes about 40

15ml/1 tbsp light soy sauce
5ml/1 tsp sesame oil
2 spring onions (scallions), finely chopped
grated rind of ½ orange
5ml/1 tsp brown sugar
275g/10oz/1½ cups chopped
    smoked duck
about 40 small wonton wrappers
15ml/1 tbsp vegetable oil
whole fresh chives, to garnish (optional)

For the mango sauce

30ml/2 tbsp vegetable oil
5ml/1 tsp ground cumin
2.5ml/½ tsp ground cardamom
1.5ml/¼ tsp ground cinnamon
250ml/8fl oz/1 cup mango purée (about
    1 large mango)
15ml/1 tbsp clear honey
2.5ml/½ tsp Chinese chilli sauce (or
    to taste)
15ml/1 tbsp cider vinegar
chopped fresh chives, to garnish

2 Stir in the mango purée, clear honey, chilli sauce and vinegar. Remove from the heat and leave to cool. Pour into a bowl and cover until ready to serve.

3 Prepare the wonton filling. In a large bowl, mix together the soy sauce, sesame oil, spring onions, orange rind and brown sugar until well blended. Add the duck and toss to coat well.

5 Preheat the oven to 190°C/ 375°F/Gas 5. Line a large baking sheet with foil and brush lightly with oil. Arrange the filled wontons in a single layer on the baking sheet and bake for about 10–12 minutes, until crisp and golden. Serve with the mango sauce garnished with chopped fresh chives. If you like, tie each wonton with a fresh chive.

1 First prepare the sauce. In a medium pan, heat the oil over a medium-low heat. Add the ground cumin, cardamom and cinnamon and cook for about 3 minutes, stirring constantly.

4 Place a teaspoonful of the duck mixture in the centre of each wonton wrapper. Brush the edges with water and then draw them up to the centre, twisting to seal and forming a pouch shape.

COOK'S TIP

Wonton wrappers, available in some large supermarkets and Asian food stores, are sold in 450g/1lb packets and can be stored in the freezer almost indefinitely. Remove as many as you need, keeping the rest frozen.

VEGETABLE
AND
CHEESE
STARTERS

~

You don't have to be a vegetarian to enjoy the recipes here.
In fact, many people prefer to serve a vegetable or cheese dish
as a first course to balance and offer a contrast to the
following meat or fish main course. If you are a vegetarian
or entertaining vegetarian guests, you will be spoilt for choice
with appetizers as diverse as terrines, risottos, tarts,
pies and fritters, all based on delicious fresh produce or
an international selection of cheeses.

V

Roast Pepper Terrine

This terrine is perfect for a dinner party because it tastes better if made ahead. Prepare the salsa on the day of serving. Serve with a warmed Italian bread, such as ciabatta or the flavoursome focaccia.

INGREDIENTS

Serves 8

8 (bell) peppers (red, yellow and orange)

675g/1½ lb/3 cups mascarpone cheese

3 eggs, separated

30ml/2 tbsp each coarsely chopped fresh
    flat leaf parsley and shredded fresh basil

2 large garlic cloves, coarsely chopped

2 red, yellow or orange (bell) peppers,
    seeded and coarsely chopped

30ml/2 tbsp extra virgin olive oil

10ml/2 tsp balsamic vinegar

a few fresh basil sprigs

salt and ground black pepper

1 Place the whole peppers under a hot grill (broiler), turning frequently, for 8–10 minutes. Then put them into a plastic bag, tie the top and leave until cold before peeling and seeding them. Chop seven of the peppers lengthways into thin strips.

2 Put the mascarpone cheese in a bowl with the egg yolks, herbs and half the garlic. Add salt and pepper to taste. Beat well. In a separate bowl, whisk the egg whites to soft peaks, then fold into the cheese mixture until they are evenly incorporated.

3 Preheat the oven to 180°C/350°F/Gas 4. Line the base of a lightly oiled 900g/2lb loaf tin (pan). Put one-third of the cheese mixture in the tin and spread level. Arrange half the pepper strips on top in an even layer. Repeat until all the cheese and peppers are used, ending with a layer of the cheese mixture.

4 Cover the tin with foil and place in a roasting pan. Pour in boiling water to come halfway up the sides of the loaf tin. Bake for 1 hour. Leave to cool in the water bath, then lift out and chill overnight.

5 A few hours before serving, make the salsa. Place the remaining peeled pepper and fresh peppers in a food processor. Add the remaining garlic, oil and vinegar. Set aside a few basil leaves for garnishing and add the rest to the processor. Process until finely chopped. Tip the mixture into a bowl, add salt and pepper to taste and mix well. Cover and chill until ready to serve.

6 Turn out the terrine, peel off the lining paper and slice thickly. Garnish with the reserved basil leaves and serve cold, with the sweet pepper salsa.

Asparagus and Egg Terrine

*For a special dinner this terrine is a
delicious choice, yet it is very light.
Make the hollandaise sauce well in
advance and warm through gently
when required.*

INGREDIENTS

Serves 8

150ml/¼ pint/⅔ cup milk

150ml/¼ pint/⅔ cup double
   (heavy) cream

40g/1½oz/3 tbsp butter

40g/1½oz/6 tbsp plain (all-purpose) flour

75g/3oz herbed or garlic cream cheese

675g/1½lb asparagus spears, cooked

a little oil

2 eggs, separated

15ml/1 tbsp chopped fresh chives

30ml/2 tbsp chopped fresh dill

salt and ground black pepper

fresh dill sprigs, to garnish

For the orange hollandaise sauce

15ml/1 tbsp white wine vinegar

15ml/1 tbsp fresh orange juice

4 black peppercorns

1 bay leaf

2 egg yolks

115g/4oz/½ cup butter, melted and
   cooled slightly

1 Put the milk and cream into a small pan and heat to just below boiling point. Melt the butter in a medium pan, stir in the flour and cook to a thick paste. Gradually whisk in the milk and beat to a smooth paste. Stir in the cream cheese, season to taste with salt and ground black pepper and leave to cool slightly.

2 Trim the asparagus to fit the width of a 1.2 litre/2 pint/ 5 cup loaf tin (pan) or terrine. Lightly oil the tin and then place a sheet of greaseproof (waxed) paper in the base, cut to fit. Preheat the oven to 180°C/350°F/Gas 4.

3 Beat the yolks into the sauce mixture. Whisk the whites until stiff and fold in with the chives, dill and seasoning. Layer the asparagus and egg mixture in the tin, starting and finishing with asparagus. Cover the top with foil.

4 Place the terrine in a roasting pan; half-fill with hot water. Cook for 50 minutes, until firm.

5 To make the sauce, put the vinegar, juice, peppercorns and bay leaf in a small pan and heat until reduced by half.

6 Cool the sauce slightly, then whisk in the egg yolks, then the butter, with a balloon whisk over a very gentle heat. Season to taste with salt and pepper and keep whisking until thick.

7 When the terrine is just firm to the touch, remove from the oven and allow to cool, then chill. Carefully invert the terrine on to a serving dish, remove the lining paper and garnish with the dill. Gently reheat the sauce over a pan of hot water. Cut the terrine into slices and pour over the sauce.

Vegetable Terrine

This colourful terrine uses all the vegetables of the Mediterranean.

INGREDIENTS

Serves 6

2 large red (bell) peppers, quartered and seeded
2 large yellow (bell) peppers, quartered and seeded
1 large aubergine (eggplant), sliced lengthways
2 large courgettes (zucchini), sliced lengthways
90ml/6 tbsp olive oil
1 large red onion, thinly sliced
75g/3oz/½ cup raisins
15ml/1 tbsp tomato purée (paste)
15ml/1 tbsp red wine vinegar
400ml/14fl oz/1⅔ cups tomato juice
15g/½oz/2 tbsp powdered gelatine or Gelozone
fresh basil leaves, to garnish

For the dressing
90ml/6 tbsp extra virgin olive oil
30ml/2 tbsp red wine vinegar
salt and ground black pepper

1 Place the peppers skin side up under a hot grill (broiler) until the skins are blackened. Transfer to a plastic bag and leave to cool.

2 Arrange the aubergine and courgette slices on separate baking sheets. Brush them with a little oil and cook under the grill, turning occasionally, until they are tender and golden.

3 Heat the remaining olive oil in a frying pan, and add the sliced onion, raisins, tomato purée and red wine vinegar. Cook gently until the mixture is soft and syrupy. Set aside and leave to cool in the frying pan.

4 Line a 1.75 litre/3 pint/7½ cup terrine with clear film (plastic wrap) – it helps if you lightly oil the terrine first – leaving a little hanging over the sides.

5 Pour half the tomato juice into a pan, and sprinkle with the gelatine or Gelozone. Dissolve gently over a low heat, stirring to prevent any lumps from forming.

6 Place a layer of red peppers in the base of the terrine, and pour in enough of the tomato juice mixture to cover. Add a layer of yellow peppers, followed by aubergine slices, then courgette slices and, finally, the onion mixture, pouring a little tomato juice mixture over each layer.

7 Continue layering all the vegetables, adding the tomato juice mixture to each layer and finishing with red peppers. Add the remaining tomato juice to the pan, and pour into the terrine. Give it a sharp tap, to disperse the juice. Cover and chill until set.

8 To make the dressing, whisk together the oil and vinegar, and season. Turn out the terrine and remove the lining. Serve in thick slices, drizzled with dressing and garnished with basil leaves.

COOK'S TIP

Ring the changes and use orange and green peppers along with or in place of the red and yellow ones. green beans, simply boiled first, would make a nice addition, as would a layer of peas or corn kernels.

Risotto Alla Milanese

This classic risotto is often served with the hearty beef stew, osso buco, but it also makes a delicious first course in its own right.

INGREDIENTS

Serves 5–6

about 1.2 litres/2 pints/5 cups Meat or
    Vegetable Stock
good pinch of saffron threads
75g/3oz/6 tbsp butter
1 onion, finely chopped
275g/10oz/1½ cups risotto rice
75g/3oz/1 cup freshly grated
    Parmesan cheese
salt and ground black pepper

1 Bring the stock to the boil, then reduce to a low simmer. Ladle a little stock into a small bowl. Add the saffron threads and leave to infuse (steep).

2 Melt 50g/2oz/4 tbsp of the butter in a large pan. Add the chopped onion and cook over a low heat for 3–5 minutes, stirring frequently, until softened and translucent, but not browned .

3 Add the rice. Stir until the grains start to swell and burst, then add a few ladlefuls of the stock, with the saffron liquid and salt and pepper to taste. Stir over a low heat until the stock has been absorbed. Add the remaining stock, a few ladlefuls at a time, allowing the rice to absorb all the liquid before adding more, and stirring constantly. After about 20–25 minutes, the rice should be just tender and the risotto golden yellow, moist and creamy.

4 Gently stir in about two-thirds of the grated Parmesan and the remaining butter. Gently heat through until the butter has melted, then taste and adjust the seasoning if necessary. Transfer the risotto to a warmed serving bowl or platter and serve immediately, with the remaining grated Parmesan served separately.

Risotto with Four Cheeses

This is a very rich dish. Serve it for a special dinner-party first course, with a light, dry sparkling white wine to accompany it.

INGREDIENTS

Serves 4–6

40g/1½oz/3 tbsp butter

1 small onion, finely chopped

1.2 litres/2 pints/5 cups Vegetable or
   Chicken Stock

350g/12oz/1¾ cups risotto rice

200ml/7fl oz/scant 1 cup dry white wine

50g/2oz/½ cup grated Gruyère cheese

50g/2oz/½ cup diced taleggio cheese

50g/2oz/½ cup diced Gorgonzola cheese

50g/2oz/⅔ cup freshly grated
   Parmesan cheese

salt and ground black pepper

chopped fresh flat leaf parsley, to garnish

1 Melt the butter in a large, heavy pan or deep frying pan and cook the onion over a gentle heat for about 4–5 minutes, stirring frequently, until softened and lightly browned. Pour the stock into a separate pan and heat it to simmering point.

2 Add the rice to the onion mixture, stir until the grains start to swell and burst, then add the wine. Stir until it stops sizzling and most of it has been absorbed by the rice, then pour in a little of the hot stock. Add salt and ground black pepper to taste. Stir the rice over a low heat until the stock has been absorbed.

3 Gradually add the remaining stock, a little at a time, allowing the rice to absorb the liquid before adding more, and stirring constantly. After about 20–25 minutes the rice will be *al dente* and the risotto will have a creamy consistency.

4 Turn off the heat under the pan, then add the Gruyère, taleggio, the Gorgonzola and 30ml/2 tbsp of the Parmesan. Stir gently until the cheeses have melted, then taste for seasoning. Spoon into a serving bowl and garnish with parsley. Serve the remaining Parmesan separately.

V

Baked Mediterranean Vegetables

Crisp and golden crunchy batter surrounds these vegetables, turning them into a substantial starter. Use other vegetables instead if you like.

INGREDIENTS

Serves 10–12

1 small aubergine (eggplant), trimmed, halved and thickly sliced

1 egg

115g/4oz/1 cup plain (all-purpose) flour

300ml/½ pint/1¼ cups milk

30ml/2 tbsp fresh thyme leaves, or 10ml/2 tsp dried thyme

1 red onion

2 large courgettes (zucchini)

1 red (bell) pepper

1 yellow (bell) pepper

60–75ml/4–5 tbsp sunflower oil

salt and ground black pepper

30ml/2 tbsp freshly grated Parmesan cheese and fresh herbs, to garnish

1 Place the aubergine in a colander or sieve, sprinkle generously with salt and leave in the sink for 10 minutes. Drain, rinse and pat dry on kitchen paper.

2 Meanwhile, to make the batter, beat the egg, then gradually beat in the flour and a little milk to make a smooth thick paste. Blend in the rest of the milk, add the thyme leaves and season to taste with salt and pepper. Blend until completely smooth. Leave in a cool place until required.

3 Quarter the onion, slice the courgettes and seed and quarter the peppers. Put the oil in a roasting pan and heat through in the oven at 220°C/425°F/Gas 7. Add all the vegetables, turn in the oil to coat them well and return to the oven for 20 minutes, until they start to cook.

4 Whisk the batter again, then pour it over the vegetables and return to the oven for 30 minutes. If well puffed up and golden, then reduce the heat to 190°C/375°F/Gas 5 and bake for 10–15 minutes more, until crisp around the edges. Sprinkle with Parmesan and herbs and serve immediately.

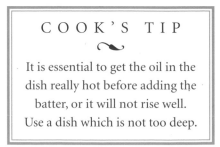

COOK'S TIP

It is essential to get the oil in the dish really hot before adding the batter, or it will not rise well. Use a dish which is not too deep.

Aubergine and Smoked Mozzarella Rolls

V

Slices of grilled aubergine are stuffed with smoked mozzarella, tomato and fresh basil to make an attractive hors d'oeuvre. The rolls are also good cooked on a barbecue.

INGREDIENTS

Serves 4

1 large aubergine (eggplant)

45ml/3 tbsp olive oil, plus extra for drizzling (optional)

165g/5½oz smoked mozzarella cheese, cut into 8 slices

2 plum tomatoes, each cut into 4 even-size slices

8 large basil leaves

balsamic vinegar, for drizzling (optional)

salt and ground black pepper

1 Cut the aubergine lengthways into 10 thin slices and discard the two outermost slices. Sprinkle the slices with salt and set them aside in a colander or sieve for 20 minutes. Rinse under cold running water, then pat dry with kitchen paper.

2 Preheat the grill (broiler) and line the rack with foil. Place the aubergine slices on the grill rack and brush liberally with oil. Grill (broil), turning once, for 8–10 minutes, until tender.

3 Remove the aubergine slices from the grill, then place a slice of mozzarella and tomato and a basil leaf in the centre of each aubergine slice, and season to taste. Fold the aubergine over the filling and cook, seam side down, under the grill until heated through and the mozzarella begins to melt. Serve drizzled with olive oil and a little balsamic vinegar, if using.

Marinated Feta Cheese with Capers

Marinating cubes of feta cheese with herbs and spices gives a marvellous flavour. Serve with toast.

INGREDIENTS

Serves 6

350g/12oz feta cheese

2 garlic cloves

2.5ml/½ tsp mixed peppercorns

8 coriander seeds

1 bay leaf

15–30ml/1–2 tbsp drained capers

fresh oregano or thyme sprigs

olive oil, to cover

hot toast, to serve

1 Cut the feta cheese into cubes. Thickly slice the garlic. Put the mixed peppercorns and coriander seeds in a mortar and crush lightly with a pestle.

2 Pack the feta cubes into a large preserving jar with the bay leaf, interspersing layers of cheese with garlic, crushed peppercorns and coriander, capers and the fresh oregano or thyme sprigs.

3 Pour in enough olive oil to cover the cheese. Close tightly and leave to marinate for 2 weeks in the refrigerator.

4 Lift out the feta cubes and serve on hot toast, with some chopped tomatoes and a little of the flavoured oil from the jar drizzled over.

COOK'S TIP

Add pitted black or green olives to the feta cheese in the marinade if you like.

Dolmades

V

If you can't locate fresh vine leaves,
use a packet or can of brined leaves.
Soak in hot water for 20 minutes,
then rinse and pat dry.

INGREDIENTS

Makes 20 to 24

24–28 fresh young vine (grape)
   leaves, soaked
30ml/2 tbsp olive oil
1 large onion, finely chopped
1 garlic clove, crushed
225g/8oz/2 cups cooked long grain rice, or
   mixed white and wild rice
about 45ml/3 tbsp pine nuts
15ml/1 tbsp flaked (sliced) almonds
40g/1½ oz/¼ cup sultanas
   (golden raisins)
15ml/1 tbsp chopped fresh chives
15ml/1 tbsp finely chopped fresh mint
juice of ½ lemon
150ml/¼ pint/⅔ cup white wine
hot Vegetable Stock
salt and ground black pepper
fresh mint sprig, to garnish
garlic yogurt and pitta bread, to serve

1 Bring a large pan of water to
the boil and cook the vine
leaves for about 2–3 minutes. They
will darken and go limp after
about 1 minute and simmering for
a further minute or so will make
sure that they are pliable. If using
packet or canned leaves, place in a
bowl, cover with boiling water and
leave for 20 minutes, until the
leaves can be separated easily.
Rinse and dry on kitchen paper.

2 Heat the oil in a small frying
pan and cook the onion and
garlic for 3–4 minutes over a gentle
heat until soft. Spoon the mixture
into a large bowl and add the
cooked rice. Stir to combine.

3 Stir in 30ml/2 tbsp of the pine
nuts, the almonds, sultanas,
chives and mint. Squeeze in the
lemon juice. Add salt and pepper
to taste and mix well.

4 Set aside four large vine leaves.
Lay a vine leaf on a clean work
surface, veined side uppermost.
Place a spoonful of filling near the
stem, fold the lower part of the
vine leaf over it and roll up, folding
in the sides as you go. Stuff the rest
of the vine leaves in the same way.

5 Line the base of a deep frying
pan with the reserved vine
leaves. Place the dolmades close
together in the pan, seam side
down, in a single layer. Pour over
the wine and enough stock just to
cover. Anchor the dolmades by
placing a plate on top of them,
then cover the pan and simmer
gently for 30 minutes.

6 Transfer the dolmades to a
plate. Cool, chill, then garnish
with the remaining pine nuts and
the mint. Serve with a little garlic
yogurt and some pitta bread.

V

Tomato and Courgette Timbales

Timbales are baked savoury custards typical of the South of France, and mainly made with light vegetables. This combination is delicious as an appetizer. It can be served warm or cool. Try other combinations, if you like.

INGREDIENTS

Serves 4

a little butter

2 courgettes (zucchini), about 175g/6oz

2 firm, ripe vine tomatoes, sliced

2 eggs plus 2 egg yolks

45ml/3 tbsp double (heavy) cream

15ml/1 tbsp fresh tomato sauce or passata (bottled strained tomatoes)

10ml/2 tsp chopped fresh basil or oregano or 5ml/1 tsp dried

salt and ground black pepper

salad leaves, to serve

1 Preheat the oven to 180°C/ 350°F/Gas 4. Lightly butter four large ramekins. Trim the courgettes, then cut them into thin slices. Put them into a steamer and steam over boiling water for 4–5 minutes. Drain well in a colander and, when cool enough to handle, layer the courgettes in the ramekins, alternating with the sliced tomatoes.

2 Whisk together the eggs, cream, tomato sauce or passata, herbs and seasoning. Pour the egg mixture into the ramekins. Place them in a roasting pan and half-fill with hot water. Bake the ramekins for 20–30 minutes, until the custard is just firm.

3 Cool slightly, then run a knife around the rims and carefully turn out on to small plates. Serve with salad leaves.

COOK'S TIP

Don't overcook the timbales or the texture of the savoury custard will become rubbery.

Wild Mushroom and Fontina Tarts

V

Italian fontina cheese gives these tarts a creamy, nutty flavour.

INGREDIENTS

Serves 4

25g/1oz/½ cup dried wild mushrooms

30ml/2 tbsp olive oil

1 red onion, chopped

2 garlic cloves, chopped

30ml/2 tbsp medium-dry sherry

1 egg

120ml/4fl oz/½ cup single (light) cream

25g/1oz fontina cheese, thinly sliced

salt and ground black pepper

rocket (arugula) leaves, to serve

For the pastry

115g/4oz/1 cup wholemeal (whole-
    wheat) flour

50g/2oz/4 tbsp unsalted (sweet) butter

25g/1oz/¼ cup walnuts, roasted
    and ground

1 egg, lightly beaten

1 To make the pastry, rub the flour and butter together until the mixture resembles fine breadcrumbs. Add the nuts, then the egg and mix to a soft dough. Wrap, then chill for 30 minutes.

2 Meanwhile, soak the dried wild mushrooms in 300ml/ ½ pint/1¼ cups boiling water for 30 minutes. Drain and reserve the liquid. Cook the onion in the oil over a low heat for 5 minutes, then add the garlic and cook for about 2 minutes, stirring frequently.

3 Add the soaked mushrooms and cook for 7 minutes over a high heat until the edges become crisp. Add the sherry and the reserved soaking liquid. Cook over a high heat for about 10 minutes, until the liquid evaporates. Season to taste and set aside to cool.

COOK'S TIP

You can prepare the pastry cases in advance, bake them blind for 10 minutes, then store in an airtight container for up to 2 days.

4 Preheat the oven to 200°C/ 400°F/Gas 6. Lightly grease four 10cm/4in tartlet tins (muffin pans). Roll out the pastry on a lightly floured work surface and use to line the tartlet tins.

5 Prick the pastry, line with greaseproof (waxed) paper and baking beans and bake blind for about 10 minutes. Remove the paper and the beans.

6 Whisk the egg and cream to mix, add to the mushroom mixture, then season to taste. Spoon into the pastry cases, top with cheese slices and bake for 18 minutes, until the filling is set. Serve warm with rocket.

V

Vegetable Tarte Tatin

This upside-down tart combines Mediterranean vegetables with rice, garlic, onions and olives.

INGREDIENTS

Serves 4

30ml/2 tbsp sunflower oil

about 25ml/1½ tbsp olive oil

1 aubergine (eggplant), sliced lengthways

1 large red (bell) pepper, seeded and cut into long strips

5 tomatoes

2 red shallots, finely chopped

1–2 garlic cloves, crushed

150ml/¼ pint/⅔ cup white wine

10ml/2 tsp chopped fresh basil

225g/8oz/2 cups cooked white or brown long grain rice

40g/1½oz/⅔ cup pitted black olives, chopped

350g/12oz puff pastry, thawed if frozen

ground black pepper

salad leaves, to serve

1 Preheat the oven to 190°C/375°F/Gas 5. Heat the sunflower oil with 15ml/1 tbsp of the olive oil and fry the aubergine slices for 4–5 minutes on each side. Drain on kitchen paper.

COOK'S TIP
~

Courgettes (zucchini) and mushrooms could be used as well, or use strips of lightly browned chicken.

---

2 Add the pepper strips to the oil remaining in the pan, turning them to coat. Cover the pan with a lid or foil and sweat the peppers over a moderately high heat for 5–6 minutes, stirring occasionally, until the pepper strips are soft and flecked with brown.

3 Slice two of the tomatoes and set them aside. Plunge the remaining tomatoes briefly into boiling water, then peel them, cut them into quarters and remove the core and seeds. Chop the tomato flesh coarsely.

4 Heat the remaining olive oil in the frying pan, add the shallots and garlic and cook over a low heat, stirring occasionally, for 3–4 minutes, until softened. Add the chopped tomatoes and cook for a few minutes, until softened. Stir in the wine and basil and season with black pepper to taste. Bring to the boil, then remove the pan from the heat and stir in the cooked rice and black olives.

5 Arrange the tomato slices, aubergine slices and peppers in a single layer on the base of a heavy, 30cm/12in, shallow ovenproof dish. Spread the rice mixture on top.

6 Roll out the pastry to a round slightly larger than the diameter of the dish and place on top of the rice, tucking the overlap down inside the dish.

7 Bake for 25–30 minutes, until the pastry is golden and risen. Cool slightly, then invert the tart on to a large, warmed serving plate. Serve in slices, with some salad leaves.

Lemon, Thyme and Bean Stuffed Mushrooms

Portabello mushrooms have a rich flavour and a meaty texture that go well with this fragrant herb-and-lemon stuffing. The garlicky pine nut accompaniment is a traditional Middle Eastern dish with a smooth, creamy consistency similar to that of hummus.

INGREDIENTS

Serves 4–6

200g/7oz/1 cup dried or 400g/14oz/2 cups
    drained, canned aduki beans
45ml/3 tbsp olive oil, plus extra
    for brushing
1 onion, finely chopped
2 garlic cloves, crushed
30ml/2 tbsp chopped fresh thyme or
    5ml/1 tsp dried thyme
8 large field mushrooms, such as
    portabello mushrooms, stalks
    finely chopped
50g/2oz/1 cup fresh wholemeal (whole-
    wheat) breadcrumbs
juice of 1 lemon
185g/6½ oz/¾ cup goat's
    cheese, crumbled
salt and ground black pepper

For the pine nut sauce
50g/2oz/½ cup pine nuts, toasted
50g/2oz/1 cup cubed white bread
2 garlic cloves, chopped
200ml/7fl oz/scant 1 cup milk
45ml/3 tbsp olive oil
15ml/1 tbsp chopped fresh parsley, to
    garnish (optional)

1 If using dried beans, place them in a bowl, add cold water to cover and soak overnight. Drain and rinse well. Place in a pan, add enough fresh water to cover and bring to the boil. Boil rapidly for 10 minutes, then reduce the heat and cook for about 1 hour, until tender, then drain. If using canned beans, rinse, drain well, then set aside.

2 Preheat the oven to 200°C/ 400°F/Gas 6. Heat the oil in a large, heavy frying pan, add the onion and garlic and cook for 5 minutes, until softened. Add the thyme and the mushroom stalks and cook for a further 3 minutes, stirring occasionally, until tender.

3 Stir in the beans, breadcrumbs and lemon juice, season well, then cook for 2 minutes, until heated through. Mash about two-thirds of the beans with a fork or potato masher.

4 Brush an ovenproof dish and the base and sides of the mushrooms with oil, then top each one with a spoonful of the bean mixture. Place the mushrooms in the dish, cover with foil and bake for 20 minutes. Remove the foil. Top each mushroom with some of the goat's cheese and bake for a further 15 minutes, or until the cheese is melted and bubbly and the mushrooms are tender.

5 To make the pine nut sauce, place all the ingredients in a food processor or blender and blend until smooth and creamy. Add more milk if the mixture appears too thick. Sprinkle with parsley, if using, and serve with the stuffed mushrooms.

Griddled Tomatoes on Soda Bread

V

Nothing could be simpler than this delightful appetizer, yet a drizzle of olive oil and balsamic vinegar and shavings of Parmesan cheese transform it into something really rather special.

INGREDIENTS

Serves 4

extra virgin olive oil, for brushing
    and drizzling
6 tomatoes, thickly sliced
4 thick slices soda bread
balsamic vinegar, for drizzling
salt and ground black pepper
freshly shaved Parmesan cheese,
    to serve

1 Brush a griddle pan with oil and heat. Add the tomato slices and cook them for 4 minutes, turning once, until softened and slightly blackened. Alternatively, heat the grill (broiler) to high and line the rack with foil. Grill (broil) the tomato slices for 4–6 minutes, turning once, until softened.

2 Meanwhile, lightly toast the soda bread. Place the tomatoes on top of the toast and drizzle each portion with a little olive oil and balsamic vinegar. Season to taste with salt and pepper and serve immediately with thin shavings of Parmesan cheese.

COOK'S TIP
～

Using a griddle pan reduces the amount of oil required for cooking the tomatoes which is useful for those watching their weight. It also gives them a delicious barbecue flavour.

V

Twice-baked Gruyère and Potato Soufflé

This recipe can be prepared in advance and given its second baking just before you serve it up.

INGREDIENTS

Serves 4

225g/8oz floury potatoes

2 eggs, separated

175g/6oz/1½ cups grated Gruyère cheese

50g/2oz/½ cup self-raising (self-rising) flour

50g/2oz spinach leaves

butter, for greasing

salt and ground black pepper

salad leaves, to serve

1 Preheat the oven to 200°C/ 400°F/Gas 6. Peel the potatoes and cook in lightly salted boiling water for 20 minutes, until very tender. Drain and mash with the egg yolks.

2 Stir in half of the Gruyère cheese and all of the flour. Season to taste with salt and ground black pepper.

VARIATION

For a different flavouring, try replacing the Gruyère with a crumbled blue cheese, such as Stilton or Shropshire Blue, which have a stronger taste.

3 Finely chop the spinach and fold into the potato mixture.

4 Whisk the egg whites until they form soft peaks. Fold a little of the egg white into the mixture to slacken it slightly. Using a large spoon, fold the remaining egg white into the mixture.

5 Grease four large ramekins. Pour the mixture into the dishes. Place on a baking sheet and bake for 20 minutes. Remove from the oven and leave to cool.

6 Turn the soufflés out on to a baking sheet and sprinkle with the remaining cheese. Bake for 5 minutes. Serve with salad leaves.

Risotto Frittata

V

*Half omelette, half risotto, this
makes a delightful and satisfying
appetizer. If possible, cook each
frittata separately, and preferably in
a small, cast-iron pan, so that the
eggs cook quickly underneath, but
stay moist on top. Or cook in one
large pan and serve in wedges.*

INGREDIENTS

Serves 4

30–45ml/2–3 tbsp olive oil

1 small onion, finely chopped

1 garlic clove, crushed

1 large red (bell) pepper, seeded and cut
   into thin strips

150g/5oz/³⁄₄ cup risotto rice

400–475ml/14–16fl oz/1²⁄₃–2 cups
   simmering Vegetable Stock

25–40g/1–1¹⁄₂ oz/2–3 tbsp butter

175g/6oz/2¹⁄₂ cups button (white)
   mushrooms, thinly sliced

60ml/4 tbsp freshly grated
   Parmesan cheese

6–8 eggs

salt and ground black pepper

1 Heat 15ml/1 tbsp oil in a large
frying pan and cook the onion
and garlic over a gentle heat for
2–3 minutes, until the onion
begins to soften but does not
brown. Add the pepper and cook,
stirring, for 4–5 minutes, until soft.

2 Stir in the rice and cook gently
for 2–3 minutes, stirring
constantly, until the grains are
evenly coated with oil.

3 Add a quarter of the vegetable
stock and season with salt and
pepper. Stir over a low heat until
the stock has been absorbed.
Continue to add more stock, a
little at a time, allowing the rice to
absorb the liquid before adding
more. Continue cooking in this
way for 20–25 minutes, until the
rice is *al dente*.

4 In a separate small pan, heat a
little of the remaining oil and
some of the butter and quickly
cook the mushrooms until golden.
Transfer to a plate.

5 When the rice is tender,
remove the pan from the heat
and stir in the cooked mushrooms
and the Parmesan cheese.

6 Beat the eggs with 40ml/8 tsp
cold water and season well with
salt and pepper. Heat the remaining
oil and butter in an omelette pan
and add the risotto mixture. Spread
the mixture out in the pan, then
immediately add the beaten egg
mixture, tilting the pan so that it is
evenly distributed. Cook the
omelette over a moderately high
heat for 1–2 minutes, then transfer
to a warmed plate and serve.

COOK'S TIP

Don't be impatient while cooking
the rice. Adding the stock
gradually guarantees a
wonderfully creamy consistency.

V

Leek and Onion Tartlets

Baking in individual tins makes for easier serving for an appetizer and it looks attractive too.

INGREDIENTS

Serves 6

25g/1oz/2 tbsp butter
1 onion, thinly sliced
2.5ml/¹⁄₂ tsp dried thyme
450g/1lb leeks, thinly sliced
50g/2oz Gruyère or Emmenthal
  cheese, grated
3 eggs
300ml/¹⁄₂ pint/1¹⁄₄ cups single
  (light) cream
pinch of freshly grated nutmeg
salt and ground black pepper
mixed salad leaves, to serve

For the pastry
175g/6oz/1¹⁄₃ cup plain (all-
  purpose) flour
75g/3oz/6 tbsp cold butter
1 egg yolk
30–45ml/2–3 tbsp cold water
2.5ml/¹⁄₂ tsp salt

1 To make the pastry, sift the flour into a bowl and rub in the butter with your fingertips until it resembles breadcrumbs. Make a well in the centre.

2 Beat the egg yolk with the water and salt, pour into the well and combine the flour and liquid until it begins to stick together. Form into a ball. Wrap and chill for 30 minutes.

3 Butter six 10cm/4in tartlet tins (muffin pans). On a lightly floured surface, roll out the dough until 3mm/¹⁄₈in thick, then using a 12.5cm/5in cutter, cut as many rounds as possible. Gently ease the rounds into the tins, pressing the pastry firmly into the base and sides. Re-roll the trimmings and line the remaining tins. Prick the bases all over and chill in the refrigerator for 30 minutes.

4 Preheat the oven to 190°C/375°F/Gas 5. Line the pastry cases with foil and fill with baking beans. Place on a baking sheet and bake for 6–8 minutes until golden at the edges. Remove the foil and beans and bake for a further 2 minutes until the bases appear dry. Transfer to a wire rack to cool. Reduce the oven temperature to 180°C/350°F/Gas 4.

5 In a large frying pan, melt the butter over a medium heat, then add the onion and thyme and cook for 3–5 minutes, until the onion is just softened, stirring frequently. Add the leeks and cook for 10–12 minutes, until they are soft and tender, stirring occasionally. Divide the leek mixture among the pastry cases and sprinkle each with cheese, dividing it evenly.

6 In a medium bowl, beat the eggs, cream, nutmeg and salt and pepper. Place the pastry cases (shells) on a baking sheet and pour in the egg and cream mixture. Bake for 15–20 minutes, until set and golden. Transfer the tartlets to a wire rack to cool slightly, then remove them from the tins and serve either warm or at room temperature with salad leaves.

Courgette Fritters with Chilli Jam

V

Chilli jam is hot, sweet and sticky –
rather like a thick chutney. It adds a
delicious piquancy to these light
courgette fritters which are always a
popular dish.

INGREDIENTS

Makes 12 Fritters

450g/1lb/3½ cups coarsely grated
  courgettes
50g/2oz/⅔ cup freshly grated
  Parmesan cheese
2 eggs, beaten
60ml/4 tbsp plain (all-purpose) flour
vegetable oil, for frying
salt and ground black pepper

For the chilli jam

75ml/5 tbsp olive oil
4 large onions, diced
4 garlic cloves, chopped
1–2 fresh green chillies, seeded and sliced
30ml/2 tbsp dark brown soft sugar

1 First make the chilli jam. Heat
the oil in a frying pan until
hot, then add the onions and the
garlic. Reduce the heat to low, then
cook for 20 minutes, stirring
frequently, until the onions are
very soft.

COOK'S TIP

Stored in an airtight jar in the
refrigerator, the chilli jam will
keep for up to 1 week

2 Leave the onion mixture to
cool, then transfer to a food
processor or blender. Add the
chillies and sugar and blend until
smooth, then return the mixture
to the pan. Cook for a further
10 minutes, stirring frequently,
until the liquid evaporates and the
mixture has the consistency of
jam. Cool slightly.

3 To make the fritters, squeeze
the courgettes in a dishtowel to
remove any excess liquid, then
combine with the Parmesan, eggs,
and flour and season to taste with
salt and pepper.

4 Heat enough oil to cover the
base of a large frying pan. Add
30ml/2 tbsp of the mixture for
each fritter and cook three fritters
at a time. Cook for 2–3 minutes on
each side until golden, then keep
warm while you cook the rest of
the fritters. Drain on kitchen paper
and serve warm with a spoonful of
the chilli jam.

V

Son-in-law Eggs

This fascinating name comes from a story about a prospective bridegroom who wanted to impress his future mother-in-law and devised a recipe from the only other dish he knew how to make – boiled eggs. The hard-boiled eggs are deep fried and then drenched with a sweet piquant tamarind sauce.

INGREDIENTS

Serves 4–6

75g/3oz/generous ⅓ cup palm sugar

60ml/4 tbsp light soy sauce

105ml/7 tbsp tamarind juice

oil, for frying

6 shallots, thinly sliced

6 garlic cloves, thinly sliced

6 fresh red chillies, seeded and sliced

6 hard-boiled eggs, shelled

fresh coriander (cilantro) sprigs,
   to garnish

lettuce, to serve

1 Combine the palm sugar, soy sauce and tamarind juice in a small pan. Bring to the boil, stirring until the sugar dissolves, then simmer the sauce for about 5 minutes.

2 Taste and add more palm sugar, soy sauce or tamarind juice, if necessary. It should be sweet, salty and slightly sour. Transfer the sauce to a bowl and set aside until needed.

3 Heat 30ml/2 tbsp of the oil in a frying pan and cook the shallots, garlic and chillies until golden brown. Transfer the mixture to a bowl and set aside.

4 Deep-fry the eggs in hot oil for 3–5 minutes, until golden brown. Drain on kitchen paper, quarter and arrange on a bed of lettuce. Sprinkle the shallot mixture over, drizzle with the sauce and garnish with coriander.

Fried Rice Balls Stuffed with Mozzarella

These deep-fried balls of risotto go by the name of Suppli al Telefono – *telephone wires – in their native Italy. Stuffed with mozzarella cheese, they are very popular snacks, which is hardly surprising as they are quite delicious. They make a wonderful start to any meal.*

INGREDIENTS

Serves 4

1 quantity Risotto alla Milanese, made without the saffron and with vegetable stock

3 eggs

breadcrumbs and plain (all-purpose) flour, to coat

115g/4oz/²⁄₃ cup mozzarella cheese, cut into small cubes

oil, for deep-frying

dressed frisée lettuce and cherry tomatoes, to serve

1 Put the risotto in a bowl and leave it to cool completely. Beat two of the eggs, and stir them into the cooled risotto until well mixed.

2 Use your hands to form the rice mixture into balls the size of a large egg. If the mixture is too moist to hold its shape well, stir in a few spoonfuls of breadcrumbs. Poke a hole in the centre of each ball with your finger, then fill it with small cubes of mozzarella, and close the hole over again with the rice mixture.

COOK'S TIP

These provide the perfect solution as to what to do with leftover risotto, as they are best made with a cold mixture, cooked the day before.

3 Heat the oil for deep-frying until a small piece of bread sizzles as soon as it is dropped in.

4 Spread some flour on a plate. Beat the remaining egg in a shallow bowl. Sprinkle another plate with breadcrumbs. Roll the balls in the flour, then in the egg, and, finally, in the breadcrumbs.

5 Fry the rice balls, a few at a time, in the hot oil until golden and crisp. Drain on kitchen paper and keep warm while the remaining balls are being fried. Serve immediately, with a simple salad of dressed frisée lettuce leaves and cherry tomatoes.

V

V

Greek Aubergine and Spinach Pie

Aubergines layered with spinach, feta cheese and rice make a flavoursome and dramatic filling for a pie. It can be served warm or cold in elegant slices.

INGREDIENTS

Serves 12

375g/13oz shortcrust (unsweetened)
    pastry, thawed if frozen
45–60ml/3–4 tbsp olive oil
1 large aubergine (eggplant), sliced
1 onion, chopped
1 garlic clove, crushed
175g/6oz spinach, washed
4 eggs
75g/3oz/½ cup crumbled feta cheese
40g/1½oz/½ cup freshly grated
    Parmesan cheese
60ml/4 tbsp natural (plain) yogurt
90ml/6 tbsp milk
225g/8oz/2 cups cooked white or brown
    long grain rice
salt and ground black pepper

2 Heat 30–45ml/2–3 tbsp of the oil in a frying pan and fry the aubergine slices for 6–8 minutes on each side, until golden. You may need to add a little more oil at first, but this will be released as the flesh softens. Lift out and drain well on kitchen paper.

3 Add the onion and garlic to the oil remaining in the pan, then cook over a gentle heat for 4–5 minutes, until soft, adding a little extra oil if necessary.

1 Preheat the oven to 180°C/ 350°F/Gas 4. Roll out the pastry thinly and use to line a 25cm/10in flan tin (quiche pan). Prick the base all over and bake for 10–12 minutes, until the pastry is pale golden. (Alternatively, bake blind, having lined the pastry with baking parchment and weighted it with a handful of baking beans.)

4 Chop the spinach finely, by hand or in a food processor. Beat the eggs in a large mixing bowl, then add the spinach, feta, Parmesan, yogurt, milk and the onion mixture. Season well with salt and ground black pepper and stir thoroughly to mix.

5 Spread the rice in an even layer over the base of the part-baked pastry case. Reserve a few aubergine slices for the top, and arrange the rest in an even layer over the rice.

6 Spoon the spinach and feta mixture over the aubergines and place the remaining slices on top. Bake for 30–40 minutes until lightly browned. Serve the pie while warm, or leave it to cool completely before transferring to a serving plate.

COOK'S TIP

Courgettes (zucchini) could be used in place of the aubergines. Cook the sliced courgettes in a little oil for 3–4 minutes, until evenly golden. You will need to use three to four standard courgettes, or choose baby courgettes instead and slice them horizontally.

FISH STARTERS

Fish is always a popular first course, not least because it is such a versatile ingredient. Recipes here range from elegant pâtés and terrines to crisp croquettes and tasty fish cakes. Dishes that are served cold can be made in advance, so they are ideal for entertaining, freeing you from the kitchen to greet your guests in the knowledge that there are no lingering fishy smells. On the other hand, the appetizing aroma as you cook Deep-fried Whitebait or Seafood Pancakes will make fish-lovers' mouths water with anticipation.

Potted Salmon with Lemon and Dill

This sophisticated dish would be ideal for a dinner party. Preparation is done well in advance, so you can concentrate on the main course, or if you are really well organized, you can enjoy a pre-dinner conversation with your guests. If you cannot find fresh dill use 5ml/1 tsp dried dill instead.

INGREDIENTS

Serves 6

350g/12oz cooked salmon, skinned
150g/5oz/⅔ cup butter, softened
rind and juice of 1 large lemon
10ml/2 tsp chopped fresh dill
salt and ground white pepper
75g/3oz/¾ cup flaked (sliced) almonds,
  coarsely chopped

1 Flake the salmon into a bowl and then place in a food processor together with two-thirds of the butter, the lemon rind and juice, half the dill, and plenty of salt and pepper. Process until the mixture is quite smooth.

2 Mix in the flaked almonds. Check the seasoning and pack the mixture into small ramekins.

3 Sprinkle the remaining dill over the top of each ramekin. Clarify the remaining butter, and pour over each ramekin to make a seal. Chill. Serve with crudités.

Salmon Rillettes

*This is an economical way of serving
a first course of salmon.*

INGREDIENTS

Serves 6

350g/12oz salmon fillets
175g/6oz/¾ cup butter, softened
1 celery stick, finely chopped
1 leek, white part only, finely chopped
1 bay leaf
150ml/¼ pint/⅔ cup dry white wine
115g/4oz smoked salmon trimmings
generous pinch of ground mace
60ml/4 tbsp fromage frais
   (farmer's cheese)
salt and ground black pepper
salad leaves, to serve

1 Lightly season the salmon.
Melt 25g/1oz/2 tbsp of the
butter in a medium sauté pan. Add
the celery and leek and cook for
about 5 minutes. Add the salmon
and bay leaf and pour the white
wine over. Cover and cook for
about 15 minutes, until tender.

2 Strain the cooking liquid into a
pan and boil until reduced to
30ml/2 tbsp. Cool. Meanwhile, melt
50g/2oz/4 tbsp of the remaining
butter and gently cook the smoked
salmon trimmings until pale pink.
Leave to cool.

3 Remove the skin and any
bones from the salmon fillets.
Flake the flesh into a bowl and add
the reduced, cooled cooking liquid.

4 Beat in the remaining butter,
with the ground mace and the
fromage frais. Break up the cooked
smoked salmon trimmings and
fold into the fresh salmon mixture
with all the juices from the pan.
Taste and adjust the seasoning.

5 Spoon the salmon mixture
into a dish or terrine and
smooth the top level. Cover with
clear film (plastic wrap) and chill.
The prepared mixture can be left
in the refrigerator for up to 2 days.

6 To serve the salmon rillettes,
shape the mixture into oval
quenelles using two dessert spoons
and arrange on individual plates
with the salad leaves. Accompany
the rillettes with brown bread or
oatcakes, if you like.

Smoked Salmon Pâté

Making this pâté in individual ramekins wrapped in extra smoked salmon gives a really special presentation. Taste the salmon pâté as you are making it, as some people prefer more lemon juice and salt and pepper.

INGREDIENTS

Serves 4

350g/12oz thinly sliced smoked salmon
150ml/¼ pint/⅔ cup double
   (heavy) cream
finely grated rind and juice of 1 lemon
salt and ground black pepper
Melba toast, to serve

1 Line four small ramekin dishes with clear film (plastic wrap). Then line the dishes with 115g/4oz of the smoked salmon cut into strips long enough to flop a little way over the edges.

2 In a food processor fitted with a metal blade, process the rest of the smoked salmon with the double cream, lemon rind and juice and season to taste with salt and plenty of pepper.

3 Pack the lined ramekins with the smoked salmon pâté and wrap over the loose strips of salmon. Cover with clear film and chill for 30 minutes. Invert on to plates and serve with Melba toast.

Brandade of Salt Cod

There are almost as many versions of this creamy salt cod purée as there are regions of France. Some contain mashed potatoes, others truffles. This fairly light recipe includes garlic, but you can omit it and serve the brandade on toasted slices of French bread rubbed with garlic.

INGREDIENTS

Serves 6

200g/7oz salt cod

250ml/8fl oz/1 cup extra virgin olive oil

4 garlic cloves, crushed

250ml/8fl oz/1 cup whipping or
    double (heavy) cream

ground white pepper

shredded spring onions (scallions),
    to garnish

herbed crispbread, to serve

1 Soak the fish in cold water for 24 hours, changing the water often. Drain. Cut into pieces, place in a shallow pan and pour in cold water to cover. Heat the water until simmering, then poach the fish for 8 minutes, until it is just cooked. Drain, then remove the skin and bone the cod carefully.

2 Combine the olive oil and garlic in a small pan and heat to just below boiling point. In another pan, heat the cream until it starts to simmer.

3 Put the cod into a food processor, process it briefly, then gradually add alternate amounts of the garlic-flavoured olive oil and cream, while keeping the machine running.

4 Once the mixture has the consistency of mashed potato, add white pepper to taste, then scoop the brandade into a serving bowl. Garnish with shredded spring onions and serve warm with herbed crispbread.

COOK'S TIP

You can purée the fish mixture in a mortar with a pestle. This gives a better texture, but is notoriously hard work.

Striped Fish Terrine

Serve this terrine cold or just warm, with a hollandaise sauce if you like.

INGREDIENTS

Serves 8

15ml/1 tbsp sunflower oil

450g/1lb salmon fillet, skinned

450g/1lb sole fillets, skinned

3 egg whites

105ml/7 tbsp double (heavy) cream

15ml/1 tbsp finely chopped fresh chives

juice of 1 lemon

115g/4oz/scant 1 cup fresh or frozen
    peas, cooked

5ml/1 tsp chopped fresh mint

salt, ground white pepper and
    grated nutmeg

thinly sliced cucumber, salad cress and
    whole chives, to garnish

1 Grease a 1 litre/1¾ pint/4 cup loaf tin (pan) or terrine with the oil. Slice the salmon thinly; cut it and the sole into long strips, 2.5cm/1in wide. Preheat the oven to 200°C/400°F/Gas 6.

2 Line the terrine neatly with alternate slices of salmon and sole, leaving the ends overhanging the edges. You should be left with about a third of the salmon and half the sole.

3 In a grease-free bowl, beat the egg whites with a pinch of salt until they form soft peaks. Process the remaining sole in a food processor. Spoon into a mixing bowl, season, then fold in two-thirds of the egg whites, followed by two-thirds of the cream. Put half the mixture into a second bowl and stir in the chives. Add nutmeg to the first bowl.

4 Process the remaining salmon, scrape it into a bowl and add the lemon juice. Fold in the remaining egg whites, then the remaining cream.

5 Process the peas with the mint. Season the mixture with salt and pepper and spread it over the base of the terrine, smoothing the surface with a spatula. Spoon over the sole with chives mixture and spread evenly.

6 Add the salmon mixture, then finish with the plain sole mixture. Cover the top with the overhanging fish fillets and make a lid of oiled foil. Stand the terrine in a roasting pan and pour in enough boiling water to come halfway up the sides.

7 Bake for 15–20 minutes, until the top fillets are just cooked and the terrine feels springy. Remove the foil, lay a wire rack over the top of the terrine and invert both rack and terrine on to a lipped baking sheet to catch the cooking juices that drain out. Keep these to make fish stock or soup.

8 Leaving the tin in place, let the terrine stand for about 15 minutes, then turn it over again, invert it on to a serving dish and lift off the tin carefully. Serve warm, or chill in the refrigerator first and serve cold. Garnish with thinly sliced cucumber, salad cress and chives before serving.

Sea Trout Mousse

*This deliciously creamy mousse
makes a little sea trout go a long
way. It is equally good made
with salmon if sea trout is
unavailable. Serve with crisp
Melba toast or toasted pitta bread.*

INGREDIENTS

Serves 6

250g/9oz sea trout fillet

120ml/4fl oz/½ cup Fish Stock

2 gelatine leaves, soaked in cold water, or
    15ml/1 tbsp powdered gelatine,
    softened in water for 5 minutes

juice of ½ lemon

30ml/2 tbsp dry sherry or dry vermouth

30ml/2 tbsp freshly grated Parmesan

300ml/½ pint/1¼ cups whipping cream

2 egg whites

15ml/1 tbsp sunflower oil, for greasing

salt and ground white pepper

For the garnish

5cm/2in piece of cucumber, with peel,
    thinly sliced and halved

fresh dill or chervil

1 Put the sea trout in a shallow
pan. Pour in the fish stock and
heat to simmering point. Poach
the fish for about 3–4 minutes,
until it is lightly cooked. Strain the
stock into a jug (pitcher) and leave
the trout to cool slightly.

2 Add the gelatine to the hot
stock and dissolve, according
to the packet instructions. Set aside
until required.

3 When the trout is cool enough
to handle, remove the skin and
flake the flesh. Pour the stock into a
food processor or blender. Process
briefly, then gradually add the
flaked trout, lemon juice, sherry or
vermouth and Parmesan through
the feeder tube, continuing to
process the mixture until it is
smooth. Scrape into a large bowl
and leave to cool completely.

4 Lightly whip the cream in a
bowl, then fold it into the cold
trout mixture. Season to taste, then
cover with clear film (plastic wrap)
and chill until the mousse is just
starting to set. It should have the
consistency of mayonnaise.

5 In a grease-free bowl, beat the
egg whites with a pinch of salt
until they are softly peaking. Then,
using a large metal spoon, stir
about one-third of the egg whites
into the sea trout mixture to
slacken it slightly, then fold in
the remainder.

6 Lightly grease six ramekins or
similar individual serving
dishes. Divide the mousse among
the dishes and level the surface.
Place in the refrigerator for
2–3 hours, until set. Just before
serving, arrange slices of cucumber
and a small herb sprig on top of
each mousse and sprinkle over a
little chopped dill or chervil too.

Ceviche

You can use almost any firm-fleshed fish for this South American dish, provided that is perfectly fresh. The fish is "cooked" by the action of the acidic lime juice. Adjust the amount of chilli according to your taste.

INGREDIENTS

Serves 6

675g/1½lb halibut, turbot, sea bass or
   salmon fillets, skinned

juice of 3 limes

1–2 fresh red chillies, seeded and very
   finely chopped

15ml/1 tbsp olive oil

salt

For the garnish

4 large tomatoes, peeled, seeded and diced

1 ripe avocado, peeled and diced

15ml/1 tbsp lemon juice

30ml/2 tbsp olive oil

30ml/2 tbsp fresh coriander
   (cilantro) leaves

1 Cut the fish into strips measuring about 5 x 1cm/ 2 x ½in. Lay these in a shallow, non-metallic dish and pour over the lime juice, turning the fish strips to coat them all over in the juice. Cover with clear film (plastic wrap) and leave for 1 hour.

2 Meanwhile, prepare the garnish. Mix together all the ingredients except the coriander leaves. Set aside.

3 Season the fish with salt and sprinkle over the chillies. Drizzle with the olive oil. Toss the fish in the mixture, then re-cover. Leave in the refrigerator to marinate for 15–30 minutes more. To serve, divide the garnish among six plates. Arrange the ceviche, then sprinkle with coriander.

Haddock and Smoked Salmon Terrine

This is a fairly substantial terrine, so serve modest slices, perhaps accompanied by fresh dill mayonnaise or a fresh mango salsa. Follow with a light main course and a fruit-based dessert.

INGREDIENTS

Serves 10–12

15ml/1 tbsp sunflower oil,
    for greasing
350g/12oz oak-smoked salmon
900g/2lb haddock fillets, skinned
2 eggs, lightly beaten
105ml/7 tbsp crème fraîche
30ml/2 tbsp drained capers
30ml/2 tbsp drained soft green or
    pink peppercorns
salt and ground white pepper
crème fraîche, peppercorns and fresh dill
    sprigs and rocket (arugula), to garnish

1 Preheat the oven to 200°C/ 400°F/Gas 6. Grease a 1 litre/ 1¾ pint/4 cup loaf tin (pan) or terrine with the sunflower oil. Use some of the smoked salmon to line the loaf tin or terrine, allowing some of the ends to overhang the edges. Reserve the remaining smoked salmon until required.

2 Cut two long slices of haddock the length of the tin or terrine and set aside. Cut the remainder of the haddock fillets into small pieces. Season all of the haddock with salt and ground white pepper to taste.

3 Combine the eggs, crème fraîche, capers and green or pink peppercorns in a bowl. Add salt and pepper; stir in the haddock pieces. Spoon the mixture into the mould until it is one-third full. Smooth the surface with a spatula.

4 Wrap the long haddock fillets in the reserved salmon. Lay them on top of the layer of the fish mixture in the tin or terrine.

5 Cover with the rest of the fish mixture, smooth the surface and fold the overhanging pieces of salmon over the top. Cover tightly with a double thickness of foil. Tap the terrine to settle the contents.

6 Stand the terrine in a roasting pan and pour in boiling water to come about halfway up the sides. Place in the oven and cook for 45 minutes–1 hour, until the filling is just set.

7 Take the terrine out of the roasting pan, but do not remove the foil cover. Place two or three large heavy cans on the foil to weight it and leave until cold. Chill in the refrigerator for 24 hours.

8 About an hour before serving, remove the terrine from the refrigerator, lift off the weights and remove the foil. Carefully invert on to a serving plate and garnish with crème fraîche, peppercorns and sprigs of dill and rocket leaves.

COOK'S TIP

Use any thick white fish fillets for this terrine; try cod, whiting, hake or hoki.

Smoked Haddock Pâté

Arbroath smokies are small haddock that are beheaded and gutted but not split before being salted and hot-smoked, creating a great flavour.

Serves 6

3 large Arbroath smokies, or smoked
    haddock fillets, about 225g/8oz each
275g/10oz/1¼ cups medium-fat
    soft cheese
3 eggs, beaten
30–45ml/2–3 tbsp lemon juice
ground black pepper
fresh chervil sprigs, to garnish
lemon wedges and lettuce leaves, to serve

1 Preheat the oven to 160°C/
325°F/Gas 3. Butter six
ramekin dishes.

2 Lay the smokies in a single
layer in an ovenproof dish and
heat through in the oven for
10 minutes. Carefully remove the
skin and bones from the smokies,
then flake the flesh into a bowl.

3 Mash the fish with a fork and
work in the cheese, then the
eggs. Add lemon the juice and
season with pepper to taste.

4 Divide the fish mixture among
the ramekins and place in a
roasting pan. Pour hot water into
the roasting pan to come halfway
up the dishes. Bake for 30 minutes,
until just set.

5 Leave to cool for 2–3 minutes,
then run a knife point around
the edge of each dish and invert on
to a warmed plate. Garnish with
chervil sprigs and serve with the
lemon wedges and lettuce.

Egg and Salmon Puff Parcels

*These crisp elegant parcels hide a
mouthwatering collection of flavours
and textures and make a delicious
appetizer or lunch dish.*

INGREDIENTS

Serves 6

75g/3oz/scant ½ cup long grain rice

300ml/½ pint/1¼ cups Fish Stock

350g/12oz piece salmon tail

juice of ½ lemon

15ml/1 tbsp chopped fresh dill

15ml/1 tbsp chopped fresh parsley

10ml/2 tsp mild curry powder

6 small (US medium) eggs, soft-boiled
    and cooled

425g/15oz flaky pastry, thawed if frozen

1 small (US medium) egg, beaten

salt and ground black pepper

1 Cook the rice in boiling fish
stock for 15 minutes. Drain
and set aside to cool. Preheat the
oven to 220°C/425°F/Gas 7.

2 Poach the salmon, then
remove the bones and skin and
flake the fish into the rice. Add the
lemon juice, herbs, curry powder
and seasoning and mix well. Peel
the soft-boiled eggs.

COOK'S TIP

~

You can also add a spoonful of
cooked chopped fresh or frozen
spinach to each parcel.

3 Roll out the pastry and cut
into six 14–15cm/5½–6in
squares. Brush the edges with the
beaten egg. Place a spoonful of rice
in the middle of each square, push
an egg into the middle and top
with a little more rice.

4 Pull over the pastry corners to
the middle to form a square
parcel, squeezing the joins together
well to seal. Brush with more egg,
place on a baking sheet and bake
the puffs for 20 minutes, then
reduce the oven temperature to
190°C/375°F/Gas 5 and cook the
puffs for a further 10 minutes, or
until golden and crisp underneath.

5 Cool slightly before serving,
with a curry flavoured
mayonnaise or hollandaise sauce,
if you like.

Seafood Pancakes

The combination of fresh and smoked haddock imparts a wonderful flavour to the filling.

INGREDIENTS

Serves 6
For the pancakes
115g/4oz/1 cup plain (all-purpose) flour
pinch of salt
1 egg plus 1 egg yolk
300ml/½ pint/1¼ cups milk
15ml/1 tbsp melted butter, plus extra
   for cooking
50–75g/2–3oz/½–¾ cup grated
   Gruyère cheese
frisée lettuce, to serve

For the filling
225g/8oz smoked haddock fillet
225g/8oz fresh haddock fillet
300ml/½ pint/1¼ cups milk
150ml/¼ pint/⅔ cup single (light) cream
40g/1½ oz/3 tbsp butter
60 ml/4 tbsp plain (all-purpose) flour
freshly grated nutmeg
2 hard-boiled eggs, peeled and chopped
salt and ground black pepper

1 To make the pancakes, sift the flour and salt into a bowl. Make a well in the centre and add the egg and yolk. Whisk the egg, starting to incorporate the flour.

2 Gradually add the milk, whisking constantly until the batter is smooth and has the consistency of thin cream. Stir in the measured melted butter.

3 Heat a small crêpe pan or omelette pan until hot, then rub around the inside of the pan with a pad of kitchen paper dipped in melted butter.

4 Pour about 30ml/2 tbsp of the batter into the pan, then tip the pan to coat the base evenly. Cook for about 30 seconds, until the underside of the pancake is brown.

5 Flip the pancake over and cook on the other side until it is lightly browned. Repeat to make 12 pancakes, rubbing the pan with melted butter between each pancake. Stack the pancakes as you make them between sheets of greaseproof (waxed) paper. Keep warm on a plate set over a pan of simmering water.

6 Put the haddock fillets in a large pan. Add the milk and poach for 6–8 minutes, until just tender. Lift out the fish using a slotted spoon and, when cool enough to handle, remove the skin and any bones. Reserve the milk.

7 Measure the single cream into a measuring jug or cup, then strain enough of the reserved milk into the cream to make up the quantity to 450ml/¾ pint/scant 2 cups in total.

8 Melt the butter in a pan, stir in the flour and cook gently for 1 minute. Gradually mix in the milk mixture, stirring constantly. Cook for 2–3 minutes, until thickened. Season with salt, black pepper and nutmeg. Coarsely flake the haddock and fold into the sauce with the eggs. Leave to cool.

9 Preheat the oven to 180°C/ 350°F/Gas 4. Divide the filling among the pancakes. Fold the sides of each pancake into the centre, then roll them up to enclose the filling completely.

10 Butter six individual ovenproof dishes and then arrange two filled pancakes in each, or butter one large dish for all the pancakes. Brush with melted butter and cook for 15 minutes. Sprinkle over the Gruyère and cook for a further 5 minutes, until warmed through. Serve hot with frisée lettuce leaves.

Three-colour Fish Kebabs

Don't leave the fish to marinate for more than an hour. The lemon juice will start to break down the protein fibres of the fish after this time and it will then be difficult to avoid overcooking it.

INGREDIENTS

Serves 4

120ml/4fl oz/½ cup olive oil

finely grated rind and juice of
   1 large lemon

5ml/1 tsp crushed chilli flakes

350g/12oz monkfish fillet, cubed

350g/12oz swordfish fillet, cubed

350g/12oz thick salmon fillet or
   steak, cubed

2 red, yellow or orange (bell) peppers,
   seeded and cut into squares

30ml/2 tbsp finely chopped fresh flat
   leaf parsley

salt and ground black pepper

For the sweet tomato and chilli salsa

225g/8oz ripe tomatoes, finely chopped

1 garlic clove, crushed

1 fresh red chilli, seeded and chopped

45ml/3 tbsp extra virgin olive oil

15ml/1 tbsp lemon juice

15ml/1 tbsp finely chopped fresh flat
   leaf parsley

pinch of sugar

1 Put the olive oil in a shallow glass or china dish and add the lemon rind and juice, the chilli flakes and pepper to taste. Whisk to combine, then add the fish chunks. Turn to coat evenly.

2 Add the pepper squares, stir, then cover with clear film (plastic wrap) and marinate in a cool place for 1 hour, turning the fish chunks occasionally with a slotted spoon.

3 Drain the fish and peppers, reserving the marinade. Thread the fish and peppers on to eight oiled metal skewers. Cook the skewered fish on a barbecue or under a grill (broiler) for 5–8 minutes, turning once.

4 Meanwhile, make the salsa by mixing all the ingredients in a bowl, and seasoning to taste with salt and pepper.

5 Heat the reserved marinade in a small pan, remove from the heat and stir in the parsley, then season with salt and pepper to taste. Serve the kebabs hot, with the marinade spooned over and accompanied by the salsa.

> ### COOK'S TIP
>
> Use tuna instead of swordfish, if you like. It has a similar meaty texture and will be equally tasty and successful.

Deep-fried Whitebait

A spicy coating on these fish gives this favourite dish a crunchy bite.

INGREDIENTS

Serves 6

115g/4oz/1 cup plain (all-purpose) flour
2.5ml/½ tsp curry powder
2.5ml/½ tsp ground ginger
2.5ml/½ tsp cayenne pepper
pinch of salt
1.2kg/2½ lb whitebait, thawed if frozen
vegetable oil, for deep-frying
lemon wedges, to garnish

1 Mix together the plain flour, curry powder, ground ginger, cayenne pepper and a little salt in a large bowl.

2 Coat the fish in the seasoned flour, covering them evenly and shaking off any excess.

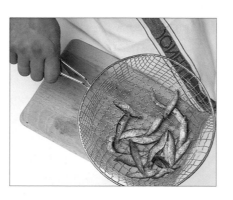

3 Heat the oil in a large, heavy pan until it reaches a temperature of 190°C/375°F. Deep-fry the whitebait, in batches, for about 2–3 minutes, until the fish is golden and crisp.

4 Drain the whitebait well on kitchen paper. Keep warm in a low oven until you have cooked all the fish. Serve immediately, garnished with lemon wedges for squeezing over.

Smoked Salmon and Rice Salad Parcels

Feta, cucumber and tomatoes give a Greek flavour to the salad in these parcels, a combination which goes well with the rice, especially if a little wild rice is added.

INGREDIENTS

Serves 4

175g/6oz/scant 1 cup mixed wild rice and basmati rice

8 slices smoked salmon, total weight about 350g/12oz

10cm/4in piece of cucumber, finely diced

about 225g/8oz feta cheese, cubed

8 cherry tomatoes, quartered

30ml/2 tbsp mayonnaise

10ml/2 tsp fresh lime juice

15ml/1 tbsp chopped fresh chervil

salt and ground black pepper

lime slices and fresh chervil, to garnish

1 Cook the rice according to the instructions on the packet. Drain, tip into a bowl and leave to cool completely.

2 Line four ramekins with clear film (plastic wrap), then line each ramekin with two slices of smoked salmon, allowing the ends to overlap the edges of the dishes.

COOK'S TIP

Use smoked sea trout in place of the salmon if you like.

---

3 Add the cucumber, feta and tomatoes to the rice and stir in the mayonnaise, lime juice and chervil. Mix together well. Season with salt and ground black pepper to taste.

4 Spoon the rice mixture into the salmon-lined ramekins. (Any leftover mixture can be used to make a rice salad.) Then fold over the overlapping ends of salmon so that the rice mixture is completely encased.

5 Place the fish parcels in the refrigerator to chill for 30–60 minutes, then invert each parcel on to a plate, using the clear film to ease them out of the ramekins. Carefully peel off the clear film, then garnish each parcel with slices of lime and a sprig of fresh chervil and serve.

Thai Fish Cakes with Cucumber Relish

These wonderful small fish cakes are very familiar and popular. They are usually accompanied with Thai beer or you could choose a robust, oaked Chardonnay instead.

INGREDIENTS

Makes about 12

300g/11oz white fish fillet, such as cod, cut into chunks
30ml/2 tbsp Thai red curry paste
1 egg
30ml/2 tbsp Thai fish sauce
5ml/1 tsp granulated sugar
30ml/2 tbsp cornflour (cornstarch)
3 kaffir lime leaves, shredded
15ml/1 tbsp chopped fresh coriander (cilantro)
50g/2oz green beans, thinly sliced
vegetable oil, for frying
Chinese mustard cress, to garnish

For the cucumber relish
60ml/4 tbsp Thai coconut or rice vinegar
60ml/4 tbsp water
50g/2oz sugar
1 bulb pickled garlic
1 cucumber, quartered and sliced
4 shallots, thinly sliced
15ml/1 tbsp chopped fresh root ginger

1 To make the relish, bring the vinegar, water and sugar to the boil. Stir until the sugar dissolves, then set aside to cool.

2 Combine the rest of the relish ingredients together in a bowl and pour the vinegar mixture over.

3 Combine the fish, curry paste and egg in a food processor and process well. Transfer the mixture to a bowl, add the rest of the ingredients, except the oil and garnish, and mix well.

4 Mould and shape the mixture into cakes about 5cm/2in in diameter and 5mm/¼in thick.

5 Heat the oil in a wok or deep-fat fryer. Deep-fry the fish cakes, working in small batches, for about 4–5 minutes, or until golden brown. Remove and drain on kitchen paper. Keep warm in a low oven. Garnish with Chinese mustard cress and serve with a little cucumber relish spooned on the side.

Salmon Cakes with Butter Sauce

Salmon fish cakes make a real treat for the start of a dinner party. They are also economical, as you could use any small tail pieces which are on special offer.

INGREDIENT

Makes 6

225g/8oz salmon tail piece, cooked

30ml/2 tbsp chopped fresh parsley

2 spring onions (scallions), trimmed
   and chopped

grated rind and juice of ½ lemon

225g/8oz mashed potato (not too soft)

1 egg, beaten

50g/2oz/1 cup fresh white breadcrumbs

75g/3oz/6 tbsp butter, plus extra for
   frying (optional)

vegetable oil, for frying (optional)

salt and ground black pepper

courgette and carrot slices and fresh
   coriander (cilantro) sprigs, to garnish

1 Remove all the skin and bones from the fish and mash or flake it well. Add the fresh parsley, spring onions and 5ml/1 tsp of the lemon rind, and season with salt and lots of black pepper.

2 Gently work in the potato and then shape into six rounds, triangles or croquettes. Chill the salmon cakes for 20 minutes.

3 Preheat the grill (broiler). When chilled, coat the salmon cakes well in beaten egg and then in the breadcrumbs. Grill (broil) gently for 5 minutes on each side, or until they are golden, or fry in a mixture of butter and oil.

4 To make the butter sauce, melt the butter, whisk in the remaining lemon rind, the lemon juice, 15–30ml/1–2 tbsp water and seasoning to taste. Simmer for a few minutes and serve with the hot fish cakes, garnished with slices of courgette and carrot and a sprig of fresh coriander.

Herbed Plaice Croquettes

Serve these baby croquettes with a tartare sauce if you like. Simply chop some capers and gherkins, and stir into home-made or good quality store-bought mayonnaise. Season to taste with salt and pepper.

INGREDIENTS

Serves 4

450g/1lb plaice or flounder fillets

300ml/½ pint/1¼ cups milk

450g/1lb cooked potatoes

1 fennel bulb, finely chopped

45ml/3 tbsp chopped fresh parsley

2 eggs

15g/½oz/1 tbsp unsalted (sweet) butter

250g/9oz/2 cups white breadcrumbs

25g/1oz/2 tbsp sesame seeds

vegetable oil, for deep-frying

salt and ground black pepper

1 Gently poach the fish fillets in the milk for about 15 minutes, until the flesh flakes easily. Drain and reserve the milk.

2 Peel the skin off the fish and remove any bones. In a food processor fitted with a metal blade, process the fish, potatoes, fennel, parsley, eggs and butter.

3 Add 30ml/2 tbsp of the reserved cooking milk and season with salt and plenty of ground black pepper. Mix well. Chill for 30 minutes, then shape into twenty even-size croquettes with your hands.

4 Mix together the breadcrumbs and sesame seeds, then roll the croquettes in this mixture to form a good coating. Heat the oil in a large, heavy pan to 190°C/375°F or until it is hot enough to brown a cube of stale bread in 30 seconds. Deep-fry the croquettes, in small batches, for about 4 minutes, until they are golden brown all over. Drain well on kitchen paper and serve the croquettes hot.

Fish Sausages

This recipe originated in Hungary during the seventeenth century. It is still popular today..

INGREDIENTS

Serves 4

375g/13oz fish fillets, such as perch, pike, carp or cod, skinned

1 white bread roll

75ml/5 tbsp milk

25ml/1½ tbsp chopped fresh flat leaf parsley

2 eggs, well beaten

50g/2oz/½ cup plain (all-purpose) flour

50g/2oz/1 cup fine fresh white breadcrumbs

vegetable oil, for shallow frying

salt and ground black pepper

deep-fried fresh parsley sprigs and lemon wedges, dusted with paprika, to garnish

1 Mince (grind) or process the fish fillets coarsely in a food processor or blender. Soak the roll in the milk for about 10 minutes, then squeeze it out. Mix the fish and bread together before adding the chopped parsley, one of the eggs and plenty of seasoning.

2 Using your fingers, shape the fish mixture into 10cm/4in long sausages, making them about 2.5cm/1in thick.

3 Carefully roll the fish "sausages" in the flour, then in the remaining egg and finally in the breadcrumbs.

4 Heat the oil in a pan, then gently cook the "sausages" until golden brown all over. (You may need to work in batches.) Drain well on crumpled kitchen paper. Garnish with the deep-fried parsley sprigs and lemon wedges dusted with paprika.

Breaded Sole Batons

Goujons of lemon sole are coated in seasoned flour and then in breadcrumbs, and fried until deliciously crisp. They are served with piquant tartare sauce.

INGREDIENTS

Serves 4

275g/10oz lemon sole fillets, skinned

2 eggs

115g/4oz/1½ cups fine fresh breadcrumbs

75g/3oz/6 tbsp plain (all-purpose) flour

salt and ground black pepper

vegetable oil, for frying

tartare sauce and lemon wedges, to serve

1 Cut the fish fillets into long diagonal strips about 2cm/¾in wide, using a sharp knife.

2 Break the eggs into a shallow dish and beat well with a fork. Place the breadcrumbs in another shallow dish. Put the flour in a large plastic bag and season with salt and plenty of freshly ground black pepper.

3 Dip the fish strips in the egg, turning to coat well. Place on a plate and then, taking a few at a time, shake them in the bag of flour. Dip the fish strips in the egg again, then in the breadcrumbs, turning to coat well. Place on a tray in a single layer, not touching. Place in the refrigerator and let the coating set for at least 10 minutes.

4 Heat 1cm/½in oil in a large frying pan over a medium-high heat. When the oil is hot (a cube of bread will sizzle), fry the fish strips for 2–2½ minutes, in batches, turning once, taking care not to overcrowd the pan. Drain on kitchen paper and keep warm. Serve the fish with tartare sauce and lemon wedges.

SHELLFISH STARTERS

~

For sheer visual appeal, shellfish appetizers are hard to beat.
There is little more tempting than a plate – or skewer – full
of plump, succulent sizzling prawns (shrimp) and there is a
uniquely naughty pleasure found in the delightful messiness
of peeling them at the table. For more formal occasions and
for those with more sophisticated table manners, serve creamy
crab meat, delicately flavoured scallops or a delicious shellfish
mousse. Even that old favourite, Prawn Cocktail, has a
fabulous, new, contemporary treatment.

Prawn Cocktail

There is no nicer appetizer than a good, fresh prawn cocktail – and nothing nastier than one in which soggy prawns swim in a thin, vinegary sauce embedded in limp lettuce. This recipe shows just how good a prawn cocktail can be.

INGREDIENTS

Serves 6

60ml/4 tbsp double (heavy) cream, lightly whipped

60ml/4 tbsp mayonnaise

60ml/4 tbsp tomato ketchup

5–10ml/1–2 tsp Worcestershire sauce

juice of 1 lemon

½ cos, romaine or other very crisp lettuce

450g/1lb/4 cups cooked peeled prawns (shrimp)

salt, ground black pepper and paprika

6 large whole cooked unpeeled prawns (shrimp), to garnish (optional)

thinly sliced brown bread and lemon wedges, to serve

1 In a bowl, mix together the whipped cream, mayonnaise and tomato ketchup. Stir in Worcestershire sauce to taste, then stir in enough lemon juice to make a really tangy cocktail sauce.

2 Finely shred the lettuce and fill six individual glasses one-third full. Stir the prawns into the sauce, then check the seasoning. Spoon the prawn mixture generously over the lettuce.

3 If you like, drape a whole cooked prawn over the edge of each glass (see Cook's Tip). Sprinkle each of the cocktails with ground black pepper and some paprika. Serve immediately, with thinly sliced brown bread and butter and lemon wedges for squeezing over.

> ### COOK'S TIP
> To prepare the garnish, peel the body shell from the prawns and leave the tail "fan" for decoration.

Piquant Prawn Salad

The Thai-inspired dressing, which includes fish sauce and sesame oil, adds a superb flavour to the rice noodles and tiger prawns. This delicious salad can be served warm; or alternatively, chill before serving.

INGREDIENTS

Serves 6

200g/7oz rice vermicelli or stir-fry
   rice noodles

8 baby corn cobs, halved

150g/5oz mangetouts (snow peas)

15ml/1 tbsp sunflower oil

2 garlic cloves, finely chopped

2.5cm/1in piece of fresh root ginger,
   finely chopped

1 fresh red or green chilli, seeded and
   finely chopped

450g/1lb raw peeled tiger prawns
   (jumbo shrimp)

4 spring onions (scallions), thinly sliced

15ml/1 tbsp sesame seeds, toasted

1 lemon grass stalk, thinly shredded,
   to garnish

For the dressing

15ml/1 tbsp chopped fresh chives

15ml/1 tbsp Thai fish sauce

5ml/1 tsp soy sauce

45ml/3 tbsp groundnut (peanut) oil

5ml/1 tsp sesame oil

30ml/2 tbsp rice vinegar

1 Put the rice vermicelli or noodles in a wide, heatproof bowl, pour over boiling water and leave for 5 minutes. Drain, refresh under cold water and drain again. Tip back into the bowl and set aside until required.

2 Boil or steam the corn cobs and mangetouts for about 3 minutes; they should still be crunchy. Refresh under cold water and drain. Now make the dressing. Mix all the ingredients in a screw-top jar, close tightly and shake well to combine.

3 Heat the oil in a large frying pan or wok. Add the garlic, ginger and red or green chilli and stir-fry for 1 minute. Add the tiger prawns and stir-fry for 3 minutes, until they have just turned pink. Add the spring onions, corn cobs, mangetouts and sesame seeds, and toss lightly to mix.

4 Tip the contents of the pan or wok over the rice vermicelli or noodles. Pour the dressing on top and toss well. Serve, garnished with lemon grass, or chill for 1 hour before serving.

King Prawns with Romesco Sauce

This sauce, originally from the Catalan region of Spain, is served with fish and shellfish. Its main ingredients are sweet pepper, tomatoes, garlic and almonds.

INGREDIENTS

Serves 6–8

24 raw king prawns (jumbo shrimp)

30–45ml/2–3 tbsp olive oil

flat leaf parsley, to garnish

lemon wedges, to serve

For the sauce

2 well-flavoured tomatoes

60ml/4 tbsp olive oil

1 onion, chopped

4 garlic cloves, chopped

1 canned pimiento, chopped

2.5ml/½ tsp dried chilli flakes or powder

75ml/5 tbsp Fish Stock

30ml/2 tbsp white wine

10 blanched almonds

15ml/1 tbsp red wine vinegar

salt

3 Toast the almonds under the grill (broiler) until golden. Leave to cool slightly, then transfer to a blender or food processor and grind coarsely. Add the remaining 30ml/2 tbsp of oil, the vinegar and the remaining garlic clove and process until evenly combined. Add the tomato and pimiento sauce and process until smooth. Season with salt, to taste.

4 Remove the heads from the prawns leaving them otherwise unpeeled and, with a sharp knife, slit each one down the back and remove the dark vein. Rinse and pat dry on kitchen paper. Preheat the grill. Toss the prawns in olive oil, then spread out in the grill pan. Grill (broil) for about 2–3 minutes on each side, until pink. Arrange on a serving platter with the lemon wedges, and the sauce in a small bowl. Serve immediately, garnished with parsley.

1 To make the sauce, immerse the tomatoes in boiling water for about 30 seconds, then refresh them under cold water. Peel away the skins and coarsely chop the tomato flesh.

2 Heat 30ml/2 tbsp of the oil in a pan, add the onion and 3 of the garlic cloves and cook until soft. Add the pimiento, tomatoes, chilli, fish stock and wine, then cover and simmer for 30 minutes.

Italian Prawn Skewers

Parsley and lemon are all that is required to create a lovely tiger prawn dish. Grill them or cook on a barbecue for an informal al fresco *summer appetizer.*

INGREDIENTS

Serves 4

900g/2lb raw tiger prawns (jumbo
   shrimp), peeled
60ml/4 tbsp olive oil
45ml/3 tbsp vegetable oil
75g/3oz/1¼ cups very fine
   dry breadcrumbs
1 garlic clove, crushed
15ml/1 tbsp chopped fresh parsley
salt and ground black pepper
lemon wedges, to serve

1 Slit the prawns down their backs and remove the dark vein. Rinse in cold water and pat dry on kitchen paper.

2 Put the olive oil and vegetable oil in a large bowl and add the prawns, mixing them to coat evenly. Add the breadcrumbs, garlic and parsley and season with salt and pepper. Toss the prawns thoroughly, to give them an even coating of breadcrumbs. Cover and leave to marinate for 1 hour.

3 Thread the tiger prawns on to four metal or wooden skewers, curling them up as you work, so that the tails are skewered neatly in the middle.

4 Preheat the grill (broiler). Place the skewers in the grill pan and cook for 2 minutes on each side, until the coating is golden. Serve with lemon wedges.

King Prawns in Sherry

This dish just couldn't be simpler. The sherry brings out the sweetness of the seafood perfectly.

INGREDIENTS

Serves 4

12 raw king prawns (jumbo
    shrimp), peeled

30ml/2 tbsp olive oil

30ml/2 tbsp medium or dry sherry

few drops of Tabasco sauce

salt and ground black pepper

1 Using a very sharp knife, make a shallow cut down the back of each prawn, then pull out and discard the dark vein.

2 Heat the oil in a frying pan and cook the prawns for about 2–3 minutes, until pink. Pour over the sherry and season to taste with Tabasco sauce and salt and pepper. Turn into a dish and serve the prawns immediately.

Sizzling Prawns

This dish works especially well with tiny prawns that can be eaten whole, but any type of unpeeled prawns will be fine. Choose a small casserole or frying pan that can be taken to the table for serving while the garlicky prawns are still sizzling.

INGREDIENTS

Serves 4

2 garlic cloves, halved

25g/1oz/2 tbsp butter

1 small fresh red chilli, seeded and sliced

115g/4oz/1 cup unpeeled cooked
    prawns (shrimp)

sea salt and coarsely ground black pepper

lime wedges, to serve

1 Rub the cut surfaces of the garlic cloves over the base and sides of a frying pan, then throw the garlic cloves away. Add the butter to the pan and melt over a fairly high heat until it just begins to turn golden brown.

2 Toss in the sliced red chilli and the prawns. Stir-fry for 1–2 minutes, until heated through, then season to taste with sea salt and plenty of black pepper. Serve directly from the pan with lime wedges for squeezing over.

COOK'S TIP

Wear gloves when handling chillies, or wash your hands thoroughly afterwards, as the juices can cause severe irritation to sensitive skin, especially around the eyes, nose or mouth.

Tiger Prawns with Mint, Dill and Lime

A wonderful combination – mint, dill and lime blend together to make a magical concoction to flavour succulent tiger prawns that will delight everyone who tries it.

INGREDIENTS

Serves 4

4 large sheets filo pastry

75g/3oz/⅓ cup butter, melted

16 large cooked peeled tiger prawns (jumbo shrimp)

15ml/1 tbsp chopped fresh mint, plus extra to garnish

15ml/1 tbsp chopped fresh dill

juice of 1 lime

8 cooked unpeeled tiger prawns (jumbo shrimp) and lime wedges, to serve

1 Keep the sheets of filo pastry covered with a dry, clean cloth to keep them moist. Cut one sheet of filo pastry in half widthways and brush with melted butter. Place one half on top of the other.

2 Preheat the oven to 230°C/ 450°F/Gas 8. Slit each of the tiger prawns in half down the back of the prawn and remove the dark vein.

3 Place four prawns in the centre of the filo pastry and sprinkle a quarter of the mint, dill and lime juice over the top. Fold over the sides, brush with butter and roll up to make a parcel.

4 Once you have filled all the parcels place them, join side down, on a greased baking sheet. Bake for 10 minutes, or until golden. Serve with whole tiger prawns, lime wedges and mint.

Scallop-stuffed Roast Peppers with Pesto

Serve these scallop-and-pesto-filled sweet red peppers with Italian bread, such as ciabatta or focaccia, to mop up the garlicky juices.

INGREDIENTS

Serves 4

4 squat red (bell) peppers

2 large garlic cloves, cut into thin slivers

60ml/4 tbsp olive oil

4 shelled scallops

45ml/3 tbsp pesto

salt and ground black pepper

freshly grated Parmesan cheese, to serve

salad leaves and fresh basil sprigs,
    to garnish

1 Preheat the oven to 180°C/ 350°F/Gas 4. Cut the peppers in half lengthways, through their stalks. Scrape out and discard the seeds. Wash the pepper shells and pat dry with kitchen paper.

2 Put the peppers, cut side up, in an oiled roasting pan. Divide the slivers of garlic equally among them and sprinkle with salt and ground black pepper to taste. Then spoon the oil into the peppers and roast for 40 minutes.

3 Using a sharp knife, carefully cut each of the shelled scallops in half horizontally to make two flat discs each with a piece of coral. When cooked, remove the peppers from the oven and place a scallop half in each pepper half. Then top with the pesto.

4 Return the pan to the oven and roast for 10 minutes more. Transfer the peppers to individual serving plates, sprinkle with grated Parmesan and garnish each plate with a few salad leaves and basil sprigs. Serve warm.

COOK'S TIP

Scallops are available from most fishmongers and supermarkets with fresh fish counters. Never cook scallops for longer than the time stated in the recipe or they will be tough and rubbery.

Prawn, Egg and Avocado Mousses

A light creamy mousse with lots of texture and a great mix of flavours. Serve chilled on the day you make it.

INGREDIENTS

Serves 6

a little olive oil

20ml/4tsp powdered gelatine

juice and rind of 1 lemon

60ml/4 tbsp mayonnaise

60ml/4 tbsp chopped fresh dill

5ml/1 tsp anchovy essence (paste)

5ml/1 tsp Worcestershire sauce

1 large avocado, ripe but just firm

4 hard-boiled eggs, peeled and chopped

175g/6oz/1 cup cooked peeled prawns
  (shrimp), coarsely chopped if large

250ml/8fl oz/1 cup double (heavy) or
  whipping cream, lightly whipped

2 egg whites, whisked

salt and ground black pepper

fresh dill or parsley sprigs, to garnish

warmed multigrain bread or toast,
  to serve

1 Prepare six small ramekins. Lightly grease the dishes with olive oil, then wrap a greaseproof (waxed) paper collar around the top of each and secure with tape. This makes sure that you can fill the dishes as high as you like and that the extra mixture will be supported while it is setting. The mousses will, therefore, look really dramatic when you remove the paper. Alternatively, prepare just one small soufflé dish.

2 Dissolve the gelatine in the lemon juice with 15ml/1 tbsp hot water in a small bowl set over hot water, until clear, stirring occasionally. Allow to cool slightly, then blend in the lemon rind, mayonnaise, dill, anchovy essence and Worcestershire sauce.

3 In a medium bowl mash the avocado flesh. Add the eggs and prawns. Stir in the gelatine mixture and then fold in the cream, egg whites and seasoning to taste. When evenly blended, spoon into the ramekins or soufflé dish and chill for 3–4 hours. Garnish with the herbs and serve with bread.

COOK'S TIP

Other fish can make a good alternative to prawns. Try substituting the same quantity of smoked trout or salmon, or cooked crab meat.

Crab and Ricotta Tartlets

Use the meat from a freshly cooked crab, weighing about 450g/1lb, if you can. Otherwise, look out for frozen brown and white crab meat.

INGREDIENTS

Serves 4

225g/8oz/2 cups plain (all-purpose) flour
pinch of salt
115g/4oz/½ cup butter, diced
225g/8oz/1 cup ricotta cheese
15ml/1 tbsp grated onion
30ml/2 tbsp freshly grated
   Parmesan cheese
2.5ml/½ tsp mustard powder
2 eggs, plus 1 egg yolk
225g/8oz crab meat
30ml/2 tbsp chopped fresh parsley
2.5ml/½ tsp anchovy essence (paste)
5–10ml/1–2 tsp lemon juice
salt and cayenne pepper
salad leaves, to garnish

1 Preheat the oven to 200°C/ 400°F/Gas 6. Sift the flour and salt into a bowl, add the butter and rub it in until the mixture resembles fine breadcrumbs. Stir in about 60ml/4 tbsp cold water to make a firm dough.

2 Turn the dough on to a floured surface and knead lightly. Roll out the pastry and use to line four 10cm/4in tartlet tins (muffin pans). Prick the bases with a fork, then chill for 30 minutes.

3 Line the pastry cases (pie shells) with greaseproof (waxed) paper and fill with baking beans. Bake for 10 minutes, then remove the paper and beans. Return to the oven and bake for a further 10 minutes.

4 Place the ricotta, grated onion, Parmesan and mustard powder in a bowl and beat until soft. Gradually beat in the eggs and egg yolk.

5 Gently stir in the crab meat and chopped parsley, then add the anchovy essence, lemon juice, salt and cayenne pepper, to taste.

6 Remove the tartlet cases from the oven and reduce the temperature to 180°C/350°F/Gas 4. Spoon the crab meat and ricotta filling into the cases and bake for 20 minutes, until set and golden brown. Serve hot with a garnish of salad leaves.

Garlic Prawns in Filo Tartlets

Tartlets made with crisp layers of filo pastry and filled with garlic prawns make a tempting appetizer.

INGREDIENTS

Serves 4
For the tartlets
50g/2oz/4 tbsp butter, melted
2–3 large sheets filo pastry

For the filling
115g/4oz/½ cup butter
2–3 garlic cloves, crushed
1 fresh red chilli, seeded and chopped
350g/12oz/3 cups cooked peeled
   prawns (shrimp)
30ml/2 tbsp chopped fresh parsley
salt and ground black pepper

1 Preheat the oven to 200°C/
400°F/Gas 6. Brush four
individual 7.5cm/3in flan tins
(quiche pans) with melted butter.

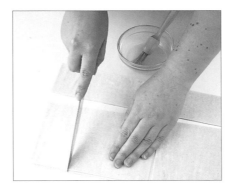

2 Cut the filo pastry into twelve
10cm/4in squares and brush
with the melted butter.

3 Place three squares inside each
tin, overlapping them at slight
angles and carefully frilling the
edges and points while forming a
good hollow in each centre. Bake
for 10–15 minutes, until crisp and
golden. Leave to cool slightly, then
remove the pastry cases (pie shells)
from the tins.

4 Meanwhile, make the filling.
Melt the butter in a large
frying pan, then add the garlic,
chilli and prawns and cook quickly
for 1–2 minutes to warm through.
Stir in the chopped fresh parsley
and season with salt and plenty of
black pepper.

5 Spoon the prawn filling
into the tartlets and serve
immediately, perhaps with some
sour cream.

Paella Croquettes

Paella is probably Spain's most famous dish, and here it is used for a tasty fried tapas. In this recipe, the paella is cooked from scratch, but you could, of course, use leftover paella instead.

INGREDIENTS

Serves 4

pinch of saffron threads
150ml/¼ pint/⅔ cup white wine
30ml/2 tbsp olive oil
1 small onion, finely chopped
1 garlic clove, finely chopped
150g/5oz/⅔ cup risotto rice
300ml/½ pint/1¼ cups hot Chicken Stock
50g/2oz /½ cup cooked peeled prawns
  (shrimp), deveined and coarsely chopped
50g/2oz cooked chicken, coarsely chopped
75g/3oz/⅔ cup petits pois (baby peas),
  thawed if frozen
30ml/2 tbsp freshly grated
  Parmesan cheese
1 egg, beaten
30ml/2 tbsp milk
75g/3oz/1½ cups fresh
  white breadcrumbs
vegetable or olive oil, for shallow frying
salt and ground black pepper
flat leaf parsley, to garnish

1 Stir the saffron into the wine in a small bowl and set aside.

2 Heat the oil in a pan and gently cook the onion and garlic for 5 minutes, until softened. Stir in the risotto rice and cook, stirring constantly, for 1 minute.

3 Keeping the heat fairly high, add the wine and saffron mixture to the pan, stirring until it is all absorbed. Gradually add the stock, about 1 ladleful at a time, stirring constantly until all the liquid has been absorbed and the rice is cooked and tender – this should take about 20 minutes.

4 Stir in the prawns, chicken, petits pois and freshly grated Parmesan. Season to taste with salt and pepper. Leave to cool slightly, then use two tablespoons to shape the mixture into 16 small lozenges.

5 Mix the egg and milk in a shallow bowl. Spread out the breadcrumbs on a sheet of foil. Dip the croquettes in the egg mixture, then coat them evenly in the breadcrumbs.

6 Heat the oil in a large frying pan. Then shallow fry the croquettes for 4–5 minutes, until crisp and golden brown. Work in batches. Drain on kitchen paper and keep hot. Serve garnished with a sprig of flat leaf parsley.

MEAT AND POULTRY STARTERS

~

Look no further for appetizers to impress even the most
discerning guest. Salads, pâtés, meaty skewers or crisp-coated
chicken – these really are starters to get your teeth into. These
tempting morsels of succulent meat and chicken have been
inspired by recipes from countries as far apart as France and
India, Poland and Indonesia and range from the hot and spicy
to the subtle and aromatic. Set the table, set the mood and
set the taste buds tingling.

Melon and Prosciutto Salad

Sections of cool fragrant melon wrapped with slices of air-dried ham make a delicious appetizer. If strawberries are in season, serve with a savoury-sweet strawberry salsa and watch it disappear.

INGREDIENTS

Serves 4

1 large melon, cantaloupe, charentais or galia
175g/6oz prosciutto or Serrano ham, thinly sliced

For the salsa

225g/8oz/2 cups strawberries
5ml/1 tsp caster (superfine) sugar
30ml/2 tbsp sunflower oil
15ml/1 tbsp orange juice
2.5ml/½ tsp finely grated orange rind
2.5ml/½ tsp finely grated fresh root ginger
salt and ground black pepper

1 Halve the melon and scoop the seeds out with a spoon. Cut the rind away with a paring knife, then slice the melon thickly. Chill until ready to serve.

2 To make the salsa, hull the strawberries and cut them into large dice. Place in a small mixing bowl with the sugar and crush lightly to release the juices. Add the oil, orange juice, orange rind and ginger. Season with salt and plenty of ground black pepper.

3 Arrange the melon on a serving plate, lay the ham over the top and serve with a bowl of salsa, handed around separately.

Prosciutto Salad with an Avocado Fan

*Avocados are amazingly versatile –
they can serve as edible containers,
be sliced or diced in a salad, or form
the foundation of a delicious soup or
sauce. However, they are at their
most elegant when sliced thinly and
fanned on a plate.*

INGREDIENTS

Serves 4

3 avocados

150g/5oz prosciutto

75–115g/3–4oz rocket (arugula) leaves

24 marinated black olives, drained

For the dressing

15ml/1 tbsp balsamic vinegar

5ml/1 tsp lemon juice

5ml/1 tsp prepared English (hot) mustard

5ml/1 tsp sugar

75ml/5 tbsp olive oil

salt and ground black pepper

1 First, make the dressing.
Combine the balsamic
vinegar, lemon juice, mustard and
sugar in a bowl. Whisk in the olive
oil, season to taste with salt and
pepper and set aside.

2 Cut two of the avocados in
half. Remove the stones (pits)
and skins, and cut the flesh into
1cm/½in thick slices. Toss with
half the dressing. Place the
prosciutto, avocado slices and
rocket on four serving plates.
Sprinkle the olives and the
remaining dressing over the top.

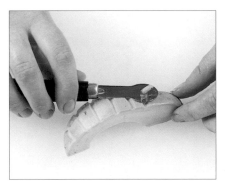

3 Halve, stone (pit) and peel the
remaining avocado. Slice each
half lengthways into eighths.
Gently draw a cannelle knife across
the quarters at 1cm/½in intervals
to create regular stripes.

4 Make four cuts lengthways
down each avocado eighth,
leaving 1cm/½in intact at the end.
Carefully fan out the slices and
arrange them on the side of
each plate.

Prosciutto with Potato Rémoulade

Rémoulade is a classic piquant dressing based on mayonnaise. The traditional French version is flavoured with mustard, gherkins, capers and herbs, but simpler variations are seasoned only with mustard. Lime juice brings a contemporary twist to this recipe for a cream-enriched dressing.

INGREDIENTS

Serves 4

2 potatoes, each weighing about 175g/6oz, quartered lengthways

150ml/¼ pint/⅔ cup mayonnaise

150ml/¼ pint/⅔ cup double (heavy) cream

5–10ml/1–2 tsp Dijon mustard

juice of ½ lime

30ml/2 tbsp olive oil

12 prosciutto slices

450g/1lb asparagus spears, halved

salt and ground black pepper

25g/1oz wild rocket (arugula), to garnish

extra virgin olive oil, to serve

1 Put the potatoes in a pan. Add cold water to cover and bring to the boil. Add a pinch of salt, then simmer over a medium-low heat for about 15 minutes, or until the potatoes are tender, but do not let them get too soft. Drain them thoroughly and leave to cool, then cut into long, thin strips.

2 Beat together the mayonnaise, cream, mustard, lime juice and seasoning in a large bowl. Add the potatoes and stir carefully to coat them with the dressing.

3 Heat the oil in a griddle or frying pan and cook the prosciutto, in batches, until crisp and golden. Use a slotted spoon to remove the ham, draining each piece well. Cook the asparagus in the fat remaining in the pan for about 3 minutes, or until tender and golden.

4 Put a generous spoonful of potato rémoulade on each plate and top with several slices of prosciutto. Add the asparagus and garnish with rocket. Serve, offering olive oil to drizzle over.

Thai Beef Salad

All the ingredients for this traditional Thai dish – known as yam nua yang – are widely available in larger supermarkets.

INGREDIENTS

Serves 4

675g/1½lb fillet or rump (round) steak

30ml/2 tbsp olive oil

2 small fresh mild red chillies, seeded
and sliced

225g/8oz/3¼ cups shiitake
mushrooms, sliced

For the dressing

3 spring onions (scallions),
finely chopped

2 garlic cloves, finely chopped

juice of 1 lime

15–30ml/1–2 tbsp fish or oyster sauce

5ml/1 tsp soft light brown sugar

30ml/2 tbsp chopped fresh
coriander (cilantro)

To serve

1 cos or romaine lettuce, torn into strips

175g/6oz cherry tomatoes, halved

5cm/2in piece of cucumber, peeled, halved
and thinly sliced

45ml/3 tbsp toasted sesame seeds

1 Preheat the grill (broiler) until hot, then cook the steak for about 2–4 minutes on each side, depending on how well done you like steak. (In Thailand, the beef is traditionally served quite rare.) Set the steak aside to cool for at least 15 minutes.

2 Use a very sharp knife to slice the meat as thinly as possible and place the slices in a bowl.

3 Heat the olive oil in a small frying pan. Add the sliced red chillies and the sliced mushrooms and cook for 5 minutes, stirring occasionally. Turn off the heat and add the grilled (broiled) steak slices to the pan, then stir well to coat the beef slices in the chilli and mushroom mixture.

4 Stir all the ingredients for the dressing together, then pour the dressing over the meat mixture and toss gently.

5 Sprinkle over the sesame seeds. Arrange the salad ingredients on a serving plate. Spoon the warm steak mixture in the centre and serve immediately.

COOK'S TIP

If you can find them, yellow chillies make a colourful addition to this dish. Substitute one for one of the red chillies.

Chopped Chicken Livers

It is said that remnants of this classic dish were found in sites dating back to 1400 and have been eaten in various guises ever since. The French love of liver-enriched pâtés is an inheritance from the Jews of Alsace, Strasbourg and the East who brought their specialities with them when they fled, and shared them.

INGREDIENTS

Serves 4–6

250g/9oz chicken livers

2–3 onions, chopped, plus ½ onion, finely chopped or grated

60ml/4 tbsp rendered chicken fat or vegetable oil

3–4 spring onions (scallions), thinly sliced

2–3 hard-boiled eggs, coarsely chopped or diced

10ml/2 tsp mayonnaise or firm chicken fat (optional)

5–10ml/1–2 tsp chopped fresh dill

salt and ground black pepper

chopped fresh dill or parsley, to garnish

lettuce, thin slices of crisp matzos or rye bread and a few slices of dill pickle, to serve

1 Grill (broil) the chicken livers lightly to bring the blood out on to the surface and render them kosher. Rinse, place in a pan, cover with cold water and bring to the boil. Reduce the heat, simmer gently for 5–10 minutes, then leave to cool in the water. (The livers should be firm but not dry and brown.)

2 In a large, heavy pan, cook the onions in the fat or oil over a medium heat, sprinkling with salt and pepper, until well browned and beginning to crisp, and caramelized around the edges.

3 To hand-chop the livers, use a round-bladed knife and chop the livers finely. Place in a bowl and mix in the fried onions and oil. If using a food processor, put the livers and fried onions in the bowl of the food processor with just enough oil from the fried onions to process to a thick paste.

4 In a bowl, combine the livers with the finely chopped or grated onion, the spring onions, hard-boiled eggs, mayonnaise or chicken fat, if using, and chopped dill. Cover and chill the livers for an hour or so until firm.

5 Mound the chopped livers on plates and garnish with the chopped fresh dill or parsley. Serve with lettuce, matzos or rye bread and dill pickles.

Herbed Liver Pâté Pie

Serve this highly flavoured pâté with a glass of Pilsner beer for a change from wine.

Serves 10

675g/1½ lb minced (ground) pork
350g/12oz pork liver
350g/12oz/2 cups diced cooked ham
1 small onion, finely chopped
30ml/2 tbsp chopped fresh parsley
5ml/1 tsp German mustard
30ml/2 tbsp kirsch
5ml/1 tsp salt
beaten egg, for sealing and glazing
25g/1oz sachet aspic jelly
250ml/8fl oz/1 cup boiling water
ground black pepper
mustard, bread and dill pickles, to serve

For the pastry

450g/1lb/4 cups plain (all-purpose) flour
pinch of salt
275g/10oz/1¼ cups butter
2 eggs plus 1 egg yolk
30ml/2 tbsp water

1 Preheat the oven to 200°C/400°F/Gas 6. To make the pastry, sift the flour and salt and rub in the butter. Beat the eggs, egg yolk and water, add to the dry ingredients and mix.

2 Knead the dough briefly until smooth. Roll out two-thirds on a lightly floured surface and use to line a 10 x 25cm/4 x 10in hinged loaf tin (pan). Trim off any excess dough.

3 Process half the pork with all of the liver until fairly smooth. Stir in the remaining minced pork, the ham, onion, parsley, mustard, kirsch and seasoning.

4 Spoon the filling into the tin, and level the surface.

5 Roll out the remaining pastry on the lightly floured surface and use it to top the pie, sealing the edges with some of the beaten egg. Decorate with the pastry trimmings and glaze with the remaining beaten egg. Using a fork, make 3 or 4 holes in the top, for the steam to escape.

6 Bake for 40 minutes, then reduce the oven temperature to 180°C/350°F/Gas 4 and cook for 1 further hour. Cover the pastry with foil if the top begins to brown too much. Remove from the oven and leave the pie to cool in the tin.

7 Make up the aspic jelly, using the boiling water. Stir to dissolve, then leave to cool.

8 Make a small hole near the edge of the pie with a skewer, then pour in the aspic through a greaseproof (waxed) paper funnel. Chill for at least 2 hours before serving the pie in slices with mustard, bread and dill pickles.

Beef Satay with a Hot Mango Dip

Strips of tender beef are flavoured with a delicious spicy marinade before being grilled, then served with a fruit dip.

INGREDIENTS

Makes 12 skewers

450g/1lb sirloin steak, trimmed

For the marinade

15ml/1 tbsp coriander seeds
5ml/1 tsp cumin seeds
50g/2oz/$\frac{1}{3}$ cup raw cashew nuts
15ml/1 tbsp vegetable oil
2 shallots or 1 small onion, finely chopped
1cm/$\frac{1}{2}$in piece fresh root ginger, finely chopped
1 garlic clove, crushed
30ml/2 tbsp tamarind sauce
30ml/2 tbsp dark soy sauce
10ml/2 tsp sugar
5ml/1 tsp rice or white wine vinegar

For the mango dip

1 ripe mango
1–2 small fresh red chillies, seeded and finely chopped
15ml/1 tbsp Thai fish sauce
juice of 1 lime
10ml/2 tsp sugar
1.5ml/$\frac{1}{4}$ tsp salt
30ml/2 tbsp chopped fresh coriander (cilantro)

1 Soak 12 bamboo skewers for 30 minutes. Slice the beef into long narrow strips and thread, zigzag-style, on to the skewers. Lay on a flat plate and set aside.

2 For the marinade, dry-fry the seeds and nuts in a large wok until evenly brown. Transfer to a mortar with a rough surface and crush finely with the pestle. Add the oil, shallots or onion, ginger, garlic, tamarind and soy sauces, sugar and rice or white wine vinegar.

3 Spread this marinade over the beef and leave to marinate for up to 8 hours. Cook the beef under a moderate grill (broiler) or over a barbecue for 6–8 minutes, turning to make sure of an even colour. Meanwhile, make the mango dip.

4 Cut away the skin and remove the stone (pit) from the mango. Process the mango flesh with the red chillies, fish sauce, lime juice, sugar and salt until smooth, then add the coriander. Serve immediately.

Barbecue-glazed Chicken Skewers

Known as yakitori in Japan, these skewers are popular throughout the country and are often served as an appetizer with drinks.

INGREDIENTS

Makes 12 skewers and 8 wing pieces

8 chicken wings

4 skinless chicken thighs,

4 spring onions (scallions), blanched and
    cut into short lengths

For the basting sauce

60ml/4 tbsp sake

75ml/5 tbsp/⅓ cup dark soy sauce

30ml/2 tbsp tamari

15ml/1 tbsp mirin, or sweet sherry

15ml/1 tbsp sugar

1 Remove the wing tip of the chicken at the first joint. Chop through the second joint, revealing the two narrow bones. Take hold of the bones with a clean cloth and pull, turning the meat around the bones inside out. Remove the smaller bone and discard. Set the wings aside.

2 Bone the chicken thighs and cut the meat into large dice. Thread the spring onions and thigh meat on to 12 skewers.

3 Measure the basting sauce ingredients into a stainless-steel or enamel pan and simmer until reduced by two-thirds. Cool.

4 Heat the grill (broiler) to a moderately high temperature. Grill (broil) the skewers without applying any oil. When juices begin to emerge from the chicken, baste liberally with the sauce. Allow a further 3 minutes for the chicken on skewers and not more than 5 minutes for the wings.

Lamb Tikka

Creamy yogurt and ground nuts go wonderfully with these spices.

Makes about 20

450g/1lb lamb fillet

2 spring onions (scallions), chopped

For the marinade

350ml/12 fl oz/1½ cups natural (plain) yogurt

15ml/1 tbsp ground almonds, cashewnuts or peanuts

15ml/1 tbsp vegetable oil

2–3 garlic cloves, finely chopped

juice of 1 lemon

5ml/1 tsp garam masala or curry powder

2.5ml/½ tsp ground cardamom

1.5ml/¼ tsp cayenne pepper

15–30ml/1–2 tbsp chopped fresh mint

1 To prepare the marinade, stir together the marinade ingredients. In a separate small bowl, reserve about 120ml/4fl oz/½ cup of the mixture to use as a dipping sauce for the meatballs.

2 Cut the lamb into small pieces and put in the bowl of a food processor with the spring onions. Process, using the pulse action, until the meat is finely chopped. Add 30–45ml/2–3 tbsp of the marinade and process again.

3 Test to see if the mixture holds together by pinching a little between your fingertips. Add a little more marinade, if necessary, but do not make the mixture too wet and soft.

4 With moistened palms, form the meat mixture into slightly oval balls, about 4cm/1½in long, and arrange in a shallow dish. Spoon over the remaining marinade, cover and chill the meatballs in the refrigerator for 8–10 hours or overnight.

5 Preheat the grill (broiler) and line a baking sheet with foil. Thread each meatball on to a skewer and arrange on the baking sheet. Grill (broil) for 4–5 minutes, turning them occasionally, until crisp and golden on all sides. Serve with the reserved marinade as a dipping sauce.

Pork Satay

Originating in Indonesia, satay are skewers of meat marinated with spices and grilled quickly over charcoal. It's street food at its best, prepared by vendors with portable grills who set up stalls at every road side and market place. It makes a great-tasting appetizer, too. It's not too filling and it's bursting with flavour. You can make satay with chicken, beef or lamb. Serve with satay sauce, and a cucumber relish if you like.

INGREDIENTS

Makes about 20

450g/1lb lean pork
5ml/1 tsp grated fresh root ginger
1 lemon grass stalk, finely chopped
3 garlic cloves, finely chopped
15ml/1 tbsp medium curry paste
5ml/1 tsp ground cumin
5ml/1 tsp ground turmeric
60ml/4 tbsp coconut cream
30ml/2 tbsp Thai fish sauce
5ml/1 tsp granulated sugar
vegetable oil, for brushing
fresh herbs, to garnish

For the satay sauce

250ml/8fl oz/1 cup coconut milk
30ml/2 tbsp Thai red curry paste
75g/3oz crunchy peanut butter
120ml/4fl oz/½ cup Chicken Stock
45ml/3 tbsp brown sugar
30ml/2 tbsp tamarind juice
15ml/1 tbsp Thai fish sauce
2.5ml/½ tsp salt

1 Cut the pork thinly into 5cm/2in strips and place in a shallow dish. Mix together the fresh root ginger, lemon grass, garlic, curry paste, cumin, turmeric, coconut cream, fish sauce and sugar.

2 Pour over the pork and leave to marinate for about 2 hours.

3 Meanwhile, make the sauce. Heat the coconut milk over a medium heat, then add the red curry paste, peanut butter, chicken stock and sugar.

4 Cook, stirring constantly, for about 5–6 minutes, until smooth. Add the tamarind juice, fish sauce and salt to taste.

5 Thread the meat on to skewers. Brush with oil and cook over charcoal or under a hot grill (broiler) for 3–4 minutes on each side, turning occasionally, until cooked and golden brown. Serve with the satay sauce garnished with fresh herbs.

Skewered Lamb with Red Onion Salsa

This summery tapas dish is ideal for outdoor eating, although, if the weather fails, the skewers can be cooked in the kitchen. The simple tomato and onion salsa makes a refreshing accompaniment – make sure that you use a mild-flavoured red onion that is fresh and crisp, and a ripe tomato that is full of flavour.

INGREDIENTS

Serves 4

225g/8oz lean lamb, cubed

2.5ml/½ tsp ground cumin

5ml/1 tsp paprika

15ml/1 tbsp olive oil

salt and ground black pepper

For the salsa

1 red onion, very thinly sliced

1 large tomato, seeded and chopped

15ml/1 tbsp red wine vinegar

3–4 fresh basil or mint leaves, coarsely torn

small mint leaves, to garnish

1 Place the lamb in a bowl with the cumin, paprika, olive oil and plenty of salt and pepper. Toss well until the lamb is coated with spices.

2 Cover the bowl with clear film (plastic wrap) and set aside in a cool place for a few hours, or in the refrigerator overnight, so that the lamb absorbs the flavours.

3 Spear the lamb cubes on four small skewers – if using wooden skewers, soak them first in cold water for 30 minutes to prevent them from burning.

4 To make the salsa, put the sliced onion, tomato, red wine vinegar and basil or mint leaves in a small bowl and stir together until thoroughly blended. Season to taste with salt, garnish with mint, then set aside while you cook the lamb skewers.

5 Cook over the barbecue or under a preheated grill (broiler) for 5–10 minutes, turning frequently, until the lamb is well browned all over, but still slightly pink in the centre. Serve hot, with the salsa.

Stuffed Garlic Mushrooms with Prosciutto

Field mushrooms can vary greatly in size. Choose similar size specimens with undamaged edges.

INGREDIENTS

Serves 4

1 onion, chopped

75g/3oz/6 tbsp unsalted (sweet) butter

8 field (portabello) mushrooms

15g/½oz/¼ cup dried ceps, bay boletus or
   saffron milk-caps, soaked in warm
   water for 20 minutes

1 garlic clove, crushed

75g/3oz/¾ cup fresh breadcrumbs

1 egg

75ml/5 tbsp chopped fresh parsley

15ml/1 tbsp chopped fresh thyme

salt and ground black pepper

115g/4oz prosciutto di Parma or San
   Daniele, thinly sliced

fresh parsley, to garnish

1 Preheat the oven to 190°C/
375°F/Gas 5. Cook the onion gently in half the butter for 6–8 minutes, until soft but not coloured. Meanwhile, break off the stems of the field mushrooms, setting the caps aside. Drain the dried mushrooms and chop these and the stems of the field mushrooms finely. Add to the onion together with the garlic and cook for a further 2–3 minutes.

2 Transfer the mixture to a bowl, add the breadcrumbs, egg, herbs and seasoning. Melt the remaining butter in a small pan and generously brush over the mushroom caps. Arrange the mushrooms on a baking sheet and spoon in the filling. Bake in the oven for 20–25 minutes, until they are well browned.

3 Top each mushroom with a slice of prosciutto, garnish with parsley and serve.

COOK'S TIP

• Garlic mushrooms can be easily prepared in advance ready to go into the oven.

• Fresh breadcrumbs can be made and then frozen. They can be taken from the freezer as they are required and do not need to be thawed first.

Chicken with Lemon and Garlic

Easy to cook and delicious to eat, serve this tapas dish with aioli.

Serves 4

225g/8oz skinless, boneless chicken
   breast portions
30ml/2 tbsp olive oil
1 shallot, finely chopped
4 garlic cloves, finely chopped
5ml/1tsp paprika
juice of 1 lemon
30ml/2 tbsp chopped fresh parsley
salt and ground black pepper
flat leaf parsley, to garnish
lemon wedges, to serve

1 Sandwich the chicken between two sheets of clear film (plastic wrap) or greaseproof (waxed) paper. Bat out with a rolling pin or meat mallet until the portions are about 5mm/¼in thick.

2 Cut the chicken into strips about 1cm/½in wide. Heat the oil in a large frying pan. Stir-fry the chicken strips with the shallot, garlic and paprika over a high heat for about 3 minutes, until lightly browned and cooked through.

3 Add the lemon juice and parsley and season with salt and pepper to taste. Serve with lemon wedges, garnished with flat leaf parsley.

Smoked Chicken with Peach Mayonnaise Tartlets

These are attractive and, because smoked chicken is sold ready cooked, they require the minimum of culinary effort. The filling can be prepared a day in advance and chilled, but do not fill the pastry cases until you are ready to serve them or they will become soggy.

INGREDIENTS

Makes 12

25g/1oz/2 tbsp butter

3 sheets filo pastry, each
    measuring 45 x 28cm /18 x 11in,
    thawed if frozen

2 skinless, boneless smoked chicken breast
    portions, thinly sliced

150ml/¼ pint/⅔ cup mayonnaise

grated rind of 1 lime

30ml/2 tbsp lime juice

2 ripe peaches, peeled, stoned (pitted)
    and chopped

salt and ground black pepper

fresh tarragon sprigs,
    lime slices and salad leaves,
    to garnish

1 Preheat the oven to 200°C/ 400°F/Gas 6. Melt the butter in a small pan. Brush 12 small individual tartlet tins (muffin pans) with a little of the melted butter. Cut each sheet of filo pastry into 12 equal rounds large enough to line the tins, allowing enough to stand up above the tops of the tins.

2 Place a round of pastry in each tin and brush with a little melted butter, then add another round of pastry. Brush each with more melted butter and add a third round of pastry.

3 Bake the tartlets for 5 minutes, or until the pastry is golden brown. Leave in the tins for a few moments before transferring to a wire rack to cool.

4 Mix the chicken, mayonnaise, lime rind and juice and peaches and season to taste with salt and pepper. Chill this chicken mixture for at least 30 minutes, or up to 12 hours. When ready to serve, spoon the chicken mixture into the filo tartlets and garnish with tarragon sprigs, lime slices and salad leaves.

Pork and Bacon Rillettes with Onion Salad

Rillettes is potted meat, the most famous of which is made in Tours, France from pork and ham. This version makes a great appetizer, delicious snack or light meal.

INGREDIENTS

Serves 8

1.8kg/4lb belly of pork, boned and cut into cubes (reserve the bones)

450g/1lb rindless streaky (fatty) bacon, finely chopped

5ml/1 tsp salt

1.5ml/¼ tsp ground black pepper

4 garlic cloves, finely chopped

1 fresh bouquet garni containing parsley, bay leaf, thyme and sage

300ml/½ pint/1¼ cups water

crusty French bread, to serve

For the onion salad

1 small red onion, halved and finely sliced

2 spring onions (scallions), cut into thin batons

2 celery sticks, cut into thin batons

15ml/1 tbsp freshly squeezed lemon juice

15ml/1 tbsp light olive oil

ground black pepper

1 In a large bowl, mix the pork, bacon and salt. Cover and leave at room temperature for 30 minutes. Preheat the oven to 150°C/300°F/Gas 2. Stir the pepper and garlic into the meat. Add the bouquet garni to the meat.

2 Spread the meat mixture in a large roasting pan and pour in the water. Place the bones from the pork on top and cover tightly with foil. Cook for 3½ hours.

3 Discard the bones and herbs, and ladle the meat mixture into a metal sieve set over a large bowl. Allow the liquid to drain. Repeat until all the meat is drained. Reserve the liquid. Use two forks to pull the meat apart into fine shreds.

4 Line a 1.5 litre/2½ pint/6¼ cup terrine or deep, straight-sided dish with clear film (plastic wrap) and spoon the shredded meat into it. Strain the reserved liquid through a sieve lined with muslin (cheesecloth) and pour it over the meat. Leave to cool. Cover and chill in the refrigerator for at least 24 hours, or until set.

5 To make the onion salad, place the sliced onion, spring onions and celery in a bowl. Add the lemon juice and olive oil and toss gently. Season with freshly ground black pepper, but do not add any salt as the rillettes is well salted.

6 Serve the rillettes, cut into thick slices, on individual plates with a little onion salad and thick slices of crusty French bread and unsalted (sweet) butter.

Deep-fried Lamb Patties

These patties are a tasty North African speciality – called kibbeh – of minced meat and bulgur wheat. They are sometimes stuffed with additional meat and deep-fried. Moderately spiced, they're good served with yogurt.

INGREDIENTS

Serves 6

450g/1lb lean lamb or lean minced
   (ground) lamb or beef
salt and ground black pepper
vegetable oil, for deep-frying
avocado slices and fresh coriander
   (cilantro) sprigs, to serve

For the patties
225g/8oz/1⅓ cups bulgur wheat
1 fresh red chilli, seeded and chopped
1 onion, coarsely chopped

For the stuffing
1 onion, finely chopped
50g/2oz/⅔ cup pine nuts
30ml/2 tbsp olive oil
7.5ml/1½ tsp ground allspice
60ml/4 tbsp chopped fresh
   coriander (cilantro)

1 If necessary, chop the lamb and process in a blender or food processor until minced. Divide into two equal portions.

2 For the patties, soak the bulgur wheat for 15 minutes in cold water. Drain, then process in a blender or a food processor with the chilli, onion, half the meat and salt and pepper.

3 For the stuffing, cook the onion and pine nuts in the oil for 5 minutes. Add the allspice and remaining meat and cook gently, breaking up the meat with a wooden spoon, until browned. Stir in the coriander and seasoning.

4 Turn the patty mixture out on to a work surface and shape into a cake. Cut into 12 wedges.

5 Flatten one piece and spoon some stuffing into the centre. Bring the edges of the patty up over the stuffing , making sure that the filling is completely encased.

6 Heat oil to a depth of 5cm/2in in a large pan until a few patty crumbs sizzle on the surface.

7 Lower half of the filled patties into the oil and deep-fry for about 5 minutes, until golden. Drain on kitchen paper and keep hot while cooking the remainder. Serve with avocado slices and coriander sprigs.

Spicy Koftas

These tasty meatballs will need to be cooked in batches.

INGREDIENTS

Makes 20–25

450g/1lb lean minced (ground) beef

30ml/2 tbsp finely ground ginger

30ml/2 tbsp finely chopped garlic

4 fresh green chillies, finely chopped

1 small onion, finely chopped

1 egg

2.5ml/½ tsp ground turmeric

5ml/1 tsp garam masala

50g/2oz/2 cups coriander (cilantro) leaves, chopped

4–6 mint leaves, chopped, or 2.5ml/½ tsp mint sauce

175g/6oz raw potato

salt

vegetable oil, for deep-frying

1 Place the beef in a large bowl with the ground ginger, garlic, chillies, onion, egg, turmeric, garam masala and herbs. Grate the potato into the bowl, and season with salt. Knead together to blend well and form a soft dough.

2 Using your fingers, shape the kofta mixture into portions the size of golf balls. You should be able to make 20–25 koftas. Set the balls aside at room temperature to rest for about 25 minutes.

3 In a wok or frying pan, heat the oil to medium-hot and deep-fry the koftas, in small batches, until they are golden brown in colour. Drain well and serve hot.

COOK'S TIP

Leftover koftas can be coarsely chopped and packed into pitta bread spread with chutney or relish for a quick and delicious snack.

Chicken Bitki

This is a popular Polish dish and makes an attractive appetizer when offset by deep red beetroot and vibrant green salad leaves.

INGREDIENTS

Makes 12

15g/½oz/1 tbsp butter, melted

115g/4oz flat mushrooms, finely chopped

50g/2oz/1 cup fresh white breadcrumbs

350g/12oz skinless, boneless chicken breast portions or guinea fowl, minced (ground) or finely chopped

2 eggs, separated

1.5ml/¼ tsp grated nutmeg

30ml/2 tbsp plain (all-purpose) flour

45ml/3 tbsp vegetable oil

salt and ground black pepper

salad leaves and grated pickled beetroot (beet), to serve

1 Melt the butter in a pan and cook the mushrooms for about 5 minutes, until soft and the juices have evaporated. Leave to cool.

2 Mix together the mushrooms, breadcrumbs, chicken or guinea fowl, egg yolks and nutmeg in a bowl and season to taste with salt and pepper.

3 Whisk the egg whites until stiff. Stir half into the chicken mixture to slacken it, then fold in the remainder.

4 Shape into 12 even-size meatballs, about 7.5cm/3in long and 2.5cm/1in wide. Roll in the flour to coat.

5 Heat the oil in a large, heavy frying pan and cook the bitki, turning frequently, for about 10 minutes, until evenly golden brown and cooked through. Serve immediately with salad leaves and pickled beetroot.

Golden Parmesan Chicken

These tasty morsels make a great appetizer for an informal dinner.

INGREDIENTS

Serves 4

4 skinless, boneless chicken
   breast portions
75g/3oz/1½ cups fresh
   white breadcrumbs
40g/1½ oz/½ cup finely grated
   Parmesan cheese
30ml/2 tbsp chopped fresh parsley
2 eggs, beaten
120ml/4fl oz/½ cup mayonnaise
120ml/4fl oz/½ cup fromage frais
   (farmer's cheese)
1–2 garlic cloves, crushed
50g/2oz/4 tbsp butter, melted
salt and ground black pepper

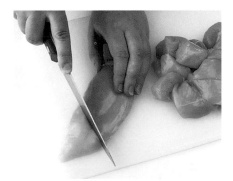

1 Cut each chicken portion into four or five chunks. Combine the breadcrumbs, Parmesan, parsley and seasoning in a dish.

2 Dip the chicken pieces in the egg, then into the breadcrumb mixture. Place in a single layer on a baking sheet. Chill for 30 minutes.

3 Meanwhile, to make the garlic mayonnaise, mix together the mayonnaise, fromage frais and garlic, and season to taste with ground black pepper. Spoon the mayonnaise into a small serving bowl. Cover and chill in the refrigerator until required.

4 Preheat the oven to 180°C/ 350°F/Gas 4. Drizzle the melted butter over the chicken pieces and cook them for about 20 minutes, until crisp and golden. Serve the chicken immediately accompanied by the garlic mayonnaise for dipping.

SALADS

Salads are among the most varied and versatile dishes.
When summer weather arrives, cold dishes are a welcome
change to the family menu, warm and cold salads make
perfect appetizers for more formal occasions and,
whether made with crisp green leaves or substantial
pulses, they are the perfect accompaniment for all kinds
of dishes all year round. This section includes a helpful
glossary of ingredients, advice on vegetable and fruit
preparation and recipes for popular dressings, besides
a collection of truly mouthwatering recipes.

Salad Vegetables

The salad vegetable is any type of vegetable that earns its keep in a salad by virtue of freshness and flavour. Vegetables for a salad can be raw or lightly cooked. If cooked, they are best served at room temperature to bring out their full flavour. Here is a selection of the most commonly used salad vegetables.

Avocado

This has a smooth, buttery flesh when ripe and is an asset to many salads, of which Guacamole is perhaps the best known. Avocados can also be served on their own as a starter, with a light vinaigrette dressing or a spoonful of lemon mayonnaise, or even just a squeeze of lemon juice and salt.

Carrots

These should be young, slender and sweet to taste. Either cooked or raw, they bring flavour and colour to a salad.

Celery

A useful salad vegetable, celery is grown year round for its robust, earthy flavour. The crisp stems should be neither stringy nor tough. Celery partners well with cooked ham, apple and walnut in Waldorf Salad and is also used as a crudité.

Courgettes (Zucchini)

These can be bitter to taste and are usually cooked before being combined with other young vegetables. Smooth in texture when cooked, they blend well with tomatoes, aubergines (eggplant), (bell) peppers and onions. Use baby courgettes for a sweeter flavour if you want to serve them raw as a crudité.

Cucumbers

A common salad ingredient that turns up, invited or not, in salad bowls everywhere. The quality of this popular vegetable is best appreciated in salads with a strong flavour.

Fennel

The bulb (or Florence) variety has a strong, aniseed flavour and looks like a squat head of celery. Because the flavour can be dominant, it may be blanched in boiling water for 6 minutes before use in a salad.

Garlic

Strong to taste, garlic is essential to the robust cooking of South America, Asia and the Mediterranean. Garlic should be used carefully as it can mask other flavours, but it is a vital part of salad preparation. To impart a very gentle hint of garlic, rub around the inside of your salad bowl with a cut clove. Another way to moderate the strength of fresh garlic is to store a few crushed cloves in a bottle of olive oil, and use the oil sparingly in dressings.

Green Beans

The varieties are too numerous to mention here, but they all have their merits as salad vegetables. To appreciate the sweet flavour of young tender green beans, cook them for 6 minutes and then refresh immediately in cold running water so that the crispness and colour are retained. An essential ingredient of Salade Niçoise, green beans are an ideal crudité and also make good partners to a spicy tomato sauce.

Mushrooms

These provide a rich tone to many salads and are eaten both raw and cooked. The oyster mushroom, which grows wild but is also cultivated, has a fine flavour and texture. White mushrooms are widely available and are often used raw, thinly sliced, in a mixed salad. Chestnut mushrooms are similar to white mushrooms but have slightly more flavour.

Onions

Several varieties are suited to salads. The strongest is the small, brown onion, which should be chopped finely and used sparingly. Less strong is the large, white Spanish onion, which has a sweeter, milder flavour and may be used coarsely chopped.

Potatoes

A staple carbohydrate ingredient to add bulk to a salad or provide a main element.

Spring Onions (Scallions)

These have a milder flavour than the common onion and give a gentle bite to many popular salads.

Baby Corn Cobs

Baby corn cobs can be eaten whole, lightly cooked or raw, and should be served warm or at room temperature.

Tomatoes

Technically a fruit rather than a vegetable, tomatoes are valued for their flavour and colour. Small varieties usually ripen more quickly than large ones and have a better flavour.

Salad Fruit

The contents of the fruit bowl offer endless possibilities for sweet and savoury salads.

Apples
This versatile fruit offers a unique flavour to both sweet and savoury salads.

Apricots
You can use apricots raw, dried or lightly poached.

Bananas
These bring a special richness to fruit salads, although their flavour can often interfere with more delicate fruit.

Blackberries
With a very short season, wild blackberries have more flavour than cultivated.

Blueberries
These tight-skinned berries combine well with the sharpness of fresh oranges.

Cherries
Cherries should be firm and glossy and are a deliciously colourful ingredient in many kinds of fruit salad.

Cranberries
Too sharp to eat raw, but very good for cooking.

Dates
Fresh dates are sweet and juicy, dried ones have a more intense flavour. Both kinds work well in fresh fruit salads.

Figs
Green- or purple-skinned fruit, with sweet, pinkish-red flesh. Eat whole or peeled.

Gooseberries
Dessert types can be eaten raw, but cooking varieties are more widely available.

Grapefruit
These can have yellow, green or pink flesh; the pink-fleshed or ruby varieties are the sweetest.

Grapes
Large Muscat varieties, whose season runs from late summer to autumn, are the most highly prized and also the most expensive.

Kiwi Fruit
Available all the year round.

Kumquats
Tiny relatives of the orange and can be eaten raw or cooked.

Lemons and Limes
Both these indispensable citrus fruits are used for flavour and to prevent fruit turning brown.

Lychees
A small fruit with a hard pink skin and sweet, juicy flesh.

Mangoes
Tropical fruit with an exotic flavour and golden-orange flesh that is wonderful in sweet or savoury salads.

Melons
These grow in abundance from mid- to late summer and provide a resource of freshness and flavour. Melon is at its most delicious served icy cold.

Nectarines
A relative of the peach with a smoother skin.

Oranges
At their best during winter, they can be segmented and added to sweet and savoury salads.

Papayas
These fruits of the tropics have a distinctive, sweet flavour. When ripe they are yellow-green.

Peaches
Choose white peaches for the sweetest flavour, and yellow for a more aromatic taste.

Pears
Perfect for savoury salads, and with strong blue cheese and toasted pecan nuts.

Physalis
Small, fragrant, pleasantly tart orange berries, wrapped in a paper cape.

Pineapples
Ripe pineapples resist firm pressure in the hand and have a sweet smell.

Plums
There are many dessert and cooking varieties.

Raspberries
Much-coveted soft fruits that partner well with ripe mango, passion fruit and strawberries.

Rhubarb
Technically a vegetable, too tart to eat raw.

Star Fruit
When sliced, this makes a pretty shape perfect for garnishes.

Strawberries
A popular summer fruit.

Lettuces and Leaves

One particular aspect of lettuce that sets it apart from any other vegetable is that you can buy it in only one form – fresh.

Lettuce has been cultivated for thousands of years. In Egyptian times it was sacred to the fertility god Min. It was then considered a powerful aphrodisiac, yet for the Greeks and the Romans it was thought to have quite the opposite effect, making one sleepy and generally soporific. Chemists today confirm that lettuce contains a hypnotic similar to opium, and in herbal remedies lettuce is recommended for insomniacs.

There are hundreds of different varieties of lettuce. Today, an increasing choice is available in stores so that the salad bowl can become a wealth of colour, taste and texture with no other ingredient than a selection of leaves.

Round (Butterhead)

These are the classic round lettuces. They have a pale heart and floppy, loosely packed leaves. They have a pleasant flavour as long as they are fresh. Choose the lettuce with the best heart by picking it up at the base and gently squeezing to check there is a firm centre.

Lollo Rosso

Lollo rosso and lollo biondo – similar in shape but a paler green without any purple edges – are both non-hearting lettuces. Although they do not have a lot of flavour, they look superb and are often used to form a nest of leaves on which to place the rest of a salad.

Cos or Romaine

The cos lettuce would have been known in antiquity. It has two names, cos, derived from the Greek island where it was found; and romaine, the name used by the French. Cos is considered to have the best flavour and is the correct lettuce for use in Caesar Salad.

Escarole

Escarole is one of the more robust lettuces in terms of flavour and texture. Like the curly-leafed frisée, escarole has a distinct bitter flavour. Served with other leaves and a well-flavoured dressing, escarole and frisée will give your salad a pleasant "bite".

Oak Leaf Lettuce

Oak leaf lettuce, together with lollo rosso and lollo biondo, is another member of the loosehead lettuce group. Oak leaf lettuce has a very gentle flavour. It is a very decorative leaf and makes a beautiful addition to any salad, and a lovely garnish.

Little Gem (Bibb)

Looking like a cross between a baby cos or romaine and a furled round (butterhead) lettuce, they have firm hearts. Their tight centres mean that they can be sliced whole and the quarters used for carrying slivers of smoked fish or anchovy as a simple appetizer.

Chinese Leaves (Chinese Cabbage)

This has pale green, crinkly leaves with long, wide, white ribs. Its shape is a little like a very fat head of celery, which gives rise to another of its names, celery cabbage. It is crunchy, and since it is available all year round, it makes a useful winter salad component.

Radicchio

This is a variety developed from wild chicory (Belgian endive). It looks like a lettuce with deep wine-red leaves and cream ribs and owes its splendid foliage to careful shading from the light. If it is grown in the dark, the leaves are marbled pink. Its flavour is quite bitter .

Lamb's Lettuce

Lamb's lettuce or corn salad is a popular winter leaf that does not actually belong to the lettuce family, but is terrific in salads. Called mâche in France, lamb's lettuce has small, attractive, dark green leaves and grows in pretty little sprigs. Its flavour is mild and nutty.

Watercress

Watercress is perhaps the most robustly flavoured of all the salad ingredients and a handful of watercress is all you need to perk up a dull salad. It has a distinctive "raw" flavour, peppery and slightly pungent, and this, together with its shiny leaves, make it a popular garnish.

Rocket (Arugula)

Rocket has a wonderful peppery flavour and is excellent in a mixed green salad. It was eaten by the Greeks and Romans as an aphrodisiac. Since it has such a striking flavour, a little goes a long way; just a few leaves will transform a green salad and liven up a sandwich.

Herbs

For as long as salads have drawn on the qualities of fresh produce, sweet herbs have played an important part in providing individual character and flavour. When herbs are used in a salad, they should be as full of life as the salad leaves they accompany. Dried herbs are no substitute for fresh ones and should be kept for cooked dishes, such as casseroles. Salad herbs are distinguished by their ability to release flavour without lengthy cooking.

Most salad herbs belong finely chopped in salad dressings and marinades, while the robust flavours of rosemary, thyme and fennel branches can be used on the barbecue to impart a smoky herb flavour. Ideally salad herbs should be picked just before use, but if you cannot use them immediately, keep them in water to retain their freshness. Parsley, mint and coriander will keep for up to a week in this way if also covered with a plastic bag and placed in the refrigerator.

Basil

Remarkable for its fresh, pungent flavour unlike that of any other herb, basil is widely used in Mediterranean salads, especially Italian recipes. Basil leaves are tender and delicate and should be gently torn or snipped with scissors, rather than chopped with a knife.

Chives

Chives belong to the onion family and have a mild onion flavour. The slender, green stems and soft mauve flowers are both edible. Chives are an indispensable flavouring for potato salads.

Coriander (Cilantro)

The chopped leaves of this pungent, distinctively flavoured herb are popular in Middle Eastern and Eastern salads.

Lavender

This soothingly fragrant herb is edible and may be used in both sweet and savoury salads, as it combines well with thyme, garlic, honey and orange.

Mint

This much-loved herb is widely used in Greek and Middle Eastern salads, such as Tzatziki and Tabbouleh. It is also a popular addition to fruit salads. Garden mint is the most common variety; others include spearmint and the round-leaf apple mint.

Clockwise from top left: thyme, coriander (cilantro), parsley, chives, lavender, rose , mint and basil.

Parsley

Curly and flat leaf parsley are both used for their fresh, green flavour. Flat leaf parsley is said to have a stronger taste. Freshly chopped parsley is used by the handful in salads and dressings.

Rose

Although it is not technically a herb, the sweet-scented rose can be used to flavour fresh fruit salads. It combines well with blackberries and raspberries.

Thyme

An asset to salads featuring rich, earthy flavours, this herb has a penetrating flavour.

Spices

Spices are the aromatic seasonings found in the seed, bark, fruit and sometimes flowers of certain plants and trees. Spices are highly valued for their warm, inviting flavours, and thankfully their price is relatively low. The flavour of a spice is contained in the volatile oils of the seed, bark or fruit; so, like herbs, spices should be used as fresh as possible. Whole spices keep better than ground ones, which tend to lose their freshness in 3–4 months.

Not all spices are suitable for salad making, although many allow us to explore the flavours of other cultures. The recipes in this book use curry spices in moderation so as not to spoil the delicate salad flavours.

Caraway

These savoury-sweet-tasting seeds are widely used in German and Austrian cooking and feature strongly in many Jewish dishes. The small ribbed seeds are similar in appearance and taste to cumin. The flavour combines especially well with German mustard in a dressing for frankfurter salad.

Cayenne Pepper

Also known as chilli powder, this is the dried and finely ground fruit of the hot chilli pepper. It is an important seasoning in South American cooking and is often used when seasoning fish and shellfish. Cayenne pepper can be blended with paprika if it is too hot and should be used with care.

Celery Salt

A combination of ground celery seed and salt, this spice is used for seasoning vegetables, especially carrots.

Cumin seeds

Often associated with Asian and North African cookery, cumin can be bought ground or as small, slender seeds. It combines well with coriander seeds.

Curry Paste

Prepared curry paste consists of a blend of Indian spices preserved in oil. It may be added to dressings, and is particularly useful in this respect for showing off the sweet qualities of fish and shellfish.

Paprika

Made from a variety of sweet red (bell) pepper, this spice is mild in flavour and adds colour.

Pepper

Undoubtedly the most popular spice used in the West, pepper features in the cooking of

Above: Flavoursome additions to salads include (clockwise from top left) celery salt, caraway seeds, curry paste, saffron threads, peppercorns and cayenne pepper.

almost every nation. Pepper-corns can be white, black, green or red and should always be freshly milled rather than bought already ground.

Saffron

The world's most expensive spice, made from the dried stigma of a crocus, real saffron has a tobacco-rich smell and gives a sweet yellow tint to liquids used for cooking. It can be used in creamy dressings and brings out the richness of fish and shellfish dishes. There are many powdered imitations which provide colour without the flavour of the real thing.

Oils, Vinegars and Flavourings

OILS

Oil is the main ingredient of most dressings and provides an important richness to salads. Neutral oils, such as sunflower, safflower or groundnut (peanut), are ideally used as a background for stronger oils. Sesame, walnut and hazelnut oils are the strongest and should be used sparingly. Olive oil is prized for its clarity of flavour and clean richness. The most significant producers of olive oil are Italy, France, Spain and Greece. These and other countries produce two main grades of olive oil: estate-grown extra virgin olive oil and semi-fine olive oil, which is of a good, basic standard.

Olive Oils

French olive oils are subtly flavoured and provide a well-balanced lightness to dressings.
Greek olive oils are typically strong in character. They are often green with quite a thick texture and are unsuitable for making mayonnaise.
Italian olive oils are noted for their vigorous Mediterranean flavours. Tuscan oils are noted for their well-rounded, spicy flavour. Sicilian oils tend to be lighter in texture, although they are often stronger in flavour.
Spanish olive oils are typically fruity and often have a nutty quality with a slight bitterness.

Nut Oils

Hazelnut and walnut oils are valued for their strong, nutty flavour. Tasting richly of the nuts from which they are pressed, both are usually blended with neutral oils for salad dressings.

Seed Oils

Groundnut (peanut) oil and sunflower oil are valued for their clean, neutral flavour.

SALAD FLAVOURINGS

Capers

These are the pickled flower buds of a bush native to the Mediterranean. Their strong, sharp flavour is well suited to richly flavoured salads.

Lemon and Lime Juice

The juice of lemons and limes is used to impart a clean acidity to oil dressings. They should be used in moderation.

Mustard

Mustard has a tendency to bring out the flavour of other ingredients. It also acts as an emulsifier in dressings and allows oil and vinegar to merge for a short period of time. The most popular mustards for use in salads are French, German, English (hot) and wholegrain.

Top left to right; Italian virgin olive oil, Spanish olive oil, Italian olive oil, safflower oil, hazelnut oil, walnut oil, groundnut (peanut) oil, French olive oil, Italian olive oil, white wine vinegar. Left to right bottom; lemon, olives, limes, capers and mustard.

Olives

Black and green olives belong in salads with a Mediterranean flavour. As a general rule, black olives are sweeter and juicier than green ones.

VINEGARS

White Wine Vinegar

This should be used in moderation to balance the richness of an oil. A good-quality white wine vinegar will serve most purposes.

Balsamic Vinegar

Sweeter than other vinegars, only a few drops of balsamic vinegar are necessary to enhance a salad or dressing. It is also a good substitute for lemon juice.

Making Herbed Oils and Vinegars

Many herbed oils and vinegars are available commercially, but you can very easily make your own. Pour the oil or vinegar into a sterilized jar and add your flavouring. Leave to steep for 2 weeks, then strain and decant into an attractive bottle which has also been sterilized properly. Add a seal and an identifying label. Flavoured vinegars should be used within 3 months, and flavoured oils within 10 days. Fresh herbs should be clean and completely dry before you use them.

TARRAGON VINEGAR

Steep tarragon in cider vinegar, then decant. Insert 2 or 3 long sprigs of tarragon into the bottle.

ROSEMARY VINEGAR

Steep a fresh rosemary sprig in red wine vinegar, then decant. Pour into a sterilized, dry bottle and add a few long stems of fresh rosemary as decoration.

LEMON AND LIME VINEGAR

Steep strips of lemon and lime rind in white wine vinegar, then decant. Pour into a sterilized, clean bottle and add fresh strips of mixed rind for colour.

RASPBERRY VINEGAR

Pour vinegar into a pan with 30ml/ 1 tbsp of pickling spices and heat gently for 5 minutes. Pour the hot mixture over the raspberries in a bowl and then add 2 fresh lemon thyme sprigs. Cover and leave the mixture to steep for 2 days in a cool, dark place. Strain the liquid and pour the flavoured vinegar into a sterilized bottle and seal.

DILL AND LEMON OIL

Steep a handful of fresh dill and a large strip of lemon rind in virgin olive oil, then decant. Use for salads containing fish or shellfish.

MEDITERRANEAN HERB OIL

Steep fresh rosemary, thyme and marjoram in extra virgin olive oil, then decant.

BASIL AND CHILLI OIL

Steep basil and 3 fresh chillies in virgin olive oil, then decant. Add to tomato and mozzarella salads.

WARNING

There is some evidence that oils containing fresh herbs and spices can grow harmful moulds, especially once the bottle has been opened and the contents are not fully covered by the oil. To protect against this, it is recommended that the herbs and spices are removed once their flavour has passed into the oil.

Left: Beautiful and delicious, herbal vinegars make exquisite gifts. From left: Tarragon vinegar, Rosemary vinegar, Raspberry vinegar and Lemon and Lime vinegar.

Vegetable Preparation

SHREDDING CABBAGE

Cabbage features in many salad recipes, such as coleslaw, and this method for shredding can be used for white, green or red varieties.

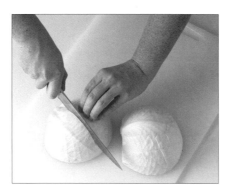

1 Use a large knife to cut the cabbage into quarters.

2 Cut the hard core from each quarter and discard; this part is not really edible when raw.

3 Slice each quarter to form fine shreds. Shredded cabbage will keep for several hours in the refrigerator, but do not dress it until you are ready to serve.

CHOPPING AN ONION

Chopped onions are used in many recipes and, whether they are finely or coarsely chopped, the method is the same; just vary the gap between cuts to give different size pieces.

1 Cut off the stalk end of the onion and cut in half through the root, leaving the root intact. Remove the skin and place the halved onion, cut side down, on the board. Make lengthways vertical cuts into the onion, taking care not to cut right through to the root.

2 Make two or three horizontal cuts from the stalk end through to the root, but without cutting all the way through.

3 Turn the onion on to its side. Cut the onion across from the stalk end to the root. The onion will fall away in small squares. Cut further apart for larger squares.

PREPARING GARLIC

Don't worry if you don't have a garlic press: try this method, which gives wonderful, juicy results.

1 Break off the clove of garlic, place the flat side of a large knife on top and strike with your fist. Remove all the papery outer skin. Begin by finely chopping the clove.

2 Sprinkle over a little table salt and, using the flat side of a large knife blade, work the salt into the garlic, until the clove softens and releases its juices. Use the garlic pulp as required.

PREPARING CHILLIES

Chillies add a distinct flavour, but remove the fiery-hot seeds.

1 Always protect your hands, as chillies can irritate the skin; wear gloves and never rub your eyes after handling chillies. Halve the chilli lengthways and remove and discard the seeds.

2 Slice, the finely chop and use as required. Wash the knife and chopping board thoroughly in hot, soapy water. Always wash your hands thoroughly after preparing chillies and avoid touching your eyes and face.

PEELING TOMATOES

If you have the time, peel tomatoes before adding them to sauces or purées. This avoids rolled-up, tough pieces of tomato skin that don't soften during cooking.

1 Make a cross in each tomato with a sharp knife and place in a bowl.

2 Pour over enough boiling water to cover and leave to stand for 30 seconds. The skins should start to come away. Slightly unripe tomatoes may take a little longer.

3 Drain the tomatoes and peel the skin away with a sharp knife. Don't leave the tomatoes in the boiling water for too long.

CHOPPING HERBS

Chop herbs just before you use them.

1 Remove the leaves and place on a clean, dry board. Use a large, sharp cook's knife.

2 Chop the herbs, as finely or as coarsely as required, by holding the tip of the blade on the board and rocking the handle up and down.

CUTTING JULIENNE STRIPS

Small julienne strips of vegetables make an attractive salad ingredient or garnish. Use this technique for carrots, cucumber and celery.

1 Peel the vegetable and use a large knife to cut it into 5cm/ 2in lengths. Cut a thin sliver from one side of the first piece so that it sits flat on the board.

2 Cut each piece into thin slices lengthwise. Stack the slices of vegetable and then cut through them again to make fine strips.

PREPARING SPRING ONIONS

Spring onions (scallions) make a crisp and tasty addition to salads. They are rather awkward to prepare, but the flavour is worth it.

1 Trim off the root of the spring onion with a sharp knife. Peel away any damaged or tough leaves.

2 For an intense flavour and an attractive green colour cut the dark green part into thin batons.

3 For a milder flavour just use the white part of the spring onion, discard the root and slice thinly on a slight diagonal.

Fruit Preparation

CITRUS FRUIT

1 To peel, cut a slice from the top and from the base. Set the fruit base down on a work surface.

2 Cut off the peel lengthways in thick strips. Take the coloured rind and all the white pith (which has a bitter taste). Cut following the curve of the fruit.

1 To remove the thin, coloured rind, use a vegetable peeler to shave off the rind in wide strips, taking none of the white pith. You can use these strips as they are or cut them into fine shreds with a sharp knife.

2 Alternatively, rub the fruit against the fine holes of a metal grater, turning the fruit so that you take just the coloured rind and not the white pith. Or use a special tool, called a citrus zester, to take fine threads of rind. Finely chop the threads with a sharp knife for tiny pieces.

1 For slices, cut across the fruit in slices with a serrated knife.

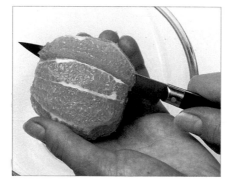

2 For segments, hold the fruit over a bowl to catch the juice. Working from the side of the fruit to the centre, slide the knife down first one side of a separating membrane and then the other. Continue cutting out segments.

FRESH CURRANTS

Pull through the tines of a fork to remove red, black or white currants from the stalks.

APPLES AND PEARS

1 For whole fruit, use an apple corer to stamp out the whole core from stalk end to base.

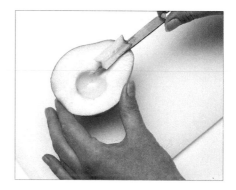

2 For halves, use a melon baller to scoop out the core. Cut out the stalk and base with a sharp knife.

3 For rings, remove the core and seeds. Set the fruit on its side and cut across, as required.

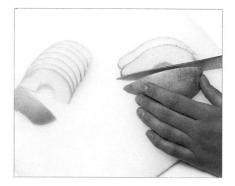

4 For slices, cut the fruit in half and remove the core and seeds. Set one half, cut side down, and cut it across into neat slices. Repeat with the other half.

FRESH DATES

Halve the fruit lengthways and lift out the stone (pit).

PAPAYAS AND MELONS

Halve the fruit. Scoop out the seeds from the central hollow, then scrape away any fibres. For slices, follow the pear technique.

KIWI FRUIT, STAR FRUIT (CARAMBOLA)

Cut the fruit across into neat slices; discard the ends.

PINEAPPLES

1 To peel the pineapple, set the pineapple on its base, hold it at the top and cut thick slices of skin from top to bottom. Dig out any eyes that remain with the point of the knife.

2 For chunks, halve the peeled fruit lengthways and then cut into quarters. Cut each quarter into spears and cut out the core. Cut each spear into chunks.

3 For rings, cut the peeled fruit across into slices and cut out the core.

KEEPING FRESH COLOUR

If exposed to the air for long, the cut flesh of fruits, such as apples, bananas and avocados, starts to turn brown. So if cut fruit has to wait before being served, sprinkle the cut surfaces with lemon juice, or immerse hard fruits in water and lemon juice, but do not soak or the fruit may become soggy.

MANGOES

1 Cut lengthways on either side of the stone (pit). Then cut from the thin ends of the stone.

2 Remove the skin and cut the flesh into slices or cubes.

PEACHES, NECTARINES, APRICOTS AND PLUMS

Cut the fruit in half, cutting around the indentation. Twist the halves apart. Lift out the stone (pit), or lever it out with the tip of a knife. Or cut the unpeeled fruit into wedges, removing the stone. Set each wedge, peel side down, and slide the knife down to peel.

Salad Dressings

Although the ingredients of a salad are important, the secret of a perfect salad is a good dressing. A French dressing made from the very best olive oil and vinegar can rescue even the dullest selection of lettuce leaves, while a home-made mayonnaise is always impressive. If you are a confident and experienced salad dresser, you might feel able to add oil and vinegar directly to your salad just before serving, but the safest way of creating a perfect dressing is to prepare it in advance. Home-made dressings can be stored in the refrigerator for up to a week and will improve in flavour. Here is a selection of dressings that should be part of every cook's repertoire.

THOUSAND ISLANDS DRESSING

This creamy dressing is great with green salads and grated carrot, hot potato, pasta and rice salads.

INGREDIENTS

Makes about 120ml/4fl oz/¹/₂ cup
60ml/4 tbsp sunflower oil
15ml/1 tbsp orange juice
15ml/1 tbsp lemon juice
10ml/2 tsp grated lemon rind
15ml/1 tbsp finely chopped onion
5ml/1 tsp paprika
5ml/1 tsp Worcestershire sauce
15ml/1 tbsp finely chopped fresh parsley
salt and ground black pepper

Put all the ingredients into a screw-top jar and season to taste. Replace the lid and shake well.

FRENCH DRESSING

French vinaigrette is the most widely used salad dressing.

INGREDIENTS

Makes about 120ml/4fl oz/¹/₂ cup
90ml/6 tbsp extra virgin olive oil
15ml/1 tbsp white wine vinegar
5ml/1 tsp French mustard
pinch of caster (superfine) sugar

1 Place the extra virgin olive oil and white wine vinegar in a clean screw-top jar.

2 Add the French mustard and a pinch of sugar.

3 Replace the lid and shake the jar vigorously.

FRENCH HERB DRESSING

The delicate scents and flavours of fresh herbs combine especially well in a French dressing. Use just one herb or a selection. Toss with a simple green salad and serve with good cheese, fresh bread and wine.

INGREDIENTS

Makes about 120ml/4fl oz/¹/₂ cup
60ml/4 tbsp extra virgin olive oil
30ml/2 tbsp sunflower oil
15ml/1 tbsp lemon juice
60ml/4 tbsp finely chopped fresh herbs
    (parsley, chives, tarragon
    and marjoram)
pinch of caster superfine sugar

1 Place the olive oil and sunflower oil in a clean screw-top jar.

2 Add the lemon juice, chopped fresh herbs and sugar.

3 Replace the lid and shake the jar vigorously.

MAYONNAISE

Mayonnaise is a simple emulsion made with egg yolks and oil. For consistent results, make sure that both egg yolks and oil are at room temperature before combining. Home-made mayonnaise is made with raw egg yolks and may therefore be considered unsuitable for young children, pregnant mothers and the elderly.

INGREDIENTS

Makes about 300ml/¹/₂ pint/1¹/₄ cups
2 egg yolks
5ml/1 tsp French mustard
150ml/¹/₄ pint/²/₃ cup extra virgin
   olive oil
150ml/¹/₄ pint/²/₃ cup groundnut (peanut)
   or sunflower oil
10ml/2 tsp white wine vinegar
salt and ground black pepper

1 Place the egg yolks and mustard in a food processor and process until smooth.

2 Add the olive oil, a little at a time, while the processor is running. When the mixture is quite thick, add the groundnut or sunflower oil in a slow, steady stream through the feeder tube.

3 Add the vinegar and season to taste with salt and pepper.

YOGURT DRESSING

This is a less rich version of a classic mayonnaise and is much easier to make. It can be used as a low-fat substitute. Change the herbs as you like, or leave them out.

INGREDIENTS

Makes about 200ml/7fl oz/scant 1 cup
150ml/¹/₄ pint/²/₃ cup natural
   (plain) yogurt
30ml/2 tbsp mayonnaise
30ml/2 tbsp milk
15ml/1 tbsp chopped fresh parsley
15ml/1 tbsp chopped fresh chives
salt and ground black pepper

Put all the ingredients together in a bowl. Season to taste with salt and pepper and mix well.

BLUE CHEESE AND CHIVE DRESSING

Blue cheese dressings have a strong, robust flavour and are well suited to winter salad leaves, such as escarole, chicory (Belgian endive) and radicchio.

INGREDIENTS

Makes about 350ml/12fl oz/1¹/₂ cups
75g/3oz blue cheese (Stilton, Bleu
   d'Auvergne or Gorgonzola)
150ml/¹/₄ pint/²/₃ cup medium-fat natural
   (plain) yogurt
45ml/3 tbsp olive oil
30ml/2 tbsp lemon juice
15ml/1 tbsp chopped fresh chives
ground black pepper

1 Remove the rind from the cheese. Combine the cheese with a third of the yogurt.

2 Add the remainder of the yogurt, the olive oil and the lemon juice.

3 Stir in the chopped chives and season to taste with ground black pepper.

BASIL AND LEMON MAYONNAISE

This luxurious dressing is flavoured with lemon juice and two types of basil. Serve with all kinds of leafy salads, crudités or coleslaws. It is also good with baked potatoes or as a delicious dip for French fries. The dressing will keep in an airtight jar for up to a week in the refrigerator.

INGREDIENTS

Makes about 300ml/½ pint/1¼ cups

2 large (US extra large) egg yolks
15ml/1 tbsp lemon juice
150ml/¼ pint/⅔ cup extra virgin
   olive oil
150ml/¼ pint/⅔ cup sunflower oil
4 garlic cloves
handful of fresh green basil
handful of fresh opal basil
salt and ground black pepper

1 Place the egg yolks and lemon juice in a blender or food processor and process briefly until lightly blended.

2 In a jug (pitcher), stir together both oils. With the machine running, pour in the oil very slowly, a little at a time.

3 Once half of the oil has been added and the dressing has successfully emulsified, the remaining oil can be incorporated a little more quickly. Continue processing until a thick, creamy mayonnaise has formed.

4 Peel and crush the garlic cloves and add them to the mayonnaise. Alternatively, place the garlic cloves on a chopping board and sprinkle with a little salt, then flatten them with the heel of a heavy-bladed knife and chop the flesh. Flatten the garlic again to make a coarse purée. Add to the mayonnaise.

5 Remove the basil stalks and tear both types of leaves into small pieces. Stir into the mayonnaise.

6 Add salt and pepper to taste, then transfer the mayonnaise to a serving dish. Cover and chill until ready to serve.

Instant Dressings and Dips

If you need an instant dressing or dip, try one of these quick and easy recipes. Most of them use store-cupboard ingredients.

CREAMY BLACK OLIVE DIP

Stir a little black olive paste into a carton of extra-thick double (heavy) cream until smooth and well blended. Add salt, ground black pepper and a squeeze of lemon juice to taste. Serve chilled.

CRÈME FRAÎCHE DRESSING WITH SPRING ONIONS

Finely chop a bunch of spring onions (scallions) and stir into a carton of crème fraîche. Add a dash of chilli sauce, a squeeze of lime juice, salt and ground black pepper.

GREEK YOGURT AND MUSTARD DIP

Mix a small carton of creamy, Greek (US strained plain) yogurt with 5–10ml/1–2 tsp wholegrain mustard. Serve with crudités.

HERB MAYONNAISE

Liven up ready-made French-style mayonnaise with a handful of chopped fresh herbs – try flat leaf parsley, basil, dill or tarragon.

PASSATA AND HORSERADISH DIP

Bring a little tang to a small carton or bottle of passata (bottled strained tomatoes) by adding some horseradish sauce or 5–10ml/ 1–2 tsp creamed horseradish and season with salt and pepper to taste. Serve with a selection of lightly-cooked vegetables.

PESTO DIP

For a simple, speedy, Italian-style dip, stir 15ml/1 tbsp ready-made red or green pesto into a carton of sour cream. Serve with crisp crudités or wedges of oven-roasted Mediterranean vegetables, such as (bell) peppers, courgettes (zucchini) and onions.

SOFT CHEESE AND CHIVE DIP

Mix a tub of soft cheese with 30–45ml/2–3 tbsp chopped fresh chives and season to taste with salt and black pepper. If the dip is too thick, stir in a little milk to soften it. Use as a dressing for all kinds of salads, especially winter coleslaws.

Above: Top row; Creamy Black Olive Dip, Crème Fraîche Dressing with Spring Onions. Second row; Herb Mayonnaise, Sun-dried Tomato Dip. Third row; Greek Yogurt and Mustard dip, Soft Cheese and Chive Dip, Spiced Yogurt Dressing. Fourth row; Pesto Dip, Passata and Horseradish dip.

SPICED YOGURT DRESSING

Stir a little curry paste and chutney into a carton of yogurt.

SUN-DRIED TOMATO DIP

Stir 15–30ml/1–2 tbsp sun-dried tomato paste into a carton of Greek (strained plain) yogurt. Season to taste.

INSTANT SALADS

~

Made in minutes, these salads are not so much thrown
together as tossed together and their harmonious
combinations of ingredients and complementary dressings
belie the speed with which they are made. They are ideal for
easy entertaining or speedy midweek meals when you are
too tired, too busy or too hot to spend much time in
the kitchen. They can all be served as appetizers and many
of them would also work well as a refreshing accompaniment
to fish or meat dishes.

V

Lettuce and Herb Salad

Stores now sell many different types of lettuce leaves all year, so try to use a mixture. Look for pre-packed bags of mixed baby lettuce leaves.

INGREDIENTS

Serves 4

½ cucumber

mixed lettuce leaves

1 bunch of watercress, about 115g/4oz

1 chicory (Belgian endive) head, sliced

45ml/3 tbsp chopped fresh herbs, such as
    parsley, thyme, tarragon, chives, chervil

For the dressing

15ml/1 tbsp white wine vinegar

5ml/1 tsp prepared mustard

75ml/5 tbsp olive oil

salt and ground black pepper

3 Either toss the cucumber, lettuce, watercress, chicory and herbs together in a bowl, or arrange them in the bowl in layers.

4 Stir the dressing, then pour over the salad and toss lightly to coat the salad vegetables and leaves. Serve immediately.

1 To make the dressing, mix the vinegar and mustard together, then whisk in the oil and seasoning.

2 Peel the cucumber, if you like, then halve it lengthways and scoop out the seeds. Thinly slice the flesh. Tear the lettuce leaves into bitesize pieces.

Fresh Spinach and Avocado Salad

*Young, tender spinach leaves make
a change from lettuce. They are
delicious served with avocado,
cherry tomatoes and radishes in
an unusual tofu sauce.*

INGREDIENTS

Serves 2–3

1 large avocado

juice of 1 lime

225g/8oz baby spinach leaves

115g/4oz cherry tomatoes

4 spring onions (scallions), sliced

½ cucumber

50g/2oz radishes, sliced

For the dressing

115g/4oz soft silken tofu

45ml/3 tbsp milk

10ml/2 tsp mustard

2.5ml/½ tsp white wine vinegar

cayenne pepper

salt and ground black pepper

radish roses and fresh herb sprigs,
   to garnish

1 Cut the avocado in half,
remove the stone (pit) and
peel. Cut the flesh into slices.
Transfer to a plate, drizzle over
the lime juice and set aside.

2 Wash and dry the baby
spinach leaves. Put them in a
mixing bowl.

3 Cut the larger cherry tomatoes
in half and add all the
tomatoes to the mixing bowl
with the spring onions. Cut the
cucumber into chunks and add to
the bowl with the sliced radishes.

COOK'S TIP

Use soft silken tofu rather than
the firm block variety. It can be
found in most supermarkets in
long-life cartons.

---

4 To make the dressing, put the
tofu, milk, mustard, vinegar
and a pinch of cayenne in a food
processor or blender. Add salt
and pepper to taste. Process for
30 seconds, until smooth. Scrape
the dressing into a bowl and add
a little extra milk if you like a
thinner dressing. Sprinkle with a
little extra cayenne, garnish with
radish roses and herb sprigs and
serve separately. Place the avocado
slices with the spinach salad on a
serving dish.

V

Mixed Green Salad

A good combination of leaves for this salad would be rocket, radicchio, lamb's lettuce and frisée lettuce, with herbs, such as chervil, basil, parsley and tarragon.

INGREDIENTS

Serves 4–6

1 garlic clove, peeled

30ml/2 tbsp red wine or sherry vinegar

5ml/1 tsp Dijon mustard (optional)

75–120ml/5–8 tbsp extra virgin olive oil

200–225g/7–8oz mixed salad leaves
    and herbs

salt and ground black pepper

1 Rub a large salad bowl with the garlic clove. Leave the garlic clove in the bowl.

2 Add the vinegar, salt and pepper and mustard, if using. Stir to mix the ingredients and dissolve the salt, then gradually whisk in the olive oil.

3 Remove and discard the garlic clove and stir the vinaigrette again to combine.

4 Add the salad leaves to the bowl and toss well. Serve the salad immediately, before it starts to wilt.

VARIATION

A salad like this should always contain some pungent leaves. Try young dandelion leaves when they are in season, but be sure to pick them well away from traffic routes and agricultural crop spraying.

Apple and Celeriac Salad

Celeriac, despite its coarse appearance, has a sweet and subtle flavour. Traditionally par-boiled in lemony water, in this salad it is served raw, allowing its unique taste and texture to come through.

INGREDIENTS

Serves 3–4

675g/1½lb celeriac, peeled

10–15ml/2–3 tsp lemon juice

5ml/1 tsp walnut oil (optional)

1 apple

45ml/3 tbsp mayonnaise

10ml/2 tsp Dijon mustard

15ml/1 tbsp chopped fresh parsley

salt and ground black pepper

1 Using a food processor or coarse cheese grater, shred the celeriac. Alternatively, cut it into very thin julienne strips, using a sharp knife.

2 Place the prepared celeriac in a bowl and sprinkle with the lemon juice and the walnut oil, if using. Stir well to mix.

3 Peel the apple if you like. Cut the apple into quarters and remove the core. Slice the apple quarters thinly crossways and toss together with the celeriac.

4 Mix together the mayonnaise, mustard, parsley and salt and pepper to taste. Add to the celeriac mixture and stir well. Chill for several hours until ready to serve.

| V |

Green Bean and Sweet Red Pepper Salad

A galaxy of colour and texture, with a jolt of heat from the chilli, will make this a favourite salad.

INGREDIENTS

Serves 4

350g/12oz cooked green beans, quartered

2 red (bell) peppers, seeded and chopped

2 spring onions (scallions), both white and green parts, chopped

1 or more drained pickled serrano chillies, well rinsed, seeded and chopped

1 iceberg lettuce, coarsely shredded, or mixed salad leaves

green olives, to garnish

For the dressing

45ml/3 tbsp red wine vinegar

135ml/9 tbsp olive oil

salt and ground black pepper

1 Combine the green beans, peppers, spring onions and chilli(es) in a salad bowl.

2 To make the dressing, pour the red wine vinegar into a bowl or jug (pitcher). Season with salt and black pepper to taste, then gradually whisk in the olive oil until well combined.

3 Pour the dressing over the prepared vegetables and toss lightly together to mix and to coat them thoroughly.

4 Line a large serving platter with the shredded lettuce or mixed salad leaves and arrange the vegetable mixture attractively on top. Garnish with the olives and serve.

Pepper and Cucumber Salad

*Generous quantities of fresh herbs
transform ordinary ingredients.*

INGREDIENTS

Serves 4

1 yellow or red (bell) pepper

1 large cucumber

4–5 tomatoes

1 bunch of spring onions (scallions)

30ml/2 tbsp fresh parsley

30ml/2 tbsp fresh mint

30ml/2 tbsp fresh coriander (cilantro)

2 pitta breads, to serve

For the dressing

2 garlic cloves, crushed

75ml/5 tbsp olive oil

juice of 2 lemons

salt and ground black pepper

1 Slice the pepper, discard the seeds and core. Coarsely chop the cucumber and tomatoes. Place in a large salad bowl.

2 Trim and slice the spring onions. Add to the cucumber, tomatoes and pepper. Finely chop the parsley, mint and coriander and add to the bowl. If you have plenty of herbs, you can add as much as you like.

3 To make the dressing, blend the garlic with the olive oil and lemon juice in a jug (pitcher), then season to taste with salt and pepper. Pour the dressing over the salad and toss lightly to mix.

4 Toast the pitta breads in a toaster or under a hot grill (broiler) until crisp and serve them alongside the salad.

VARIATION

If you like, serve this Middle Eastern salad in the traditional way. After toasting the pitta breads, crush them in your hand and then sprinkle the pieces over the salad before serving.

V

Classic Greek Salad

If you have ever visited Greece, you'll know that this salad accompanied by a chunk of bread makes a delicious first course.

INGREDIENTS

Serves 4

1 cos or romaine lettuce

½ cucumber, halved lengthways

4 tomatoes

8 spring onions (scallions), sliced

black olives

115g/4oz feta cheese

For the dressing

90ml/6 tbsp white wine vinegar

150ml/¼ pint/⅔ cup extra virgin
   olive oil

salt and ground black pepper

1 Tear the lettuce leaves into pieces and place in a large bowl. Slice the cucumber and add to the bowl.

2 Cut the tomatoes into wedges and put them into the bowl.

COOK'S TIP

◠

The salad can be assembled in advance and chilled, but should be dressed only just before serving. Keep the dressing at room temperature as chilling deadens the flavour.

3 Add the spring onions to the bowl together with the olives, and toss well.

4 Cut the feta cheese into cubes and add to the salad.

5 Put the vinegar, olive oil and seasoning into a small bowl and whisk well. Pour the dressing over the salad and toss to combine. Serve immediately, with extra olives and chunks of bread.

V

Tomato and Feta Cheese Salad

Sweet, sun-ripened tomatoes are rarely more delicious than when served with feta cheese and olive oil.

INGREDIENTS

Serves 4

900g/2lb tomatoes

200g/7oz feta cheese

120ml/4fl oz/½ cup olive oil

12 black olives

4 fresh basil sprigs

ground black pepper

2 Slice the tomatoes thickly and arrange them attractively in a shallow serving dish.

3 Crumble the feta over the tomatoes, sprinkle with oil, then strew with the olives and basil sprigs. Season to taste with pepper and serve at room temperature.

1 Remove the tough cores from the tomatoes, using a small, sharp knife.

COOK'S TIP

Feta cheese has a strong flavour and can be salty. The least salty variety is imported from Greece and Turkey, and is available from specialist delicatessens.

V

Spinach and Mushroom Salad

This nutritious salad goes well with strongly flavoured dishes. If served alone as a light lunch, it could be dressed with a French vinaigrette and served with warm, crusty French bread.

INGREDIENTS

Serves 4

10 baby corn cobs

2 tomatoes

115g/4oz/1½ cups mushrooms

1 onion cut into rings

20 small spinach leaves

25g/1oz salad cress (optional)

salt and ground black pepper

1 Using a sharp knife, halve the baby corn cobs lengthways and slice the tomatoes.

2 Trim the mushrooms and cut them into thin slices.

3 Arrange all the salad ingredients attractively in a large bowl. Season with salt and pepper to taste and serve.

Nutty Salad

A delicious salad with a tangy bite to it which can be served as an accompaniment to a main meal, or as an appetizer. For wholesome finger food at a party, serve mini pitta breads stuffed with the salad.

INGREDIENTS

Serves 4

1 onion, cut into 12 rings

115g/4oz/¾ cup canned red kidney beans, drained and rinsed

1 green courgette (zucchini), sliced

1 yellow courgette (zucchini), sliced

50g/2oz/½ cup pasta shells, cooked

50g/2oz/½ cup cashew nuts

25g/1oz/¼ cup peanuts

lime wedges and fresh coriander (cilantro) sprigs, to garnish

For the dressing

120ml/4fl oz/½ cup fromage frais (farmer's cheese)

30ml/2 tbsp natural (plain) yogurt

1 fresh green chilli, seeded and chopped

15ml/1 tbsp chopped fresh coriander (cilantro)

2.5ml/½ tsp crushed black peppercorns

2.5ml/½ tsp crushed dried red chillies

15ml/1 tbsp lemon juice

2.5ml/½ tsp salt

1 Arrange the onion rings, red kidney beans, green and yellow courgette slices and pasta shells in a salad dish, ready for serving. Sprinkle the cashew nuts and peanuts over the top.

2 In a separate bowl, blend together the fromage frais, yogurt, green chilli, coriander and salt and beat well using a fork.

3 Sprinkle the crushed black pepper, red chillies and lemon juice over the dressing. Garnish the salad with the lime wedges and coriander sprigs and serve with the dressing in a separate bowl or poured over the salad.

V

Rocket and Pear Salad

For a sophisticated start to an elaborate meal, try this simple salad of honey-rich pears, fresh Parmesan and aromatic rocket leaves.

INGREDIENTS

Serves 4

3 ripe pears (Williams or Packhams)
10ml/2 tsp lemon juice
45ml/3 tbsp hazelnut or walnut oil
115g/4oz rocket (arugula) leaves
75g/3oz piece of Parmesan cheese
ground black pepper

2 Combine the hazelnut or walnut oil with the pears. Add the rocket leaves and toss.

3 Turn the salad out on to four small serving plates and top with thin shavings of Parmesan cheese. Season with pepper and serve immediately.

1 Peel and core the pears and slice thickly. Moisten with lemon juice to keep the flesh white.

COOK'S TIP

Parmesan cheese is a delicious main ingredient in a salad. Buy a chunk of fresh Parmesan and shave strips off the side, using a vegetable peeler. The distinctive flavour is quite strong. Store the rest of the Parmesan wrapped in foil in the refrigerator.

Radish, Mango and Apple Salad

V

Radish is a year-round vegetable and this salad, with its clean, crisp tastes and mellow flavours, can be served at any time of year. Serve with smoked fish, such as rolls of smoked salmon, or with flavourful ham or salami.

INGREDIENTS

Serves 4

10–15 radishes

1 apple, peeled, cored and thinly sliced

2 celery sticks, thinly sliced

1 small ripe mango

fresh dill sprigs, to garnish

For the dressing

120ml/4fl oz/½ cup sour cream

10ml/2 tsp creamed horseradish

15ml/1 tbsp chopped fresh dill

salt and ground black pepper

1 To prepare the dressing, blend together the sour cream, horseradish and dill in a small bowl and season with a little salt and pepper.

2 Trim the radishes and slice them thinly. Put in a bowl together with the apple and celery.

3 Halve the mango lengthways, cutting either side of the stone pit. Make even, criss-cross cuts through the flesh of each side section and bend it back to separate the cubes. Remove the cubes with a small knife and add to the bowl.

4 Stir the dressing again, then pour it over the vegetables and fruit and stir gently so that all the ingredients are well coated without breaking up the mango. Garnish with dill sprigs and serve.

Egg, Bacon and Avocado Salad

A glorious medley of colours, flavours and textures to delight the eye and the taste buds.

INGREDIENTS

Serves 4

1 large cos or romaine lettuce

8 bacon rashers (strips), fried until crisp

2 large avocados, peeled and diced

6 hard-boiled eggs, chopped

2 beefsteak tomatoes, peeled, seeded
   and chopped

175g/6oz blue cheese, crumbled

For the dressing

1 garlic clove, crushed

5ml/1 tsp sugar

7.5ml/1½ tsp lemon juice

25ml/1½ tbsp red wine vinegar

120ml/4fl oz/½ cup groundnut
   (peanut) oil

salt and ground black pepper

1 Slice the lettuce into strips across the leaves. Crumble the fried bacon rashers.

2 To make the dressing, put the garlic, sugar, lemon juice, vinegar and oil in a screw-top jar, add salt and pepper to taste and shake the jar vigorously. On a large, rectangular or oval platter, spread out the strips of lettuce to make a bed.

3 Arrange the avocados, eggs, tomatoes and cheese neatly in rows on top of the lettuce. Sprinkle the bacon on top.

4 Pour the dressing carefully and evenly over the salad just before serving.

Spicy Corn Salad

This brilliant, sweet-flavoured salad is served warm with a delicious, spicy dressing.

INGREDIENTS

Serves 4

30ml/2 tbsp vegetable oil

450g/1lb drained canned corn kernels, or
   frozen corn kernels, thawed

1 green (bell) pepper, seeded and diced

1 small fresh red chilli, seeded and diced

4 spring onions (scallions), sliced

45ml/3 tbsp chopped fresh parsley

225g/8oz cherry tomatoes, halved

salt and ground black pepper

For the dressing

2.5ml/½ tsp sugar

30ml/2 tbsp white wine vinegar

2.5ml/½ tsp Dijon mustard

15ml/1 tbsp chopped fresh basil

15ml/1 tbsp mayonnaise

1.5ml/¼ tsp chilli sauce

1 Heat the vegetable oil in a frying pan. Add the corn, green pepper, chilli and spring onions. Cook over a medium heat, stirring frequently, for about 5 minutes, until softened.

2 Transfer the vegetables to a salad bowl. Stir in the parsley and the cherry tomatoes.

3 To make the dressing, combine all the ingredients in a small bowl and whisk together until thoroughly combined.

4 Pour the dressing over the corn mixture. Season to taste with salt and pepper. Toss well to combine, then serve immediately, while the salad is still warm.

WARM
SALADS

~

A relatively recent food fashion that is destined to last, warm
salads offer the best of both worlds. Colourful salad leaves
and crisp vegetables may be served with a topping of freshly
pan-fried meat or a rich warm dressing or, alternatively,
just-cooked vegetables or pasta can be tossed with salad
ingredients and cold dressings. The result is not only a
delicious combination of flavours and textures, but also
a stimulating and appetizing contrast of temperatures.

V

Warm Broad Bean and Feta Salad

This medley of fresh-tasting salad ingredients is lovely served warm or cold as an appetizer or makes a good accompaniment to a main course.

INGREDIENTS

Serves 4–6

900g/2lb broad (fava) beans, shelled, or
    350g/12oz shelled frozen beans
60ml/4 tbsp olive oil
175g/6oz fresh plum tomatoes, halved,
    or quartered if large
4 garlic cloves, crushed
115g/4oz firm feta cheese, cut
    into chunks
45ml/3 tbsp chopped fresh dill
12 black olives
salt and ground black pepper
chopped fresh dill, to garnish

1 Cook the broad beans in salted, boiling water until just tender. Drain and set aside.

2 Meanwhile, heat the olive oil in a heavy frying pan and add the tomatoes and garlic. Cook until the tomatoes are beginning to change colour.

3 Add the feta to the pan and toss the ingredients together for 1 minute. Mix with the drained beans, dill and olives and season to taste with salt and pepper. Serve garnished with chopped dill.

COOK'S TIP

Plum tomatoes are now widely available in supermarkets fresh as well as canned. Their deep red, oval shapes are very attractive in salads and they have a sweet, rich flavour.

V

Halloumi and Grape Salad

In this recipe firm, salty halloumi cheese is fried and then tossed with sweet, juicy grapes which really complement its distinctive flavour.

INGREDIENTS

Serves 4

150g/5oz mixed green salad leaves
75g/3oz seedless green grapes
75g/3oz seedless black grapes
250g/9oz halloumi cheese
45ml/3 tbsp olive oil
fresh young thyme leaves or fresh dill,
    to garnish

For the dressing
60ml/4 tbsp olive oil
15ml/1 tbsp lemon juice
2.5ml/½ tsp caster (superfine) sugar
15ml/1 tbsp chopped fresh thyme or dill
salt and ground black pepper

1 To make the dressing, mix together the olive oil, lemon juice and sugar. Season with salt and pepper. Stir in the chopped thyme or dill and set aside.

2 Toss together the salad leaves and the green and black grapes, then transfer to a large serving plate.

3 Thinly slice the cheese. Heat the oil in a large frying pan. Add the cheese and fry briefly until golden on the underside. Turn the cheese with a fish slice or metal spatula and cook the other side.

4 Arrange the cheese over the salad. Pour over the dressing and garnish with sprigs of fresh thyme or dill.

V

Green Bean Salad

Green beans are delicious served with a simple vinaigrette dressing, but this dish is a little more elaborate.

INGREDIENTS

Serves 4

450g/1lb green beans
15ml/1 tbsp olive oil
25g/1oz/2 tbsp butter
½ garlic clove, crushed
50g/2 oz/1 cup fresh white breadcrumbs
15ml/1 tbsp chopped fresh parsley
1 hard-boiled egg, finely chopped

For the dressing
30ml/2 tbsp olive oil
30ml/2 tbsp sunflower oil
10ml/2 tsp white wine vinegar
½ garlic clove, crushed
1.5ml/¼ tsp Dijon mustard
pinch of sugar
pinch of salt

1 Cook the green beans in salted boiling water for 5–6 minutes, until tender. Drain, refresh under cold running water and place in a serving bowl.

2 To make the dressing, mix all the ingredients thoroughly together. Pour the dressing over the beans and toss.

3 Heat the oil and butter in a heavy frying pan and cook the garlic for 1 minute. Stir in the breadcrumbs and cook over a medium heat for 3–4 minutes, until golden brown, stirring frequently.

4 Remove the pan from the heat and stir in the parsley and then the chopped egg. Sprinkle the breadcrumb mixture over the green beans. Serve warm or at room temperature.

Lentil and Cabbage Salad

A warm, crunchy salad that makes a satisfying meal if served with crusty French bread or fresh rolls.

V

INGREDIENTS

Serves 4–6

225g/8 oz/1 cup Puy lentils

3 garlic cloves

1 bay leaf

1 small onion, peeled and studded with
　2 cloves

15ml/1 tbsp olive oil

1 red onion, thinly sliced

15ml/1 tbsp fresh thyme leaves

350g/12oz cabbage, finely shredded

finely grated rind and juice of 1 lemon

15ml/1 tbsp raspberry vinegar

salt and ground black pepper

1 Rinse the lentils in cold water and place in a large pan with 1.5 litres/2½ pints/6¼ cups cold water, 1 of the garlic cloves, the bay leaf and clove-studded onion. Bring to the boil and cook for 10 minutes. Reduce the heat, cover and simmer gently for about 15–20 minutes. Drain and discard the onion, garlic and bay leaf.

2 Crush the remaining garlic cloves. Heat the oil in a large pan. Add the red onion, crushed garlic and thyme and cook over a medium heat, stirring occasionally, for 5 minutes, until softened.

3 Add the cabbage and cook for 3–5 minutes, until just cooked but still crunchy.

4 Stir in the cooked lentils, lemon rind and juice and the raspberry vinegar. Season to taste with salt and pepper and serve immediately while still warm.

V

Sweet Potato and Carrot Salad

This warm salad has a sweet-and-sour taste, and several unusual ingredients. It is attractively garnished with whole walnuts, sultanas and onion rings.

INGREDIENTS

Serves 4

1 sweet potato

2 carrots, cut into thick diagonal slices

3 tomatoes

8–10 iceberg lettuce leaves

75g/3oz/½ cup canned chickpeas, drained

For the dressing

15ml/1 tbsp clear honey

90ml/6 tbsp natural (plain) yogurt

2.5ml/½ tsp salt

5ml/1 tsp ground black pepper

For the garnish

15ml/1 tbsp walnuts

15ml/1 tbsp sultanas (golden raisins)

1 small onion, cut into rings

1 Peel the sweet potato and cut coarsely into cubes. Boil it until it is soft but not mushy, then cover the pan and set aside.

2 Boil the carrots for just a few minutes, making sure that they remain crunchy. Add the carrots to the sweet potato.

3 Drain the water from the sweet potato and carrots and place them together in a bowl.

4 Slice the tops off the tomatoes, then scoop out the seeds with a spoon and discard. Coarsely chop the flesh. Slice the lettuce into strips across the leaves.

5 Line a salad bowl with the shredded lettuce leaves. Mix together the sweet potato, carrots, chickpeas and tomatoes and place the mixture in the centre.

6 To make the dressing, mix together all the ingredients and beat well, using a fork.

7 Garnish the salad with the walnuts, sultanas and onion rings. Pour the dressing over the top just before serving, or serve it in a separate bowl.

COOK'S TIP

This salad makes an excellent main course for lunch or a family supper. Serve it with a sweet mango chutney and warm naan bread.

Chicken Liver, Bacon and Tomato Salad

Warm salads are especially welcome during the autumn months when the days are growing shorter and cooler. This rich salad includes sweet spinach and the bitter leaves of frisée lettuce.

Serves 4

225g/8oz young spinach, stems removed

1 frisée lettuce

105ml/7 tbsp sunflower oil

175g/6oz rindless unsmoked bacon, cut into thin strips

75g/3oz day-old bread, crusts removed and cut into short fingers

450g/1lb chicken livers

115g/4oz cherry tomatoes

salt and ground black pepper

1 Place the spinach and lettuce leaves in a salad bowl. Heat 60ml/4 tbsp of the oil in a large frying pan, add the bacon and cook for 3–4 minutes, or until crisp and brown. Remove the bacon with a slotted spoon and drain on kitchen paper.

2 To make croûtons, fry the bread in the bacon-flavoured oil, tossing until crisp and golden. Drain on kitchen paper.

3 Heat the remaining 45ml/ 3 tbsp oil in the frying pan, add the chicken livers and cook briskly for 2–3 minutes. Turn the chicken livers out over the salad leaves and add the bacon, croûtons and tomatoes. Season, toss and serve warm.

VARIATION

If you can't find any baby spinach leaves you can use lamb's lettuce. Watercress would make a deliciously peppery substitute, but you should use less of it and bulk the salad out with a milder leaf so that the watercress doesn't overwhelm the other flavours.

Warm Pasta Salad with Asparagus

This warm salad is served with ham, eggs and Parmesan. A mustard dressing made from the thick part of the asparagus stalks provides a rich accompaniment.

INGREDIENTS

Serves 4

450g/1lb asparagus

450g/1lb dried tagliatelle

225g/8oz cooked ham, sliced 5mm/¼in thick, and cut into fingers

2 eggs, hard-boiled and sliced

50g/2oz piece Parmesan cheese

For the dressing

50g/2oz cooked potato

75ml/5 tbsp olive oil

15ml/1 tbsp lemon juice

10ml/2 tsp Dijon mustard

120ml/4fl oz/½ cup Vegetable Stock

salt and ground black pepper

1 Bring a pan of salted water to the boil. Trim and discard the tough, woody part of the asparagus stalks. Cut the asparagus in half and boil the thicker halves for 12 minutes, adding the asparagus tips after 6 minutes. Refresh under cold water until warm, then drain.

2 Finely chop 150g/5oz of the thicker asparagus pieces. Place in a food processor together with the dressing ingredients and process until smooth. Season the dressing to taste.

3 Boil the pasta in a large pan of salted water until *al dente*. Refresh under cold water.

4 Dress with the asparagus sauce and turn out into four pasta bowls. Top each pile of pasta with some of the ham, eggs and asparagus tips. Using a vegetable peeler, make thin shavings of Parmesan cheese to garnish the salad and serve warm.

Gado Gado

This classic Indonesian vegetable salad is served with a delicious hot peanut sauce.

INGREDIENTS

Serves 4–6

2 potatoes

175g/6oz green beans, trimmed

175g/6oz Chinese leaves (Chinese cabbage), shredded

1 iceberg lettuce

175g/6oz beansprouts

½ cucumber, cut into fingers

150g/5oz mooli (daikon), shredded

3 spring onions (scallions)

225g/8oz tofu, cut into large slices

3 hard-boiled eggs, shelled and quartered

1 small bunch of fresh coriander (cilantro)

prawn (shrimp) crackers, to serve

For the peanut sauce

150g/5 oz/1¼ cups raw peanuts

15ml/1 tbsp vegetable oil

2 shallots or 1 small onion, finely chopped

1 garlic clove, crushed

1–2 small fresh chillies, seeded and finely chopped

1cm/½in square shrimp paste or 15ml/ 1 tbsp Thai fish sauce (optional)

30ml/2 tbsp tamarind sauce

120ml/4fl oz/½ cup canned coconut milk

15ml/1 tbsp clear honey

1 Peel the potatoes. Bring to the boil in salted water and simmer for about 15 minutes, or until tender. Cook the green beans for 3–4 minutes. Drain the potatoes and beans and refresh under cold running water.

2 To make the peanut sauce, dry-fry the peanuts in a wok, or place under a moderate grill (broiler), tossing them all the time to prevent them from burning.

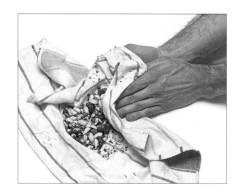

3 Turn the peanuts on to a clean cloth and rub them vigorously with your hands to remove the papery skins. Place the peanuts in a food processor and blend for 2 minutes, until finely crushed.

4 Heat the vegetable oil in a wok and cook the shallots or onion, garlic and chillies without letting them colour. Add the shrimp paste or fish sauce, if using, together with the tamarind sauce, coconut milk and honey.

5 Simmer briefly, add to the blended peanuts and process to form a thick sauce. Transfer to a small serving bowl and keep hot.

6 Arrange the potatoes, green beans and all the other salad ingredients on a large serving platter. Serve with the bowl of peanut sauce and prawn crackers.

Chicken Liver Salad

This delicious salad may be served as a main course for a summer lunch party, or as a tasty first course served on individual plates. The richness of the chicken livers is complemented perfectly by the sweet tangy wholegrain mustard dressing. Serve with warm crusty bread to mop up the dressing.

INGREDIENTS

Serves 4

mixed salad leaves such as frisée, oak leaf
   lettuce, radicchio
1 avocado, diced
30ml/2 tbsp lemon juice
2 pink grapefruit
350g/12oz chicken livers
30ml/2 tbsp olive oil
1 garlic clove, crushed
salt and ground black pepper
whole fresh chives, to garnish

For the dressing
30ml/2 tbsp lemon juice
60ml/4 tbsp olive oil
2.5ml/½ tsp wholegrain mustard
2.5ml/½ tsp clear honey
15ml/1 tbsp chopped fresh chives
salt and ground black pepper

1 To make the dressing, put the lemon juice, olive oil, mustard, honey and chopped fresh chives into a screw-top jar, and shake vigorously. Season to taste with salt and freshly ground black pepper.

2 Arrange the previously washed and well-drained mixed salad leaves attractively on a large serving plate.

3 Peel and dice the avocado and mix with the lemon juice to prevent browning. Add to the plate of mixed leaves.

4 Peel the grapefruit, removing as much of the white pith as possible. Split into segments and arrange with the leaves and avocado on the serving plate.

5 Dry the chicken livers on kitchen paper and remove any unwanted pieces.

6 Using a sharp knife, cut the larger chicken livers in half. Leave the smaller ones whole.

7 Heat the oil in a large frying pan. Stir-fry the chicken livers and garlic briskly until the livers are brown all over (they should be slightly pink inside).

8 Season the chicken livers to taste with salt and black pepper, remove from the pan and drain on kitchen paper.

9 Place the chicken livers, while still warm, on to the salad leaves and spoon over the dressing. Garnish with the whole chives and serve immediately.

VEGETARIAN SALADS

~

This exciting collection of salads features an array of
cheeses, boiled and poached eggs, and nuts combined with
a breathtaking mixture of vegetables and fruit. Serve them as
tempting hors d'oeuvres before any kind of main course,
as a lovely, light vegetarian lunch – perhaps with crusty
bread or fresh rolls – or, in many instances, as a refreshing
accompaniment. Whether based on fresh mushrooms,
asparagus or summer herbs, these are gourmet salads for
the discerning palate.

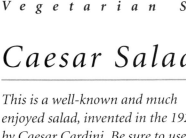

Caesar Salad

This is a well-known and much enjoyed salad, invented in the 1920s by Caesar Cardini. Be sure to use cos or romaine lettuce and add the very soft eggs at the last minute.

INGREDIENTS

Serves 6

175ml/6fl oz/³⁄₄ cup salad oil, preferably olive oil

115g/4oz French or Italian bread, cut in 2.5cm/1in cubes

1 large garlic clove, crushed with the flat side of a knife

1 cos or romaine lettuce

2 eggs, boiled for 1 minute

120ml/4fl oz/¹⁄₂ cup lemon juice

50g/2oz/²⁄₃ cup freshly grated Parmesan cheese

salt and ground black pepper

1 Heat 50ml/2fl oz/¹⁄₄ cup of the oil in a large, heavy frying pan. Add the bread cubes and garlic. Cook over a medium heat, stirring and turning constantly, until the cubes are golden brown all over. Remove with a slotted spoon and drain well on kitchen paper. Discard the garlic.

2 Tear large lettuce leaves into smaller pieces. Then put all the lettuce in a bowl.

3 Add the remaining oil to the lettuce and season with salt and plenty of ground black pepper. Toss well to coat the leaves.

4 Break the eggs on top. Sprinkle with the lemon juice. Toss well again to combine.

5 Add the Parmesan cheese and toss gently to mix.

6 Sprinkle the fried bread cubes over the top and serve the salad immediately.

COOK'S TIP

To make a tangier dressing mix 30ml/2 tbsp white wine vinegar, 15ml/1 tbsp Worcestershire sauce, 2.5ml/¹⁄₂ tsp mustard powder, 5ml/1 tsp sugar, salt and pepper in a screw-top jar, then add the oil and shake well.

Tricolour Salad

V

A popular salad, this dish depends for its success on the quality of its ingredients. Mozzarella di bufala is the best cheese to serve uncooked. Whole ripe plum tomatoes give up their juice to blend with extra virgin olive oil for a natural dressing.

INGREDIENTS

Serves 2–3

150g/5oz mozzarella di bufala cheese, thinly sliced

4 large plum tomatoes, sliced

1 large avocado

about 12 basil leaves or a small handful of flat leaf parsley leaves

45–60ml/3–4 tbsp extra virgin olive oil

sea salt flakes ground black pepper

ciabatta, to serve

1 Arrange the sliced mozzarella cheese and tomatoes randomly on two salad plates. Crush over a few good pinches of sea salt flakes. This will help to draw out some of the juices from the plum tomatoes. Cover and set aside in a cool place and leave to marinate for about 30 minutes.

2 Just before serving, cut the avocado in half using a large sharp knife and twist the halves to separate. Lift out the stone (pit) and remove the peel.

3 Carefully slice the avocado flesh crossways into half moons, or cut it into large chunks if that is easier.

4 Place the avocado on the salad, then sprinkle with the basil or parsley. Drizzle over the olive oil, add a little more salt, if you like, and some black pepper. Serve at room temperature, with chunks of crusty Italian ciabatta for mopping up the dressing.

Goat's Cheese and Fig Salad

Fresh figs and walnuts are perfect partners for goat's cheese and toasted buckwheat. The olive and nut oil dressing contains no vinegar, depending instead on the acidity of the goat's cheese.

INGREDIENTS

Serves 4

175g/6 oz/1 cup couscous

30ml/2 tbsp toasted buckwheat

1 egg, hard-boiled

30ml/2 tbsp chopped fresh parsley

60ml/4 tbsp olive oil

45ml/3 tbsp walnut oil

115g/4oz rocket (arugula) leaves

½ frisée lettuce

175g/6oz crumbly white goat's cheese

50g/2oz/½ cup broken walnuts, toasted

4 ripe figs, trimmed and almost cut into
    four (leave the pieces joined at the base)

1 Place the couscous and toasted buckwheat in a bowl, cover with boiling water and leave to soak for 15 minutes. Place in a sieve to drain off any remaining water, then spread out on a metal tray and leave to cool.

2 Shell the hard-boiled egg and grate finely.

3 Toss the grated egg, parsley, couscous and buckwheat together in a bowl. Combine the olive and walnut oils, using half to moisten the couscous mixture.

4 Toss the salad leaves in the remaining oil and distribute among four large serving plates.

5 Pile the couscous mixture in the centre of each plate and crumble the goat's cheese over the top. Sprinkle with toasted walnuts, place a fig in the centre of each plate and serve.

COOK'S TIP

Goat's cheeses vary in strength from the youngest, which are soft and mild, to strongly flavoured, mature cheeses, which have a firm and crumbly texture. The crumbly varieties are best suited to salads.

V

Spinach and Roast Garlic Salad

Don't worry about the amount of garlic in this salad. During roasting, the garlic becomes sweet and subtle and loses its pungent taste.

INGREDIENTS

Serves 4

12 garlic cloves, unpeeled

60ml/4 tbsp extra virgin olive oil

450g/1lb baby spinach leaves

50g/2 oz/½ cup pine nuts,
   lightly toasted

juice of ½ lemon

salt and ground black pepper

1 Preheat the oven to 190°C/ 375°F/Gas 5. Place the garlic in a small roasting pan, add 30ml/ 2 tbsp of the olive oil, tossing well to coat all over, and roast for about 15 minutes, until the garlic cloves are softened and slightly charred around the edges.

2 While still warm, tip the garlic into a salad bowl. Add the spinach, pine nuts, lemon juice, remaining olive oil and a little salt. Toss well and add black pepper to taste. Serve immediately, inviting guests to squeeze the softened garlic purée out of the skin to eat.

V

Marinated Cucumber Salad

A wonderfully cooling salad for the summer, with the distinctive flavour of fresh dill.

INGREDIENTS

Serves 4–6

2 medium cucumbers

15ml/1 tbsp salt

90g/3½oz/½ cup granulated sugar

175ml/6fl oz/¾ cup dry (hard) cider

15ml/1 tbsp cider vinegar

45ml/3 tbsp chopped fresh dill

ground black pepper

1 Slice the cucumbers thinly and place them in a colander, sprinkling salt between each layer. Put the colander over a bowl and leave to drain for 1 hour.

2 Thoroughly rinse the cucumber under cold running water to remove excess salt, then pat dry with kitchen paper.

3 Gently heat the sugar, cider and vinegar in a pan until the sugar has dissolved. Remove from the heat and leave to cool. Put the cucumber slices in a bowl, pour over the cider mixture and leave to marinate for 2 hours.

COOK'S TIP

The salad would be a perfect accompaniment for fresh salmon.

4 Drain the cucumber and sprinkle with the dill and pepper to taste. Mix well and transfer to a serving dish. Chill until ready to serve.

V

Flower Garden Salad

Dress a colourful mixture of salad leaves with good olive oil and lemon juice, then top it with crisp croûtons.

Serves 4–6

3 thick slices day-old bread, such
    as ciabatta
120ml/4fl oz/½ cup extra virgin olive oil
1 garlic clove, halved
½ small cos or romaine lettuce
½ small oak leaf lettuce
25g/1oz rocket (arugula) leaves or
    salad cress
25g/1oz fresh flat leaf parsley
a small handful of young dandelion leaves
juice of 1 lemon
a few nasturtium leaves and flowers
pansy and pot marigold flowers
sea salt flakes and ground black pepper

1 Cut the slices of bread into 1cm/½in cubes.

2 Heat half the oil gently in a frying pan and cook the bread cubes in it, tossing them until they are well coated and lightly browned. Remove and cool.

3 Rub the inside of a large salad bowl with the cut sides of the garlic clove, then discard. Pour the remaining oil into the base of the bowl.

4 Tear all the salad leaves into bitesize pieces and pile them into the bowl with the oil. Season with salt and pepper. Cover and keep chilled until you are ready to serve the salad.

5 To serve, toss the leaves in the oil at the base of the bowl, then sprinkle with the lemon juice and toss again. Sprinkle the croûtons and the flowers over the top and serve immediately.

Panzanella Salad

If sliced juicy tomatoes layered with day-old bread sounds strange for a salad, don't be deceived – it's quite delicious. A popular Italian salad, this dish is ideal for serving as an appetizer. Use full-flavoured tomatoes for the best result.

INGREDIENTS

Serves 4–6

4 thick slices day-old bread, white, brown
   or rye
1 small red onion, thinly sliced
450g/1lb ripe tomatoes, thinly sliced
115g/4oz mozzarella cheese, thinly sliced
5ml/1 tbsp fresh basil, shredded, or
   fresh marjoram
120ml/4fl oz/½ cup extra virgin olive oil
45ml/3 tbsp balsamic vinegar
juice of 1 small lemon
salt and ground black pepper
pitted and sliced black olives or salted
   capers, to garnish

1 Dip the bread briefly in cold water, then carefully squeeze out the excess water. Arrange the bread in the base of a shallow salad bowl.

2 Soak the onion slices in cold water for about 10 minutes while you prepare the other ingredients. Drain and reserve.

3 Layer the tomatoes, cheese, onion, basil or marjoram in the bowl, seasoning well with salt and pepper in between each layer. Sprinkle with oil, vinegar and lemon juice.

4 Top the salad with the olives or capers, cover with clear film (plastic wrap) and chill in the refrigerator for at least 2 hours or overnight, if possible.

Poached Egg Salad with Croûtons

[V]

Soft poached eggs, hot garlic croûtons and cool, crisp salad leaves make a great combination.

INGREDIENTS

Serves 2

½ small loaf white bread

75ml/5 tbsp/⅓ cup extra virgin olive oil

2 eggs

115g/4oz mixed salad leaves

2 garlic cloves, crushed

7.5ml/½ tbsp white wine vinegar

25g/1oz piece Parmesan cheese

ground black pepper

1 Remove the crust from the loaf of bread. Cut the bread into 2.5cm/1in cubes.

2 Heat 30ml/2 tbsp of the oil in a frying pan. Cook the bread for about 5 minutes, tossing the cubes occasionally, until they are golden brown.

3 Meanwhile, bring a pan of water to the boil. Carefully slide in the eggs, one at a time. Gently poach the eggs for 4 minutes until lightly cooked.

4 Divide the salad leaves between two plates. Remove the croûtons from the frying pan and arrange them over the leaves. Wipe the frying pan clean with kitchen paper.

5 Heat the remaining oil in the pan, add the garlic and vinegar and cook over a high heat for 1 minute. Pour the warm dressing over each salad.

6 Place a poached egg on each plate of salad. Sprinkle with shavings of Parmesan and a little black pepper and serve.

COOK'S TIP

Add a dash of vinegar to the water before poaching the eggs. This helps to keep the whites together.

To make sure that a poached egg has a good shape, swirl the water with a spoon, whirlpool-fashion, before sliding in the egg.

Before serving trim the edges of the egg for a neat finish.

Fresh Ceps Salad

V

To capture the just-picked flavour of a cep, this delicious salad is enriched with an egg yolk and walnut oil dressing. Choose small ceps which will have a firm texture and the very best flavour.

INGREDIENTS

Serves 4

350g/12oz fresh ceps

175g/6oz mixed salad leaves, including Batavia, young spinach and frisée

50g/2oz/½ cup broken walnut pieces, toasted

50g/2oz piece Parmesan cheese

salt and ground black pepper

For the dressing

2 egg yolks

2.5ml/½ tsp French mustard

75ml/5 tbsp groundnut (peanut) oil

45ml/3 tbsp walnut oil

30ml/2 tbsp lemon juice

30ml/2 tbsp chopped fresh parsley

pinch of caster (superfine) sugar

1 To make the dressing, place the egg yolks in a screw-top jar with the mustard, groundnut and walnut oils, lemon juice, parsley and sugar. Shake well.

2 Trim the ceps and cut them into thin slices.

3 Place the ceps in a large salad bowl and combine with the dressing. Leave for 10–15 minutes for the flavours to mingle.

4 Wash and dry the salad leaves, then toss them together with the ceps.

5 Turn the salad out on to four large serving plates. Season well, sprinkle with the toasted walnuts and shavings of Parmesan cheese, then serve.

Beansprout and Mooli Salad

V

Thin slices of crisp vegetables mixed with beansprouts make the perfect foil for an unusual Asian dressing.

INGREDIENTS

Serves 4

225g/8 oz/1 cup beansprouts
1 cucumber
2 carrots
1 small mooli (daikon)
1 small red onion, thinly sliced
2.5cm/1in piece of fresh root ginger, cut
    into thin batons
1 small fresh red chilli, seeded and sliced
handful of fresh coriander (cilantro) or
    mint leaves

For the dressing

15ml/1 tbsp rice wine vinegar
15ml/1 tbsp light soy sauce
15ml/1 tbsp Thai fish sauce
1 garlic clove, finely chopped
15ml/1 tbsp sesame oil
45ml/3 tbsp groundnut (peanut) oil
30ml/2 tbsp sesame seeds, lightly toasted

1 First make the dressing. Place all the dressing ingredients in a bottle or screw-top jar and shake well. The dressing may be made in advance and will keep well for a couple of days if stored in the refrigerator or a cool place.

2 Wash the beansprouts and drain thoroughly in a colander.

3 Peel the cucumber, cut in half lengthways and scoop out the seeds. Peel the cucumber flesh into long ribbon strips using a vegetable peeler or mandoline.

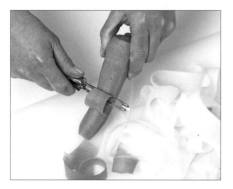

4 Peel the carrots and mooli radish into long strips in the same way as for the cucumber.

5 Place the carrots, mooli radish and cucumber in a large, shallow serving dish, add the red onion, ginger batons, chilli and coriander or mint leaves and toss to mix. Pour the dressing over just before serving.

V

Asparagus and Orange Salad

A slightly unusual combination of ingredients with a simple dressing based on good-quality olive oil.

INGREDIENTS

Serves 4

225g/8oz asparagus, trimmed and cut into
    5cm/2in lengths

2 large oranges

2 well-flavoured tomatoes, cut
    into eighths

50g/2oz cos or romaine lettuce leaves

30ml/2 tbsp extra virgin olive oil

2.5ml/½ tsp sherry vinegar

salt and ground black pepper

1 Cook the asparagus in salted, boiling water for 3–4 minutes, until just tender. The cooking time may vary according to the size of the asparagus stems. Drain and refresh under cold water, then leave to cool.

2 Grate the rind from half an orange and reserve. Peel both the oranges and cut into segments over a bowl to catch any juice. Squeeze the juice from the membrane into the bowl and reserve for the dressing.

3 Put the asparagus, orange segments, tomatoes and lettuce into a salad bowl.

4 Mix together the olive oil and sherry vinegar, and add 15ml/ 1 tbsp of the reserved orange juice and 5ml/1 tsp of the grated orange rind. Season to taste with salt and pepper. Just before serving, pour the dressing over the salad and mix gently to coat all the ingredients.

Coronation Salad

The famous salad dressing used in this dish was created especially for the coronation dinner of Queen Elizabeth II. It is a wonderful accompaniment to hard-boiled eggs and vegetables.

INGREDIENTS

Serves 6

450g/1lb new potatoes

45ml/3 tbsp French Dressing

3 spring onions (scallions), chopped

6 eggs, hard-boiled and halved

frisée lettuce leaves

¼ cucumber, cut into thin strips

6 large radishes, sliced

1 carton salad cress

salt and ground black pepper

For the coronation dressing

30ml/2 tbsp olive oil

1 small onion, chopped

15ml/1 tbsp mild curry powder or korma
    spice mix

10ml/2 tsp tomato purée (paste)

30ml/2 tbsp lemon juice

30ml/2 tbsp sherry

300ml/½ pint/1¼ cups mayonnaise

150ml/¼ pint/⅔ cup natural
    (plain) yogurt

1 Boil the potatoes in salted water until tender. Drain them, transfer to a large bowl and toss in the French dressing.

2 Stir in the spring onions and salt and pepper to taste and leave to cool thoroughly.

3 Meanwhile, make the coronation dressing. Heat the oil in a small pan and cook the onion for 3 minutes, until soft. Stir in the curry powder or spice mix and cook for 1 further minute. Remove from the heat and mix in all the other dressing ingredients.

4 Stir the dressing into the potatoes, add the eggs, then chill. Line a serving platter with lettuce leaves and pile the salad in the centre. Sprinkle over the cucumber, radishes and cress.

V

Potato Salad with Curry Plant Mayonnaise

Potato salad can be made well in advance and is therefore a useful dish for serving as an unusual appetizer at a party. Its popularity means that there are very rarely any leftovers to be cleared away at the end of the day.

INGREDIENTS

Serves 6

1kg/2¼lb new potatoes, in skins

300ml/½ pint/1¼ cups mayonnaise

6 curry plant leaves,
    coarsely chopped

salt and ground black pepper

mixed lettuce leaves or other salad leaves,
    to serve

1 Place the unpeeled potatoes in a large pan of lightly salted water, bring to the boil and cook over a low heat for 15 minutes, or until tender. Drain well in a colander, place in a large bowl and leave to cool slightly.

2 Mix the mayonnaise with the curry plant leaves and black pepper. Stir this mixture into the potatoes while they are still warm. Leave to cool completely, then serve on a bed of mixed lettuce leaves or other salad leaves.

Pear and Pecan Nut Salad

V

Toasted pecan nuts have a special affinity with crisp white pears. Their robust flavours combine well with a rich Blue Cheese and Chive dressing to make this a salad to remember.

INGREDIENTS

Serves 4

75g/3 oz/½ cup shelled pecan nuts, coarsely chopped

3 crisp pears

175g/6oz young spinach, stems removed

1 escarole or round (butterhead) lettuce

1 radicchio

30ml/2 tbsp Blue Cheese and Chive Dressing

salt and ground black pepper

crusty bread, to serve

1 Toast the pecan nuts under a moderate grill (broiler) to bring out their flavour.

COOK'S TIP
~

The pecan nuts will burn very quickly under the grill (broiler), so keep constant watch over them and remove them as soon as they change colour.

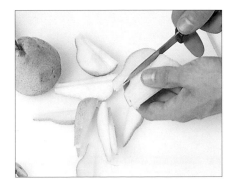

2 Cut the pears into even slices, leaving the skins intact but discarding the cores.

3 Place the spinach, lettuce and radicchio leaves in a large bowl. Add the pears and toasted pecans, pour over the Blue Cheese and Chive Dressing and toss well. Distribute among four large serving plates and season to taste with salt and pepper. Serve the salad with warm crusty bread.

Black and Orange Salad

This dramatically colourful salad, with its spicy dressing, is very unusual. It is a feast for the eyes as well as for the taste buds.

INGREDIENTS

Serves 4

3 oranges

115g/4oz/1 cup pitted black olives

15ml/1 tbsp chopped fresh
    coriander (cilantro)

15ml/1 tbsp chopped fresh parsley

For the dressing

30ml/2 tbsp olive oil

15ml/1 tbsp lemon juice

2.5ml/½ tsp paprika

2.5ml/½ tsp ground cumin

1 With a sharp knife, cut away the peel and pith from the oranges and divide the fruit into segments.

2 Place the oranges in a salad bowl and add the black olives, coriander and parsley.

3 Blend together the olive oil, lemon juice, paprika and cumin. Pour the dressing over the salad and toss gently. Cover with clear film (plastic wrap) and chill for about 30 minutes, then serve.

Rocket and Coriander Salad

Rocket leaves have a wonderful, peppery flavour. However, unless you have a plentiful supply of rocket, you may well have to use extra spinach or another green leaf to pad out this salad.

INGREDIENTS

Serves 4

115g/4oz or more rocket (arugula) leaves

115g/4oz young spinach leaves

1 large bunch fresh coriander (cilantro),
    about 25g/1oz

2–3 fresh parsley sprigs

For the dressing

1 garlic clove, crushed

45ml/3 tbsp olive oil

10ml/2 tsp white wine vinegar

pinch of paprika

cayenne pepper

salt

1 Place the rocket and spinach leaves in a salad bowl. Chop the coriander and parsley and sprinkle them over the top.

2 In a small jug (pitcher), blend together the garlic, olive oil, vinegar, paprika, cayenne pepper and salt.

3 Pour the dressing over the salad and serve immediately.

V

Orange and Water Chestnut Salad

Crunchy water chestnuts combine with radicchio or red lettuce and oranges in this unusual salad.

INGREDIENTS

Serves 4

1 red onion, thinly sliced
    into rings
2 oranges, peeled and cut into segments
1 can drained water chestnuts, peeled and
    cut into strips
2 radicchio heads, cored, or 1 red-leaf
    lettuce, leaves separated
45ml/3 tbsp chopped fresh parsley
45ml/3 tbsp chopped fresh basil
15ml/1 tbsp white wine vinegar
50ml/2fl oz/¼ cup walnut oil
salt and ground black pepper
1 fresh basil sprig, to garnish

1 Put the onion in a colander and sprinkle with 5ml/1 tsp salt. Leave to drain for 15 minutes.

2 In a large mixing bowl combine the oranges and water chestnuts.

3 Spread out the radicchio or red-leaf lettuce leaves in a large, shallow bowl or on a serving platter.

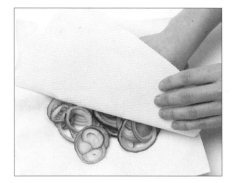

4 Rinse the onion to remove excess salt and dry on kitchen paper. Toss it with the water chestnuts and oranges.

5 Arrange the water chestnut, orange and onion mixture on top of the radicchio or lettuce leaves. Sprinkle with the chopped parsley and basil.

6 Put the vinegar, oil and salt and pepper to taste in a screw-top jar and shake well to combine. Pour the dressing over the salad and serve immediately, garnished with a sprig of basil.

V

Plantain and Green Banana Salad

Cook the plantains and bananas in their skins to retain their soft texture. They will then absorb all the flavour of the dressing.

INGREDIENTS

Serves 4

2 firm yellow plantains

3 green bananas

1 garlic clove, crushed

1 red onion

15–30ml/1–2 tbsp chopped fresh coriander (cilantro)

45ml/3 tbsp sunflower oil

25ml/1½ tbsp malt vinegar

salt and ground black pepper

1 Slit the plantains and bananas lengthways along their natural ridges, then cut in half and place in a large pan.

2 Cover the plantains and bananas with water, add a little salt and bring to the boil. Boil gently for 20 minutes, until tender, then remove from the water. When they are cool enough to handle, peel and cut into medium-size slices.

3 Put the plantain and banana slices into a bowl and add the garlic, turning them with a wooden spoon to distribute the garlic evenly.

4 Halve the onion and slice thinly. Add to the bowl with the coriander, oil and vinegar and season with salt and pepper to taste. Toss together to mix, then transfer to a serving bowl.

PASTA, NOODLE AND PULSE SALADS

These are substantial salads with plenty of texture. They make good main course dishes, but are equally delicious, served in smaller quantities, as appetizers and accompaniments. Great family favourites, pasta salads are especially popular with children if you use interesting shapes. Noodle salads, particularly with exotic dressings, ring a welcome change at mealtimes, while salads made with pulses are the perfect choice in the winter, when the more usual green vegetables are not in season.

V

Pasta, Avocado, Tomato and Cheese Salad

This popular salad is made from ingredients representing the colours of the Italian flag – a sunny, cheerful dish! The addition of pasta turns it into a main course meal for a light summer lunch.

Serves 4

175g/6oz pasta bows (farfalle)

6 ripe red tomatoes

225g/8oz mozzarella cheese

1 large ripe avocado

30ml/2 tbsp chopped fresh basil

30ml/2 tbsp pine nuts, toasted

fresh basil sprig, to garnish

For the dressing

90ml/6 tbsp olive oil

30ml/2 tbsp wine vinegar

5ml/1 tsp balsamic vinegar (optional)

5ml/1 tsp wholegrain mustard

pinch of sugar

salt and ground black pepper

1 Cook the pasta bows in in a large pan of lightly salted, boiling water until *al dente*.

2 Slice the tomatoes and mozzarella cheese into thin rounds.

3 Halve the avocado, remove the stone (pit) and peel off the skin. Slice the flesh lengthways.

4 To make the dressing, whisk the oil, vinegars, mustard and sugar in a small bowl and season to taste with salt and pepper.

5 Arrange the tomato, mozzarella and avocado slices in overlapping slices around the edge of a flat serving plate.

6 Toss the pasta with half of the dressing and the chopped basil. Pile into the centre of the plate. Pour over the remaining dressing, sprinkle over the pine nuts and garnish with a sprig of fresh basil. Serve immediately.

COOK'S TIP

The pale green flesh of the avocado quickly discolours once it is cut. Prepare it at the last minute and place immediately in dressing. If you do have to prepare it ahead, squeeze lemon juice over the cut side and cover with clear film (plastic wrap).

V

Pasta, Olive and Avocado Salad

The ingredients of this salad are united by a wonderful sun-dried tomato and fresh basil dressing.

INGREDIENTS

Serves 6

225g/8oz pasta spirals (fusilli) or other small pasta shapes

115g/4oz can corn, drained, or frozen corn, thawed

½ red (bell) pepper, seeded and diced

8 black olives, pitted and sliced

3 spring onions (scallions), finely chopped

2 medium avocados

For the dressing

2 sun-dried tomato halves, loose-packed (not preserved in oil)

25ml/1½ tbsp balsamic or white wine vinegar

25ml/1½ tbsp red wine vinegar

½ garlic clove, crushed

2.5ml/½ tsp salt

75ml/5 tbsp olive oil

15ml/1 tbsp chopped fresh basil

1 To make the dressing, drop the sun-dried tomatoes into a small pan containing 2.5cm/1in boiling water and simmer for about 3 minutes, until tender. Drain and chop finely.

2 Process the sun-dried tomatoes, both types of vinegar, garlic and salt in a food processor. With the machine running, add the olive oil in a stream. Stir in the basil.

3 Cook the pasta in a large pan of lightly salted, boiling water until *al dente*. Drain well. In a large bowl, combine the pasta, corn, red pepper, black olives and spring onions. Add the dressing and toss well to mix.

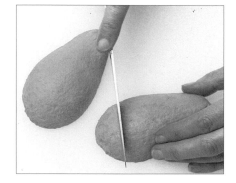

4 Just before serving, peel and stone (pit) the avocados and cut the flesh into cubes. Gently stir the cubes into the pasta mixture, then transfer the salad to a large serving dish. Serve immediately at room temperature.

Pasta, Asparagus and Potato Salad

V

Made with wholewheat pasta, this delicious salad is a real treat, especially when made with fresh asparagus just in season.

Serves 4

225g/8oz wholewheat pasta shapes

60ml/4 tbsp extra virgin olive oil

350g/12oz baby new potatoes

225g/8oz asparagus

115g/4oz piece Parmesan cheese

salt and ground black pepper

1 Cook the pasta in lightly salted, boiling water until *al dente*.

2 Drain well and toss with the olive oil while the pasta is still warm. Season with salt and ground black pepper.

3 Scrub the potatoes and cook in salted, boiling water for about 15 minutes, or until tender. Drain the potatoes and toss together with the pasta.

4 Trim any woody ends off the asparagus and halve the stalks if very long. Blanch in salted, boiling water for 6 minutes, until bright green and still crunchy. Drain. Plunge into cold water to stop the asparagus cooking and leave to cool. Drain and dry on kitchen paper.

5 Toss the asparagus with the potatoes and pasta, adjust the seasoning to taste and transfer to a shallow serving bowl. Using a vegetable peeler, thinly shave the Parmesan over the salad.

V

Roquefort and Walnut Pasta Salad

This is a simple, earthy salad, relying totally on the quality of the ingredients. There is no real substitute for the Roquefort – a blue-veined ewe's-milk cheese from south-western France.

INGREDIENTS

Serves 4

225g/8oz pasta shapes

selection of salad leaves such as rocket (arugula), frisée lettuce, lamb's lettuce, baby spinach, radicchio

30ml/2 tbsp walnut oil

60ml/4 tbsp sunflower oil

30ml/2 tbsp red wine vinegar or sherry vinegar

225g/8oz Roquefort cheese, coarsely crumbled

115g/4oz/1 cup walnut halves

salt and ground black pepper

1 Cook the pasta in plenty of salted, boiling water until *al dente*. Drain well and cool. Place the salad leaves in a bowl.

2 Whisk together the walnut oil, sunflower oil and vinegar. Season with salt and pepper to taste.

COOK'S TIP

Toast the walnuts under the grill (broiler) to add extra flavour.

3 Pile the pasta in the centre of the salad leaves, sprinkle over the crumbled Roquefort and pour over the dressing.

4 Sprinkle the walnuts over the top. Toss the salad just before serving at room temperature.

Roast Pepper and Mushroom Pasta Salad

A combination of grilled peppers and two different kinds of mushroom makes this salad colourful as well as nutritious.

INGREDIENTS

Serves 6

1 red (bell) pepper, halved

1 yellow (bell) pepper, halved

1 green (bell) pepper, halved

350g/12oz wholewheat pasta shells

30ml/2 tbsp olive oil

45ml/3 tbsp balsamic vinegar

75ml/5 tbsp tomato juice

30ml/2 tbsp chopped fresh basil

15ml/1 tbsp chopped fresh thyme

175g/6oz/2¼ cups shiitake
    mushrooms, diced

175g/6oz/2¼ cups oyster
    mushrooms, sliced

400g/14oz can black-eyed beans (peas),
    drained and rinsed

115g/4oz/¾ cup sultanas (golden raisins)

2 bunches of spring onions (scallions),
    finely chopped

salt and ground black pepper

1 Preheat the grill (broiler) to hot. Put the peppers cut side down on a grill pan rack and place under the grill for 10–15 minutes, until the skins are charred. Cover the peppers with a clean, damp dishtowel and set aside to cool.

2 Meanwhile, cook the pasta shells in a large pan of lightly salted, boiling water until *al dente*, then drain thoroughly.

3 Mix together the oil, vinegar, tomato juice, basil and thyme, add to the warm pasta and toss.

4 Remove and discard the skins from the peppers. Seed and slice and add to the pasta.

5 Add the mushrooms, beans, sultanas, spring onions and seasoning. Toss the ingredients to mix and serve immediately. Alternatively, cover with clear film (plastic wrap) and chill in the refrigerator before serving.

Mediterranean Pasta Salad

A type of Salade Niçoise with pasta, conjuring up all the sunny flavours of the Mediterranean.

INGREDIENTS

Serves 4

225g/8oz chunky pasta shapes

175g/6oz fine green beans

2 large ripe tomatoes

50g/2oz fresh basil leaves

200g/7oz can tuna in oil, drained

2 hard-boiled eggs, shelled and sliced
   or quartered

50g/2oz can anchovy fillets, drained

capers and black olives, to taste

For the dressing

90ml/6 tbsp extra virgin olive oil

30ml/2 tbsp white wine vinegar or
   lemon juice

2 garlic cloves, crushed

2.5ml/½ tsp Dijon mustard

30ml/2 tbsp chopped fresh basil

salt and ground black pepper

1 To make the dressing, whisk all the ingredients together in a small bowl. Leave to infuse (steep) while you prepare the salad.

COOK'S TIP

Don't be tempted to chill this salad – the flavour will be dulled.

2 Cook the pasta in plenty of salted, boiling water until *al dente*. Drain well and cool.

3 Trim the green beans and blanch in lightly salted, boiling water for 3 minutes. Drain and refresh in cold water.

4 Slice the tomatoes and arrange on the base of a serving bowl. Moisten with a little dressing and cover with a quarter of the basil leaves. Then cover with the beans. Moisten with a little more dressing and cover with a third of the remaining basil.

5 Cover the vegetables with the pasta tossed in a little more dressing, half the remaining basil and the coarsely flaked tuna.

6 Arrange the eggs on top, then finally sprinkle over the anchovy fillets, capers and olives. Spoon over the remaining dressing and garnish with the remaining basil. Serve immediately.

Smoked Bacon and Green Bean Pasta Salad

A tasty pasta salad, subtly flavoured with smoked bacon.

INGREDIENTS

Serves 4

350g/12oz wholewheat pasta twists

225g/8oz green beans

8 rashers (strips) smoked bacon

2 bunches of spring onions (scallions)

350g/12oz cherry tomatoes, halved

400g/14oz can chickpeas, drained

For the dressing

90ml/6 tbsp tomato juice

30ml/2 tbsp balsamic vinegar

5ml/1 tsp ground cumin

5ml/1 tsp ground coriander

30ml/2 tbsp chopped fresh
coriander (cilantro)

salt and ground black pepper

2 Preheat the grill (broiler) and cook the bacon for 2–3 minutes on each side, until cooked. Dice and add to the beans.

3 Chop the spring onions and put them in a large bowl with the tomatoes and chickpeas. In a small bowl, mix together the tomato juice, vinegar, spices, fresh coriander and seasoning.

4 Pour the dressing into the large bowl. Drain the cooked pasta thoroughly and add to the tomato mixture with the green beans and bacon. Toss all the ingredients together to mix thoroughly. Serve warm or cold.

1 Cook the pasta in a large pan of lightly salted, boiling water until *al dente*. Meanwhile, trim and halve the green beans and cook them in boiling water for about 5 minutes, until tender. Drain thoroughly and keep warm.

COOK'S TIP

Always rinse canned beans and pulses well before using, to remove as much of the brine (salt water) as possible.

Devilled Ham and Pineapple Salad

This tasty salad, with a crunchy topping of toasted almonds, can be quickly prepared. It is delicious served with crusty bread.

INGREDIENTS

Serves 4

225g/8oz wholewheat penne

150ml/¼ pint/⅔ cup natural (plain) yogurt

15ml/1 tbsp cider vinegar

5ml/1 tsp wholegrain mustard

large pinch of caster (superfine) sugar

30ml/2 tbsp hot mango chutney

115g/4oz cooked lean ham, cubed

200g/7oz can pineapple chunks, drained

2 celery sticks, chopped

½ green (bell) pepper, seeded and diced

15ml/1 tbsp toasted flaked (sliced) almonds, coarsely chopped

salt and ground black pepper

1 Cook the pasta in a large pan of salted boiling water until *al dente*. Drain and rinse thoroughly. Leave to cool.

2 To make the dressing, mix the yogurt, vinegar, mustard, sugar and mango chutney together. Season with salt and pepper. Add the pasta and toss lightly together.

3 Transfer the pasta to a serving dish. Add the ham, pineapple, celery and green pepper.

4 Sprinkle the toasted almonds over the top of the salad to garnish. Serve immediately.

Spicy Pasta and Chicken Salad

Marinate the chicken in advance for this tasty salad, which is otherwise quick to prepare.

INGREDIENTS

Serves 6

5ml/1 tsp ground cumin seeds
5ml/1 tsp paprika
5ml/1 tsp ground turmeric
1–2 garlic cloves, crushed
30ml/2 tbsp lime juice
4 skinless, boneless chicken breast portions
225g/8oz rigatoni
1 red (bell) pepper, seeded and chopped
2 celery sticks, thinly sliced
1 shallot or small onion, finely chopped
25g/1oz/¼ cup stuffed green
   olives, halved
30ml/2 tbsp clear honey
15ml/1 tbsp wholegrain mustard
15–30ml/1–2 tbsp lime juice
mixed salad leaves
salt and ground black pepper

1 Mix the cumin, paprika, turmeric, garlic and lime juice in a bowl. Season with salt and pepper. Rub this mixture over the chicken portions. Lay these in a shallow dish, cover with clear film (plastic wrap) and leave in a cool place for 3 hours or overnight.

2 Preheat the oven to 200°C/ 400°F/Gas 6. Put the chicken on a grill (broiler) rack and bake for 20 minutes. (Alternatively grill (broil) for 8–10 minutes on each side.)

3 Cook the rigatoni pasta in a large pan of lightly salted, boiling water until *al dente*. Drain and rinse under cold water. Leave to drain thoroughly.

4 Put the red pepper, celery, shallot or small onion and olives into a large bowl with the pasta. Mix together.

5 Mix the honey, mustard and lime juice together in a small bowl and pour over the pasta mixture. Toss to coat.

6 Cut the chicken into bitesize pieces. Arrange the mixed salad leaves on a serving dish, spoon the pasta mixture into the centre and top with the spicy chicken pieces.

Smoked Trout Pasta Salad

The little pasta shells catch the trout creating tasty mouthfuls.

INGREDIENTS

Serves 8

15g/½oz/1 tbsp butter

175g/6oz/1 cup minced (ground)
    bulb fennel

6 spring onions (scallions), 2 minced
    (ground) and the rest thinly sliced

225g/8oz skinless smoked trout
    fillets, flaked

45ml/3 tbsp chopped fresh dill

120ml/4fl oz/½ cup mayonnaise

10ml/2 tsp fresh lemon juice

30ml/2 tbsp whipping cream

450g/1lb/4 cups small pasta shapes

salt and ground black pepper

fresh dill sprigs, to garnish

1 Melt the butter in a small pan. Cook the fennel and minced onions for 3–5 minutes. Transfer to a large bowl and cool slightly.

2 Add the sliced spring onions, trout, dill, mayonnaise, lemon juice and cream. Season with salt and pepper and mix.

3 Bring a large pan of lightly salted water to the boil and add the pasta. Cook according to the instructions on the packet until just *al dente*. Drain thoroughly and leave to cool.

4 Add the pasta to the vegetable and trout mixture and toss to coat evenly. Taste for seasoning. Serve the salad lightly chilled or at room temperature, garnished with sprigs of dill.

Smoked Trout and Noodle Salad

It is important to use ripe, juicy tomatoes for this fresh-tasting salad. For a special occasion you could use smoked salmon.

INGREDIENTS

Serves 4

225g/8oz somen noodles

2 smoked trout, skinned and boned

2 hard-boiled eggs, coarsely chopped

30ml/2 tbsp chopped fresh chives

lime halves, to serve (optional)

For the dressing

6 ripe plum tomatoes

2 shallots, finely chopped

30ml/2 tbsp tiny capers, rinsed

30ml/2 tbsp chopped fresh tarragon

finely grated rind and juice of ½ orange

60ml/4 tbsp extra virgin olive oil

salt and ground black pepper

1 To make the dressing, cut the tomatoes in half, remove the cores and cut the flesh into chunks.

2 Place in a bowl with the shallots, capers, tarragon, orange rind and juice and olive oil. Season with salt and pepper and mix well. Leave to marinate at room temperature for 1–2 hours.

3 Cook the noodles in a large pan of boiling water, following the directions on the packet, until just tender. Drain and rinse under cold running water. Drain well.

4 Toss the noodles with the dressing, then adjust the seasoning to taste. Arrange the noodles on a large serving platter or individual plates.

5 Flake the smoked trout over the noodles, then sprinkle the eggs and chives over the top. Serve, with lime halves on the side of the plate, if you like.

Noodles with Pineapple, Ginger and Chillies

A coconut, lime and fish sauce dressing is the perfect partner to this fruity and spicy salad.

INGREDIENTS

Serves 4

275g/10oz dried udon noodles

½ pineapple, peeled, cored and sliced into 4cm/1½in rings

45ml/3 tbsp soft light brown sugar

60ml/4 tbsp lime juice

60ml/4 tbsp coconut milk

30ml/2 tbsp Thai fish sauce

30ml/2 tbsp grated fresh root ginger

2 garlic cloves, finely chopped

1 ripe mango or 2 peaches peeled, stoned (pitted) and finely diced

ground black pepper

2 spring onions (scallions), finely sliced, 2 fresh red chillies, seeded and finely shredded, and fresh mint leaves, to garnish

1 Cook the noodles in a large pan of boiling water until tender, following the directions on the packet. Drain, refresh under cold water and drain again.

2 Place the pineapple rings in a flameproof dish, sprinkle with 30ml/2 tbsp of the sugar and grill (broil) for about 5 minutes, or until golden. Cool slightly and cut into small dice.

3 Mix the lime juice, coconut milk and fish sauce in a salad bowl. Add the remaining brown sugar with the ginger, garlic and black pepper and whisk well. Add the noodles and pineapple.

4 Add the mango or peaches and toss. Sprinkle over the spring onions, chillies and mint leaves before serving.

Buckwheat Noodles with Smoked Salmon

Young pea sprouts are available for only a short time. You can substitute watercress, salad cress, young leeks or your favourite green vegetable or herb in this dish.

INGREDIENTS

Serves 4

225g/8oz buckwheat or soba noodles

15ml/1 tbsp oyster sauce

juice of ½ lemon

30–45ml/2–3 tbsp light olive oil

115g/4oz smoked salmon, cut into fine strips

115g/4oz young pea sprouts

2 ripe tomatoes, peeled, seeded and cut into strips

15ml/1 tbsp chopped chives

ground black pepper

1 Cook the buckwheat or soba noodles in a large pan of boiling water until tender, following the directions on the packet. Drain, then rinse under cold running water and drain well.

2 Tip the noodles into a large bowl. Add the oyster sauce and lemon juice and season with pepper to taste. Moisten the noodles with the olive oil.

3 Add the smoked salmon, pea sprouts, tomatoes and chives. Mix well and serve immediately.

Thai Noodle Salad

V

The addition of coconut milk and sesame oil gives an unusual nutty flavour to the dressing for this colourful noodle salad.

INGREDIENTS

Serves 4–6

350g/12oz somen noodles

1 large carrot, cut into thin strips

1 bunch of asparagus, trimmed and cut into 4cm/1½in lengths

1 red (bell) pepper, seeded and cut into fine strips

115g/4oz mangetouts (snow peas), trimmed and halved

115g/4oz baby corn cobs, halved lengthways

115g/4oz beansprouts

115g/4oz can water chestnuts, drained and thinly sliced

lime wedges, 50g/2oz/½ cup roasted peanuts, coarsely chopped, and fresh coriander (cilantro) leaves, to garnish

For the dressing

45ml/3 tbsp coarsely torn fresh basil

75ml/5 tbsp coarsely chopped fresh mint

250ml/8fl oz/1 cup coconut milk

30ml/2 tbsp dark sesame oil

15ml/1 tbsp grated fresh root ginger

2 garlic cloves, finely chopped

juice of 1 lime

2 spring onions (scallions), finely chopped

salt and cayenne pepper

1 To make the dressing, combine all the ingredients in a bowl and mix well. Season to taste with salt and cayenne pepper.

2 Cook the noodles in a pan of boiling water, following the directions on the packet, until just tender. Drain, rinse under cold running water and drain again.

3 Cook all the vegetables, except the water chestnuts, in separate pans of boiling, lightly salted water until they are tender, but still crisp. Drain, plunge them immediately into cold water and drain again.

4 Toss the noodles, vegetables, water chestnuts and dressing together. Arrange on individual serving plates and garnish with the lime wedges, chopped peanuts and coriander leaves.

Prawn Noodle Salad with Fragrant Herbs

A light, refreshing salad with all the tangy flavour of the sea. Instead of prawns, you can also use squid, scallops, mussels or crab.

INGREDIENTS

Serves 4

115g/4oz cellophane noodles, soaked in hot water until soft

1 small green (bell) pepper, seeded and cut into strips

¹/₂ cucumber, cut into strips

1 tomato, cut into strips

2 shallots, thinly sliced

16 cooked peeled prawns (shrimp)

salt and ground black pepper

fresh coriander (cilantro) leaves, to garnish

For the dressing

15ml/1 tbsp rice wine vinegar

30ml/2 tbsp Thai fish sauce

30ml/2 tbsp lime juice

2.5ml/¹/₂ tsp grated fresh root ginger

1 lemon grass stalk, finely chopped

1 fresh red chilli, seeded and finely sliced

30ml/2 tbsp coarsely chopped fresh mint

few tarragon, sprigs coarsely chopped

15ml/1 tbsp chopped fresh chives

1 To make the dressing, combine all the ingredients in a small bowl or jug (pitcher) and whisk.

2 Drain the noodles, then plunge them into a pan of boiling water for 1 minute. Drain, rinse under cold running water and drain again well.

3 In a large bowl, combine the noodles with the green pepper, cucumber, tomato and shallots. Lightly season with salt and pepper, then toss with the dressing.

COOK'S TIP

Prawns (shrimp) are available ready-cooked and often peeled. To cook prawns, boil them for 5 minutes. Leave them to cool in the cooking liquid, then gently pull off the tail shell and twist off the head.

4 Spoon the noodles on to individual serving plates, arranging the prawns on top. Garnish with a few coriander leaves and serve immediately.

Egg Noodle Salad with Sesame Chicken

Quickly stir-fried chicken is served warm in a nest of noodles.

Serves 4–6

400g/14oz fresh thin egg noodles

1 carrot, cut into long fine strips

50g/2oz mangetouts (snow peas), cut into fine strips and blanched

115g/4oz/½ cup beansprouts, blanched

30ml/2 tbsp olive oil

225g/8oz skinless, boneless chicken breast portions, thinly sliced

30ml/2 tbsp sesame seeds, toasted

2 spring onions (scallions), finely sliced diagonally, and fresh coriander (cilantro) leaves, to garnish

For the dressing

45ml/3 tbsp sherry vinegar

75ml/5 tbsp soy sauce

60ml/4 tbsp sesame oil

90ml/6 tbsp light olive oil

1 garlic clove, finely chopped

5ml/1 tsp grated fresh root ginger

salt and ground black pepper

1 To make the dressing, whisk together all the ingredients in a small bowl. Season to taste.

2 Cook the noodles in a large pan of boiling water. Stir them occasionally to separate. They will take only a few minutes to cook; be careful not to overcook them. Drain the noodles, rinse under cold running water and drain well. Tip into a bowl.

3 Add the carrot, mangetouts and beansprouts to the noodles. Pour in about half the dressing, then toss the mixture well and adjust the seasoning according to taste.

4 Heat the oil in a large frying pan. Add the chicken and stir-fry for 3 minutes, or until cooked and golden. Remove from the heat. Add the sesame seeds and drizzle in some of the remaining dressing.

5 Arrange the noodle mixture on individual serving plates, making a nest on each plate. Spoon the chicken on top. Sprinkle with the spring onions and coriander leaves and serve any remaining dressing separately.

Sesame Duck and Noodle Salad

This salad is complete in itself and makes a lovely summer lunch. The marinade is a marvellous blend of Asian flavours.

INGREDIENTS

Serves 4

2 boneless duck breasts

15ml/1 tbsp oil

150g/5oz sugar snap peas

2 carrots, cut into 7.5cm/3in sticks

225g/8oz medium egg noodles

6 spring onions (scallions), sliced

salt

30ml/2 tbsp fresh coriander (cilantro) leaves, to garnish

For the marinade

15ml/1 tbsp sesame oil

5ml/1 tsp ground coriander

5ml/1 tsp Chinese five-spice powder

For the dressing

15ml/1 tbsp rice wine vinegar

5ml/1 tsp soft light brown sugar

5ml/1 tsp soy sauce

1 garlic clove, crushed

15ml/1 tbsp sesame seeds, toasted

45ml/3 tbsp sunflower oil

30ml/2 tbsp sesame oil

ground black pepper

1 Slice the duck breasts thinly across and place in a shallow dish. Mix together the ingredients for the marinade, pour over the duck and turn well to coat thoroughly. Cover with clear film (plastic wrap) and leave in a cool place for 30 minutes.

2 Heat the oil in a frying pan, add the slices of duck breast and stir-fry for 3–4 minutes, until cooked. Set aside.

3 Bring a pan of lightly salted water to the boil. Place the sugar snap peas and carrots in a steamer that will fit on top of the pan. When the water boils, add the noodles. Place the steamer on top and steam the vegetables while cooking the noodles.

4 Set the steamed vegetables aside. Drain the noodles, refresh under cold running water and drain again. Place them in a large serving bowl.

5 To make the dressing, mix the vinegar, sugar, soy sauce, garlic and sesame seeds in a bowl. Add a generous grinding of pepper, then whisk in the oils.

6 Pour the dressing over the noodles and mix well. Add the peas, carrots, spring onions and duck slices and toss to mix. Sprinkle the coriander leaves over the top and serve immediately.

V

Peppery Bean Salad

This pretty salad uses canned beans for speed and convenience.

INGREDIENTS

Serves 4–6

425g/15oz can red kidney beans

425g/15oz can black-eyed beans (peas)

425g/15oz can chickpeas

¼ red (bell) pepper

¼ green (bell) pepper

6 radishes

2 spring onions (scallions), chopped

For the dressing

5ml/1 tsp ground cumin

15ml/1 tbsp tomato ketchup

30ml/2 tbsp olive oil

15ml/1 tbsp white wine vinegar

1 garlic clove, crushed

2.5ml/½ tsp hot pepper sauce

1 Drain the canned red kidney beans, black-eyed beans and chickpeas and rinse well under cold running water. Shake off the excess water and tip them into a large bowl.

2 Core, seed and chop the red and green peppers. Trim the radishes and slice thinly. Add the peppers, radishes and spring onions to the beans.

3 Mix together the cumin, tomato ketchup, oil, vinegar and garlic in a small bowl. Add a little salt and hot pepper sauce to taste and stir again thoroughly.

4 Pour the dressing over the salad and mix. Chill the salad for at least 1 hour before serving, garnished with extra slices of spring onion.

Green Green Salad

You could make this dish any time of the year with frozen vegetables and still get a pretty salad.

INGREDIENTS

Serves 4

175g/6oz shelled broad (fava) beans

115g/4oz green beans, quartered

115g/4oz mangetouts (snow peas)

8–10 small fresh mint leaves

3 spring onions, (scallions) chopped

For the dressing

60ml/4 tbsp green olive oil

15ml/1 tbsp cider vinegar

15ml/1 tbsp chopped fresh mint

1 garlic clove, crushed

salt and ground black pepper

1 Plunge the broad beans into a pan of boiling water and bring back to the boil. Remove from the heat immediately and plunge into cold water. Drain. Repeat with the green beans.

COOK'S TIP

Frozen broad (fava) beans are a good stand-by, but for this salad it is worth shelling fresh beans for the extra flavour.

2 In a large bowl, mix the blanched broad beans and green beans with the raw mangetouts, mint leaves and spring onions.

3 In another bowl, mix together the olive oil, vinegar, chopped or dried mint, garlic and salt and pepper. Pour over the salad and toss well. Chill until ready to serve.

V

White Bean and Celery Salad

This simple bean salad is a delicious alternative to the potato salad that seems to appear on every salad menu. If you do not have time to soak and cook dried beans, you can use canned ones.

INGREDIENTS

Serves 4

450g/1lb dried white beans (haricot, navy, cannellini, butter or lima beans) or

3 x 400g/14oz cans white beans

1 litre/1¾ pints/4 cups Vegetable Stock

3 celery sticks, cut into 1cm/½in strips

120ml/4fl oz/½ cup French Dressing

45ml/3 tbsp chopped fresh parsley

salt and ground black pepper

1 If you are using dried beans, cover them with plenty of cold water and soak for at least 4 hours. Discard the soaking water, then place the beans in a heavy pan. Cover with water.

2 Bring to the boil and simmer without a lid for 1½ hours, or until the skins are broken. Cooked beans will squash readily between a thumb and forefinger. Drain the beans. If using canned beans, drain and rinse.

3 Place the cooked beans in a large pan. Add the vegetable stock and celery, bring to the boil, cover and simmer for 15 minutes. Drain thoroughly. Moisten the beans with the French dressing and leave to cool.

4 Add the chopped parsley and mix. Season to taste with salt and pepper, transfer to a salad bowl and serve.

Smoked Ham and Bean Salad

A fairly substantial salad that should be served in small quantities if intended as an accompaniment.

INGREDIENTS

Serves 8

175g/6oz black-eyed beans (peas)

1 onion

1 carrot

225g/8oz smoked ham, diced

3 tomatoes, peeled, seeded and diced

salt and ground black pepper

For the dressing

2 garlic cloves, crushed

45ml/3 tbsp olive oil

45ml/3 tbsp red wine vinegar

30ml/2 tbsp vegetable oil

15ml/1 tbsp lemon juice

15ml/1 tbsp chopped fresh or 5ml/1 tsp dried basil

15ml/1 tbsp wholegrain mustard

5ml/1 tsp soy sauce

2.5ml/½ tsp dried oregano

2.5ml/½ tsp caster (superfine) sugar

1.5ml/¼ tsp Worcestershire sauce

2.5ml/½ tsp chilli sauce

1 Soak the beans in cold water to cover overnight. Drain.

2 Put the beans in a large pan and add the onion and carrot. Cover with fresh cold water and bring to the boil. Lower the heat and simmer for about 1 hour, until the beans are tender.

3 Drain the beans, reserving the onion and carrot. Transfer the beans to a salad bowl.

4 Finely chop the onion and carrot. Toss with the beans. Stir in the ham and tomatoes.

5 For the dressing, combine all the ingredients in a small bowl and whisk to mix.

6 Pour the dressing over the ham and beans. Season with salt and pepper. Toss to combine, then serve.

FISH, MEAT AND POULTRY SALADS

~

If you ever doubted that salads could be considered culinary
masterpieces, the recipes here will certainly convince you of
their true splendour. Fish and shellfish, steak and chicken,
ham and bacon are combined with tropical fruit, tender
vegetables or crisp salad leaves, then served with a "designer"
dressing to complement them perfectly. Whether classic salads
or imaginative innovations, these are dishes for a special
occasion and a cause for celebration in themselves.

Thai Scented Fish Salad

For a tropical taste of the Far East, try this delicious fish salad scented with coconut, exotic fruits and warm Thai spices.

INGREDIENTS

Serves 4

350g/12oz red mullet or snapper fillets

1 cos or romaine lettuce

½ lollo biondo lettuce

1 papaya or mango, peeled and sliced

1 pithaya, peeled and sliced

1 large ripe tomato, cut into wedges

½ cucumber, peeled and cut into strips

3 spring onions (scallions), sliced

For the marinade

5ml/1 tsp coriander seeds

5ml/1 tsp fennel seeds

2.5ml/½ tsp cumin seeds

5ml/1 tsp caster (superfine) sugar

2.5ml/½ tsp hot chilli sauce

30ml/2 tbsp garlic oil

salt

For the dressing

15ml/1 tbsp creamed coconut
    (coconut cream)

60ml/4 tbsp safflower oil

finely grated rind and juice of 1 lime

1 fresh red chilli, seeded and chopped

5ml/1 tsp sugar

45ml/3 tbsp chopped fresh
    coriander (cilantro)

1 Cut the fish into even strips and place them on a plate or in a shallow bowl.

2 To make the marinade, crush the coriander, fennel and cumin seeds together with the sugar. Add the chilli sauce, garlic oil and salt and combine.

3 Spread the marinade over the fish, cover with clear film (plastic wrap) and leave to stand in a cool place for at least 20 minutes.

4 To make the dressing, place the creamed coconut in a screw-top jar with 45ml/3 tbsp boiling water and leave to dissolve. Add the safflower oil, lime rind and juice, red chilli, sugar and chopped coriander. Shake well and set aside.

5 Combine the lettuce leaves with the papaya or mango, pithaya, tomato, cucumber and spring onions. Toss with the dressing, then distribute among four large serving plates.

6 Heat a large non-stick frying-pan, add the fish and cook for 5 minutes, turning once. Place the cooked fish over the salad and serve immediately.

COOK'S TIP

If planning ahead, you can leave the fish in the marinade for up to 8 hours. The dressing can also be made in advance, minus the fresh coriander (cilantro). Store at room temperature and add the coriander when you are ready to assemble the salad.

Prawn and Artichoke Salad

The mild flavours of prawns and artichoke hearts are complemented by a zingy herb dressing.

Serves 4

1 garlic clove

10ml/2 tsp Dijon mustard

60ml/4 tbsp red wine vinegar

150ml/¼ pint/⅔ cup olive oil

45ml/3 tbsp shredded fresh basil leaves or
    30ml/2 tbsp finely chopped
    fresh parsley

1 red onion, very finely sliced

350g/12oz cooked peeled prawns (shrimp)

400g/14oz can artichoke hearts

½ iceberg lettuce

salt and ground black pepper

1 Chop the garlic, then crush it to a pulp with 5ml/1 tsp salt, using the flat edge of a heavy knife blade. Mix the garlic and mustard to a paste in a small bowl.

2 Beat in the vinegar and, finally, the olive oil, beating hard to make a thick, creamy dressing. Season with black pepper and, if necessary, additional salt.

3 Stir the basil or parsley into the dressing, followed by the sliced onion. Leave the mixture to stand for 30 minutes at room temperature, then stir in the prawns and chill for 1 hour, or until ready to serve.

4 Drain the artichoke hearts and halve each one. Shred the lettuce finely.

5 Make a bed of lettuce on a serving platter or on four individual salad plates and spread the artichoke hearts over it.

6 Immediately before serving, pour the prawns and their marinade over the top of the salad.

Salade Niçoise

Made with the freshest ingredients, this classic Provençal salad makes a simple yet unbeatable summer dish. Serve with country-style bread and chilled white wine for a substantial starter.

INGREDIENTS

Serves 4–6

115g/4oz green beans

1 tuna steak, about 175g/6oz

olive oil, for brushing

115g/4oz mixed salad leaves

½ small cucumber, thinly sliced

4 ripe tomatoes, quartered

50g/2oz can anchovies, drained and
    halved lengthways

4 hard-boiled eggs, quartered

½ bunch radishes, trimmed

50g/2oz/½ cup small black olives

salt and ground black pepper

flat leaf parsley, to garnish

For the dressing

90ml/6 tbsp virgin olive oil

2 garlic cloves, crushed

15ml/1 tbsp white wine vinegar

salt and ground black pepper

1 Whisk together the oil, garlic and vinegar, then season to taste with salt and pepper.

2 Preheat the grill (broiler). Brush the tuna steak with olive oil and season with salt and black pepper. Grill (broil) for 3–4 minutes on each side until cooked through. Set aside to cool.

3 Trim and halve the green beans. Cook them in a pan of boiling water for 2 minutes, until only just tender, then drain, refresh and leave to cool.

4 Mix together the salad leaves, sliced cucumber, tomatoes and green beans in a large, shallow bowl. Flake the tuna steak with your fingers or two forks.

5 Sprinkle the tuna, anchovies, eggs, radishes and olives over the salad. Pour over the dressing and toss together lightly. Serve garnished with parsley.

San Francisco Salad

California is a salad-maker's paradise and is renowned for the healthiness of its produce. San Francisco has become the salad capital of California, although this recipe is, in fact, based on a salad served at the Chez Panisse restaurant in Berkeley.

INGREDIENTS

Serves 4

900g/2 lb langoustines or Dublin
    Bay prawns (jumbo shrimp)

50g/2oz bulb fennel, sliced

2 ripe medium tomatoes, quartered, and
    4 small tomatoes

30ml/2 tbsp olive oil, plus extra for
    moistening the salad leaves

60ml/4 tbsp brandy

150ml/¼ pint/⅔ cup dry white wine

200ml/7fl oz can lobster or crab bisque

30ml/2 tbsp chopped fresh tarragon

45ml/3 tbsp double (heavy) cream

225g/8oz green beans, trimmed

2 oranges

175g/6oz lamb's lettuce

115g/4oz rocket (arugula) leaves

½ frisée lettuce

salt and cayenne pepper

1 Bring a large pan of salted water to the boil, add the langoustines or Dublin Bay prawns and simmer for 10 minutes. Refresh under cold running water.

2 Pre-heat the oven to 220°C/ 425°F/Gas 7. Twist off the tails from all but four of the langoustines or prawns – reserve these to garnish the dish. Peel the outer shell from the tail meat. Put the tail peelings, carapace and claws in a heavy roasting pan with the fennel and medium tomatoes. Toss with the olive oil and roast near the top of the oven for 20 minutes.

3 Remove the roasting pan from the oven and place it over a medium heat on top of the stove. Add the brandy and ignite to release the flavour of the alcohol. Add the wine and simmer briefly.

4 Transfer the contents of the roasting pan to a food processor and process to a coarse purée: this will take 10–15 seconds. Rub the purée through a fine nylon sieve into a bowl. Add the lobster or crab bisque, tarragon and cream. Season to taste with salt and a little cayenne pepper.

5 Bring a pan of salted water to the boil and cook the beans for 6 minutes. Drain and cool under running water. To segment the oranges, cut the peel from the top and bottom, and then from the sides, with a serrated knife. Loosen the segments by cutting between the membranes and the flesh with a small knife.

6 Moisten the salad leaves with olive oil and distribute among four serving plates. Fold the langoustine or prawn tails into the dressing and distribute among the plates. Add the beans, orange segments and small tomatoes. Garnish each plate with a whole langoustine or prawn and serve the salad warm.

Hot Coconut, Prawn and Papaya Salad

Transport yourself to the Far East with this wonderful dish of juicy papaya and succulent prawn tails.

INGREDIENTS

Serves 4–6

225g/8oz raw or cooked prawn (shrimp) tails, peeled and deveined

2 ripe papayas

225g/8oz cos, romaine or iceberg lettuce leaves, Chinese leaves (Chinese cabbage) and young spinach leaves

1 firm tomato, peeled, seeded and coarsely chopped

3 spring onions (scallions), shredded

1 small bunch fresh coriander (cilantro), shredded, and 1 large fresh chilli, sliced, to garnish

For the dressing

15ml/1 tbsp creamed coconut (coconut cream)

90ml/6 tbsp vegetable oil

juice of 1 lime

2.5ml/½ tsp hot chilli sauce

10ml/2 tsp Thai fish sauce (optional)

5ml/1 tsp sugar

2 If using raw prawn tails, cover with cold water in a pan, bring to the boil and simmer for no longer than 2 minutes. Drain well and set aside.

3 Cut the papayas in half from top to bottom and remove the black seeds. Peel away the skin and cut the flesh into equal-size pieces.

4 Place the salad leaves in a bowl. Add the prawn tails, papayas, tomato and spring onions. Pour over the dressing, garnish with the coriander and chilli and serve.

1 To make the dressing, place the creamed coconut in a screw-top jar and add 30ml/2 tbsp boiling water to soften it. Add the oil, lime juice, chilli sauce, fish sauce, if using, and sugar. Shake well and set aside. Do not chill.

Russian Salad

Russian salad became fashionable in the hotel dining rooms of the 1920s and 1930s. Originally it consisted of lightly-cooked vegetables, egg, shellfish and mayonnaise. Today we find it diced in plastic pots in supermarkets. This version recalls better days and plays on the theme of the Fabergé egg.

INGREDIENTS

Serves 4

115g/4oz large button
  (white) mushrooms
120ml/4fl oz/½ cup mayonnaise
15ml/1 tbsp lemon juice
350g/12oz cooked peeled
  prawns (shrimp)
1 large gherkin, chopped, or
  30ml/2 tbsp capers
115g/4oz broad (fava) beans
  (shelled weight)
115g/4oz small new potatoes, scrubbed
  or scraped
115g/4oz young carrots, trimmed
  and peeled
115g/4oz baby corn cobs
115g/4oz baby turnips, trimmed
15ml/1 tbsp olive oil
4 eggs, hard-boiled and shelled
25g/1oz canned anchovy fillets, drained
  and cut into fine strips
ground paprika
salt, and ground black pepper

1 Slice the mushrooms thinly, then cut into thin batons. Combine the mayonnaise and lemon juice. Fold the mayonnaise into the mushrooms, then add the prawns, gherkin or capers, and seasoning to taste.

2 Bring a large pan of lightly salted water to the boil, add the broad beans and cook for 3 minutes. Drain and cool under running water, then pinch the beans between thumb and forefinger to release them from their tough skins.

3 Boil the potatoes for about 15 minutes, and the remaining vegetables for 6 minutes. Drain and cool under running water. Moisten the vegetables with oil and divide among four shallow bowls.

4 Spoon on the prawn mixture and place a hard-boiled egg in the centre. Decorate the egg with strips of anchovy, sprinkle with paprika and serve.

Prawn and Mint Salad

Fresh, uncooked prawns make all the difference to this salad, as cooking them in butter adds to the piquant flavour. Garnish with shavings of fresh coconut for a tropical topping, if you like.

INGREDIENTS

Serves 4

12 large fresh, raw prawns (shrimp)
15ml/1 tbsp unsalted (sweet) butter
15ml/1 tbsp Thai fish sauce
juice of 1 lime
45ml/3 tbsp thin coconut milk
5ml/1 tsp caster (superfine) sugar
1 garlic clove, crushed
2.5cm/1in piece of fresh root
    ginger, grated
2 red fresh chillies, seeded and chopped
30ml/2 tbsp fresh mint leaves
225g/8oz light green lettuce leaves
ground black pepper

1 Carefully peel the raw prawns, removing and discarding the heads and outer shells, but leaving the tails intact.

2 Using a sharp knife, carefully remove the dark-coloured vein that runs along the back of each prawn.

3 Melt the butter in a large frying pan. When the melted butter is foaming add the prawns and toss over a high heat until they turn pink. Remove the pan from the heat; it is important not to cook them for too long so that their tenderness is retained.

4 In a small bowl mix the fish sauce, lime juice, coconut milk, sugar, garlic, ginger and chillies together. Season to taste with freshly ground black pepper.

5 Toss the warm prawns into the sauce with the mint leaves. Arrange the lettuce leaves on a serving plate and place the prawn and mint mixture in the centre.

VARIATION

Instead of prawns, this dish also works very well with lobster tails if you are feeling very extravagant.

COOK'S TIP

If you can't find any fresh, raw prawns, you could use frozen ones. To make the most of their flavour, toss very quickly in the hot butter when they are completely thawed.

Genoese Squid Salad

This is a good salad for summer, when green beans and new potatoes are at their best. Serve it for a first course or light lunch.

INGREDIENTS

Serves 4–6

450g/1lb prepared squid, cut into rings

4 garlic cloves, coarsely chopped

300ml/½ pint/1¼ cups Italian red wine

450g/1lb waxy new potatoes, scrubbed

225g/8oz green beans, trimmed and cut into short lengths

2–3 sun-dried tomatoes in oil, drained and thinly sliced lengthways

60ml/4 tbsp extra virgin olive oil

15ml/1 tbsp red wine vinegar

salt and ground black pepper

1 Preheat the oven to 180°C/ 350°F/Gas 4. Put the squid rings in an earthenware dish with half the garlic, the wine and pepper to taste. Cover and cook for 45 minutes, or until the squid is tender.

2 Put the potatoes in a pan, cover with cold water and add a good pinch of salt. Bring to the boil, cover and simmer for about 15 minutes, until tender. Using a slotted spoon, lift out the potatoes and set aside. Add the beans to the boiling water and cook for 3 minutes. Drain.

3 When the potatoes are cool enough to handle, slice them thickly on the diagonal and place them in a bowl with the warm beans and sun-dried tomatoes. Whisk the oil, vinegar and the remaining garlic in a jug (pitcher) and add salt and pepper to taste. Pour over the potato mixture.

4 Drain the squid and discard the liquid. Add the squid to the potato mixture and mix very gently. Arrange on individual plates and season liberally with pepper.

COOK'S TIP

The French potato called Charlotte is perfect for this salad because it retains its shape when boiled. Prepared squid can be bought from supermarkets with fresh fish counters, and from fishmongers.

Tuscan Tuna and Bean Salad

A great store-cupboard dish which can be put together in very little time. Served with crusty bread, this salad makes a meal in itself.

INGREDIENTS

Serves 4

1 red onion

30ml/2 tbsp smooth French mustard

300ml/½ pint/1¼ cups olive oil

60ml/4 tbsp white wine vinegar

30ml/2 tbsp chopped fresh parsley

30ml/2 tbsp chopped fresh chives

30ml/2 tbsp chopped fresh tarragon
or chervil

400g/14oz can haricot (navy) beans

400g/14oz can kidney beans

225g/8oz canned tuna in oil, drained and
lightly flaked

fresh chives and tarragon sprigs,
to garnish

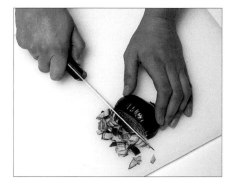

1 Chop the red onion finely, using a sharp knife.

2 To make the dressing, whisk together the mustard, oil, vinegar, parsley, chives and tarragon or chervil.

3 Drain the haricot and kidney beans in a colander, then rinse well in fresh water.

4 Mix the chopped onion, beans and dressing together thoroughly, then carefully fold in the tuna. Garnish with chives and tarragon sprigs and serve.

Mixed Seafood Salad

Use fresh seafood that is in season, or you can use a combination of fresh and frozen seafood.

INGREDIENTS

Serves 6–8

350g/12oz small squid

1 small onion, cut into quarters

1 bay leaf

200g/7oz raw prawns (shrimp), in their shells

750g/1½lb fresh mussels, in their shells

450g/1lb fresh small clams

175ml/6fl oz/¾ cup white wine

1 fennel bulb

For the dressing

75ml/5 tbsp extra virgin olive oil

45ml/3 tbsp lemon juice

1 garlic clove, finely chopped

salt and ground black pepper

1 Working near the sink, clean the squid by first peeling off the thin skin from the body section. Rinse well.

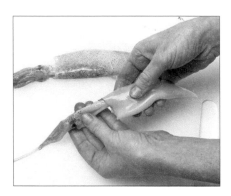

2 Pull the head and tentacles away from the sac section. Remove and discard the translucent quill and any remaining insides from the sac. Sever the tentacles and head.

3 Discard the head and intestines. Remove the small, hard beak from the base of the tentacles. Rinse the tentacles and sac under cold water. Drain.

4 Bring a large pan of water to the boil. Add the onion and bay leaf. Drop in the squid and cook for about 10 minutes, until tender. Remove with a slotted spoon and leave to cool before slicing into rings 1cm/½in wide. Cut each tentacle section into two pieces. Set aside.

5 Drop the prawns into the same boiling water and cook for about 2 minutes, until they turn pink. Remove with a slotted spoon. Shell and devein. (The cooking liquid may be strained and kept for soup.)

6 Cut the "beards" from the mussels. Scrub and rinse the mussels and clams well in several changes of cold water. Any that are open should close if given a sharp tap; if they fail to do so, discard. Place in a large pan with the wine. Cover and steam until all the shells have opened. (Discard any that do not open.) Lift the clams and mussels out of the pan.

7 Remove all the clams from their shells with a small spoon. Place in a large serving bowl. Remove all but eight of the mussels from their shells and add them to the clams in the bowl. Leave the remaining mussels in their half-shells, and set aside.

8 Cut the green, fronds of the fennel away from the bulb. Chop finely and set aside. Chop the bulb into bitesize pieces and add it to the serving bowl together with the squid and prawns.

9 To make the dressing, combine the oil, lemon juice and garlic in a bowl. Add the reserved chopped fennel fronds and salt and pepper to taste. Pour over the salad, and toss well. Decorate with the remaining mussels in their half-shells. Serve the salad at room temperature or lightly chilled.

"Poor Boy" Steak Salad

"Poor Boy" started life in New Orleans when the poor survived on sandwiches filled with left-over scraps. Times have improved since then, and today the "Poor Boy" sandwich is commonly filled with tender beef steak and other goodies. This is a salad version of "Poor Boy".

INGREDIENTS

Serves 4

4 sirloin or rump (round) steaks, each
    about 175g/6oz
1 escarole lettuce
1 bunch of watercress
4 tomatoes, quartered
4 large gherkins, sliced
4 spring onions (scallions), sliced
4 canned artichoke hearts, halved
175g/6oz button (white)
    mushrooms, sliced
12 green olives
120ml/4fl oz/½ cup French Dressing
salt and ground black pepper

1 Season the steaks with black pepper. Cook under a medium grill (broiler) for 6–8 minutes, turning once, until they are medium-rare. Cover and leave to rest in a warm place.

2 Combine the lettuce and watercress leaves with the tomatoes, gherkins, spring onions, artichoke hearts, mushrooms and olives and toss with the French Dressing.

3 Divide the salad among four serving plates. Slice each steak diagonally and arrange over the salad. Season to taste with salt and serve immediately.

Mushroom Salad with Prosciutto

Pancake ribbons create a lovely light texture to this salad. Use whatever edible wild mushrooms you can find, or substitute interesting cultivated varieties if you need to.

INGREDIENTS

Serves 4

40g/1½oz/3 tbsp unsalted (sweet) butter
450g/1lb assorted wild and cultivated
    mushrooms, such as chanterelles, ceps,
    bay boletus, Caesar's mushrooms,
    oyster, field (portabello) and Paris
    mushrooms, trimmed and sliced
60ml/4 tbsp Madeira or sherry
juice of ½ lemon
½ oak leaf lettuce
½ frisée lettuce
30ml/2 tbsp walnut oil
salt and ground black pepper

For the pancake and ham ribbons
25g/1oz/3 tbsp plain (all-purpose) flour
75ml/5 tbsp milk
1 egg
60ml/4 tbsp freshly grated
    Parmesan cheese
60ml/4 tbsp chopped fresh herbs, such as
    parsley, thyme, marjoram or chives
salt and pepper
butter, for frying
175g/6oz prosciutto, thickly sliced

1 To make the pancakes, blend the flour and the milk. Beat in the egg, cheese, herbs and some seasoning. Heat the butter in a frying pan and pour enough of the mixture to coat the base. When the batter has set, turn the pancake over and cook until firm.

2 Turn out and cool. Roll up the pancake and slice to make 1cm/½in ribbons. Cook the remaining batter the same way and cut the prosciutto into similar size ribbons. Toss with the pancake ribbons. Set aside.

3 Gently soften the mushrooms in the butter for 6–8 minutes until the moisture has evaporated. Add the Madeira or sherry and lemon juice and season.

4 Toss the salad leaves in the oil and arrange on four plates. Place the prosciutto and pancake ribbons in the centre, spoon on the mushrooms and serve.

Wilted Spinach and Bacon Salad

The hot dressing wilts the spinach and provides a taste sensation.

Serves 6

450g/1lb fresh young spinach leaves

225g/8oz streaky (fatty) bacon rashers (strips)

25ml/1½ tbsp vegetable oil

60ml/4 tbsp red wine vinegar

60ml/4 tbsp water

20ml/4 tsp caster (superfine) sugar

5ml/1 tsp dry mustard

8 spring onions (scallions), thinly sliced

6 radishes, thinly sliced

2 hard-boiled eggs, coarsely grated

salt and ground black pepper

1 Pull any coarse stalks from the spinach leaves and rinse well and pat dry with kitchen paper. Put the leaves in a large salad bowl.

2 Fry the bacon rashers in the oil until crisp and brown. Remove with tongs and drain on kitchen paper. Reserve the cooking fat in the pan. Chop the bacon and set aside until needed.

3 Combine the vinegar, water, sugar, mustard, and salt and ground black pepper in a bowl and stir until smoothly blended. Add to the fat in the frying pan and stir to mix. Bring the dressing to the boil, stirring constantly.

4 Pour the hot dressing over the spinach leaves. Sprinkle the bacon, spring onions, radishes and eggs over and toss, then serve.

Waldorf Ham Salad

Waldorf Salad first appeared at the Waldorf-Astoria Hotel, New York, in the 1890s. Originally, it consisted of apples, celery and mayonnaise, and was commonly served with duck, ham and goose. This modern-day version often includes meat and is something of a meal in itself.

INGREDIENTS

Serves 4

3 apples

15ml/1 tbsp lemon juice

2 slices cooked ham, each about 175g/6oz

2 celery sticks

150ml/¼ pint/⅔ cup mayonnaise

1 escarole or frisée lettuce

1 small radicchio, finely shredded

½ bunch of watercress

45ml/3 tbsp walnut or olive oil

50g/2 oz/½ cup broken walnuts, toasted

salt and ground black pepper

1 Peel, core, slice and finely shred the apples. Moisten with lemon juice to keep them white. Cut the ham into 5cm/2in strips. Cut the celery sticks into similar-size pieces. Combine the apples, ham and celery in a bowl.

2 Add the mayonnaise and mix thoroughly.

3 Shred all the salad leaves finely, then moisten with oil. Distribute the leaves among four serving plates. Pile the mayonnaise mixture in the centre, sprinkle with the walnuts, season and serve.

Corn-fed Chicken Salad with Garlic Bread

This makes a light first course for eight people or a substantial main course for four.

INGREDIENTS

Serves 4

1.75 kg/4–4½lb corn-fed chicken

300ml/½ pint/1¼ cups white wine and water, mixed

24 slices French bread, 5mm/¼in thick

1 garlic clove, peeled

225g/8oz green beans

115g/4oz young spinach leaves

2 celery sticks, thinly sliced

2 sun-dried tomatoes, chopped

2 spring onions (scallions), thinly sliced

fresh chives and parsley, to garnish

For the vinaigrette

30ml/2 tbsp red wine vinegar

90ml/6 tbsp olive oil

15ml/1 tbsp wholegrain mustard

15ml/1 tbsp clear honey

30ml/2 tbsp chopped fresh mixed herbs, such as thyme, parsley, chives

10ml/2 tsp finely chopped capers

salt and ground black pepper

1 Preheat the oven to 190°C/ 375°F/Gas 5. Put the chicken into a casserole with the wine and water. Cook in the oven for 1½ hours, until tender. Leave to cool in the liquid. Discard the skin and bones and cut the flesh into small pieces.

2 To make the vinaigrette, put all the ingredients into a screw-top jar and shake vigorously to combine. Adjust the seasoning to taste if necessary.

3 Toast the French bread under the grill (broiler) or in the oven until dry and golden, then lightly rub with the garlic clove.

4 Trim the green beans, cut into 5cm/2in lengths and cook in boiling water until just tender. Drain well and rinse under cold running water. Drain again.

5 Wash the spinach, discarding the stalks, and tear into small pieces. Arrange on individual serving plates with the celery, green beans, sun-dried tomatoes, chicken and spring onions.

6 Spoon over the vinaigrette dressing. Arrange the toasted slices of French bread on top, garnish with fresh chives and parsley and serve immediately.

Frisée Lettuce Salad with Bacon

This delicious salad may also be sprinkled with chopped hard-boiled egg.

INGREDIENTS

Serves 4

50g/2oz white bread
225g/8oz frisée lettuce or escarole leaves
75–90ml/5–6 tbsp extra virgin olive oil
175g/6oz piece smoked bacon, diced, or
    6 thick-cut smoked bacon rashers
    (strips), cut crossways into thin strips
1 small garlic clove, finely chopped
15ml/1 tbsp red wine vinegar
10ml/2 tsp Dijon mustard
salt and ground black pepper

1 Cut the crusts off the white bread, then cut the bread into small cubes. Tear the frisée lettuce or escarole into bitesize pieces and put into a salad bowl.

2 Heat 15ml/1 tbsp of the oil in a medium, non-stick frying pan over a medium-low heat and add the bacon. Cook gently, stirring occasionally, until well browned. Remove with a slotted spoon and drain on kitchen paper.

3 Add another 30ml/2 tbsp of the oil to the pan and cook the bread cubes over a medium-high heat, turning frequently, until evenly browned. Remove the bread cubes with a slotted spoon and drain on kitchen paper. Discard any remaining fat.

4 Stir the garlic, vinegar and Dijon mustard into the pan with the remaining oil and heat gently until just warm, whisking to combine. Season to taste with salt and pepper, then pour the dressing over the salad and sprinkle with the fried bacon and croûtons. Serve the salad immediately while still warm.

Roasted Chicken and Walnut Salad

The chickens may be cooked the day before eating and the salad finished on the day itself. Serve with warm garlic bread.

INGREDIENTS

Serves 8

4 fresh tarragon or rosemary sprigs
2 x 1.75 kg/4–4½lb chickens
65g/2½oz/5 tbsp softened butter
150ml/¼ pint/⅔ cup Chicken Stock
150ml/¼ pint/⅔ cup white wine
115g/4oz/1 cup walnut pieces
1 small cantaloupe melon
lettuce leaves
450g/1lb seedless grapes or
  pitted cherries
salt and ground black pepper

For the dressing
30ml/2 tbsp tarragon vinegar
120ml/4fl oz/½ cup light olive oil
30ml/2 tbsp chopped fresh mixed herbs,
  such as parsley, mint, tarragon

1 Preheat the oven to 200°C/400°F/Gas 6. Put the sprigs of tarragon or rosemary inside the chickens and season with salt and pepper.

2 Spread the chickens with 50g/2oz/4 tbsp of the butter, place in a roasting pan and pour the stock around. Cover loosely with foil and roast for about 1½ hours, basting twice, until browned and the juices run clear. Remove from the roasting pan and leave to cool.

3 Add the wine to the roasting pan. Bring to the boil on the top of the stove and cook until syrupy. Strain and leave to cool. Heat the remaining butter in a frying pan and cook the walnuts until lightly browned. Scoop the melon flesh into balls or cut into cubes. Cut the chickens into serving pieces.

4 To make the dressing, whisk the vinegar and olive oil together with a little salt and pepper. Remove the fat from the chicken juices and add the juices to the dressing with the herbs. Adjust the seasoning to taste.

5 Arrange the chicken pieces on a bed of lettuce leaves, sprinkle over the grapes or cherries and melon, and spoon over the dressing. Sprinkle with the toasted walnuts and serve.

Duck Salad with Orange Sauce

The rich, gamey flavour of duck provides the foundation for this delicious salad. Serve it in late summer or autumn and enjoy the warm flavours of orange and coriander. Garlic croûtons add extra crunchy texture.

INGREDIENTS

Serves 4

1 small orange
2 boneless duck breasts
150ml/¼ pint/⅔ cup dry white wine
5ml/1 tsp ground coriander seeds
2.5ml/½ tsp ground cumin or fennel seeds
30ml/2 tbsp caster (superfine) sugar
juice of ½ small lime or lemon
75g/3oz day-old bread, thickly sliced
45ml/3 tbsp garlic oil
½ escarole lettuce
½ frisée lettuce
30ml/2 tbsp sunflower or oil
salt and cayenne pepper
4 fresh coriander (cilantro) sprigs,
    to garnish

1 Halve the orange and slice thickly. Discard any pips (seeds) and place the slices in a small pan. Cover with water, bring to the boil and simmer gently for 5 minutes. Drain the orange slices and set aside.

2 Pierce the skin of the duck breasts diagonally with a small knife (this will help release the fat). Rub the skin with salt.

3 Place a steel or cast-iron frying pan over a steady heat and cook the duck for 20 minutes, turning once, until it is medium-rare. Transfer to a warm plate, cover and keep warm.

4 Heat the sediment in the frying pan until it begins to darken and caramelize. Add the wine and stir to loosen the sediment. Add the ground coriander, cumin or fennel seeds, sugar and orange slices.

5 Boil quickly and reduce to a coating consistency. Sharpen with the lime or lemon juice and season to taste with salt and cayenne pepper. Transfer the orange sauce to a bowl, cover and keep warm.

6 Remove the crusts from the bread and cut the bread into short fingers. Heat the garlic oil in a heavy frying pan and brown the croûtons. Season with salt, then turn out on to kitchen paper.

7 Moisten the salad leaves with a little sunflower oil and distribute them among four large serving plates.

8 Slice the duck breasts diagonally with a carving knife. Divide the meat into four and lift on to each salad plate. Spoon on the orange sauce, sprinkle with croûtons, decorate with a sprig of fresh coriander and serve warm.

Index